TEACHING
FOR JOY AND
JUSTICE

RE-IMAGINING THE LANGUAGE ARTS CLASSROOM

Linda Christensen

A Rethinking Schools Publication

Rethinking Schools, Ltd., is a nonprofit educational publisher of books, booklets, and a quarterly magazine on school reform, with a focus on issues of equity and social justice. To request additional copies of this book or a catalog of other publications, or to subscribe to *Rethinking Schools* magazine, contact:

Rethinking Schools
1001 East Keefe Avenue
Milwaukee, Wisconsin 53212
800-669-4192
www.rethinkingschools.org

Cover Design: Mary Jane Karp
Cover Illustration: "Kindred Spirits" by Jane Murray Lewis
Used with permission
Production Editor: Bill Bigelow
Book Design: Mary Jane Karp
Proofreading: Jennifer Morales
Business Manager: Michael Trokan

Library of Congress Cataloging-in-Publication Data
Christensen, Linda.
Teaching for joy and justice : re-imagining the language arts classroom / Linda Christensen.
— 1st ed.
p. cm.
ISBN 978-0-942961-43-0
1. Language arts (Secondary)—Social aspects—United States. 2. Literature—Study and teaching (Secondary)—Social aspects—United States. 3. Social justice—Study and teaching (Secondary)—United States. I. Title.
LB1631.C4492 2009
428.0071'2—dc22
2009019887

Acknowledgments

To acknowledge the thousands of people whose work has influenced this book would take another book. *Teaching for Joy and Justice* was nurtured from first page to last page during classes with my students and conversations with teachers, administrators, family, friends and even foes, illuminated by reading both literary and educational texts, and strengthened through collaboration with colleagues—local and global.

I have the great fortune of working with several communities of teachers and activists—the Oregon Writing Project, the National Writing Project, especially the Urban Sites Network, and our local Portland Area Rethinking Schools—whose teaching and insights and words have supported me for decades. To single out a few is to leave out the many, but without Pam Hooten, long-time English teacher and friend, I would not have found the time to bring this book to completion. Her efficiency and laughter made it possible for me to slide writing time into my schedule.

Carole Campbell, Margaret Calvert, Andy Clark, and Kim Patterson tackled me with their questions and education insights and courage. Toni Hunter, Neville Alexander, Diallo Lewis, John Rickford, Dyan Watson, and my colleagues at Urban Sites Network continue to shape my consciousness about issues of race and education.

Many colleagues as well as former students read and provided critique at key points during my work: Gloria Canson, Santha Cassell, Therese Cooper, Stefanie Goldbloom, Mark Hansen, Katharine Johnson, Andy Kulak, Dianne Leahy, Dylan Leeman, Jim Mayer, Anne Novinger, Penny Patrick, Russ Peterson, Mary Rodeback, Ruth Shagoury, Mira Shimabukuru, and Joann Tsohonis. I owe a special debt to Allen Webb at Western Michigan State University, who read many chapters and gave me wise and timely counsel on every one of them.

Many of the essays in this book first appeared in *Rethinking Schools* and were improved by the magazine's rigorous editorial process. The staff and editors of *Rethinking Schools*—Wayne Au, Bill Bigelow, Terry Burant, Kelley Dawson Salas, Stan Karp, David Levine, Fred McKissack, Larry Miller, Hyung Nam, Bob Peterson and Stephanie Walters—have been constant companions for years, cheering me on as well as sharpening my critique, and certainly making me a better teacher and writer than I could ever be on my own.

For any book to hit the shelves, invisible hands make the impossible possible. For this book, Jennifer Morales not only caught my errors, she taught me new proofreading and editing skills along the way. Mike Trokan, Rethinking Schools' business manager, deserves credit for lining up funding, resources, as well as willpower. His push has been the wind at my back for the past three years.

Photographer Jim Whitney generously videotaped and photographed my classes at Grant High School over a two-year period. His footage allowed me to revisit my classes several times as I wrote chapters. His beautiful photographs celebrate my students throughout the book. Dorothy Seymour, friend and colleague from Jefferson, took amazing photographs at the Daniel Beaty poetry workshop and kindly shared them with me. Barbara Miner, Rethinking Schools comrade, writer, and photographer extraordinaire opened her archives for the book. In the final stages of production, Alan Wieder graciously allowed us to use his remarkable photographs.

Mary Jane (MJ) Karp supplied more than layout design and artistic sensibility to the book. She read and reread every word, helped me rethink passages and ideas along the way. Her artistic vision and her wordsmithing made this book better. Whether walking along the Klickitat River or humming through keyboards, she provided both friendship and insight to the lonely work of writing.

Bill Bigelow, my husband, hiking partner, comrade, and best friend, took on the daunting task of "managing" the editorial work of his wife. While I will share no family secrets, let me say that he learned to duck wadded up drafts and withstand temper tantrums while pushing me to write the next draft and the draft after that. I take full responsibility for any errors in the book, but let there be no doubt that without Bill's honest feedback, the teaching and writing that appear in this book would not have happened. Bill initiated my journey into social justice teaching when we first taught together in 1986. He continues to be my mentor and critical friend, the first and the last teacher I turn to in my work.

And finally, my daughters—Anna and Gretchen Hereford—have provided me joy from the moment they arrived in my life. Their stories and laughter, walks, holidays, bike rides, and visits to farmers' markets sustain me. As I write this last piece of *Teaching for Joy and Justice*, our first grandchild, Xavier King Hereford-Hertel, is about to make his way into the world. My wish for Xavier is that, when he enters school, joy and justice will be the story of his education.

Contents

Alan Wieder

Introduction

I believe we need to create a pedagogy of joy and justice. When Michael writes a stunning essay about language policy in Native American boarding schools, there is joy because he finally nails this form of academic writing, but there is also justice in talking back to years of essays filled with red marks and scarred with low grades. There is joy because he's learned a craft that he felt beyond his reach; there's justice because Michael and his classmates learned to question policies that award or deny status based on race and class. When Bree writes a poem so sassy that we all laugh and applaud in admiration, we rejoice in her verbal dexterity, but we recognize the justice of affirming the beauty of black/brown women whose loveliness has too often gone unpraised in our society. When Jacoa speaks to a class of graduate students at a local college, she exudes joy in taking what she learned about Ebonics out of our high school classroom and into the university, but she speaks about justice when she tells the linguistic history of a language deemed inferior in the halls of power—including schools.

I begin my teaching with the understanding that anyone who has lived has stories to tell, but in order for these stories to emerge, I must construct a classroom where students feel safe enough to be wild and risky in their work. My curriculum uses students' lives as critical texts we mine for stories, celebrate with poetry, and analyze through essays that affirm their right to a place in our society. I attempt to craft a curriculum that focuses on key moral and ethical issues of our time because I have discovered that students care more about learning when the content matters. Writing and talking about these issues—like race, class, gender, and solidarity—takes them out of the shadow world and into the light of day, so students can understand why things are fair or unfair and how to change them. When I "correct" student writing, I embed the instruction about conventions, nitty-gritty skills, in the context of

1

students' writing about their lives and the broader world. I make their growth transparent, and we celebrate it inch-by-inch. Teaching for joy and justice makes students the subject of their own education.

Uncovering Brilliance

Teaching for joy and justice also begins with the non-negotiable belief that all students are capable of brilliance. Some students arrive in my classroom trailing years of failure behind them. Students in low-income communities are often tossed like loose change into overcrowded and underfunded classrooms where elementary teachers didn't have enough hands, materials, or time to build every student's literacy skills. Then we blame those students for arriving in our secondary classrooms without the tools they need to succeed. It's not uncommon for my high school students to read at a 2nd- or 3rd-grade level, according to unreliable reading tests,

My curriculum uses students' lives as critical texts we mine for stories, celebrate with poetry, and analyze through essays that affirm their right to a place in our society.

and to write without a punctuation mark on the page. But just because students lack skills doesn't mean they lack intelligence. My duty as a teacher is to attempt to coax the brilliance out of them.

After teaching for 24 years at Jefferson High School, located in an African American working-class neighborhood in Portland, Ore., and for a few years at Grant High School, where rich and poor, white, black, and Asian rub elbows in the hallways, I came to know that kids' lives are deep and delightful—even when they have low test scores. Their language is a history inherited from their parents, their grandparents, and their great-grandparents—a treasure of words and memories and the sounds of home, not a social fungus to be scraped from their mouths and papers.

When we begin from the premise that students need to be "fixed," invariably we design curriculum that erases students' home language and culture; we fail to find the strength and beauty in the experience and heritage that students bring with them to school. When our curriculum attempts to "correct" their supposed faults, ultimately, students will resist.

When I think of my students whose voices have been strangled and made small by overcorrection, I think of the poet Jimmy Santiago Baca, who captures this experience in his powerful essay, "Coming into Language," from the anthology *Doing Time: 25 Years of Prison Writing:*

Ashamed of not understanding and fearful of asking questions, I dropped out of school in the ninth grade. . . . Most of my life I felt like a target in the crosshairs of a hunter's rifle. When strangers and outsiders questioned me I felt the hang-rope tighten around my neck and the trapdoor creak beneath my feet. There was nothing so humiliating as being unable to express myself, and my inarticulateness increased my sense of jeopardy. Behind a mask of humility, I seethed with mute rebellion . . .

My student Jerald taught me the importance of searching for a student's talents instead of lining up his writing in the crosshairs of my weapon—a red pen. Jerald entered my classroom years behind his grade level. One day he sat at the computer behind my desk working on a piece of writing—a narrative, an imaginative story, I can't remember. Jerald knew how to write stories and essays in the big ways that matter. He knew how to catch the reader-listener by creating characters and dialogue so real and funny or tragic that we leaned in when he read his pieces out loud. And the boy could out-argue anyone, so essays were a matter of lassoing and reining

My student Jerald taught me the importance of searching for a student's talents instead of lining up his writing in the crosshairs of my weapon—a red pen.

in a thesis and lining up his arguments. Jerald had been kicked out of most of his classes, so he came to my class about four times a day. He was placed in special education, and clearly, Jerald lacked the conventional skills that mark literacy—sentences, spelling, paragraphs—but he didn't lack intelligence.

One morning during my prep period, I decided that I would teach Jerald how to punctuate. I printed out his piece where verbs not only didn't agree, they argued. And Jerald, depending on his mood, either loved the comma or left it out completely. So on this day, I was determined that I would teach him where the periods and capitals went once and for all. "Come here, Jerald," I said. "Let's go over your paper. I want to show you how to correct your punctuation." I bent over his dot-matrix print-out and covered it with cross-outs, marks, and arrows.

When I looked up, Jerald, instead of hovering, pulled away from me, from his paper. He looked at me as if I had betrayed him. I had become every teacher he'd had over the years, the ones who told him what he couldn't do instead of showing him what he knew and understood about writing. Instead of telling him how beautiful his writing was, instead of finding what worked in his piece, I found every single thing that was wrong.

Ultimately, students like Jerald taught me to teach the writer, not the paper. Locating his brilliance doesn't mean that I ignore what needs to be fixed in his writing, but I start the conversation in a different place, and I measure my critique. I show him one or two things he needs to develop in order to become a more competent essay or narrative writer. With each piece, I teach him a bit more about punctuation or grammar. He doesn't have to learn everything in one draft. If we write frequently enough, he can practice and improve his writing, one essay, one narrative, one poem at a time.

When I begin my work with the belief that all students can write and that they have something important to say, I build writers by illuminating their gifts instead of burying them.

To create dazzling, adept writers, I must rethink how I spend class time. Honing our craft takes time and multiple drafts. I can't assign writing; I have to teach it. Students need to know how to use writers' tools—from snappy openings to anecdotal evidence to flashbacks to semicolons. I can't expect that students know how to write when they enter my classroom, especially when so many children these days have been pressed like tarnished pennies through mechanical curriculum that promises increased test scores and delivers thin imitation writing without a hint of originality anywhere on the page.

When we create writing assignments that call students' memories into the classroom, we honor their heritage and their stories as worthy of study.

Students' Lives at the Center

Teaching for joy and justice also means locating the curriculum in students' lives. Many of my students experience injustice. Sometimes this mistreatment arrives in the form of an unkind comment about a person's weight, facial features, hair, or clothes. But often my students and their families are targeted because of their race or language or immigration status. Their families are denied housing, jobs, fair wages, health care, or access to decent education. Connecting these issues to the literature that we read, as well as writing and talking about their concerns makes them visible, not just the stuff of nightmares that haunt us throughout the day. I want students to examine why things are unfair, to analyze the systemic roots of that injustice, and to use their writing to talk back.

Putting students' lives at the center of the curriculum also tells them they matter—their lives, their ancestors' lives are important. When we create writing assignments that call students' memories into the classroom, we honor

Michael S. Yamashita/CORBIS

their heritage and their stories as worthy of study. Throughout the year, my students write poetry and narratives about people and events that link to the curriculum. I create opportunities to celebrate the joy of my students' daily lives. This writing is a transformative act where they build their literacy skills at the same time as they build a place for themselves in the world. Jimmy Santiago Baca's description of the island rising beneath his feet is the image I carry into my classroom:

> But when at last I wrote my first words on the page, I felt an island rising beneath my feet like the back of a whale. As more and more words emerged, I could finally rest: I had a place to stand for the first time in my life. The island grew, with each page, into a continent inhabited by people I knew and mapped with the life I lived.

My unit on "reading without words" illustrates this point. I had been struck over the years by how much school devalues the lives of blue-collar workers, divorcing manual work from "intellectual" work. In fact, I did this myself on occasion. I recall once saying to a class, "Study or you'll end up sweeping someone's floors or pumping gas." One of my students, Byron, raised his hand and said, "Ms. Christensen, my father cleans offices every night. That's how he's supported our family. There's no shame in that." Byron was right. I had insulted his family and reinforced the class lines built into the structure of our educational system.

To prepare for this "reading without words" assignment, I interviewed my Uncle Einar, who fished the Pacific for salmon and tuna his entire life, about how he "read" the ocean when he fished. My uncle flexed his intellectual muscles every time he climbed aboard the *Arctic* and left Astoria's harbor. He said he fished at the point where the water changed color, because fish school at the edge of the color change. He also told me that blue water meant albacore; brown water indicated bait was present and so were salmon. Birds diving overhead signaled schools of fish, and he put his boat on full throttle to get there.

I shared my interview with my students and asked them to interview members of their families about ways they read the world without words. Students shared delightful pieces. This assignment marked the first time Troy shared in class. He wrote about how his father, a long-haul truck driver, read his engine and the highway. Mario wrote about how his mother, a hairdresser, read hair and heads. Carl wrote about how his grandfather read rivers when he took him fishing. When students write about their lives, they have more incentive to revise the paper, and they care more about learning about mechanics.

Creating Social Justice Curriculum

Teaching for joy and justice means creating a curriculum peopled with authors and characters who not only represent our students' roots, but who also provide a window to the world. The books we choose to bring into our classroom say a lot about what we think is important, whose stories get told, whose voices are heard, whose are marginalized. When I was a young woman, I remember thinking that nobody like me had ever done anything worthwhile. Important people were men or they were rich. As a social justice educator in a language arts classroom, I look for stories where the protagonists refuse to accept "their place" in society; I try to find fiction and nonfiction

The books we choose to bring into our classroom say a lot about what we think is important, whose stories get told, whose voices are heard, whose are marginalized.

about people who disrupt the script society set for them. I want students to see that history is not inevitable, that there are spaces where it can bend, change, become more just.

All students need to see themselves reflected in the curriculum. Nelson Mandela, in his memoir, *Long Walk to Freedom*, describes the affirming moment that occurred "like a comet streaking across the night sky" when Krune Mqhayi comes on stage dressed in traditional Xhosa clothing and speaks his language. Poet, playwright, and actor Daniel Beaty told students at Jefferson High School that his life changed when he saw a videotape of Dr. Martin Luther King speaking. King's speech gave him a vision of a black man in the world that he was missing in his own life. When a student asked if he liked performing for a majority African American audience, he said, "Most of my life I read literature written by white people and watched plays written and performed by white people. I saw pieces of myself in their words. I love that people from other backgrounds can watch my plays and see themselves reflected in my work."

His words reminded me of a beautiful moment after Beaty performed his play, "Emergency," at Grant High School. A few students from the African American Literature class came to the faculty meeting the following Monday to share poems they had written during a workshop with Beaty. One of the students said, "We always read literature by white people, like Shakespeare. This is the first time everyone in the school had to read a play by a black man."

I write this 30 years after Portland's Black United Front demanded a multicultural curriculum that honors and celebrates the accomplishments, literature, and history of our diverse and unequal nation and community. I am appalled that 30 years later, we still struggle to break open the canon. Teaching and discussing and writing about the plays of

Teaching the works of writers of color and working-class writers allows students to understand that no matter their gender, skin color, or social class, they can write.

Luis Valdez and August Wilson, the stories or novels of Louise Erdrich and Raymond Carver, the poetry of Lucille Clifton and Li-Young Lee, or any other writer of color or working-class writer, allows students to understand a wider human experience, to know that no matter their gender, skin color, or social class, they can write.

Building a Curriculum That Matters

Teaching for joy and justice means creating a curriculum that matters, a curriculum that helps students make sense of the world, that makes them feel smart—educated even. Historian Howard Zinn talks about how too often the teaching of history gets lost in a narrow, fact-finding game about the past. The same is true of language arts. We can get lost in the minutiae of memorizing literary terms instead of analyzing, questioning, and creating. When I center my curriculum on key moral and ethical issues, students care more because the content matters. The study of literature and composition, which should be a study of society and ideas, can get reduced to a search for technical details—chasing motifs and symbols at the expense of the big ideas. How do we live our lives as moral citizens of the world, how do we make the world a better place? What can we learn from literature and history that helps us understand the complex problems confronting us today: Gender violence, the corruption and inequality exposed by Hurricane Katrina, the rise of gangs and youth violence, the skyrocketing incarceration of men of color?

We need a curriculum that matters in order to address the roots of inequality that allows some students to arrive in our classrooms without literacy skills. Students, no matter what their reading and writing ability, are capable of amazing intellectual work. They act up and get surly when the curriculum feels insulting. Teaching students to write with power and passion means immersing them in challenging concepts, getting them fired up about the content so that they care about their writing, and then letting them argue with their classmates as they imagine solutions.

If we intend to create citizens of the world, as most school districts claim in their mission statements, then we need to teach students how to use their knowledge to create change.

Great writing doesn't take place in isolation from the world. Global warming? Getting pulled over by the police because you're black and young and running down the street? Plant closures? Domestic abuse? Forest, river, and salmon loss? Toxic dump in your back yard? Students will rise to the "challenge" of a rigorous curriculum about important issues if that rigor reflects the real challenges in their lives. Too often the rigor offered students is a "rigor" of memorization and piling up of facts in order to earn high scores on end-of-course tests.

And students need to act on their new knowledge. If we intend to create citizens of the world, as most school districts claim in their mission statements, then we need to teach students how to use their knowledge to create change. By this I don't mean taking students out to demonstrations and picket lines, although they might end up there of their own accord. I mean we must construct academic ways for students to use the curriculum, to authentically tie student learning to the world. Over the years my students have traveled to local colleges to teach graduate education students about the history of the SATs, the politics of language, and the power of praise poetry in the Harlem Renaissance. They have also walked to elementary and middle schools to read books they've written about abolitionists, Native American treaties, and Ebonics. They've created poetry posters for local store windows, distributed report cards on cartoon videos to video stores and local newspapers. They've created table-tents for elementary schools about women we should honor, and they've testified about changes that need to happen in their schools.

Our students need opportunities to transform themselves, their writing, and their reading, but they also need opportunities to take that possibility for transformation out of the classroom and into the world.

Easier Said Than Done

Teaching for joy and justice isn't an individual endeavor. We can't do this work alone. It takes time to find the just-right reading material, to build a role play or tea party, to invent a curriculum from scratch that encompasses literature, history, and students' lives—while we're teaching. As my mother used to say, "Many hands make light work." And it is true, whether we're cleaning up after a family dinner or creating a unit for a literature circle on the politics of food.

From the first moment I entered Jefferson High School in 1974, I learned the importance of working with my colleagues. From our spontaneous discussions in the hallways to our department meetings to our arguments during faculty meetings, I found teachers whose curriculum and pedagogy helped me evolve as a teacher.

Twenty-five years ago, my husband and teaching partner, Bill Bigelow, and I became members of a critical pedagogy group with like-minded teachers from the Portland area. We got together every other Sunday night to discuss books on critical pedagogy. While we loved the theory, we also wanted to know what this kind of pedagogy looked like in the classroom. In teaching, as in writing, we need models. In our group we used each other as a sounding board as we developed curriculum to engage our students in literacy and history by critically examining their lives and the world. The group became my curricular conscience. Instead of leaping from book to book, my years of working in a critical collaborative community taught me to construct curriculum around ideas that matter and that connect students to their community and world. I learned to pull books, stories, poems, and essays that helped students critically examine the world.

Years of working in a critical collaborative community taught me to construct curriculum around ideas that connect students to their community and world.

During my years in the Portland Public Schools curriculum department and in my work with the Oregon Writing Project, I have experienced the joy of collaboratively developing units with other teachers. Whether it's learning how Sandra Childs sets up response groups, or how Mark Hansen gets his 3rd-grade students to move from a community walk to passionate persuasive essays about the need for change in their neighborhood, or how Katharine Johnson uses color-coding to teach students how to write cumulative sentences, my students have benefited from the new skills and ideas I've collected.

I attempt to keep my vision—and hope—alive by continuing to participate in critical teaching groups—including my local Portland Area Rethinking Schools group, the Rethinking Schools editorial board, my Oregon Writing Project community, and language arts teachers in the Portland area. To use Toni Morrison's words, these "friends of my mind" help me think more carefully about social justice issues inside as well as outside of the classroom, from literacy practices to top-down curricular

I attempt to keep my vision—and hope—alive by continuing to participate in critical teaching groups, including my local Rethinking Schools group.

policies. Our sometimes-heated discussions about articles, books, and curriculum hone my ability to evaluate my work. I carry these voices—and the solidarity of these teachers—like a Greek chorus in my mind. They remind me to question and sometimes to defy those in authority when I'm told to participate in practices that harm children. They nettle me when I fall into easy patterns and point out when I deliver glib answers to difficult problems. They help me choose the more courageous path because I know I'm not alone.

And We're Never Done

After my home school, Jefferson, was reconstituted in 1998, I spent several years in the district curriculum office. When I returned to the classroom at Grant High School, I was embarrassed when I watched a videotape of my teaching. I had romanticized the classroom when I worked in the central office, so when I returned to teach tracked sophomore and junior English, I had to regain my teaching moves, remember the importance of building community, and the hard work of engaging the disengaged. Some days, to use Bill Bigelow's description from the years when we taught together, it seemed like the students had thrown a party and I was the uninvited guest. It was a cold reminder of how demanding and complex good teaching is.

Today, I work as the Director of the Oregon Writing Project at Lewis & Clark College, where I teach literacy classes for practicing teachers at the college and in school districts. I also returned home to my beloved Jefferson High School where I co-teach classes and work with teachers as part of a university-school collaboration. Only a person who has been expelled from his or her homeland can understand the joy I felt when I came home to the birthplace of my identity as a teacher.

Teaching is like life, filled with daily routines—laundry, cooking, cleaning the bathtub—and then moments of brilliance. We get up intending to create the classroom of our imagination and ideals. Sometimes we reach that place, but often we're doing the spade work that makes those moments possible: mining student lives for stories, building a community where risk-taking can happen, teaching historical background in preparation for insights and connections, or revising drafts—again and again. Those moments of empowerment and illumination are built on the foundation of hard work that often doesn't look either shining or glorious.

Teaching, really teaching, in a classroom with too many students—both the engaged and the unengaged—is both difficult and rewarding. Teachers don't make enough money; we're treated as intellectually inferior, in need of external "accountability" programs and "training." We don't have adequate time or authority to plan our curriculum, engage in conversations with our colleagues, go to the bathroom, or digest our lunch. But the joy

Teaching is like life, filled with daily routines—laundry, cooking, cleaning the bathtub—and then moments of brilliance.

of watching a student write a moving essay that sends chills up and down my spine or a narrative that brings the class to tears or a poem that makes us laugh out loud or the pride as a student teaches a class about the abolition movement at the elementary school across the street—that's the life I choose—again and again.

Teaching for joy and justice. It's what our students need. But it's also what we need. ■

1: TEACHING FOR JOY AND JUSTICE
Writing Poetry

Said Belloumi/CORBIS SYGMA

The Role of Poetry: Community Builder, Grammar Text, and Literary Tutor

Poetry is the synthesis of hyacinths and biscuits.
— Carl Sandberg

Poetry levels the writing playing field. Students who struggle in other areas of literacy education often succeed in poetry—if it's not taught as a memory Olympics for literary terminology: assonance, dissonance, dactyl, couplet, enjambement, hexameter, pentameter. Many of my students who wrestle with essays write amazing poetry. Poetry unleashes their verbal dexterity—it's break dancing for the tongue.

Poetry is lively, accessible. And poetry, especially spoken word or performance poetry, has close ties to music and the hip hop community that

Poetry unleashes my students' verbal dexterity—

it's break dancing for the tongue.

many of my students love. I agree with poet Ruth Forman who wrote in her poem "Poetry Should Ride the Bus": "poetry should hopscotch in a polka dot dress/wheel cartwheels/n hold your hand/when you walk past the yellow crackhouse." Because of the rise in popularity of Slam Poetry, poems have slid out of the academy and into the streets. Now, poetry needs to move back into the classroom "n not be so educated that it don't stop in/every now n then to sit on the porch/and talk about the comins and goins of the world." Poetry can heal, teach, and unite.

Although poetry month is celebrated in April, we write poetry all year— it's part of every unit I teach. Poetry helps me build community and teach literary analysis. I call poetry my language weightlifting. Students learn to play with language, develop strong verbs, and saturate their readers with details. Through students' poetic responses, I glean insights into their knowledge about literature and history that quizzes and tests don't surrender.

Poetry as Community Builder: Sharing Our Lives—Laughter and Tears

We don't build communities *instead* of working on academics. We build communities *while* we work on academics. Students need to feel safe enough to ask for help, but a safe community is also essential if students are going to take academic risks, to care enough about their writing to persist in working through a number of drafts. As the poet Adrienne Rich wrote, "When those who have the power to name and to socially construct reality choose not to see you or hear you, whether you are dark-skinned, old, disabled, female, or speak with a different accent or dialect than theirs, when someone with the authority of a teacher, say, describes the world and you are not in it, there is a moment of psychic disequilibrium, as if you looked into a mirror and saw nothing." Too often when I see student failure, I see students who have looked into the mirror of their school and their image is not reflected—in the curriculum, in the portraits that line the hallways, in the choir, in the theater productions, or on the honor society roster.

Through poetry, the mirror we hold up in class reflects students' lives. When we write "Raised by Women" poems, for example, we celebrate students' roots, multiple heritages, and languages that tie them to their families. When I teach Margaret Walker's "For My People," students' histories as members of a particular race, class, or even illness become part of our classroom anthology. The smell of curry, the shape of matzo balls, and the tang of tropical Kool-Aid fill the class as students write praise poems to traditional family foods. Through poetry, we reclaim any part of our lives that society has degraded, humiliated, or shamed.

When school becomes one grim, rainy day after another, tied together with due dates and hard work, I construct activities so that students can laugh and play together—and still tackle their literacy skills. Both the "Age Poem" and the "I Love" writing evoke shared memories from students who grew up in this culture and opportunities to learn about other societies when immigrant students share their experiences.

Many of my students have not had easy lives, so to create real communities also means sharing our hardships as well as our joys. Growing up I felt that I had to mask who I really was in order to fit in. When I was 13, my father died of a heart attack brought about by an alcoholic binge, and my mother started dating other men. When I looked around, it seemed that other people had "normal" families—mothers and fathers who ate dinner together and said grace. Once a classmate said, "I saw your mom walking on Broadway with some man." My mother was single. Lonely. She had a right to have a relationship with men, but Mike pulled her out like dirty laundry to humiliate me in front of our friends.

We don't build communities *instead* of working on academics. We build communities *while* we work on academics.

My two best friends both had alcoholic parents. Trudy became her mother's keeper after her father moved out when we were in junior high school. She picked her mother up off the heater vent where she passed out, and she put ointment on the waffle-like burns on her mother's back. She learned to keep vanilla and cough medicines out of the house; she cooked dinner for her younger sister and made sure she did her homework. At 13 she became the parent in her family. Alcoholism bound the three of us. But no one talked about these issues at school. We read literature. We wrote essays. We pretended like everyone went home to dinner and happy lives.

I want my students to know that they are not alone in their struggles, that other people face similar challenges, so I share my stories about my father's battle with alcoholism, my niece's struggle with Tourette's syndrome and drug addiction, and the physical abuse I ran away from during my first marriage. Of course, not all students—or teachers—face these problems, but over my 30 years in schools, I've discovered that sharing our lives gives students hope, courage, strategies, and allies as they wrestle with hard times. Lakeitha Elliot, one of my former students and now an education activist, talks openly about her father's imprisonment and her mother's drug addiction. She said, "It helped to know that I wasn't the only one with problems. When you shared your stories, I could see a teacher who made it out." Students—and teachers—who don't face these struggles gain compassion by listening to their classmates' stories.

Poetry takes that pain and makes it art. In her interview with Bill Moyers during the *Fooling with Words* series, Jane Hirschfield says, "A good poem takes something you already know as a human being and raises your ability to feel that to a higher degree so you can know your own life more intensely. When you meet your own life in a great poem, your life becomes expanded, extended, clarified, magnified, deeper in color, deeper in feeling. I feel like almost all I know about being a human being has been deepened by the poems I've read. They have taught me how to be a human being." Daniel Beaty's poem "Knock Knock" helps students turn their pain into power and poetry. (See "Knock Knock: Turning Pain into Power," p. 33.) Sharing these stories helps lay our burdens down and makes us feel less lonely.

Poetry: Literary Tutor

When I stopped trying to turn my language arts classroom into graduate seminars for literary critics, I discovered that writing poetry brings a different level of critical examination of literature to the classroom. After students have written odes, elegies, sonnets, as well as free verse, they enter literary analysis with greater understanding, patience, and knowledge. The difference between the praise of an ode and the sorrow of an elegy is manifest in their own writing. They know the terms from the inside out.

Their study of poetry is enlarged because they know how poetry works. Instead of drilling them on literary terms or taking a scalpel to dissect Adrienne Rich or Richard Hugo's poems, students learn how pace, line breaks, and allusion work in their poems, so they can take that knowledge and language back to their work when they analyze poetry. Too often in the name of "rigor," we separate the naming of literature from the creation of literature, and it doesn't have to be that way. ■

"Raised by Women": Celebrating Our Homes

Ken Weingart/GETTY IMAGES

When I first read "Raised by Women" by Kelly Norman Ellis, I knew the poem would be a hit with my students. I love Ellis' celebration of the women in her life, her use of home language, and the wit and wisdom of her rhythmic lines. And from reading student tributes to their mothers over the years, I knew most of my students would relate to the topic. "Raised by Women" also had qualities I look for in poems I use to build community and teach poetic traits: a repeating line that lays down a heartbeat for the students to follow, delicious details from the writer's life that could evoke delicious details from my students' lives, and a rhythm so alive, I want to dance when I read it.

Part of my job as a teacher is to awaken students to the joy and love that they may take for granted, so I use poetry and narrative prompts that help them "see" daily gifts, to celebrate their homes and heritages. Ellis' poetry provides a perfect example. As she wrote, "I was just lucky enough to have been born into a loving southern, black family. I want these poems to stand as witness to the beauty and abundance of that life: a black southern woman's life, a good life, a proud life, a life as rich and sweet as the pies I bake with Mississippi pecans. There are others like me, folks raised in the brown loving arms of family."

Part of my job as a teacher is to awaken students to the joy and love that they may take for granted, so I use poetry and narrative prompts that help them "see" daily gifts, to celebrate their homes and heritages.

I also use poetry to build relationships with students and between students. Ellis' smart and sassy poem helped launch our yearlong journey to establish relationships as the students and I learned about each other, but also their journey in developing their writing.

In each stanza of the poem, Ellis lists the kinds of women who raised her—from "chitterling eating" to "some PhD toten" kind of women. Ellis' poem follows a repeating but changing pattern. She writes that she was raised by women, sisters, and queens. She includes both description and dialogue in most stanzas:

I was raised by
Chitterling eating,
Vegetarian cooking,
Cornbread so good you want to lay
down and die baking
"Go on baby, get yo'self a plate"
Kind of Women.

The full poem, as well as a video clip of Ellis reading the poem, can be found at the Coal Black Voices website, which was developed by Media Working Group to "honor contemporary African American culture and celebrate regional expressions of the African Diaspora through the works of the Affrilachian Poets."

Filling the Bucket with Delicious Details and Style

After reading "Raised by Women" twice, I asked students, "Who were you raised by?" Although Ellis discusses only women, I wanted to open other possibilities. I salted the pot by generating a few: mother, father, coaches, church. I also wanted them to reach out beyond the traditional, so I encouraged them to think about neighbors, neighborhoods, musicians, novelists, civil rights activists, the halls at Grant.

After students wrote their lists, we shared them out loud so they could "steal" more ideas from each other. I pushed students to get more specific as they shared. For example, when Melvin said, "Coaches," I asked which coaches raised him—all of them? What did his football coach say or do that helped raise him? When Alex said the men at the barbershop, I asked which men and what did they contribute. Because the best poetry—and writing in general—resides in specific details, I pushed students to move beyond their first response and get deeper.

I wanted them to see that they weren't limited by the original verb, raised, so I asked, "The verb is the workhorse of the sentence. Look at how it harnesses the rest of the stanza and moves it forward. Think about your verbs. What other verbs could you use besides raised?" We played around with alternatives: brought up, taught, educated, nurtured. This is the weightlifting function of teaching poetry. Instead of grammar worksheets, I teach students about the functions of language as we discuss how verbs work in the poem.

When we completed our initial brainstorming about the repeating line, we went back to the poem. I asked, "What kinds of specific kinds of details does Ellis include?" The first stanza was about food, the second stanza focused on hair, the third was about physical appearance—skin color and clothes—the fourth about choices, the fifth about music, the sixth about attitude, and the seventh about professions. Because I didn't want each poem to turn out the same, I said, "When you write your poem, you can use these as potential categories, but you can use other categories as well. What else could you list in your poem?" Students shouted out: cars, songs, languages. I encouraged them to create a list of categories like Ellis'—food, clothes, music—and to fill in each category with specific details.

After they brainstormed, we returned to the form. "What do you notice about how Ellis developed the poem? Look at the lines. Where does it repeat? Does it repeat in the same way?" Kamaria noticed the repeating, but changing line. Damon talked about how Ellis' dialogue gives her poem flavor. Tanisha noted that she named specific people—Angela Davis and James Brown. Destiny pointed out that Ellis used home language rather than Standard English. As students noticed these details, I listed them on the board. "Take a look at this list—a repeating but changing line, dialogue, naming people, home language. When you write your poems, I want you to try to include some of these techniques. I know some of you speak another language at home. Experiment with using pieces of that language in your poems. Also, notice how Ellis catches a rhythm in her poem. See if you can create a heartbeat when you write."

The Read-around and Collective Text: Structuring Response

Before students read their poems, we arranged the desks in a circle, so they could see and hear the reader. I asked students to pull out a piece of paper to take notes on what they learned about each classmate through their poem: "Who raised them? What's important to them? Who's important to them?" I discovered that students pay more attention during the read-around if I give them a specific task. For the most part, student poems were stellar, and even those that lacked the style and sassiness of their classmates' gave us a glimpse into their lives.

Students found their own ways into the poems by celebrating more than one person. Anaiah Rhodes, for example, wrote a stanza each for her mother and father, grandmother and grandfather, church folk, music, cousins, and track. Her classmates loved how she used language and details to capture each one in turn, but they especially loved how Anaiah wrote about her church:

I was taught by a tongue talkin'
Sanctified, holy ghost filled, fire baptized, shoutin'
"'Member to keep God first, Baby!"
Kinda church folk

Some aisle runnin', teary-eyed, joy jumpin',
Devil rebukin', seed sowin'
"How you doin, Baby?"
Type of church folk

Ellis' poem provided an opportunity for us to celebrate the brilliance and linguistic richness of my students' cultures. Destinee Sanders, who also chose to write about a variety of people in her family—mother, aunts, sisters, and "abuelita"—switched languages throughout her poem:

I was raised by Mi Abuelita,
Es mi abuela favorita,
Ella es mi corazón, mi amor, mi amiga
Mi noche, mi todos los días, mi siempre.
Yo amo a mi abuelita

[I was raised by my Grandma,
My favorite grandmother
She is my heart, my love, my friend
My night, my everyday, my always.
I love my grandma]

Like Destinee, students shared information in the poem that helped us know their family and backgrounds. Jessica Chavez wrote about her "tortilla making/Grease usin'/cumbia dancin'" family. Adiana Wilmot wrote, "I was raised by that/curry goat and chicken cookin'/ 'Eat your vegetables, pickney,'/type of Jamaican woman." Kirk Allen wrote about his family—the Allens—rather than selecting out individuals:

I was raised by the gas, brake dipp'n,
Cadillac whip'n, Wood grain grip'n,
Old school, big body, pimp'n,
Ain't you bullshit'n Allens

I was raised by the show stopp'n,
Hater droppin',
Hat tilted to the side,
Look like a bad mutha,
Shut yo mouth Allens

In this and all class writing, I encouraged students to abandon the prompt and my suggestions and find their own passion and their own way into the assignment. Shona Curtis did that and forged her way to a poem about music instead of people:

I was raised by smooth jazz
Make you want to sit down and
Cry kind of music

Some move your feet and shake
Those hips feel like you dancin'
Down the streets of Argentina
Kind of music

When students wrote at the end of the assignment, many pointed to Shona's straying from the prompt as a strength in her poem.

Details from poems brought shouts of laughter or nods as students recognized their own family in Destiny Spruill's description of her family's "Found Jesus/Church goin'/You mouth can get you in trouble" and "Gumbo makin'/Hat wearin'/Mother of the church/Kinda grandmothers." They understood Ebony Ross' "I was raised to get the belt/If I was talking that lip." But it was Jessica's repeating line, "I wasn't raised by my daddy," that brought the most affirmations from other students.

Framing Reflection: Milking the Learning

After students shared, I handed out note cards and asked them to look back over their notes and write about what they learned about each other and poetry through our lesson. Kayla Anderson wrote that she learned "that you can completely change a poem but still keep the meaning. Shona made her poem fun by using words like 'hip-hoppin', pop lockin', shake your dreads.'" She noted that many students used strong verbs and imagery. Shona pointed out that "when you say your poem with attitude it sounds better."

But it was students' revelations about each other that made me realize this poetry assignment is a keeper. Students wrote about how much they learned about each other in a short amount of time. "I learned that Adiana is from Jamaica, that Bree was raised by foster parents, and that a lot of us have been let down by our fathers." Destinee wrote:

I learned that I have something in common with every single person in this room. I realize that we have all been through a lot of the same things. I learned that most of us weren't raised by our dads. I learned that Shaquala loves soul food. I learned that although Bree is Latino like me, she was raised by different types of Latinos, and I can relate to that....I learned that we're different...yet we're the same.

Out of the 30 students in the class, the majority were raised without fathers. This became a repeating "aha" for most of the class. Virginia Hankins, for example, wrote that she "learned a lot about my classmates that I would have never known. I was surprised that so many of us were raised without our fathers."

Knitting together poetry that teaches about our lives as well as the craft of writing builds the kind of caring, risk-taking community I hope to create. ■

Raised

by Anaiah Rhodes

I was raised by a lovin'
Church goin', home cookin', belt whoppin',
Non-stop children bearin'
Money arguin',
"You're going to be something great one day,"
Mom and Dad

I was raised by a Jesus lovin', behind tearin'
Bomb cookin', hair pressin', garage sale givin'
Grandma

A politic lovin', money givin', pipe puffin',
Fish fryin', Cadillac whippin', wine sippin',
"Study hard now!"
Grandpa

I was taught by a tongue talkin',
Sanctified, holy ghost filled, fire baptized,
  shoutin',
"'Member to keep God first, Baby!"
Kinda church folk

Some aisle runnin', teary-eyed, joy jumpin',
Devil rebukin', seed sowin',
"How you doin', Baby?"
Type of church folk

I was brought up with that hold on,
Wait on God, don't give up,
Weepin' may endure for the night,

But joy comes in the mornin'
What a friend we have in Jesus, music

By some double darin', house playin',
Fightin', scratchin', teasin', tauntin',
Crumb snatchin'
To football playin' and track runnin'
"I got cha back!"
Cousins

I was brought up by that race
Everybody on the block, barefoot, wind in my
  face, win or lose, spirit of runnin'
To that sweatin', trainin', muscle tearin',
Shin splintin', intense burnin',
Heavy workout, deep breathin' crazy
Type of runnin'.

Raised.

Music

by Shona Curtis

I was raised by smooth jazz
Make you want to sit down and
Cry kind of music

Some move your feet and shake
Those hips feel like you dancin'
Down the streets of Argentina
Kind of music

Some hip hop and you don't stop
Movin' to those beats feel the energy
Comin' out of the radio
Kind of music

Some hit right where you need it soul
Music make you think of the old days
When that was all we had
Kind of music

Some jump up and down slam to
The beat of the rock
Kind of music

Some poppin' pop grab your
Best friend and put on your
Favorite costume and dance
Kind of music

I was raised by music

I Was Raised by Video Games

by Seth Lee

Some x tappin'
Joystick swirlin'
"Drive me crazy til I
throw my controller"
type of videogames.

I was raised by cuts and bruises.

Some knee scrapin'
bone breakin'
fallin' out of trees
and landing on my head
kinds of cuts and bruises.

I was raised by roughnecks.

Those country music listenin'
playing football on the gravel road
pickin' blackberries from the neighbors
wrestlin' in the mud 'til dinner's ready
kind of roughnecks.

I was raised by transformers.

Some Decepticon terrorizin'
optimist prime ass kickin'
Megatron losin' day in and day out
transformers.

I was raised by sports.

Those ball kickin'
ball throwin'
ball hittin'
stick fools so hard they cry
for their mamas sort of sports.

Raised by Women

by Kelly Norman Ellis

I was raised by
Chitterling eating
Vegetarian cooking
Cornbread so good you want to lay
down and die baking
"Go on baby, get yo'self a plate"
Kind of Women.

Some thick haired
Angela Davis afro styling
"Girl, lay back
and let me scratch yo head"
Sorta Women.

Some big legged
High yellow, mocha brown
Hip shaking
Miniskirt wearing
Hip huggers hugging
Daring debutantes
Groovin
"I know I look good"
Type of Women.

Some tea sipping
White glove wearing
Got married too soon
Divorced
in just the nick of time
"Better say yes ma'am to me"
Type of Sisters.

Some fingerpopping
Boogaloo dancing
Say it loud

I'm black and I'm proud
James Brown listening
"Go on girl shake that thing"
Kind of Sisters.

Some face slapping
Hands on hips
"Don't mess with me,
Pack your bags and
get the hell out of my house"
Sort of Women.

Some PhD toten
Poetry writing
Portrait painting
"I'll see you in court"
World traveling
Stand back, I'm creating
Type of Queens.

I was raised by
Women.

Sami Sarkis/GETTY IMAGES

The Age Poem:
Building a Community of Trust

*Poetry is a political action undertaken for the sake of information,
the faith, the exorcism, and the lyrical invention, that telling the truth
makes possible. Poetry means taking control of the language of your
life. Good poems can interdict a suicide, rescue a love affair, and build
a revolution in which speaking and listening to somebody becomes
the first and last purpose to every social encounter. I would hope that
folks throughout the U.S.A. would consider the creation of poems as
a foundation for true community: a fearless democratic society.*

From the introduction to June Jordan's
Poetry for the People: A Revolutionary Blueprint

Building a community that might contribute to Jordan's "fearless democratic society" is no small accomplishment in most classrooms. Over the
years I've learned that poetry helps move students to listen and care about
each other while they build literacy skills.

Too often community building happens in the opening days of the school
year. Teachers and students engage in a series of games designed to foster
group skills and bonding, but in my experi-
ence, these activities drop off after the first
week—as if community is established with
one or two activities. In addition, these opening strategies are frequently divorced from
the course content. Creating a community of learners is not at odds with
building literacy skills in a language arts classroom. We don't need to put aside
words to develop a classroom where students can share their lives.

**We don't need to put aside words to develop a
classroom where students can share their lives.**

The age poem is a great community-building activity. Students get to talk about childhood memories—big wheel bikes, the smell of glue in kindergarten, songs, and games—that connect them and allow them to acknowledge their common bonds. This activity also brings in their family stories, languages, and customs that shape their lives. The structured approach to the poem gives students lots of choice—from the age they choose to the details about their lives that they want to reveal.

I start this activity by using Garrett Hongo's poem "What For" from *Yellow Light*. Hongo's poem is rich with details; it tells stories, names foods, uses his grandparents' language: "At six I lived for spells:/how a few Hawaiian words could call/up the rain, could hymn like the sea." In later stanzas, he evokes his grandfather: "I lived for stories about the war/my grandfather told over *hana* cards;" and his grandmother, "I lived for songs my grandmother sang/stirring curry into a thick stew." "What For" also has a repeating line that helps students scaffold their own poem from stanza to stanza. Hongo's use of verbs and imagery provides a strong model for student writing.

The age poem teaches students some basic facts about poetry—the power of specifics and repeating lines—two writing "tools" that they can carry over into essay and narrative writing. It teaches them to collect "evidence" prior to writing, to sort their details and then to select the best ones. They learn to shape their poem through the use of a repeating line, followed by a list of specific details.

The age poem teaches some basic facts about poetry—the power of specifics and repeating lines—two writing "tools" that students can carry over into essay and narrative writing.

After reading Hongo's and several student poems (see p. 26), we talk about what the poets valued, what was important enough for them to include in a poem. We also look at the kinds of details the poets used—names of family members, teachers, games they played. After we read, I ask students to write lists that match the ones in the poems we read, and I add a few other categories:

- Names of games they played, including outdoor games like freeze tag, cartoon tag, hide and seek, school games, imaginary games.
- Names of clothes—especially the weird or wacky clothes like days of the week underwear or superhero t-shirts, special occasion clothes.

Sophomores Mario Martinez-Perez and Bruk Alkadir.

- School memories from early years—teachers' names, books, special projects.
- Memories of things they were too small to reach, or things they could do because they were small—reaching the light switch, playing with the big kids, going on rides at the carnival.
- Family memories—parents, grandparents, special stories, food, ceremonies. (Hongo's poem pays special tribute to his Hawaiian grandparents.)
- Strong memories—a memory frozen from that time that replays for them.
- Music they loved, television shows they watched.

Students share their lists out loud after they each brainstorm. This is a huge piece of the community-building aspect of poetry writing. It is time consuming, but it performs several functions. One student's memory sparks memories for other students, so they can add details to their lists. But students also share common memories and laughter as they tell stories about playing freeze tag at dusk or wearing their Superman t-shirt every day of the week. Sometimes they attended the same elementary school or church, so their collective memory becomes part of the classroom story. This is also the time when students talk about their cultural heritage, including food, religious holidays, names of family members, and words from the language of their ancestors.

After students have compiled their brainstorming, I ask them to review their lists and either highlight or circle some of the best items—those details that help the reader understand how the child they were at 5 or 6 became the person they are today. I also encourage them to include words in their "home language" when appropriate.

Once students have selected their best details, I write Garrett Hongo's and Bea Clark's opening lines on the board (see p. 26): "At _____ I lived for…" and "I am in the winter of my _____ year." We play with variations—changing the age, changing the season. I encourage them to incorporate one of these lines into their poem as a repeating line or to create their own repeating line to help move the poem forward. I also tell them to surprise the reader with a memory like Tim McGarry includes in his poem "Six": "I lived for a year when/Mom's temper got hidden/behind school and/a new lover."

After students have written a draft, we "read around." Seated in our circle, students read their poems. After each student reads, classmates raise their hands to comment on what they like about the piece. The writer calls on his/her classmates and receives feedback about what is good in the poem. I stop from time to time to point out that the use of a list is a technique they might "borrow" from their peer's poem and include in their next poem or in a revision. I might note that the use of Spanish or their home language adds authenticity to their piece and ask them to see if they could add some to their poem. After a few read-around sessions, I can spot writing techniques that students have "borrowed" from each other and included in their revisions or in their next piece.

Creating community in our classrooms is not at odds with developing student skills. To the contrary. Learning to share pieces of our personal history and listening closely while others share theirs is absolutely necessary if I want students to write deeply and passionately about their lives. This authenticity lays the groundwork for both academic achievement and social insight. ∎

Resources

Hongo, Garrett Karou. *Yellow Light*. Connecticut: Wesleyan University Press, 1982.

Mueller, Lauren, ed. June Jordan's *Poetry for the People: A Revolutionary Blueprint*. New York, NY: Routledge, 1995.

Other good models for age poems:

"Eleven" by Sandra Cisneros from her book *Woman Hollering Creek* and "The Thirty-eighth Year" by Lucille Clifton from *Good Woman*.

"The Summer I Was Sixteen" by Geraldine Connolly can be downloaded from Billy Collins Poetry 180: a poem a day for American high schools (http://www.loc.gov/poetry/180/003.html.)

Five

by Bea Clark

I am in the winter of my fifth year.
My days are filled with kindergarten
And brown readers.
We sit at tiny desks,
In tiny rows
Surrounded by a scaled down world
With giant alphabet men and woodblocks.
We make paper angels, wrapping circles into cones,
Using styrofoam balls for heads,
Silver and gold glitter on heavenly
Tissue paper wings.
Too much glue makes no difference.
Add more glitter, stiffer wings—sharp wings.
We have paper angel fights.
Glitter flies into our hair, on our red faces.
Mrs. Hasselbacker calms us down.
It's time for the next activity.

The juice is gone.
And Denise ate glue on her chocolate.

We climb onto the Magic Carpet
And Mrs. Hasselbacker reads stories
From beat up hardback books.
We clap and laugh and fall asleep
On each other's shoulders.

It's time to go home,
To play,
To build snowmen that glow at night
And wink up at my window
When the moon is out.

Time to sleep,
And dream,
Of reindeer biting my toes,
Pirates' booty found in the yard,
And smiling alligators.

Six

by Tim McGarry

At six I lived for Evel Knievel
and pop rocks.
Japanese monster movies
on channel 12
flavored our fantasies
of guts and glory

I lived for Donny & Marie
and waited for their plate-class smiles
to lock in a deep kiss

I lived for the snake
at school
that ate white mice whole

I lived for a year when
Mom's temper got hidden
behind school and
a new lover

I lived for Banquet fried chicken
and rocky road ice cream
I lived to be seven
and one day eight

I lived for a security
I never knew again

Lawrence Manning/CORBIS

For My People

"I don't understand how you could walk into that building day after day for 24 years," the older woman standing at the school copier told me. "I have to go in there once a week, and I fear for my life every time I walk up those stairs. All of those black boys with their hoodlum clothes—sweatshirt hoods pulled up over their heads, baggy pants—I'm afraid they're going to knock me down the steps and steal my purse."

I look at her and remember Damon and Sekou, young black men I taught at "that building"—Jefferson High School. I remember their brilliance, imagine their faces— one in graduate school, one at NASA. I think of Kanaan's huge heart, of Frank's humor. I think of Aaron Wheeler-Kay's poem written after we visited an art museum exhibit of Carrie Mae Weems' "I Went Looking for Africa" artwork. Using Weems' phrase as a starting point, Aaron Wheeler-Kay wrote:

Many people sized up those of us who attended or worked at Jefferson based on stereotyped images and counted us out, usually without ever venturing inside to our classrooms.

I Went Looking for Jefferson
> and I found...
all the nations of the world
> wrapped in baggy jeans
> sweatshirts
> braids.
Closed minds slowly opening
> like doors under water.
Jefferson is our whetstone
> the blade is our mind.

There was no blade to open the mind of the woman at the copy machine. I'd met her before, in countless other closed minds. Many people—teachers, parents, reporters, students from other schools—sized up those of us who attended or worked at Jefferson based on stereotyped images and counted us out, usually without ever venturing inside to our classrooms. Their comments disrespected our school, our students, our community. And even when they weren't as blatant in their comments, their looks or their body language spoke bluntly.

The classroom can be a safe place for students to not only talk back, but to affirm their right to a place in the world.

Students, particularly students who don't fit the social norm because of their race, language, class, sexual orientation, weight, or ability to purchase the latest fashions, have plenty of reasons to share their anger and frustration— sometimes at inappropriate times and in inappropriate ways when they feel they've been disrespected. The classroom can be a safe place for students to not only talk back, but to affirm their right to a place in the world. During the years I worked at Jefferson, I found it necessary to talk back to those disrespectful and untrue images that the media and popular opinion formed about my students, my school, and the faculty.

I begin by reading Margaret Walker's powerful poem "For My People." Walker's poem teaches about the hardship that African Americans endured, but she also celebrates the triumphs of her people. She ends the poem with an exhortation—"Let a new earth rise. Let another world be born … Let a race of men now rise and take control!" It's the perfect poem to both examine our history and to talk back to the disrespect.

After we read the poem through a couple of times, we notice how Walker constructs her poem with the repeating phrase "For my people." We examine how she uses the phrase as an introduction to her theme for that stanza and follows it with a list. For example:

For my people everywhere singing their slave songs repeatedly: their dirges and their ditties and their blues and jubilees, praying their prayers nightly to an unknown god, bending their knees humbly to an unseen power.

Walker's poem teaches the strength of using repetition and lists in poetry. If students don't notice her delicious language on their own, I point out the rhythm of the line—"their dirges and their ditties and their blues and jubilees"—as well as the repetition of sounds in each

of the phrases: singing slave songs, dirges and ditties, and praying prayers. For beginning poets the format of a repeating line followed by a list as well as repeating sounds is a helpful link into the poem.

Then I ask students to create a list of their "people." I tell them to think of all of the communities they belong to. I list mine on the board as a way to stimulate them to think beyond their immediate categories. My list includes: Jefferson, poor whites, working class, Norwegians, Germans, teachers, feminists, social activists, women, mothers, overweight people, environmentalists.

I often use Jefferson as a model because it's the one community we all share. We catalogue reasons to celebrate our school: its diverse student body, the many languages heard in the halls, the Jefferson dancers and the gospel singers, Michele Stemler's Spanish classes, the powerful student-created murals on the walls. Then I say, "Pick one of your communities and list what you can praise about it. Think about any common misconceptions people have about any of your people. You might want to 'talk back' to those judgments in your poem."

In this, as in any assignment, some students might immediately get an idea, while others need more time to figure out who their "people" are, or what they want to say about them. This is a time when I circle the room, noticing whose writing is flowing and whose writing is stuck. I often conference with students who look stumped.

My student Cang Dao was stuck initially. We discussed how kids made fun of his newcomer English, but we also talked about how he can speak more languages than most of the student body. He embedded pieces of that talk in his poem:

People don't know how I feel
"You can't talk like us."
The words hurt me more than
It hurts them to say.

I'm getting an attitude.
Too many jokes,
I can't accept it.
What's wrong about me
That may not be accepted by them?
Is it the way I look or
The way I talk?

How many languages can you speak?
I speak four.

Is there something from
Me that you want?

My beautiful brown eyes or
My lovely skin?
Don't get jealous.

Cang's poem, "Race," talks back to those have put him down, but his poem also celebrates some of the attributes he shares with his people.

Sophia Farrier takes the opening lines from Walker and uses them to describe her pain in her poem "This is for..." She writes:

This is for the people who believed I was nothing,
that I would never be special in anyone's mind.
This is for the people who said they were my friends,
but always put me down ...
This is for the people who took my self-esteem away,
for those who never cared,
who ignored me because I wasn't "fashionable."

At the end of her poem, she attempts to find strength in herself. She changes the line from "This is for the people" to "This is for me ..."

This is for me because I didn't believe in myself.
For me because I tried too hard to be who I wasn't and
*   couldn't be ...*
And this is for my blood that rushes thick and thin
that sometimes stands tall,
but sometimes cowers away.

Lori Ann Durbin, a senior in my Writing for Publication class, was a transplanted cowgirl who ended up at Jefferson High School. Her poem celebrates that heritage:

Country Folk

For my folk, two-steppin', shit-kickin' pioneers.
Blue collar, redneck, bowlegged horsemen ...
This is my song to you.
Moonshiners, horse ranchers, hillbilly roots,
wild women, bare feet, it's nothin' or it's boots,
twangy sweet fiddle, songs about our lives,
maybe sappy to everyone else, but that's how we survive.
Fishin', singin', ridin' bareback in the field,
tight cowboy butts and Wranglers.
I love the way they feel.
Tailgate parties, couples in the barn, hay in our hair.
It's not just music.
It's a way of life.

Justin Morris, another senior, took stereotypes about black people and used them in his celebration. His poem demonstrates an in-your-face love for all aspects of his heritage. One night I was at a local copy store making huge posters of these poems to hang around the school. Several African American men from the community were copying on a machine close to my oversize machine. They laughed when they read Justin's poem and took one of the copies to hang in their office.

For My People

This is for my people
who are "colored"
who are proud.

For my people
who cause white women to clutch their purses
who white men look down on
who drank from different fountains
who fought prejudice.

For my people
with kinky afros
and gheri curls.

For my people
with big lips
and wide noses.

For my people
with black power
fingertips drenched with barbecue sauce.

For the people
with pink hearts
and brown/black skins.
For my people:
Stay strong.

The woman who feared for her life each time she walked Jefferson's halls "confessed" her racism—which is perhaps the first step toward change. I want her to read my students' poems. I want her to see beyond the baggy pants and sweatshirts to the whetstone that sharpened their minds. I hope that by reading their words, she'll see the "pink hearts" inside the "brown/black" skin, she'll hear the intelligence that ricochets off Jefferson's walls, and know she doesn't have to be afraid. ■

Resources:

Walker, Margaret, "For My People." *This Is My Century: New and Collected Poems.* Athens: University of Georgia Press, 1989.

For My People

by Shona Curtis

This is for my people
Curly hair, big noses, latkes making
Temple going torah reading shalom saying
White fish and blinsies eating
Jewish people

This is for my people
Traveling all the time won't stay in one place
Dancing around a big fire
Singing songs about their past
Gypsy people

This is for my people
Moccasin and headdress wearing
Flute and drum playing
Watching the stars from within a tent
Welcoming people into their homes
Native American people

This for my people
Hula dancing, poi eating, beat making
Fighting for their right to speak their language
Hawaiian people

This is for my people
Gospel singing get down on your knees and praise the lord
Making the best soul food you eva' had
Playing the blues and dancing to the beat of their souls
Black people

This is for my people
Surviving the holocaust
Surviving slavery
Surviving people taking their land
This is my people, the ones that live within me
My people

A Shout Out to My Black AP Students

by Alex Melson

This is a shout out to my
  Questioned
  Outstanding
  All eyes on me
  Alone brothers and sisters

To my
  Out of place
  Out of race
  Lookin' like a piece of pepper in a salt
  Shaker brothers and sisters

To my
  Unique
  Makin' it work
  Eyes on the prize
  It will all pay off in the end

This is a shout out to
  The ones who step
  Out of their comfort zone
  Who thrive under pressure
  And represent
  What it's all about

To the
  True role models
  Who prove them wrong
  And make it
  Making their own path

This is a shout out to my black AP students

For My People

by Candice Kelsey

For my people
Who are the first on this land
The ones who were strong, smart, and useful
The ones who welcomed strangers
The ones who are inside me...
A tribe unknown
This is for the Native American I have within.

For my people
of color; the brown, black, and light skinned
Beautiful people
The strong, hard working, and never-give-up people
The ones whose hands ached in pain
The ones who were stuck in the fields, never gave up hope
The ones who fought for their rights
This is for the African American I have within.

For my people
The ones who knew right from wrong
The ones who helped another
The ones who risked their lives to save another
This is for the Caucasian I have within.

For my people
All the colors, cultures, and races
For my people
The ones who came so far
For my people
Who stayed strong
For my people
That I have inside me, I am proud.

"Knock Knock": Turning Pain into Power

Poet and playwright, Daniel Beaty.

Too often today, schools are about "power standards" and common curriculum: *Scarlet Letter* and *Huck Finn* first quarter, move on to *Great Gatsby*... And too often, I get caught up in that land too. Then my heart gets cracked open by students, and I remember that first I must teach the child who is in the class. By structuring a curriculum that allows room for their lives and by listening to their stories, I can locate the right book, the right poem that turns pain into power—while I teach reading and writing. Unless I consciously build these opportunities into the curriculum, there is little opportunity to get authenticity from students.

Daniel Beaty, poet and playwright, came to life for me one New Year's Eve when my husband, Bill, and I watched hour after hour of the HBO show "Def Poetry Jam." I fell in love with many poets that night, but when I watched Daniel Beaty perform "Knock Knock," I knew I was witnessing a poet whose performance and words would inspire my students. I bought the "Def Poetry" DVD, transcribed the words, and carried Beaty with me to class. Partly autobiographical, the poem speaks directly to many of my students because Beaty's drive-home message in everything he does is that in order to heal ourselves, our society, and our world, we must turn our pain into power. (Beaty's "Def Poetry Jam" performance of "Knock Knock" is posted on YouTube: http://www.youtube.com/watch?v=nktBsI0PYPs.)

By structuring a curriculum that allows room for their lives and by listening to their stories, I can locate the right book, the right poem that turns pain into power— while I teach reading and writing.

I taught the poem to several classes at Portland's Jefferson High School days before Barack Obama was elected president. I'd spent 24 years teaching high school language arts at this predominantly African American school, and I returned to work with the faculty. I left each class in tears because when poetry, like Beaty's, cracks open students' lives in real ways, I am reminded of both the pain and the hope that schools harbor.

"Knock Knock" is constructed in three parts. Beaty begins with the story of the father's imprisonment, moves to a direct address to the father, "Papa, come home 'cause I miss you," and ends in a letter that the poet writes to "heal" and "father" himself. The poem, and Beaty's performance, are so powerful that I didn't want to interrupt it with instruction or teacher talk before they watched it the first time. I wanted them to feel the poem. My only instruction was, "As you watch the poem, notice what works for you or doesn't work. Just jot notes, so we can talk about it after we watch it a couple of times."

After students watched the poem twice, I asked them to take a few silent minutes to write their thoughts about the poem. "Look at the copy of the poem. Think about what you notice about the poem, how you connect with the poem, what poetic devices Beaty used." Students started off by talking about what they liked about the poem—from content to form: Greg said, "I like how the poem progresses from when he was young and dependent to the point when he got older and stronger." Jerome said, "He used repetition by repeating the words 'knock

Mark said, "A lot of black men could relate to this poem. Like having to teach themselves things because of an absent father."

knock.' Nothing was sugarcoated. I also like that it tells a story of pain. The story wasn't a nice-feeling, sweet one talking about love or flowers and moonlight. I connected to the story." Theresa liked "how the end of the poem is like a letter from his father that he wrote himself." When Shontay said, "I loved the line, 'Knock, knock down the doors of racism and poverty that I could not,'" many students nodded in agreement. Demetrius spoke up, "This last part makes me think of how much positive things our generation can do. How much potential we have."

Harriet said, "You know, I really like the part during the letter where he says, 'We are our fathers' sons and daughters/But we are not their choices.' We aren't the reason they made bad choices. We aren't part of their choices, and their decisions aren't our fault." I was stunned. I had taught this poem for several years with my classes at Grant High School, and I'd never thought about how a child might feel like they might bear the burden of guilt for their parents' "choices." But Harriet's comment reminded me that as a child I shouldered a lot of fear about my future based on my family's history: Would I graduate from high school? Would I go to college when no one else in my family had? Would I get pregnant and be chained to a minimum-wage job? Was my father's alcoholism a genetic stain that could explode my dreams and shackle me to relive my parents' story?

Harriet's comment prompted me to share my fears when I was their age, and I asked, "What are your fears? What chains of the past do you drag around with you? What are you afraid of? What do you worry about?"

Students wrote lists of their fears. Then we shared. Harriet said, "The women in my family have all had children before they graduated from high school, and I'm going to break that cycle." When one student opens the door for an honest conversation, others follow, especially if I create the space by responding to the student remark instead of rushing past it. So I said, "Yes, I was afraid of that too. Does anyone else have that fear?" A few other young women raised their hands.

Mark said, "My father went to jail, so I can relate to how he felt when his father never came home. A lot of black men could relate to this poem. Like having to teach themselves things because of an absent father."

Larry said, "My dad went to school at Jefferson. He never graduated, and now he's in prison. I'm going to break that cycle." Another student added, "My mother went here too. She had a bad temper and she got expelled for fighting. I don't want to get expelled for fighting." Other students shared their fears: Getting shot, becoming a drug addict, not graduating, losing a parent, not measuring up to their parents' expectations.

Writing the Poem

To move students to write the poem, I asked students to look at these three parts of the poem, "Read back over each part and write in the margin what the poet is writing about, how you connect to that part, and why you think it changes his writing style in each section." With a little nudging, students picked up on the story, the direct address, and the letter format of the poem. I didn't labor over this part of the lesson. I wanted to call attention to it, so students could build their poems in a similar style.

I gave them the following assignment: "Taking a page from Daniel Beaty, write a letter poem to yourself, giving yourself the advice you need to hear. Notice how Beaty begins with a story, then moves into the letter part of the poem that he writes to heal himself. In his letter, he lists advice to himself: 'Shave in one direction, dribble the page with your brilliance...'

"What advice do you need to hear? What do you need to do differently to succeed in school? In life? Beaty writes of the obstacles that need to be knocked down in his life: Racism, lack of opportunity. Are there obstacles in your life? Perhaps you have your school, friend, and home life together, then think of someone else who might need to hear a few words of advice.

"As an adult, there are things I wish my mother would have told me. This is not an indictment against her. Sometimes, children aren't ready to hear their parents. Also, we grow up in different times, different social periods."

Then I shared the beginnings of my poem and showed how I started with the apology, then moved from the negative to the positive in the second stanza. I also highlighted Beaty's lines to use as a frame for the poem:

Dear Linda,

I'm sorry for *the nights I left you alone*
after your father died.
I'm sorry for the solitary dinners
you ate those nights I chose a man over you.

For every lesson I failed to teach, hear these words:
Don't marry a man who drinks.
He'll spend money on booze
instead of the family.
If a man hits you once,
he'll hit you again.
Pack your bags and leave.
Move on.
When school gets hard,
remember your brilliance.
Diamonds require hard work ...

While most students wrote to themselves, a few wrote poems to other people who they thought needed advice. Andrew wrote from his father's point of view, "As I sit in a tiny cell, it amazes me how the two of us can hardly ever speak or see each other in 16 years, and yet still go through so much together.... Don't do the same idiotic decisions as me. Don't let the girls, gangs, and drugs ruin both of our lives.... I apologize for choosing the streets over my own son...."

Another student's father had died the night before our assignment. Lester wrote, "I'm sorry for leaving you five years ago without saying goodbye.... Son, do all you can to be better than me. Go to school and learn until your skull cracks. Grow up to be a wonderful father to your kids. Be there for them before they walk to the edge.... Son, I'm glad you're not here because I'm on a bed with wires attached to me and a machine that beeps every 3 seconds. I have to go because heaven is open, and I got to get in because this is the only way I can see you from a different angle."

Another student wrote a paragraph in response: "It's crazy how you love a man who was never there. I just learned not to care when you say you're going to come to my games. When you don't come, there's no disappointment. When you don't call on my birthday, there's no disappointment. Don't get me wrong, I love you, but you showed me everything I don't need to do.... Can you imagine the look on a little boy's face when the man he looks up to goes to the store for milk and never comes home.... Because of all those broken promises, I love you because you showed me how not to cry. I'm no longer weak."

Noah's poem followed the format and broke it at the same time. I love the way he played with the credit card commercial:

Dear Father,

Pay me!
Pay me well and
pay me now.
Not with your hundreds of thousands
of millions of dollars.
Pay me some damn attention!

My first bike: $87.00
Varsity basketball: $175.00
Having a care: Priceless.

Charge to your card, a hug or even a pat on the back.
Write me a check for some words of encouragement.
Send me a money order for the missed birthdays.
Your dollars will never be enough, but
Your time is priceless.
Your love is priceless.

Noah Koné

Students need opportunities to hone their skills, to write essays, to practice becoming academics. They also need opportunities to write about the tough issues in their lives that rarely surface in schools. Beaty's work opened their veins, so they could write with the blood of their lives. ∎

Knock Knock

by Daniel Beaty

As a boy I shared a game with my father.
Played it every morning 'til I was 3.
He would knock knock on my door,
and I'd pretend to be asleep
'til he got right next to the bed,
Then I would get up and jump into his arms.
"Good morning, Papa."
And my papa he would tell me that he loved me.
We shared a game.
Knock Knock

Until that day when the knock never came
and my momma takes me on a ride past corn fields
on this never ending highway 'til we reach a place of high rusty gates.
A confused little boy,
I entered the building carried in my mama's arms.
Knock Knock

We reach a room of windows and brown faces
behind one of the windows sits my father.
I jump out of my mama's arms
and run joyously towards my papa
only to be confronted by this window.
I knock knock trying to break through the glass,
trying to get to my father.
I knock knock as my mama pulls me away
before my papa even says a word.

And for years he has never said a word.
And so twenty-five years later, I write these words
for the little boy in me who still awaits his papa's knock.

Papa, come home 'cause I miss you.
I miss you waking me up in the morning and telling me you love me.
Papa, come home, 'cause there's things I don't know,
and I thought maybe you could teach me:
How to shave;
how to dribble a ball;
how to talk to a lady;
how to walk like a man.

Papa, come home because I decided a while back
I wanted to be just like you,
but I'm forgetting who you are.

And twenty-five years later a little boy cries,
and so I write these words and try to heal
and try to father myself
and I dream up a father who says the words my father did not.

Dear Son,

I'm sorry I never came home.
For every lesson I failed to teach, hear these words:
Shave in one direction in strong deliberate strokes to avoid irritation.
Dribble the page with the brilliance of your ballpoint pen.
Walk like a god and your goddess will come to you.
No longer will I be there to knock on your door,
so you must learn to knock for yourself.
Knock knock down doors of racism and poverty that I could not.
Knock knock on doors of opportunity
for the lost brilliance of the black men who crowd these cells.
Knock knock with diligence of the sake of your children.
Knock knock for me for as long as you are free,
these prison gates cannot contain my spirit.
The best of me still lives in you.
Knock knock with the knowledge that you are my son, but you are not my choices.
Yes, we are our fathers' sons and daughters,
But we are not their choices.
For despite their absences we are still here.
Still alive, still breathing
With the power to change this world,
One little boy and girl at a time.
Knock knock
Who's there?
We are.

Romilly Lockyer/GETTY IMAGES

Teaching Writing: Making Every Lesson Count

When I was a waitress at the Vista Del Mar, Elma Schwartz, the head cook, gave me valuable advice, "Make every trip count." Pouring coffee? Pick up empty plates as you circle your station. Taking out an order? Take a full load and bus the tables on your way back to the kitchen.

Although I'm no longer serving clam burgers or chicken fried steaks in that diner on Humboldt Bay, I've found that Elma's advice works in the classroom as well. My teaching needs to serve multiple purposes: I help students learn to "talk back" to the world while I teach them how to write essays. I select multicultural novels, practice close reading, and root the lessons in students' lives through narrative writing prompts.

There are times when I like to pause the critique and remind students — and myself — of what's good, what's right, what needs to be celebrated in the world.

The "I love" writing prompt that I stole from one of my student's essays uses Elma's practical advice. The lesson creates classroom community as students share their passions, and I teach the use of poetic language in prose by examining the use of listing, rhythm, and repetition in an essay. While this lesson doesn't promote a critical reading of the world, there are times when I like to pause the critique and remind students—and myself—of what's good, what's right, what needs to be celebrated in the world.

What Do You Love?

This lesson started by accident. During our college essay-writing unit, Andrew Kafoury, a senior in my Writing for Publication class, wrote a passionate essay to win acceptance into a college known for its theater program. He wrote:

When [the admissions officer] asked me to tell him why I was interested in the College of Santa Fe, I froze up. It must have been the way he was looking at me, doubtful and unimpressed. I sort of mumbled and stumbled on sentences, trying to find 10-letter words to impress him, when I should have told him the simple truth:

I love acting. I love putting on costumes and becoming creatures I am not. I love my skin sweating as bright lights send heat soaking through my body. I love getting to know my cast, watching the drama behind the drama. I love the quick change, the blackout, the dry ice and stage combat. I love cranky stage managers and quiet co-stars. I love watching ego-stricken actors fall into decline while a new face emerges from the shadows. I love the monster special effects that steal the show, and that oh-so-precious moment when you, the actor, send the audience head over heels with laughter. I love the call sheet with my name on it, and the director who calls to say I'm perfect for the part. I love the shows that I wish would go on forever, and even the ones I can't stand till they're over.

I love sitting backstage, exhausted from the matinee, and knowing in another two hours I'll go out there and do it again. I love to play the bad guy, and I love getting that killer role I've always wanted. Hell, I love it when they toss a spear in my hand and say, "Go stand in the corner." I love classical and contemporary, tragedy and comedy, romance and swashbuckling! I live for the moment when I run on stage for curtain call and the applause gets just a little bit louder. I love the smooth feeling of steady memorization, and those intense moments when something unexpected happens, like an actor not showing up two minutes before curtain, so the stage hands have to make a split-second decision because, damn it, man, the show MUST go on.

After Andrew read his essay to fourth period, I decided the rest of the students should all experiment with an "I love…" piece to potentially add to their college essays. It was just too much of a teachable moment to waste. Some ended up in my students' college essays—like my daughter, Gretchen Hereford's, below—while others turned into prose poetry.

I admit it: I love Outdoor School. I love the rain, the mud, and the mushrooms growing in the dark womb of the forest. I love the skits. I love the silly name games. I love the stories, the songs, and the hand gestures students share. I love the cabins and the smell of fir trees. I love the sound of a student's voice when she answers a question right. I love explaining why there are no pinecones in a fir forest. I love being a person

someone looks up to. I love the sound of laughter. I love slipping and falling in mud. I love breathing in fresh air, and I love getting away from car exhaust. I love Outdoor School.

Since Andrew's initial reading a number of years ago, I have used his prompt again and again. (As I point out in "Move Over, Sisyphus," I use Andrew's piece to teach poetic lists in prose.) Sometimes students write about their own passions. Other times they use the topic to write from the point of view of historical or literary characters because the prompt forces them to recall specific details from the text. What does Janie in *Their Eyes Were Watching God* love? Charlotte in *Charlotte's Web*? How about Emma Goldman? Bayard Rustin?

Elementary through high school teachers in the Portland Writing Project use variations of this piece with their students. Some elementary teachers use this prompt to get students to write from the perspectives of ants, spiders, bears, or thunderstorms. Some early elementary teachers use Eloise Greenfield's poem "Honey, I Love" to prompt their students' writing. The pattern in Greenfield's poem works great with younger students.

Putting Clothes on the Ghost

One huge problem that crops up in student papers is the lack of specific details. They love in abstract—their mothers, fathers, best friends—who are "always there for them." Their papers are bland because they don't provide enough details to create images in the reader's mind. I can discuss abstract nouns until the cows come home, but Andrew's piece shows students how to put clothes on those ghost nouns and make them dance.

Before reading Andrew's piece together, I give each student two colored highlighters. I ask them to highlight repeating words or phrases in one color and the vocabulary of theatre in another color. Students note the way Andrew repeats the words "I love." Then I ask students to call out all of the language that Andrew uses about theatre. I want students to see that one of the strengths of Andrew's piece is his use of specific details and language about theater—the dry ice, stage combat, memorization, audience, stage, drama, comedy, tragedy. He is an insider in this world, and he is giving us a guided tour.

Then I ask students to write lists of what they love. They love skateboarding, chocolate, singing in the church choir, Saturday mornings, and summer vacation. They love snow days and hot chocolate, skiing and baseball, video games and ice skating. They love summer days playing basketball at Irving Park, fishing for steelhead in the Willamette River, and eating Grandma's sweet potato pie. After they list, I encourage them to share a few out loud, so that students who are stuck can get more ideas. But this spontaneous sharing also leads us to discover new insights about each other.

Teaching Grammar in Context

Once they have shared, students each choose one item from their list and brainstorm specific evidence. "Write all of the verbs for what you love in one column. For example, if you love baseball, what verbs would you need to have on your list?" Students shout out: hit, run, slide, catch, strike, throw, bunt.

After students list verbs to include in their piece, I move to those delicious, specific details that insiders know. We repeat the group listing of baseball vocabulary as a class: glove, uniform, bat, games, bases, mound, dugout. I point out that generally these are nouns. Then students write a list of the vocabulary for their passion.

Developing Sentence Agility

I return to Andrew's piece to study sentence structure. I read the piece out loud again and ask students to listen to the rhythm of the lines. How does he make that happen? We count the words. We take note of how he shifts between long and short sentences, the way he uses items in a series to move the sentence: "I love the quick change, the blackout, the dry ice, and stage combat." I point out the way he sometimes balances the sentence over the word *and*: "I love cranky stage managers *and* quiet co-stars." And other times he pairs a series of two items and creates another list: "I love classical and contemporary, tragedy and comedy, romance and swashbuckling!"

Students take Andrew's piece as a case study of why and how writers vary sentence structure to alter pacing, and then they revise their pieces to move to that punchy language. Sean Jacobsen, a Grant sophomore, used the list, sentence variation, word length, and word sound in his piece about the recording studio:

> I love the studio. I love the computer screens and track bars. I love the speakers and the subs. I love the never-ending keyboards. I love the producers and co-artists. I love the beat and the *a cappella*. I love the pen and the pad. I love the mike and the booth. I love the glass window that separates me from the world. I love the feeling of freedom, passion, love, and vengeance. I love the finished product. I love the memory within it. I love the studio.

Once students have a large stash of language, reasons, and phrases, I point out that writers use the list, the rush of repetitions, the sharp, specific nouns, the cumulative sentence in many forms of writing—from essay to fiction to poetry. Then I return students to Andrew's piece. "Look at this sentence again: 'I love the quick change, the blackout, the dry ice, and stage combat.' Underline that. Somewhere in your piece, I want you to try to include a line that lists. Notice how he uses those details that only insiders know. What list can you include in yours? Now, look at the sentence: 'I love classical and contemporary, tragedy and comedy, romance and swashbuckling!' Underline that sentence. I want you to include a sentence like that in your piece. If you get stuck, go back to Andrew's piece and pick out a technique that he uses to get unstuck."

Before students head into the writing, I say, "I need you to get quiet now. As a writer, I need a quiet space in my mind to calm the chatter, so I can focus on my writing. I'm asking you for 15 minutes of silence, so you and your classmates can find that silent spot and write from it. I encourage you to be wild, to write fast and furious—to put it all in, to dare to be outrageous. I also want you to be specific, like Andrew. I want you to name the park, name the bait, the boat, and the gas station. What is the language of your love? Don't worry about spelling, grammar, or punctuation. Just spill the words out on the page."

After students play around with the words and phrases on their lists, we share our pieces out loud in a read-around, pausing to laugh and to point out what we *love* about each other's writing.

Writing Prose Like a Poet

I often share a few examples from my favorite writers because I want students to pay attention to how writers use these strategies. When I teach writing, I am also teaching reading. Notice how Tom Robbins in his delightful essay "Why I Live in Northwest Washington" uses a list, repetition, and lively language soaked in the Northwest:

> I'm here for the weather.
>   Well, yes, I'm also here for the volcanoes and the salmon, and the exciting possibility that at any moment the volcanoes could erupt and pre-poach the salmon. I'm here for the rust and the mildew, for webbed feet and twin peaks, spotted owls and obscene clams… blackberries and public art… for the ritual of the pot-latch and the espresso cart, for bridges that pratfall into the drink and ferries that keep ramming the dock.

I'm here because the Wobblies used to be here, and sometimes in Pioneer Square you can still find bright-eyed old anarchists singing their moldering ballads of camaraderie and revolt.... I'm here for the forests (what's left of them), for the world's best bookstores and movie theaters; for the informality, anonymity, general lack of hidebound tradition, and the fact that here and nowhere else grunge rubs shoulders in the half-mean streets with a pervasive yet subtle mysticism. The shore of Puget Sound is where electric guitars cut their teeth, and old haiku go to die.

Charlotte's Web has an unforgettable description where a sheep explains to Templeton the rat how a county fair is a "rat's paradise":

Everybody spills food at a fair. A rat can creep out late at night and have a feast. In the horse barn you will find oats that the trotters and pacers have spilled. In the trampled grass of the infield you will find old discarded lunchboxes containing the foul remains of peanut butter sandwiches, hard-boiled eggs, cracker crumbs, bits of donuts, and particles of cheese. In the hard-packed dirt of the midway, after the glaring lights are out and the people have gone home to bed, you will find a veritable treasure of popcorn fragments, frozen custard dribblings, candied apples abandoned by tired children, sugar fluff crystals, salted almonds, popsicles, partially gnawed ice cream cones, and the wooden sticks of lollypops.

Susan Orlean's, *The Orchid Thief,* takes listing and cumulative sentences to a new art form. For a follow-up homework assignment, I send students out to find lists in books, song lyrics, magazines, or newspaper articles.

Beloved: Loving Ourselves

The language in Toni Morrison's *Beloved* extends this lesson into literature and history. Baby Suggs, an "unchurched preacher, one who opened her great heart to those who could use it" holds "church" in a clearing, exhorting her followers to love themselves. Morrison uses lists, repetition, and strong verbs in this excerpt, but Morrison does more than write proficient prose; she teaches writers how to dance with language. Her message about loving yourself, her admonition to celebrate and love in you what others do not love, is both a history lesson, and reminder that students need to hear:

"Here," [Baby Suggs] said, "in this here place, we flesh; flesh that weeps, laughs; flesh that dances on bare feet in grass. Love it. Love it hard. Yonder they do not love your flesh. They despise it. They don't love your eyes; they'd just as soon pick em out. No more do they love the skin on your back. Yonder they flay it. And O my people they do not love your hands. Those they only use, tie, bind, chop off and leave empty. Love your hands! Love them. Raise them up and kiss them. Touch others with them, pat them together, stroke them on your face 'cause they don't love that either. *You* got to love it, *you!* And no, they ain't in love with your mouth. Yonder, out there, they will see it broken and break it again. What you say out of it they will not heed. What you scream from it they do not hear. What you put into it to nourish your body they will snatch away and give you leavins instead. No, they don't love your mouth. *You* got to love it. This is flesh I'm talking about here. Flesh that needs to be loved. Feet that need to rest and to dance; backs that need support; shoulders that need arms, strong arms I'm telling you. And O my people, out yonder, hear me, they do not love your neck unnoosed and straight. So love your neck; put a hand on it, grace it, stroke it and hold it up. And all your inside parts that they'd just as soon slop for hogs, you got to love them. The dark, dark liver—love it, love it, and the beat and beating heart, love that too. More than eyes or feet. More than lungs that have yet to draw free air. More than your life-holding womb and your life-giving private parts, hear me now, love your heart. For this is the prize." Saying no more, she stood up then and danced with her twisted hip the rest of what her heart had to say while others opened their mouths and gave her the music. Long notes held until the four-part harmony was perfect enough for their deeply loved flesh.

Over the years I've discovered that grammar and language books have their place as references, but to learn how to use language effectively, students need to pay attention to how writers, like Andrew Kafoury, E.B. White, Tom Robbins, and Sean Jacobsen pull them into their pieces. Students also need to experiment with their own writing, to get playful, to practice making words sing.

Elma's mantra about making every trip count lives on in my work today. When we have so much to teach, we can't afford to deliver lessons one item at a time. My students at Jefferson and Grant High School didn't have the time or patience for repetitious language and sentence drills. The work of becoming writers—and skillful readers—requires a playful attention to detail while writing a piece that matters in a room where experimenting is honored. ■

I Love Baseball

by Juan Mauleon

I love baseball. I love playing games all throughout the warm summers. I love staying close to my teammates, growing stronger as a team, while the season goes on. I love the quick innings, the long innings, the blowouts, and the one-run games. I love the sound of cheering fans as the game is on the line. I love victories. I love playing games against our rivals like Westview, Sherwood, and Scappoose. I love traveling far away from home to play in tournaments. I love having the ball in my hand on the mound when the last out is recorded. I love striking kids out and watching them return to the dugout with an angry look on their faces. I love throwing a nasty curve ball in the dirt, knowing that my catcher will stop the ball. I love the food at the concession stands: hot dogs, burgers, and Gatorade. I love my family supporting me through every practice, game, tournament, and season.

I Love Skiing

by Kyle Fish

I love skiing. I love getting up early on a cold winter morning and heading to the mountain with a cup of hot chocolate cradled in my hands. I love the turns, the jumps, the rails and the black diamond runs. I love being the first one on the slopes in the morning and the last one off at night. I love my skis gliding over knee-deep powder and eating snow as I wait in line for the lift. I love the moment in the air after a jump that I wish could last forever. I love eating my lunch on the lift, so I don't have to stop. I love a quick cut on a backcountry run to narrowly dodge a tree and finally landing a trick that I have tried so many times before. I love racing my dad down a crazy steep run, and I love the mogul field on the Magic Mile. I love the ride up the lift, and I love not being able to wait to get to the top, so I can come down again.

Carol Kohen/GETTY IMAGES

Move Over, Sisyphus: Teaching Grammar and Poetry

Let me surrender to a moment of truth telling: I still struggle to name the parts of speech and identify what's wrong in multiple-choice sentences on grammar tests. I still don't know how to use lie and lay correctly, and once in a while, I get the apostrophe in the wrong spot. But I know how to write—most of the time. And, when I'm "done" with a piece of writing, I know where to go to fix my problems. My students also suffer from gaps in their grammar and punctuation knowledge.

As a teacher, I can spend time either drilling students over and over again on the same grammar rules they seem to forget when it comes time to write, or I can spend my precious minutes teaching them how to use language more effectively.

Poetry as Grammar Text

When I was a new teacher, I dutifully pulled out the grammar textbooks, taught—and learned—parts of speech and grammar "demons" lessons. I noticed that students could get questions right on my ditto sheets (old days) and even pass end-of-chapter grammar tests, and still make the same errors in their writing. My students' writing was as stiff and unnatural as if they were wearing a too-small suit. Over the years I learned that my work with students on their poetry led to a stronger grasp of parts of speech, especially verbs, nouns, and adjectives, than my old worksheets did. But, even more significantly, my students' language jumped off the page. They slide their verbal dexterity from poetry to essays and narratives.

When students warm up their tongues through poetry, they carry that language play into their essays and narratives. Khalilah Joseph, for example, uses juicy language, full of rhythm, action, alliteration, and attitude in her essay "Tar Baby":

> I can watch a video by a given artist and before the end of it, the object of desire will prance across the screen, and, of course, she'll be a honey dipped, barely-brown bombshell.... Be gone with those tiny waisted, no-hip-having heifers. Bring on the models who range in color from caramel to dark chocolate.

(The full essay is included in *Reading, Writing, and Rising Up*, p. 70.)

My work with students on their poetry led to a stronger grasp of parts of speech, especially verbs, nouns, and adjectives, than my old worksheets did. But, even more significantly, my students' language jumped off the page.

In her essay about the education of black students, Valentina Harold uses the poetic devices of listing, repetition, and metaphor as she pushes her point: "Few people of color at Grant High School take AP classes. I understand why: They are afraid of failing, afraid of looking bad, and afraid of being the only black in a sea of white."

By letting go of the rules and the mandates about teaching grammar, I freed my students to find their voices, to learn how to write instead of how to answer multiple-choice tests about parts of speech or how to correct someone else's language.

I do my serious work of teaching students how to use language more effectively through poetry, a skill we transfer from our poetry to our prose. I want my students to pay attention to words, to use lists and imagery, to give up everyday, shopworn words for words that surprise, sing, provoke. I urge them to scrutinize their verbs to make them more active and to avoid adverbs and adjectives, which one writer called "the potbelly of poetry." When writers use generic nouns or verbs, they sometimes add an adjective or adverb to describe the action more fully, but frequently, those words make "fat" sentences because the combinations produce such flat and predictable phrases that the words barely register for the reader. For example: James walked slowly to class. If the writer used a more precise verb, she wouldn't need the adverb: James limped to class or James flirted his way to class or James crept to class.

I also encourage students to highlight all was, were, are in their poetry, as well as their narratives and essays, and see if they can create a more poetic sentence. For example, "It was a hot day" might become "the day sweated."

Verbs and Language Play

Too often, grammar study is the dull naming of parts of speech that students have difficulty remembering beyond the simple recitation, "A noun is a person, place, or thing." Well-meaning teachers, administrators, and parents who push the idea of high expectations for all students, sometimes equate the naming of parts of speech with writing. I rarely attend a meeting about improving writing where someone doesn't lament, "In the old days, kids knew what a verb was." Teachers hold struggling writers hostage to learning grammar before they can write papers. Under the mistaken notion that students who have a tentative grasp of writing conventions will benefit from studying the names of things—from sentence parts to types of sentences—struggling writers

Marc Romanelli/GETTY IMAGES

return year after year to the basic sentence before they move to the paragraph and finally to a narrative or essay. Like Sisyphus, ceaselessly rolling a rock to the top of a mountain, unskilled writers are condemned to the hopeless labor of naming instead of doing. Albert Camus presents Sisyphus' efforts as a metaphor for modern lives spent toiling at futile jobs in factories and offices: "The workman of today works every day in his life at the same tasks, and this fate is no less absurd. But it is tragic only at the rare moments when it becomes conscious." Camus encourages revolt. So do I. Real rigor is not memorizing terms isolated from their work in the world.

Instead, I put students to work creating poetry that teaches them how to use grammar in context, to examine how writers use grammar as a tool in their pieces. As I tell students, "Verbs make your poetry (and essays) strut and dance, or they make your audience snore." We examine the verbs in poems, like Quincy Troupe's "Poem for Magic," a poem so lively, we can hear the rhythm of the ball as Magic crosses the court, watch him wipe the glass, and pause before he dishes out the ball. I start with sports poems because verbs dominate the pieces. We read the poem out loud, so students can hear how rapidly Troupe's poem moves, like a basketball up and down the court. He uses quick-paced language to simulate movement.

POEM FOR MAGIC

by Quincy Troupe

take it to the hoop, "magic" johnson,
take the ball dazzling down the open lane
herk & jerk & raise your six-feet, nine-inch frame
into the air sweating screams of your neon name
"magic" johnson, nicknamed "windex" way back
in high school
cause you wiped glass backboards
so clean, where you first juked and shook
wiled your way to glory
a new-style fusion of shake-&-bake
energy, using everything possible, you created your own
space to fly through — any moment now
we expect your wings to spread feathers for that spooky takeoff
of yours — then, shake & glide & ride up in space
till you hammer home a clothes-lining deuce off glass
now, come back down with a reverse hoodoo gem
off the spin & stick in sweet, popping nets clean
from twenty feet, right side ...

After we've read the poem, I ask students to appreciate Troupe's work: "What do you love about this poem? What works for you?" Then I hand out two different colors of highlighters to each student. I ask them, "What is a verb? Give me some examples." After it seems like they get the gist of a verb, I say, "Look at the first three lines of Troupe's poem. Highlight the verbs." After they call out the verbs in those lines, I tell them to highlight the verbs in the rest of the stanza. Of course, frequently, students highlight adjectives and nouns as well as verbs, and this is an opportunity to discuss the differences, in context, while they write.

As the students call out verbs, I ask, "What verbs made you 'see' Magic Johnson?" Students read out: herk and jerk, wiped, juked and shoot, shake and glide, hammer. I tell them, "Notice how he doesn't stick dull, old stale combinations of verbs that one would expect in a poem about basketball; he shakes us with surprises and makes us see Magic Johnson on the court. Troupe saturates us in the language of the basketball court. Now go back to the poem and using your second highlighter color, I want you to color all of the basketball vocabulary he uses." Students note the lane, backboards, and nets, which leads us to a discussion about nouns and the work they do in a sentence or poem. I ask students to keep Troupe's poem handy, so they can look back and see how Troupe handled verbs or line breaks.

I also bring in other sports poems, "Analysis of Baseball" by Mae Swenson, "Fast Break" by Edward Hirsch, and "The Base Stealer" by Robert Francis. In each of these poems, I push students to examine how the writers have slowed the motion of action so they can see the extension of an arm, the slide of a hand, the rotation of a ball. They use verbs to take the reader through each step, each movement as they record it in the poem. For example, in "Fast Break," Hirsch writes, "A hook shot kisses the rim and/hangs there, helplessly, but doesn't drop,/and for once our gangly starting center/boxes out his man and times his jump/perfectly, gathering the orange leather/from the air like a cherished possession." Again, the writing soars with tight language and crisp verbs.

I tell students to write their own movement poems—giving, as always, room for inspiration and surprise as well as riverbanks (parameters or gentle directions) to help the writing flow. Through this poem, I want students to bring their lives, their passions into the classroom. I tell them: "Make a list of people you know who are really good at something. Include yourself. If you are a pitcher, let us see how you throw the ball. If you dance, take us through a piece. List the person and their passion. For example, my nephew Lee is crazy about fishing. My mother was an artist in the garden. Think big. This doesn't have to be about sports. Lucille Clifton wrote a poem for Malcolm X. Martín Espada wrote a poem celebrating a custodian. Naomi Shihab Nye wrote a poem about her father making Arabic coffee. Think of creating a poem about an organizer, a field worker, a cafeteria worker, a parent preparing dinner." Once students have created a list, I say, "Let's hear some of your thoughts. Anyone who's stuck, steal these ideas. Let these ideas jumpstart yours."

Then we move to the next piece of the activity—focusing on the language of the art/craft, including verbs. We take one of the potential items on a student's list, and we brainstorm together a list of verbs, then a list of other words that could be used in the poem. "Pete said, fishing. Let's help him out. Let's list fishing words on the board." The students generate a list: line, lure, dock, boat, bait, hook, fly, lunker, tubeworms, bass, trout, steelhead. Then I push, "What verbs will move this poem?" Toss, spin, cast, reel, catch, release, flick, drift.

Students write poems about basketball, baseball, dance, as well as poems about people immersed in their art or craft. Each poetry exercise works towards the goal of writing and reading poetry and learning to use language. In

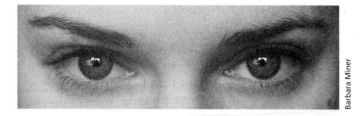

Barbara Miner

other words, I don't obsess if students write a poem where verbs aren't the focus because the bigger piece of instruction is to discover how to find voice and passion and a way to show us their lives. (See "Bottom of the Ninth.")

When they work on revision, I remind students to read their poems out loud and notice where the rhythm works and where it stalls. I encourage them to use short, one syllable words when they want to quicken the pace, like Quincy Troupe ("herk, jerk, take it to the hoop") and to interrupt the pace of longer lines. We go back to the original poems, so they can see how other poets used the rhythm of the list in their poetry.

The List Links the Work Forward

Many writers use listing as a poetic device in both poetry and prose. Lists push the writer beyond the known into new territory. Poems that use lists create a great warm-up activity and sometimes result in stunning new poems. The listing poem can also teach students to use cumulative sentences, noun and verb phrases.

I use the poem "I Got the Blues," by former Jefferson student Aaron Wheeler-Kay, to get students into the listing mood. I like his piece because he keeps pushing the list. The reader can feel him changing as he explores words, like a blues riff, caught and held, then discarded as he finds a new word.

I Got the Blues

Blue eyes.
Yes, ma'am.
Blue.
Like the ocean —
No, blue like new jeans,
Stiff and comfy —
No, blue like hard times.
Yeah.
Blue like cold steel and oil.
Blue like the caress of jazz at a funeral.
The azure ice cubes in my head
Melt hearts.
Yes, blue like lightning in a desert storm.
Blue like my baby.

Like my baby blues.
Blue like cold lips in winter,
Indigo stains
In an optical vein.
I got the blues
And they got a tale to tell.

Of course, teaching poetry doesn't mean that I abandon my social justice perspective. I also use the poem "Brown Dreams" by Paul Flores that tells a story about immigrants who join the military in order to gain U.S. citizenship. I start by showing Flores perform his poem on HBO's "Def Poetry Jam," then we read the poem out loud, and talk about the content of the poem. (The poem is posted online at http://www.youtube.com/watch?v=hhttoJwALoA.) Once we discuss the idea of "Brown Dreams," I ask students to look at how Flores uses the list throughout his poem. He starts with a list of phrases beginning with the word "who": "Brown boy who wasn't even a citizen,/Who'd barely been a resident five years,/Who didn't know much about education,/Was now willing to die to become a student." Then he shifts to a list of similes in the final stanza of his poem:

This is a brown dream,
Brown as the bus riders' union,
Brown as gasoline,
Brown as the Tigris, the Euphrates, the Mississippi,
and the Rio Grande,
Brown as coyotes,
Brown as the blood-soaked sands of Iraq
And the ranches of Arizona border vigilantes
Brown
Brown as affirmative action in the military
But not the university.

This is a brown dream.

I point out the repetition of brown in "Brown Dreams" and blue in "I Got the Blues." We also read "Yellow" by Charles Wright, which includes a list, then pushes the list with more details: "Yellow is for regret, the distal, the second hand;/The grasshopper's wing, that yellow, the slur of dust;/Back light, the yellow of loneliness." Wright's poem demonstrates how to add phrases to create rhythm and pause in a line. But we also look at how he uses commas in a series for those phrases. Students sometimes stop at the first part of a line, with the initial comparison, but the sentence or line becomes more interesting if the student adds on phrases. My student Bree Levine-DeSpain wrote a praise poem about herself, "Just Thick":

Just thick,
Thick like North Carolina sweet grained
Sun-kissed cornbread,
Melt in your mouth, smothered with
Butter and honey thick.

She pulses the description forward, drawing it out, like Wright, until she moves to the next stanza and a new comparison. Bree's poem plays with language, but it is also about content. In this praise poem, Bree talks back to the images of thin women paraded on the glossy covers of magazines by glorifying her "thick thighs/thick hips" which she connects to her African American/Latina heritage.

I also use a section of the slam poet Patricia Smith's poem, "Left Memories" where she repeats the words "I can't" then moves into a tight list of who she is, a black woman, by listing all of the things she can't stop doing, like "walking in a straight line without my hips wailing hallelujah." (Available online at http://poetry.about.com/library/weekly/aa061202b.htm.)

I can't
stop listening to blues songs where some checkertoothed
*   growler*
informs me that my heart is worthless or missing altogether.
I can't unravel the mystery of me, and it's growing late.
I can't walk in a straight line without my hips wailing
*   hallelujah.*
I can't stop dancing like a colored girl with a lit match at
*   her backside.*
I can't believe that I will be 50 before I am 40 again.
I can't find anyone to jump doubledutch with me.
I can't make my poems be happy. I have tried neon ink,
perfumed paper and writing naked under a silver-spilling
*   moon.*
I can't hold my mother close long enough for her body
*   to realize*
how completely it once harbored mine.

I encourage students to write their own list poem. I tell them, "Think of a color or a word or a phrase as the springboard for your list. Remember how Aaron Wheeler-Kay used the word 'blues,' then pushed the word. Remember how Bree took the idea, but instead of a color, she used the word 'thick?' You might also try using a phrase like Patricia Smith's 'I can't.' Then extend your list by thinking about the politics of color or the story behind the list: What else are you saying? Go beyond the typical, the usual." This is where we evoke both the poetic and political imagination. I encourage students to mix their lists—to include the known, blue is for water, but to extend the list to bring in the unusual, the unexpected—"brown as the bus riders' union"—a reference to the inspirational Los Angeles organization formed to press for greater access to affordable transportation.

For example, Grant High School student Anaiah Rhodes' poem "Black" is about the color, but also a tribute to being black. Her work was influenced by the work of Dudley Randall's "Black Girl" and other Harlem Renaissance poets we studied who praised and reclaimed the beauty of their color and features when white society demeaned and denigrated blacks. For Anaiah, "Black is harmony/Like the notes in a symphony/The hymns my mama hums to me." She takes the word harmony and keeps expanding the concept—a symphony, hymns.

When I give this assignment, I encourage students by telling them, "If you are listing why you love your grandmother's buttermilk biscuits, go for it. Add as many items as you can to the list: sights, smells, butter dripping over the edge, the way they feel in your mouth. This is a love poem to those biscuits. Make us all want them. You can weed later. Get it all down now."

When I discovered that I could give up grammar ditto sheets, I became a teacher. Instead of following mindless mandates and old-school rules, I started observing my students' writing, and I dared to say, "What happens when students are treated as intellectuals instead of intellectually challenged?" Through poetry students not only learn to harness their sassy, audacious playfulness into art, they learn a few parts of speech and ways to work with language along the way. ■

Bottom of the Ninth

by Scott Steele

Fingernails glide smoothly
across seams,
rosin absorbing
sweat from palms,
dirt skyrocketing
from the intrusion
of cleats,
signals encoded
in fingers,
an imperceptible nod,
the slow and deliberate
bringing together of the hands.

A pause.

A furtive glance.
The knee ascends
then swings,
the arm plummets
then arcs upward,
the leg kicks,
the elbow
leads the wrist
expelling the ball
between the
middle and the forefingers.
The ball in
violent revolution
crosses the plate.
Strike out.

I Got the Blues

by Aaron Wheeler-Kay

Blue eyes.
Yes, ma'am.
Blue.
Like the ocean—
No, blue like new jeans,
Stiff and comfy—
No, blue like hard times.
Yeah.
Blue like cold steel and oil.
Blue like the caress of jazz at a funeral.
The azure ice cubes in my head
Melt hearts.
Yes, blue like lightning in a desert storm.
Blue like my baby.
Like my baby blues.
Blue like cold lips in winter,
Indigo stains
In an optical vein.
I got the blues
And they got a tale to tell.

Black

by Anaiah Rhodes

Black is beautiful
Black is bold
Like the peppa in the salt shaker
Black words on white paper

Black is harmony
Like the notes in a symphony
The hymns my mama hums to me

Black is love
Courage in hard times
To tell it like it is

Black on the ledger
Makes the money flow
Black is success

Black magic
Elegant and classy
The feeling before the curtain pulls back
Black entourage

Black is the heartbeat
Of the soul
Like still waters
Riches untold
Black is beautiful

Just Thick

by Bree Levine-DeSpain

Just thick
Thick like North Carolina sweet grained
Sun-kissed cornbread thick,
Melt in your mouth, smothered
With butter and honey thick.

Thick
Thick like homemade pancake batter
Smooth to the touch
Yet creamy and delectable
To the tongue.

Thick
Thick like caramel sauce
Mouthwatering, sweet, and sticky
To the touch.

Thick
Thick thighs
Thick hips
Just thick.

Good ol' Southern style, eat what tastes good
"You wanna go to Popeye's?"
"Naw, I'll have a milkshake!"
Cornbread, pancakes, caramel sauce.
I'm thick.

Fox Photos/GETTY IMAGES

Unleashing Sorrow and Joy: Writing Poetry from History and Literature

Lila wrote that Celie, from *The Color Purple*, was a "record/on your shelf/ the one/dressed/in dust and age/... the one/your liquor-heavy fingers/find/ on days/your red water eyes/don't know the difference..." Don wrote that she was the "cold hard black floor/everyone walked on." Both students capture the essence of Celie through their poetry. Over the years, I have learned that sometimes writing a poem or interior monologue from history or literature can create a space in the classroom for a different way of knowing, a different way of expressing knowledge about a fictional character or a historical decision. My skin, my blood, my bones understand events before my mind catches up and processes the information. Too often learning becomes recitation, the dull retelling of facts, but writing poetry helps unleash sorrow or joy, the human understanding of loss and creation across cultures, centuries, and continents, so I try to create opportunities for students to demonstrate their knowledge through poetry and interior monologues as well as essays. Because my units extend for five to 10 weeks, poetry also provides new venues for students to explore their understanding

> **Sometimes writing a poem or interior monologue from history or literature can create a space in the classroom for a different way of knowing, a different way of expressing knowledge about a fictional character or a historical decision.**

of the unit. Writing poetry creates breaks for us to review concepts, materials, and re-engage in our studies with new sensibilities.

I don't give quizzes. They feel like a "gotcha" set up to catch students who haven't read. I know who hasn't read, and I'm trying to entice students in rather than push them out. These poetry pit stops help students get caught up, and re-engage them in the content so they can learn from their classmates, but they also provide structures for the students who have read to catch their breath and talk about the "texts" in new ways.

I experiment with new poetry frequently, but I've found three "frames" for content-driven poetry that help students capture details from the unit and herd those facts into poetry. The frames I use most often are: Metaphor poem, "Write that I …" poem, and the "Mirror" poem. With each of the poems, I find a pause point during the first quarter when I introduce the poetry format by encouraging students to write a "gift" poem about someone in their life. Daniel Clark-Rizzio's poem about "Grandpa Joe" provides a model of the metaphorical poem. I use the same procedure as I move through the exercise whether it is personal or literary: Steep students in the models, point out key features in the poems, write, and share in a read-around about form and content.

Metaphor Poems

I begin by reading Don Pendleton and Lila Johnson's poems about Celie. As we read each poem, I ask, "What comparison does the writer use?" Students point out that Don Pendleton compares Celie to the floor, then to the ceiling. I ask, "What is he saying about her? What does that metaphor imply about how Celie changes?" As we move to Lila Johnson's poem, we talk about how Lila compares Celie to a worn record "full of cracked songs… the one your liquor-heavy fingers find." I ask, "What story does Lila tell us through this metaphor?" As we examine and talk about the poems, I encourage students to notice that Lila's comparison isn't random; she informs the reader about Celie's life.

We look at how the initial metaphor in Lila's poem — Celie is a record — is expanded by the vocabulary and language the writer chooses: cracked songs, jackets, golden sounds, record. As a class, we brainstorm metaphors for the character and play with expanding the language in the same way Lila and Don did in their poems. In *Their Eyes Were Watching God*, for example, I asked, "How would you describe Janie's relationship with her husbands?" Kirk

said she was like a possession for Joe. He wanted to show her off. "How would you draw that? What metaphor could you use to show that relationship?" Stephanie said Janie was like a ring on Joe's finger. Emma said Joe put her on pedestal, which kept her away from the other people in town. "So if she's a ring or she's on a pedestal, what other words would you use to extend the poem? What words go with ring and pedestal? Look back at how Lila used words related to records. What words can you use? List those words and then weave those words in as you write your poem."

Once students have a sense of how to proceed with the poem, I pass out paper and crayons, which is always a big hit in the high school classroom. I ask students to create a metaphorical drawing for one of the characters (literary or historical depending on the unit). I say, "I'm not concerned about your artistic ability. I want to see your thinking about the characters. Think metaphorically." I've discovered that the time students spend drawing allows them to think more deeply about their work. It's not unusual for students to get stuck, so as I travel around the room, I ask a few students to share their drawings and discuss the comparison in order to get other students started.

After students create their metaphorical drawings, they expand the language of the metaphor in the same way that Don and Lila did in their poetry. I say, "On the back of your paper, write an explanation of your metaphor. Then list the vocabulary or language to expand the metaphor. If it's a garden, go for flowers, hose, water, vegetables, etc." Students share their drawings and metaphors in a quick whip around the classroom. I encourage classmates to help those who are struggling with the expansion and vocabulary. By this time, the students who were stuck have a good idea of how to proceed.

Then students write their poems. I encourage them to look back at the models. "When you are not sure how to move forward, look back at how Lila, Don, Jessica, and others wrote their poems [see pp. 54-55]. Think about whether you want to use first person like Lila and Don. If you do, then you begin your poem with either the name or the metaphor: 'I am Celie.' Or you can begin in third person like Daniel Clark-Rizzio, 'Grandpa Joe was a boxer.'"

The creation of the metaphor pushes students to develop a stronger understanding of characters because they have to explain how the metaphor works. While I like the poetry that comes from this exercise, I also appreciate that the activity helps students develop a frame for a potential essay. (See "Slavery and Resistance.")

Write That I...

Many years ago, I found a wonderful poem about a woman on a balcony. The poem started, "Write that I..." In the jumble of my file cabinets and my moves, I lost the original poem, but I didn't lose my love for this opening, so I wrote a poem from the point of view of Molly Craig, the main character in the movie *Rabbit Proof Fence* to use as a model with students. *Rabbit Proof Fence* is a film about the Australian government's policy of placing mixed-race Aboriginal children in boarding schools.

I begin by reading my poem "Molly Craig" out loud. I ask students to highlight the poem with two colors of highlighters: "Highlight the repeating lines in one color. For example, 'Write that I' is a repeating line. What other lines repeat? Highlight the details about Molly's life in the other color." Students usually identify the lines "write that I," and "tell them," etc. But if they don't, I point out that the poem uses a series of phrases that help weave the content together: Write that I; tell them that I; when you write my story, say that I. Students are also quick to point out all of the details from the movie. If they don't notice, I show them that I use specific information: Names of people and places, dialogue from the movie, characters' actions.

Now that they have student models, I ask students to look at how Jayme Causey used the repeating line, "Write that I..." in his poem about the Soweto Uprising.

Once students understand that frame of repeating lines—write that I, say that I, when you tell my story—I encourage them to add phrases that would hook their poem forward. "What other phrases could you use to anchor your stanza?"

Then we generate a list of characters for their poems. As we make the list, I encourage them to think about minor characters, bystanders, as well as objects in the landscape. For example, when we studied about the Soweto Uprising (see "Uncovering the Legacy of Language and Power"), students listed Hector Pieterson, who was killed by the police during the uprising, Hector's sister, the photographer, and a teacher whose students walked out, but they also listed the school building, the flag, the bullet that killed Hector.

BoB King/CORBIS

Mirror Poems

Lucille Clifton is one of my favorite poets. I love the way her poem, "what the mirror said," celebrates her beauty and strength instead of her flaws. Her poem is sassy and talks back to the traditional standards that measure a woman's beauty:

> listen,
> you a wonder.
> you a city
> of a woman.
> listen,
> somebody need a map
> to understand you.
> somebody need directions
> to move around you.

Originally, I used this poem as a praise poem, telling students, "Make a list of what you can praise about yourself: Be extraordinary, go all out. Imagine you are Lucille Clifton. This is the time to brag about your culture, your language, your hair, your skin tones, your brain, your school, your neighborhood."

Using Clifton as a model, I asked students to notice how Clifton entered the poem. They noted that her poem begins with the title, "what the mirror said." Curtina talked about how Clifton personifies the mirror, so the mirror is telling her how great she is. Sabrina talked about how Clifton's mirror is the opposite of the mirror in Disney's *Snow White* that ranks the women. Instead of telling them their strengths, *that* mirror demands comparison, "Who is the fairest of us all?"

Using Lucille Clifton's poem as a frame, I ask students first to write a praise poem about themselves, as Chetan Patel does in his poem "Tiger Eyes." I give them three potential openings to use or to inspire them to create their own: "Listen,/You a _____" or "The mirror told me,/" or "I look into the mirror/And watch the history inside of me." Chetan's poem provides an excellent model for students' personal poems. Students can see their heritage, history, or language, and use the specifics of their neighborhood home or their historical home, as Chetan does, naming rivers, mountains, and food. The repeating line, "I see," links his poem forward as he stacks detail after detail in lists.

> I look into a mirror
> and watch the history inside of me
> flood out.
> I see the Kshatriya *warrior*,
> sword in hand,
> the Sudra *laborer*,
> working hard at his feet.
> I see the stories passed
> under the Banyan tree
> and the cleansing Ganges,
> slicing down the Himalayas.

Once students have a grasp on the idea of the poem personally, I use it as a frame for their literary and historical poems. Franchesca Naimi's poem "Jackie Robinson" demonstrates how to take the same model of opening line, and repeating line with details, to write about a historical or literary figure. (See Bigelow, "Teaching Unsung Heroes.") After researching Robinson for her unsung hero project, Franchesca used details from his life to build her poem—from the racist epithets when he entered the field to the fastballs pitched at his head.

My student Robin researched Bob Moses, the Civil Rights organizer and educator. He wrote in the first person from Bob Moses' point of view:

> I organized the Mississippi Freedom Summer.
> I witnessed people being beaten
> for registering to vote.
> I was arrested.
> I was beaten.
> I was jailed.
> I saw good friends murdered
> because they were part of the movement.
> Through the years I have lost
> friends and possessions,
> but I have never lost hope.

As always, we end with a read-around, but in addition to pointing out what is working in the poem, we also use the poetry as a way to deepen our discussion about the literature or history we're studying. ∎

References:

Bigelow, Bill, "Teaching Unsung Heroes," *A People's History for the Classroom.* Rethinking Schools. 2008.

Celie

by Don Pendleton

I am Celie.
I am the cold hard black floor
everyone walked on.
People have stained me and laughed
but I stayed solid under them
and did not squeak.
I am the floor now
but once you go downstairs
I become the ceiling.

Celie

by Lila Johnson

I am a record
on your shelf
the one
dressed
in dust and age
full
of cracked songs
you play
when you are blue
the one
pushed
behind the others
cool black jackets
smooth golden sounds
the one
your liquor-heavy fingers
find
on days
your red water eyes
don't know the difference
just an old record
you play me
when you are blue

Temperamental Rainfall

by Erika Miller

I am Shug.
I am the rain.
I come when I want to.
When you are on your hands
and knees begging for me,
I'll be showering someone else.
When you are able
to exist without me,
I'll show up.
I might sprinkle you
or flood you.
And when the ground dries,
I'll be gone.

Shug Avery

by Jessica Rawlins

I am Shug.
I am the sweet breath
every man holds onto at night.
I am the lingering scent that stays
to bring memories of violets
and lily kisses.
I am the sugar perfume
that comes on strong,
burns the senses,
then vanishes,
leaving nothing,
but the life of a stolen thought.

Grandpa Joe

by Daniel Clark-Rizzio

Grandpa Joe was like a boxer,
except that he fought for others.
He swung hard at tycoons
to help the labor unions.
With a quick jab to the politicians
who did not let blacks vote.

Grandpa Joe was a boxer
who pounded on his typewriter
to let everyone know how he felt.
He trained for years for his battles.
He fought, sometimes forgetting
to make himself happy.

Grandpa Joe was like a boxer
who had soft hands when he rocked his kids.
He helped his family stay out of the ring,
so they could watch safely, but never step in.

Molly Craig

by Linda Christensen

Write that I grew up in Jigalong
With my mother and grandmother.
Say that it was my home,
No there weren't walls,
And no there weren't beds,
And yes, we were poor,
But when did love come in units
Counted up in dollar bills?
When did family become something you could count
Instead of something you could count on?

Tell them that I learned to read animal tracks,
Filter water from roots in a desert, cook over an open fire,
And find my spirit bird
Before most kids learn to read words.
And yet, Mr. Devil calls me uneducated.

He wants to teach me to sweep, empty buckets,
Wring water from white people's sheets.

Tell them instead of beating me and shaming me
For my color, my dirty hair, my language,
My mother taught me through praise,
"Good tracker," she said,
"You brought us a fat one."

When you write my story, tell Mr. Devil that my mother's grief
Could not be counted, not tallied up in his books,
My mother's grief strummed along 1200 miles of rabbit proof fence
And hummed me home.

Say that I wasn't half anything,
Not half caste, not half black, not half white,
Yes, when you tell my story,
Say that when I'm home,
I'm whole.

Soweto Uprising

Group poem from Grant
African American English, 2007

Write that I
Had the stone,
Cupped in my palm.
It was hard.
It was cold.
Just like the white man's heart.
Remembering the Afrikaans
They stuffed down
My throat
I threw the stone
Just like they tried
To throw away
My culture.

Soweto Uprising

by Jayme Causey

Write that I
sang as loud as I could
in unison with my brothers and sisters
until a deafening "Nkosi Sikeleli'
   iAfrika"
was all that could be heard.
Write that I,
along with my people,
posed no threat to the police
except for
the threat of our knowledge
the threat of our desire
the threat of our power
marching united and strong
like a pack of lions.

Tiger Eyes
by Chetan Patel

I look into a mirror
and watch the history inside of me
flood out.
I see the *Kshatriya* warrior,
sword in hand,
the *Sudra* laborer,
working hard at his feet.
I see the stories passed
under the *Banyan* tree
and the cleansing Ganges,
slicing down the Himalayas.
I see the village *Panchayat*,
the *Lok Sabha*,
the House of People.
I see the deep fried *Samosas*,
full of carrots and peas,
wrapped in flour,
ready to eat.
I see the river flooding
in the monsoons,
the locusts lying
in the fields of Jammu.
I see the tiger eyes
waiting in the high grass,
for me to come back
and relive the past.

Jackie Robinson
by Franchesca Naimi

I look in the mirror
and watch the history inside of me flood out.
I see the warrior from within
walk onto the baseball field.
I hear the hateful words from bigots.
I feel the spikes of a runner's cleats
cut my legs.
I see my son's eyes looking up to me,
admiring his heroic father.
I see the 100 mph fast pitch
drive straight at my head.
At last I see my dreams come true:
Major League baseball is integrated.

TEACHING FOR JOY AND JUSTICE

2: Narrative Writing

Patricia Cruz and Elena Nelson-Rivera compose narratives that matter.

Dorothy Seymour

Teaching Narrative Writing: Why It Matters

Under our superintendent's reign, Portland Public Schools required all students to write a literary analysis essay starting in the 3rd grade. The assignment privileged essay writing as the only genre worth teaching. As one consultant said during an elementary workshop, "The days of children lying on the carpet writing their little stories are over."

A number of high school teachers also scoff at teaching narratives in the high school classroom. The narrative seems self-indulgent, like recess or poetry or finger painting, an unruly playful child in a world of adults. Students can study narratives, otherwise known as literature, but they shouldn't spend time writing them. After all, essay, especially literary analysis, is the genre students need to know once they get to college. Students learn to write narratives in elementary school; in high school, they need to move up to essays.

Students who learn to skillfully employ the elements of fiction in their narrative writing come to the study of literature with a better understanding of how authors construct stories and use literary tools.

This genre-apartheid approach to teaching writing is wrong-headed for many reasons. First, students who learn to skillfully employ the elements of fiction in their narrative writing come to the study of literature with a better understanding of how authors construct stories and use literary tools, like characterization, flashback, interior monologues, and figurative language. Also, the division between narrative and essay is fluid. Most great essayists, like George Orwell, Joan Didion, Henry Louis

Gates, bell hooks, and Annie Dillard, employ narrative strategies in their work. They weave anecdotes into their essays to illuminate their points, as Judith Ortiz Cofer does in the following passage from her essay, "Silent Dancing":

> It seems that Father had learned some painful lessons about prejudice while searching for an apartment in Paterson....."You Cuban?" one man had asked my father, pointing at his name tag on the navy uniform—even though my father had the fair skin and light brown hair of his northern Spanish background, and the name Ortiz is as common in Puerto Rico as Johnson is in the United States.
>
> "No," my father had answered, looking past the finger into his adversary's angry eyes. "I'm Puerto Rican."
>
> "Same shit." And the door closed.

The craft of the sentence, from the hefting of verbs to the playfulness of commas and dashes, can be taught in both essay and narrative writing.

But more than that, especially in a social justice classroom, the narrative is the heart of the class. Students' stories build community and connect their lives to the curriculum. As students analyze their own experiences and hear stories from their classmates' lives, we make it possible to "challenge the myths of our society, to perceive more clearly its realities, and to find alternatives, and ultimately, new directions for action" as the conveners of the Mississippi Freedom Schools wrote in a memo to teachers. Through these "little" stories and sharing, we create communities in our classrooms where students feel safe enough to take academic risks.

I take narrative teaching seriously. Over the years I have discovered that students learn best when I embed writing assignments in a rich curriculum. When I give students time to grapple with big concepts in their lives or the lives of historical and fictional characters by talking, brainstorming, and studying the characteristics of a genre, they are more likely to write with passion and power. So I rarely teach narrative writing in isolation.

When we enter a new unit, we explore the unit's themes by examining how those subjects intersect and resonate in our own lives and contemporary society. During my "Women and Men in Literature and Society" unit, students write narratives about growing up male or female, and we discuss how family roles, advertising, and the media have shaped our gender identity. During our study of "Slavery and Resistance," students write narratives about times they stood up or wish they had, and we consider the conditions that either allow us to resist or that

strangle our voices. When we read Tim O'Brien's book *The Things They Carried*, students write about a time they had to make a difficult choice. In August Wilson's play, *Fences*, we parallel the title by writing about the fences, or obstacles, we have faced or overcome in our lives. And in all cases, our classroom conversations move between students' lives, the literature, and the broader society.

Selecting Prompts that Matter

In my experience, students enjoy writing narratives. Telling stories from their lives opens opportunities to talk about meaningful, important, sometimes life-changing events with their classmates. Given the fact-packing, pace-and-test curriculum mode of education today, narratives provide one of the few opportunities for students to write or talk about their lives in school.

So what makes a good prompt? Typically, good assignments ask students to write about important events in their lives, like the ones I listed above—choices, resistance, moments that shaped them. The subjects are broad; they give students room for choice within the topic, and they offer multiple entry points. I try to choose stories that open dialogue between students about how their race, gender, and class have affected their lives. For example, in the "Writing for Justice" prompt, I ask students to write a personal story about injustice. This is a prompt that I use with *Warriors Don't Cry* and the Civil Rights Movement, but I have also used it with *Grapes of Wrath* and other novels where an injustice occurs—which is just about any book. Students write about times when they were allies, perpetrators, targets, or bystanders during a critical moment in their lives. This narrative helps students probe the connections between their stories and historic (and continuing) inequalities during the Jim Crow era of segregated schools and society.

In the "Can't Buy Me Love" narrative, I want students' stories to help them understand that their lack of money or their lack of skills are not personal deficits, but rather the result of a system that has routinely distributed privileges unfairly.

In the introduction to *Rethinking Our Classrooms*, Rethinking Schools editors wrote, "Classrooms can be places of hope, where students and teachers gain glimpses of the kind of society we could live in and where students learn the academic and critical skills needed to make it a reality." Student narratives and discussions that flow from them provide students with moments of hope, with glimpses of the kind of society we could live in, while they

Khalilah (Joseph) Jones makes a point during class discussion.

Robert Reynolds

learn academic skills. So maybe we should reconsider the teaching of those "little stories" about their lives.

Locating Writers' Tools

When I first started teaching, I didn't explicitly teach students to identify writers' tools because I drew an artificial line between literature study and writing. When we studied literary texts, we looked at how an author developed characters through dialogue, action, and description, but I didn't transfer that language to crafting our own writing. Once I did, students' ability to write narratives exploded because they developed their writing by studying how professional, and student, writers used dialogue, description, and figurative language in their stories. This also meant that students entered literature study with a much greater appreciation and knowledge as fellow writers.

The real work of locating writers' tools comes as we examine a piece of short fiction to see those tools in action. I hand out the Narrative Criteria sheet, and the appropriate story or model for whatever narrative we're writing. (See p. 113) In the "Can't Buy Me Love," narrative, we color-highlight "Thank You, Ma'm," a short story by Langston Hughes about a boy who attempts to steal a woman's purse. (See "Can't Buy Me Love," for a full description of this lesson in action, p. 70.) Students pick up four different colors of highlighters, crayons, or colored pencils. I tell them, "Select one color to represent the first of the four elements of fiction listed on the Narrative Criteria sheet. Start with dialogue. Take your dialogue color and mark all of the dialogue in the story in one color." After students have marked the dialogue, I say, "Let's share a few pieces of dialogue out loud." Then we talk about what we learn about the character by reading the dialogue.

While most students know that dialogue is the character's words, few know the term "blocking." I didn't either until Reginald McKnight, award-winning author of the short story collection *The Kind of Light That Shines on Texas*, came to my class. He explained that blocking is a theater term, meaning information that gives actors stage directions: where to stand, how to deliver their lines, what to do while they are delivering the lines. McKnight's piece of writerly advice was a gift that changed my teaching of narrative writing. Blocking helps students "see" their story as theater rather than words on a page. To help students understand blocking, I ask students to act out the blocking while speaking the dialogue. For example, in this scene

The real work of locating writers' tools comes as we examine a piece of short fiction to see those tools in action.

from Langston Hughes' "Thank You, Ma'm," which I use during the "Can't Buy Me Love" narrative, I invite two students to come to the center of the circle. We reread the scene together as a class, then I ask the students to say the lines while "acting out" the blocking.

> After that the woman said, "Pick up my pocketbook, boy, and give it here." She still held him. But she bent down enough to permit him to stoop and pick up her purse. Then she said, "Now ain't you ashamed of yourself?"
>
> Firmly gripped by his shirt front, the boy said, "Yes'm."
>
> The woman said, "What did you want to do it for?"
>
> The boy said, "I didn't aim to."
>
> She said, "You a lie!"
>
> By that time two or three people passed, stopped, turned to look, and some stood watching.
>
> "If I turn you loose, will you run?" asked the woman.
>
> "Yes'm," said the boy.
>
> "Then I won't turn you loose," said the woman. She did not release him.

Of course, this produces a great deal of laughter, but by acting out the scene, students come to see how blocking functions in the narrative.

We repeat the highlighting process with characterization. I tell students that writers use description, dialogue, actions, as well as other characters' comments to develop their characters. As readers, we learn to become detectives, discovering what those "character clues" reveal. We read Hughes' description of Mrs. Luella Bates Washington Jones and the purse-snatcher Roger:

> She was a large woman with a large purse that had everything in it but hammer and nails. It had a long strap, and she carried it slung across her shoulder. It was about eleven o'clock at night, and she was walking alone, when a boy ran up behind her and tried to snatch her purse. The strap broke with the single tug the boy gave it from behind. But the boy's weight and the weight of the purse combined caused him to lose his balance so, instead of taking off full blast as he had hoped, the boy fell on his back on the sidewalk, and his legs flew up. The large woman simply turned around and kicked him right square in his blue-jeaned sitter. Then she reached down, picked the boy up by his shirt front, and shook him until his teeth rattled.

Mrs. Luella Bates Washington Jones makes for great character detection because she is a larger-than-life woman who surprises us with her compassion as well as her tough talk.

We also examine the story for setting. I ask students to become detectives again and to search the piece for language and details that help us understand not only the time of night, but also the time period when this story took place. The terms "ice box" and "hot plate" help place the time. Students also point out that she must live in an apartment. They aren't familiar with "boarding houses," but they get the gist when Hughes describes how Mrs. Jones drags Roger down a hall, and "into a large kitchenette-furnished room at the rear of the house. She switched on the light and left the door open. The boy could hear other roomers laughing and talking in the large house."

We also look at stories where authors used flashbacks and figurative language. With middle and high school students, we color all of the elements at one time. My colleagues who teach elementary school focus on one or two elements at a time. We come back to this coloring activity later in the narrative writing process. This activity helps students literally see how writers use these tools to develop their stories. Their papers are a rainbow of colors, showing how character description, setting description, dialogue, and blocking function in building a story.

Guided Visualization

I find the visualizations provide a good segue from one activity to another. I use this technique after students have listed stories they want to write about. For some students, the visualization helps them collect sensory details from their memories. One student, Larry, who had slow neurological processing, told me that the visualization made him understand that the movies of his memory were the stories he needed to write. It was a breakthrough for his writing. For other students, the visualization slows down the class, clears away the previous activity, and prepares them for quiet writing time.

I close the blinds and tell students that I am going to turn out the lights as a way of helping them "see and hear" the story in their heads. After I turn out the lights, I ask them to put their heads on the desk. This requires some trust. Usually I joke around with them, ask them to stretch, take a big breath; I try to put them at ease. I ask questions and leave about 60 seconds between them so that students have time to visualize. My monologue goes something like this: "You are going to be both the videographer and the actor in the scene. I want you to remember the place where the story happened. Think of the setting where the story happened. What time of year did the story take place? Do you remember any smells? Look around and soak in the details. [Pause for

Langston Hughes

60 seconds.] Now bring on the actors. Who was there? Visualize their faces. Remember details about them: Do they wear glasses? What kind of shoes do they wear? [Pause for 60 seconds.] Now, put the scene in motion. Try to see and hear the story as it took place." My questions and directions change slightly depending on the prompt.

After I finish the questions, I tell them to keep their heads down until I turn on the lights. When the lights go on, it signals quiet writing time. I say, "Write fast to get the story out. Write in a whoosh. Don't worry about grammar, punctuation, or spelling. You can fix those later. Now I want

It is critically important that struggling writers get a big chunk of writing time in class where I'm on hand to help them.

you to get as much of the story down as you can. I only want to hear the sound of writing instruments for the next 20 minutes." Over the course of the year, I build students' writing stamina, so they can write for longer stretches of time. They finish the pieces that night for homework. And mostly they do, but I do want to stress that it is critically important that struggling writers get a big chunk of writing time in class where I'm on hand to help them.

Read-Around, Revision, and Craft Lessons

Once students have a draft of their narrative, the real writing instruction can begin. Because the writing of this chapter is linear, I'm tempted to write that I always work on revision at this point, but the truth is: I don't. Depending on the time of the year—early, late, near the end of a quarter or semester or the beginning of a holiday break—or the point in a curriculum unit, I do one of the following after students have a draft: Read-around, revise, or teach a craft lesson. I'm including all three here, but this writing process is more circular than linear. Sometimes, I jump to a read-around at this point because I want to use the student stories and collective texts as part of the unit's larger narrative. Also, the stories are heart-pounding personal stories, and I don't want to pick apart that heartbeat when it's still aching. The "Writing for Justice" narratives fall into this category. Knowing that they will read their draft out loud fires students up to write stronger first drafts. Sometimes I linger on the story, teaching revision techniques through craft lessons and polishing the drafts, and follow the revisions with a read-around. The clothing story described in "Can't Buy

Me Love" falls more in this category. Sometimes students collect three or four narratives during a quarter and then choose one to revise and polish.

Narrative Revisions and Craft Lessons

In my first years of teaching, I struggled to get students to revise their writing. I'd encourage them to take their drafts home and revise them. If I was lucky, they came back with some spelling and grammar errors fixed, but more often they just copied their drafts more neatly. Then, as I mentioned earlier, I introduced students to literary elements, and I discovered that my students, for the most part, weren't lazy, they simply lacked the tools to change their writing. Without guidance, they wrote the best drafts they could at the time, but they needed more teaching to revise those drafts.

Before we start our first major revision, I discuss the craft of writing as a circular process. I draw a circle on the board, beginning with pre-writing, moving to draft, then to the first revision. "Your first revision is a big revision. This is where writing gets fun, where the real writing begins. This is where you add big chunks of writing, take out big chunks, or move them around. Sometimes in my writing I abandon my first two or three pages because as I wrote, I found my story, and I no longer need those pages." I post three or four drafts of my writing on the board. I also show them drafts from Hemingway and Richard Wright, so they can see the cross-outs and arrows that published writers have in their manuscripts.

Then I teach them how to revise "big" by returning to the Narrative Criteria sheet. In this revision, students add the elements of a narrative they might not have included in the first draft. Earlier, I described how students color-highlighted student and literary models. During our revision day, they repeat the color-highlighting activity with their own writing. Using the criteria sheet again, they highlight each of the narrative elements in a different color. We start with dialogue. I say, "Select one color for dialogue and highlight all of your dialogue in this color." Once it looks like students have completed the task, I ask a few to share examples of their dialogue so that the students who don't have any can gather some ideas. After a few share, I tell students, "Now, if you don't have any dialogue, read back over your piece and find a place where you can add it. One of the things you can look for is the word *told*. Often this is a place where you can easily insert dialogue. Instead of writing, 'My mother told me to clean my room,' write, 'Mom yelled from the bottom of the stairs, "You better clean that room before I come home from work."' Use the characters' words instead of reporting on their words. If you do have dialogue, reread your piece to see if you can add more or to make sure your characters have distinct voices." I give students time right then to make notes in the margins of their drafts about where they will add the dialogue.

Then I move to blocking. "Select a second color to highlight your blocking. Locate your dialogue. Your blocking should be right next to it. If you don't have any blocking, now is the time to add it. Maybe you wrote, 'he said' or 'she said.' Now is the time to bump it up. How did your character deliver the line? What was the character doing while talking? Leaning against the window? Opening up a candy bar? Show us the writer in action." I repeat this highlighting, sharing, and giving time for immediate revision as students locate or add character and setting description. After students have highlighted their entire paper, I say, "Look at your paper. If it's not full of colors, you haven't used all of your writing tools. This is how you revise on your own. You see what color or what tool is missing and you add it. I want those papers to look like peacocks when you are finished."

After students rewrite their papers, including missing narrative components, I ask them to color-highlight any changes they made on their new draft. "When I read your paper, I will have both copies in front of me. I want to be able to easily locate those changes because that's where I can see your growth in writing." As a final piece of the revision process, I ask students to return to their drafts and revision and write a reflection about what kinds of changes they made in their drafts and what they learned about writing narratives from their revision.

As the year progresses, I add other pieces to the revision process by teaching craft lessons—effective narrative openings, using flashbacks and interior monologues, developing character through dialogue. These lessons connect the teaching of writing directly to the teaching of literature. By learning the craft of writing, they learn to use—and recognize—writers' tools in constructing memoirs, short stories, and novels. These lessons include using language more effectively as well—from building sentence fluency to using poetic language.

Bruk Alkadir, Linda Christensen, and Wakitu Wotcha listen during a read-around.

Jim Whitney

I discovered that students care more about their writing when it becomes public. The read-around offers an immediate audience and a way to expose students to different writing styles.

On Responding to Student Work

When students turn in their writing, they attach the narrative criteria sheet, reflection, revision, and their rough, highlighted drafts. Because they highlight all of the changes they made in their most recent draft, I can quickly scan to see what kinds of revisions they made—additions, moves, cuts—as well as sentence and word level transformations. Typically, at this point, I'm looking for the students' strengths and for what they learned between drafts. I comment on these changes— something like, "Great addition of dialogue here. This brings the character to life." I also note what they might want to change if they decide to work on this draft again. "I love the way you used dialogue to develop your grandmother, but I wondered what she looked like. Does she look over her glasses when she talks? What does she do with her hands? Make us see her. I want to be able to recognize her when she walks into a room. Also, I wanted to know more about where the story took place. Could you describe her kitchen in more detail?" Sometimes, I note where I'm confused and need more information. My comments mirror the lessons we're working on in class.

I also pay attention to sentence structure, especially the effective use of clauses, parallel use of verbs, or items in a series—anything that I want the student to notice and repeat. I point out effective and strong verbs. I try to make my notes a conversation with the writer. If the student didn't make changes between their drafts, I return their writing. As I explain in "My Dirty Little Secret: I Don't Grade Student Papers" (see p. 272), I don't grade student papers, but I do give them credit for each draft—but only if they make significant revisions.

The Read-Around and Collective Text

When I first started teaching at Jefferson High School, I noticed that both performing arts students and athletes who slacked off in my class took on a different, more animated persona when they were on the stage, field, or court. I wanted to bring that level of engagement to my classroom. These dancers, actors, and athletes shared a commitment to their craft, but they also performed for an audience, a missing component in my writing class. I created that much-needed audience in two ways—the in-class read-around and publication of student work. I discovered that students care more about their writing when it becomes public. The read-around offers an immediate audience and a way to expose students to different writing styles.

The term "read-around" accurately describes this activity. Because my classroom is usually arranged in a circle, students read their pieces around the circle of our room. After each student reads, we clap to appreciate the writer, then we pause to write notes about the writing, and then we look at the writer as we discuss the poem, narrative, or essay. The feedback is always positive. We talk about what we love about the piece, what's working—a great opening, the use of humor, the rhythm in a certain line, a flashback that builds the reader's understanding of character. During the opening days of class, I model how to talk with writers. Students soon take over and I only speak to point out techniques writers are using intuitively—like a flashback or an extended metaphor, so that students can pick up the strategy and consciously use it in their writing. (See "Read-Around Procedure," p. 69.)

Over the years, my students may or may not remember every unit I taught, but they remember the read-around, because it's where we become human, where we put aside the masks we wear in the outside world and share our lives. It's the fire in the belly of our room. Sometimes the read-around creates moments of laughter as we read stories about wearing high water pants or singing silly songs

Celine Yip reads her poem.

Dorothy Seymour

at Outdoor School. Other times we cry together as students share the loss of a loved one or a beautiful moment of solidarity.

The read-around also presents teachable moments about both writing techniques and content. Sometimes, for example, I ask a student to reread a section, so I can point out a fresh metaphor, vibrant verbs, or a flashback that develops character. Students who struggle with a piece find answers in their classmates' words and passages.

The read-around is also a place for me to informally examine common problems in class papers—lack of evidence, sloppy transitions, weak introductions—as well as individual problems. The read-around allows me to teach, assess, and move students to the next draft. Students in every class I've taught have made it clear that the read-around was the best part of our work. Adam wrote:

There is so much to learn about good writing. I know that a lot of what shaped my writing was not the diagramming sentences or finding the subject and verb that we learned in grade school, but the desire to learn more about what I'm hearing around me. Just hearing the work of good writers makes an incredible difference. When I find something I really like, I ask myself, "What was it about that piece that made me get all goose-bumpy?" That's why I think it is really important to have those read-arounds in class. Not only does the author get to hear comments about his/her work, but the rest of the class gets a chance to hear some pretty amazing stuff. Like when we heard Nicole's home language paper, I don't think there was anyone who wasn't touched by it. Everyone had felt, at some point, like that and her paper was able to capture those feelings and describe them perfectly. At the same time, everyone thought, "How can I write like that?" We all learned from the paper. Now, this is only one example, but almost every day we share, something like this happens.

At the risk of putting too much on the shoulders of this activity, I also believe that the read-around is one of the places in my class where students learn about their own potential as writers and scholars. As classmates praise their stories, poems, and essays, students are forced to rearrange their ideas about their capacity as intellectuals. Obviously, this happens through the writing, revisions, readings, and discussions throughout the year. But, in particular, to be center of attention, to be praised for all that is right and beautiful about their story and their life helps build up that confidence and willingness to persist in difficult tasks, which often has been torn down and belittled through years of education.

Students move from grade-based motivation (which is in low supply with struggling writers) to working on "getting it right."

After students finish reading their pieces and receive feedback from the class, I might also use the story to prompt a discussion about the topic in a student's narrative. For example, after Kirk read his "Writing for Justice" piece about a woman pulling out a canister of mace when he was walking home behind her, I asked the class, "Has anyone else had someone act as if they are afraid of you?" This opened the conversation for Raul to talk about how he can hear car doors lock when someone at traffic light sees him on the sidewalk, which prompted a class discussion about where those fears originate.

Good writing raises the achievement bar in real ways. Instead of examining rubrics, students hold out Seth's deft insights into literature or Bree's description of her grandmother's fence or Kirk's use of metaphors in his narrative as the models they want to emulate. Students learn to become dissatisfied with first drafts. Students move from grade-based motivation (which is in low supply with struggling writers) to working on "getting it right," which anyone who writes can understand—writing until we find that train that takes the writing home.

Students take more risks in their writing because they no longer write for the teacher; they write for themselves and their classmates—or other audiences. Of course, this implies creating assignments that students care about, moving beyond writing for the teacher as the only audience or writing as an end-of-unit check-up or writing with rigid

timelines. My favorite line at the end of a read-around is, "Can I take this home and work on it some more?"

Of course, the downside is that read-arounds take time, and often teachers worry about taking such a big chunk of class time for this activity. Truthfully, so do I, but after we complete the read-around, I'm reminded how much students learn about writing, each other, and their observations about society. My friend and colleague Russ Peterson, a member of our Oregon Writing Project Teacher Research group, wrote about this in an email note, "I had my freshmen read parts of their essays to the class—yes, it took time. I don't know why I had been previously so concerned about 'instructional time.' It WAS instructive, but it was so worth it not only in terms of community building, but also in terms of validating our kids and the work they did, and in terms of 'showing' the craft lessons we have been working on."

Anne Voegtlin, a middle school teacher, told me, "The first time I did read-arounds, I wasn't sure I wanted to devote so much time to them. It takes time to have 30 or so students per class share their narratives. When we had finished, though, I felt the experience was one of the most valuable chunks of time we'd spent in our writing curriculum. Students heard their stories come to life. They heard others' stories come to life. They heard and saw problems in their own writing and were able to revise as they read. It was important to me that we learned something from each other. The read-arounds helped to develop a sense of community in my classrooms."

Writing the "Collective Text"

The collective text strategy grew out of the Literature and U.S. History class Bill Bigelow and I taught together at Jefferson. We realized that these "collective texts" helped students make connections between their lives and our content. Because the read-around provides an oral "text" of our lives, we started asking students to keep track of ideas and content in their classmates' stories, so they could reflect on what they learned from listening to these narratives. Students write about the common themes that emerge or questions they are left with after hearing each other's stories. Depending on the prompt, I might pose a particular question for students to think about as they listen. For example, after the clothing story, I ask students to write about how people felt about their clothes, why they thought buying a certain pair of shoes or pants was important. Together, most students learned that they tried to "buy acceptance" at the mall, as Chetan wrote in his collective text. By explicitly asking students to make observations about the content of each other's stories, beyond technique and craft, I attempt to drive home the point that they have a great deal to learn from each other.

In a social justice classroom, this activity helps students empathize with one another, but also encourages them to analyze how their own lives have been marked by the race, class, or gender issues we encounter in literature and history. For example, when writing their "Honoring Our Ancestors" essays, students learned that many of their grandmothers raised them. One student started her story, "I was abandoned at birth by my mother, but I've learned to forgive her." This led to an animated discussion about the hardships young mothers face. These kinds of conversations help students see beyond stereotypes they might carry about themselves and others, but also help them discover the courage to find alternative paths.

Sure, students will write better if we take the time to teach them how to write instead of expecting that they already know how and blaming them if they don't. Their writing scores on state tests might even improve. But taking the time to teach students the craft of writing narratives about their lives and taking the time to listen to their writing makes the same kind of good sense that cooking a meal with fresh, locally grown ingredients makes, instead of grabbing fast food. Its benefits extend from individuals to the whole society.

Perhaps the most profound work we can do in school is to learn how to listen, how to bring students' lives into the world of the classroom. As we attempt to construct a critical, multicultural curriculum, we need to remember to include the personal stories that help us see the impact of social policies on our lives. Students need opportunities to care about each other and the world. Narratives are a good place to start. ■

Read-Around Procedure

I use the read-around with all genres of writing, including poetry, narrative, and essay. This is the procedure I use for the first read-around, to establish procedure.

1. I seat the students in a circle—or the nearest approximation. I don't want students to have their backs to each other. They should see each other and be seen as they read. All students' attention should be focused on the reader.

2. I forage in the recycling bin for enough paper so that I can distribute to each student as many blank strips of paper as there are students in my class. These are for students to write a specific, positive comment about each writer's piece.

3. I ask students to write the name of the student who is about to share his or her writing on the paper strip. So if Lakeitha volunteers to read her paper first, everyone in the class writes Lakeitha's name on their strips. (At the beginning of the school year, this is also a way for students to learn their classmates' names.)

4. I tell students they must respond with a positive comment to each writer. "People are sharing their lives with you. Be a hungry listener. Listen with your head and your heart." I write a list of ways to respond on the board:

   Respond to the writer's content. What did the writer say that you liked? Did you like the way Ayanna used a story about her mother to point out how gender roles have changed?

   Respond to the writer's style of writing. What do you like about how the piece was written? Do you like the rhyme? Repeating lines? Humor? (I also tie these to genre-based writing, like introductions, transitions, and evidence in an essay.)

   Respond by sharing a memory that surfaced for you. Did you have a similar experience? Did this remind you of something from your life?

   As the writer reads, write down lines, ideas, words or phrases that you like. Remember: you must compliment the writer.

5. As students write each compliment, I tell them to sign their slips so the writer knows who praised them.

6. After a student shares, I ask a few volunteers to share their praise with the writer. This is slow at first, so I model it. This is an opportunity to teach writing: point out dialogue, description, attention to detail.

7. I ask students to look at the writer and give that person the compliment. At first, students look at me and tell me what they liked about the student's piece. I sidestep this by telling the writer to call on students who have raised their hands. I establish early on that all dialogue in the class does not funnel through me.

8. I offer extra credit for positive oral comments. In my classes where defiance is a badge of honor, I give points. This allows some people a "cover" for giving positive feedback: "I just do it for the points." Whether they actually do it for the extra credit or not, their compliments contribute to a positive classroom climate.

9. After everyone has read, I ask students to hand out their compliment strips to each other. (This is usually chaotic, but it's another way for students to identify who's who in the class and to connect with each other.)

10. After the first few read-arounds, I drop the strips of paper and rely on oral feedback. Students do take notes for the collective text. Each piece of writing students complete has a different theme, so collective text questions vary from assignment to assignment. In each instance, I want to draw students' attention to broad "lessons" from their lives or topics.

Color Day Production/GETTY IMAGES

Can't Buy Me Love: Teaching About Clothes, Class, and Consumption

Anne challenged a group of girls during my senior year at Eureka High School to see who could go the longest without wearing the same outfit twice. Anne and her friends had attended Zane Junior High School. Most of their parents were doctors and lawyers; they either lived in the old lumber baron homes or the fancy new houses that hugged the sides of gullies filled with redwood trees and small streams. My friends and I attended Jacobs Junior High School. Our parents were mostly working-class folks, who toiled as electricians, butchers, or pulled green chain at the lumber mills. We lived in modest ranch-style homes or rented on the side of town where the stink of the pulp mill became a perfume we wore on windy days.

Equating success with wealth starts early — think of Cinderella's magical transformation. Through clothes we can move from scullery maid to princess.

Anne's challenge wasn't realistic from the get-go. The Zane girls bought clothes at Daly's and Bistrin's, or their mothers took them on shopping trips to Santa Rosa or San Francisco. Janet's mother made most of her clothes, and Janice sewed her own dresses and skirts. I took jobs washing dishes or babysitting to buy a few outfits from Daly's. My mom sewed as well, but not with the finesse of Janet's mother. I learned to make long skirts that required only two seams and to wear a shirt long enough to cover my problematic zipper installation. I ran out of clothes after the first week. Anne won. Did she go four weeks? Seven weeks?

Clothes are class markers. And coming from my class background, I wanted desperately to fit into Anne's world, a world where people bought clothes at department stores and went to beauty shops for haircuts and permanents.

I've watched this same drama play out daily in my classrooms at Jefferson and Grant High Schools in Portland, Ore., a cruel world where one-liner jokes fly across hallways and locker rooms. "Where did you buy those shoes? Volume?" Teenagers spend nights and weekends deep-frying French fries, scooping ice cream, and selling clothing dreams to other teens so they can buy shoes or a pair of jeans that might pay a good chunk of their parents' rent. Some risk stealing from Macy's or Nike Town so that they can look like they have money. School becomes a preparation for a lifelong job of consumption, buying the next television, the next phone, the next house—ever bigger and ever better, to compete, to be successful, to be OK.

Equating success with wealth starts early—think of Cinderella's magical transformation. Through clothes we can move from scullery maid to princess. With the right clothes we will be accepted and loved. The prince will fall in love with us, we'll dance all night, and we'll live happily ever after. The story is told again and again in cartoons, literature, television shows, movies, lotto games, and advertisements. Remember how Julia Roberts moves from prostitute to socialite with a change of clothes and a bit of advice about fork etiquette in the movie *Pretty Woman?* In Bernard Shaw's *Pygmalion*, Professor Henry Higgins instructs his maid, Mrs. Pearce, to burn Eliza's clothes and buy her some new ones. "Take all her clothes off and burn them. Ring up Whiteley or somebody for new ones. Wrap her up in brown paper til they come."

Students play out this story on a daily basis. Children begin ranking and sorting each other based on those material possessions: clothes, toys, electronic gear, cars. Whose is best? Who has the most? They make jokes about each other's clothes, shoes, hair. They brag about how much they paid for their shoes or hats. For a while, my students even wore the sales tags on their hats and coats. Students purchase social cachet by wearing the right clothes, the right styles, as if they are imbued with magical power. If they have the thing, they have the status. But even if they don't gain acceptance in the inner circle, wearing the right clothes guards them from peers' humiliating judgments.

I realized when I first stumbled on this writing assignment that I had touched a place of pain and shame that needed to be explored more fully. Students knew they hurt, but they didn't have a social critique to help them understand their humiliation. They internalized the shame of poverty and blamed themselves or their families instead of criticizing a society that places more value on what we own than on our capacity for compassion or good work. In every lesson I construct, I want to puncture holes in the myths that make my students feel shame and doubt about themselves and their families.

Working in a high-poverty high school like Jefferson or a high school like Grant, where rich and poor rub elbows, I needed to help students shape a critique of that insistent voice that says, "Buy more," so students could understand the origins of both the shame and the need to equate success with money.

I feel that I can get to more honest discussions if I initiate the conversation "a little to one side," by extracting the lesson from student stories.

William Stafford, Oregon's poet laureate, wrote: "Poetry is the kind of thing you have to see from the corner of your eye. … It's like a very faint star. If you look straight at it you can't see it, but if you look a little to one side it is there." Stafford's image holds true for prying open tough conversations in the classroom. Sometimes I feel that I can get to more honest discussions if I initiate the conversation "a little to one side," by extracting the lesson from student stories. When I come in with pronouncements instead of engaging students in discovering, students resist. They fight back against the idea that the web of advertising and consumption has snared them, even though they sport name brand shoes, shirts, pants, and bags. By using literature and their lives, I set the scene for them to make their own discoveries, to learn their own lessons without teacher lectures about how they are pawns in a society so consumed with consumption that after the 9/11 attacks, President Bush encouraged citizens to show their patriotism by going shopping.

Despite having serious themes that I want students to confront, this lesson leads to lots of laughter as students recall their own stories about their brushes with clothes or class. Of course, the lesson also teaches students how to read and write more effectively.

Reading Langston Hughes

We begin by reading Langston Hughes' story, "Thank You, Ma'm." Hughes' story tells about Roger, a young man who attempted to snatch a woman's purse so he could buy a pair of blue suede shoes. Mrs. Louella Bates Washington Jones caught Roger, "put a half nelson about his neck," and took him home to her apartment where he learned a valuable lesson about compassion and forgiveness. The story prompts our discussion about why we buy—or steal—things we can't afford.

Hughes constructs his story through a series of small scenes. As we read, I ask students to note how Hughes shows the toughness and compassion of Mrs. Jones. Mrs. Jones surprised Roger with her actions, maternal banter, and generosity. Through short dialogue sequences, Mrs. Jones also uncovers Roger's living situation:

> "Are you going to take me to jail?" asked the boy, bending over the sink.
>
> "Not with that face, I would not take you nowhere," said the woman. "Here I am trying to get home to cook me a bite to eat and you snatch my pocketbook! Maybe you ain't been to your supper either, late as it is. Have you?"
>
> "There's nobody home at my house," said the boy.
>
> "Then we'll eat," said the woman. "I believe you're hungry—or been hungry—to try to snatch my pocketbook."

When Roger confesses that he wanted a pair of blue suede shoes, Mrs. Jones surprises him by saying, "Well, you didn't have to snatch my pocketbook to get some suede shoes....You could have asked me....I was young once and wanted things I could not get."

In this exchange, Hughes shows Mrs. Jones' understanding that Roger's poverty, not a character defect, played a role in his aborted attempt at purse snatching. This admission opens the door for student discussion about why someone would risk stealing for a pair of shoes. But the dialogue and actions also show students the art of developing characters through small scenes.

After reading this story, a student I'll call Randy talked about stealing jewelry at Meier & Frank, a local department store, because he couldn't afford to buy the gold chains he wanted. To move the story beyond clothes and accessories to the bigger issue of social class, I told the story about how I tried to make Judd, a family friend who took me to school on rainy days, drop me off on the other side of school so no one would see me arrive in his beat-up car. Judd, being stubborn and proud, refused. He

Brad Wilson/GETTY IMAGES

always stopped right in front of the double doors leading to the main hall of Eureka High School. This story opened up Jessica to talk about her mother's old car, and how she asked her mother to drop her off two blocks from her school so no one would see the car and make fun of her. Felicia told the story of being stuck without a ride after school. A wealthy student from the other side of town offered her a ride home. Felicia took it, but had the student drop her off in front of a big house down the street from her small, sagging house, then waited until they drove off to walk the rest of the way home.

Reading Gary Soto

We also read Gary Soto's short story, "The Jacket," which offers another example of a young man who believes that clothes will help him gain acceptance with his peers. In this story, a boy tells his mother that he wants a jacket "something like bikers wear: black leather and silver studs, with enough belts to hold down a small town." Instead his mother gets him a jacket "the color of day-old guacamole." Soto's story prompts discussion about those clothes we've been forced to wear that make us feel like outcasts.

Soto's is the anti-Cinderella story. Instead of love and acceptance, his ugly coat brings him shame and humiliation:

> The next day I wore it to sixth grade and got a D on a math quiz. During the morning recess Frankie T., the playground terrorist, pushed me to the ground and told me to stay there until recess was over. My best friend,

Steve Negrete, ate an apple while looking at me, and the girls turned away to whisper on the monkey bars. The teachers were no help: they looked my way and talked about how foolish I looked in my new jacket. I saw their heads bob with laughter, their hands half covering their mouths.

Soto endows the coat with a miraculous ability to harm him. "So embarrassed, so hurt, I couldn't even do my homework. I received C's on quizzes and forgot the state capitals and the rivers of South America.... Even the girls who had been friendly blew away like loose flowers to follow the boys in neat jackets." Soto's use of hyperbole loosens up the students to talk about their own fashion disasters.

Each of these stories prompt clothing memories—not all bad. Because the students are the same age, they share some common memories. While I remember days-of-the-week panties, they remember Underoos. I talk about Buster Brown shoes that Mom bought to last—and they did. They laugh about "jellies," a common plastic shoe that girls wore for a period of time. I loved my Annie Oakley skirt and vest, and they loved their superhero capes or pajamas.

But we also talk about the clothes that failed us. Frank talked about the day he was forced to wear grey leather pants. "I had to go to school looking like a moving couch." He described how one boy mocked him, "Hey, Frank, your legs look like two old bananas." Andrew wrote about the bellbottoms that made him the target of student laughter: "'I hate these clothes,' I said to myself as I looked in the mirror. The thought of the day ahead was the most dreaded thing of all: classroom ridicule was my worst enemy."

After reading the stories by Hughes and Soto, I tell students I want them to write narratives from their lives about clothing, shoes, or haircuts. The story might reveal something about the significance of the clothes: Did we believe they would give us magical power, like the Cinderella story? Did the clothes shame us like the Soto story? Did the clothes show something about class, like my story about the competition with the senior girls or Hughes' story? Because a prompt sometimes elicits blank stares rather than furious writing, I use student as well as Hughes' and Soto's published models to show how different writers addressed the topic.

Examining the Craft of Writing

As we continue our discussion of clothes, class, and fitting in, as well as writing styles, we return to Hughes' and Soto's stories to examine the narrative characteristics each writer uses. Students highlight the dialogue in one color, and the blocking in another. I reminded students that in theater, blocking tells actors where to stand or how to deliver their lines. In literature, it serves a similar function. In the section of "Thank You, Ma'm" I quoted earlier, when Roger bends over the sink as he asks a question, his action is blocking. We also look at the ways both authors develop character through physical description, but also through dialogue and actions.

We read "Pro Wings," by my student Sarah LePage, to examine how she details the humiliation she suffered when her mother bought her shoes from a discount store through a series of short scenes. As we color-highlight narrative criteria in the story, we learn about both Sarah and her mother through their dialogue and blocking. I ask students to notice what the blocking tells us about both characters, how Sarah's mother snaps and grabs her arm, how Sarah crosses her arms, and shakes her head:

"I'm not getting any shoes from here," I announced, as my mother led the way down the aisle crammed with my size shoes.

"You'll do what you're told or else!" she snapped back.

I crossed my arms, planted my feet, narrowed my eyes, and shook my head in defiance. "I said I want Jellies!"

She stopped cold, whirled around and grabbed me by the arm. She dragged me within inches of her beet red face and spoke in a hard, terrifying voice, "I said you'll do what you are told! Now go sit down and take off your shoes, 'cause these are the ones that you are getting." She forced a pair of gray Pro Wings with matching Velcro into my clenched fists.

Dorothy Seymour

The first few times I introduce blocking to students, I have them act the scene out. I tell them, "These are stage directions. Through blocking, the writer tells us how the character needs to deliver the line or what they are doing while they speak." For this scene, I bring two students to the front of the class. "What does Sarah sound like when she says, 'I'm not getting any shoes from here'? Is she whining? Is she shouting? What is her mother doing while Sarah says this? Put the scene in motion." The physical movement demonstrates the power of blocking to "show, not tell."

Sarah uses an extended metaphor in her story that I point out. She places her Jellies on the bed "as if burying a wounded soldier." Later, she offers her mother "the corpses" of her shoes. Soto also models the use of metaphorical language in narratives that I want my students to attempt in their writing. In the first line Soto writes, "My clothes had failed me. I remember the green coat that I wore in fifth and sixth grade when you either danced like a champ or pressed yourself against a greasy wall, bitter as a penny toward the happy couples." Bringing these literary tools to my students' attention increases the use figurative language in their writing.

I also want my students to consider their classmates as teachers and to learn from each other's stories and storytelling techniques.

After color-highlighting the pieces for literary devices, I ask students to make a list of stories that have surfaced for them, including how they got the clothes, the significance of the clothing, and a story connected to the item. When most students have generated a few stories, I ask a few students to share. This time for talk is important. Our conversations not only stir up stories for those who are stuck, our talk helps create community in the classroom. Prior to moving into writing, I lead students in a guided visualization.

Sharing Stories—Read-Arounds and Collective Text

These stories aren't written simply for me to read, grade, mark off, and return. The stories comprise part of the literature we read in class. It's worth repeating that students need real audiences for their writing. Reading the narratives out loud brings those private moments of shame or humiliation, of humanity, into the open, so we can soften the pain and examine why we believed we needed to have the latest jeans to be accepted. It is the public airing of these stories that helps us excavate those private feelings of doubt, that helps develop the ability to question why our society pushes us to look a certain way, to question why we believe that the right clothes or shoes or address will make us a better person.

But I also want my students to consider their classmates as teachers and to learn from each other's stories and storytelling techniques. So while each student reads, I tell the class to listen and take notes about how the story illuminates injustice, the need to buy acceptance, as well as the use of language, dialogue, blocking, metaphor, or characterization.

For example, Deshawn Holden's story, "Shoes," provides an example of redemption, of an ally who steps forward, offering refuge from the onslaught of criticism, as well as a great model for the use of humorous interior monologue also found in Gary Soto's piece. When DeShawn's sister leaves a pair of cheap, white shoes from Volume on his desk instead of the Nikes he hoped for, he is saved from humiliation by another student:

> The most popular boy in the school, the boy who had the three f's—fashions, friends, and fans—came up to me. Everybody looked up to him, including me.
>
> "Those shoes are fresh, man. Here, let me lace them up for you." He said this with such sincerity that no one else could laugh. I took him for his word as he laced those shoes up.

Chetan Patel's story, "Baby Oil," pushes the story beyond consumption to look at how students abandon cultural ties to assimilate into school culture. (See p. 80.) Throughout his childhood, Chetan's mother put baby oil in his black hair as a daily ritual.

> In 3rd grade, a fellow student, Anh, asked the teacher, "Why do Nimesh and Chetan have shiny heads?"
>
> "I put baby oil in my hair," Nimesh announced without hesitation.
>
> "What about you, Chetan?" Anh asked, her eyes taunting me. What she really wanted was for me to say that I used baby oil. She wanted me to be humiliated in front of the class. I wasn't going to let her have that pleasure.
>
> "I used water," I lied.
>
> "And it gets that shiny?" Mrs. Todd asked, frowning.
>
> "Yup." Mrs. Todd stared at me, trying to pry the truth out of me.

When Chetan reaches 6th grade, he abandons his morning baby oil ritual and instead, "squirted out my brother's LA Looks gel and ran it through my hair....I marched to school and held my head up high in Ockley Green's crowded hallways."

Kanaan's story about the Chuck Taylor high tops his mother kept buying him demonstrates children's fear of being taunted for their clothes: "I hated to put them on. I was already little. They looked like they covered up my whole calf. They were too flexible. High tops were supposed to support my ankle, but these didn't. I was embarrassed to go out in those old Chuck Taylors.... Nobody ever talked about them, but I still didn't feel comfortable. If I'd a been them kids, and I seen someone wear those same red Chuck Taylors everyday, I would have talked about them. They probably did talk behind my back because little kids don't let anything go past without speaking on it."

Jessica's piece directly confronts the class aspect of clothes. She is a poor student at a wealthy middle school, desperate to fit in. She wants a pair of jeans like the other girls at school, but after her mother sees the price of the jeans, she tells Jessica, "I'm sorry, honey, but I really can't afford these." Her mother takes her to Value Village, a used clothing store, to find a pair. Jessica's interior monologue shows her fear of ridicule:

Value Village? I was appalled. Obviously, she understood nothing and did not care about me or how I felt. Value Village was the place the popular kids ridiculed. They yelled at kids in the halls with insults, "You buy your clothes at Value Village!" They said it was a place for homeless people and welfare recipients.

These stories open students to talk about similar issues: going to the welfare office with their mothers, using food stamps to buy food at grocery stores, the humiliation of being the kid who receives the Thanksgiving basket of food. When I open my class to talk about real issues that affect students' lives, we can get to real learning. This gathering of "collective text" during the read-around is where the class moves beyond sharing writing as a "strut-

Barbara Miner

your-stuff" exercise and into collecting evidence about our lives. As one student said years after she graduated, the read-around and collective text helped her look beyond the cardboard stereotypes of "basketball player" and "Jefferson Dancer" to see our common humanity.

This lesson is part of my yearlong campaign to get students to examine what is taken for granted and normalized. Writing stories about clothes, hair, or fitting in becomes part of our study of literature, advertising, cartoons, and history where we ask questions about race, class, and power. As a language arts teacher, I want to shine a light on the places in my students' lives that make them feel small and vulnerable.

Too often, school allows students to stay isolated in their private feelings and observations. Their emotions and interpretations of those emotions are at the mercy of advertisers and a culture industry that rarely have young people's best interests at heart. Writing about and discussing personal issues that have social ramifications can help overcome this isolation. As they listen to one another's stories, students begin to recognize how they often chase dreams and compete in ways that may make some people lots of money, but leave them feeling empty. ■

Pro Wings

by Sarah LePage

I grasped my seashell blue Jellies and walked over to my bed. I placed them down on my bedspread as if burying a wounded soldier. Their sides had long ago come undone, their heels were ground down and filled with rocks, and their pearly blue appearance was dulled by many hours of being scuffed on pavement. In vain I tried to save them; tape wouldn't seem to hold the sides together long enough for me to take three steps and glue was far more trouble than it was worth. It formed a pasty river down my arm and cascaded over to splat against the floor. I knew what I had to do.

Tucking my exhausted Jellies under my arm, I set out to find my mom. I found her minutes later sitting in front of the TV.

"Mommy, can I have some new Jellies?" I asked, offering her the corpses of the ones I owned.

"Didn't I just buy those damn things?"

"Uh, I think it was almost two months ago," I sighed.

"I'm not going to spend any more of my hard-earned money on those cheap things. Tomorrow we'll go to Volume and get some shoes that will last."

What?? Volume? Shoes that would last? What was she saying? All I wanted was a shiny new $2.99 pair of pearly blue Jellies. "Momma, can't we just get some Jellies?" I cried.

"Girl, I ain't wastin' no more of my money on those cheap plastic things, and I think it's past your bedtime anyway!"

I sulked back to my room, a tear slipping down my cheek as I buried my beloved Jellies underneath the paper in my wastebasket.

That night, visions of Volume haunted my dreams. I heard the other children laughing. I saw the ugliest pair of shoes that resembled twin boats more than they did shoes, and I saw my mom buying those very same shoes saying, "Now, these will last ya."

The next morning Mom dragged my sleep-deprived body out of bed and said that we were going to buy my new shoes.

"Mom, do I have to go to Volume? Wouldn't it be cheaper if we just went and bought me some new Jellies?" I whined.

"Stop pestering me about those worthless things," she snapped.

Worthless? That single word stung worse than the slap of a hand. My prized shoes weren't worthless. How could she talk about them like that, and in front of me?

"I'm not getting any shoes from here," I announced, as my mother led the way down the aisle crammed with my size shoes.

"You'll do what you're told or else!" she snapped back.

I crossed my arms, planted my feet, narrowed my eyes, and shook my head in defiance. "I said I want Jellies!"

She stopped cold, whirled around and grabbed me by the arm. She dragged me within inches of her beet red face and spoke in a hard, terrifying voice, "I said you'll do what you are told! Now go sit down and take off your shoes, 'cause these are the ones that you are getting." She forced a pair of gray Pro Wings with matching Velcro into my clenched fists.

The next week at school, it was torture, as I knew it would be.

"Hey, Sarah, are those new shoes?" Jennifer asked. "I got new shoes too, but mine don't fly."

Everyone in the class started laughing, even Michael, the class dork, the boy everyone made fun of.

"Yeah, I bet you'd have no problems making the track team," he smirked. It wasn't even funny, yet everyone laughed. I walked home humiliated, with kids flapping their arms in my direction like birds, but Mom was right, those shoes lasted a long time. Too long.

Shoes

by DeShawn Holden

"Mr. Harris! Mr. Harris!" I called out desperately with my hand raised in the air. He turned around with his full-bloom belly, full mustache, and hairy beard where camouflaged dandruff hid itself.

"Yes, Mr. Holden. What can I do for you?" he answered in his deep, baritone voice.

"I need to call my mother. It's an emergency. I forgot to get my white shoes for the parade today." I was part of the Woodlawn Elementary Jump Rope Team as a 4th grader. I was the only boy, but I didn't let that deter me. I liked to jump rope.

"Come and get this pass, so you won't get caught in the halls without one." He sounded confident in me when he gave me the pass.

I took the pass, ran down the hallway to the phone. I nearly felt like passing out because nothing was functioning. I dialed the numbers quickly 2-2-2-8-8-2-2. My brain was moving faster than my fingers that acted like they were so slow they couldn't catch on. Finally, the number moved out of my brain and into my fingers and onto the number pad.

"Mom, I need you to get me some white shoes. Fast!" I said.

"Shoes for what?" she asked irritated.

"Mom, I need some shoes. I forgot to tell you about the parade I'm in."

"Shawn, I don't have no money for you to get some shoes." She sounded disappointed. We both set on the phone silent for a straight minute trying to figure out how I could get these shoes.

"Mom, Michelle said she would buy me some shoes. Can you call her and ask her can she bring my shoes up to the school within the next two hours?"

I walked back to class, happy and excited that my sister was going to bring me the shoes that I needed for the parade. I just knew my sister was going to bring me some nice shoes, some Nikes.

Two hours had come and gone and all I could think was, "Where in the world is Michelle Holden?" I was thinking about divorcing her; she was losing her place as my sister. She'd lost that privilege. The parade would start in twenty minutes. I paced and pondered so much you would have thought the Oregon Trail came through Woodlawn School. I walked myself right out of the classroom and into the restroom across the hallway. I needed a break from worrying, and I didn't want any of my classmates to realize that I didn't have the situation under control.

When I completed the job of calming my nerves, I walked back to class. I saw everybody looking at me. Some kids were snickering; some were just laughing out loud. I had no clue what they were laughing at until I turned the corner to my desk, and there it was. All my fame, fans, and friends vanished. There it sat. The brown bag with the yellow and orange lettering marked Volume Shoe Stores. The class burst into laughter. I looked around in embarrassment.

"Your sister brought these here for you," Mr. Harris said.

I don't want these shoes, I thought to myself. I opened the bag to find the XK-900's slap me in the face. I should have known that she was going to get me these because I told her that her XK-900's were fresh. But I really didn't like them, I just said that to be nice. Me and my big mouth. Now I had to wear these shoes in the parade.

The most popular boy in the school, the boy who had the three f's—fashion, friends, and fans—came up to me. Everybody looked up to him, including me.

"Those shoes are fresh, man. Here, let me lace them up for you." He said this with such sincerity that no one else could laugh. I took him for his word as he laced those shoes up.

Baby Oil

by Chetan Patel

"Chetan! Get the baby oil and come here. Now!" My mother's voice echoed through the house, waking up the neighbors and stirring their cat. I rushed out of the bathroom, comb in hand, into my mother's room and snatched the Johnson's Baby Oil off her desk. I skipped to the living room and plopped down in front of my mother who sat crisscross on the couch. The back of my head faced hers as I stared aimlessly into the kitchen, watching my brother slurp up a bowl of Frosted Flakes. I heard the squirting of baby oil into my mother's hand, and the gurgling sound as she rubbed her hands together. I shrugged as she rubbed her hands through my hair, fearing she'd get my new blue shirt wet and oily. She snatched the comb out of my hand and after three strokes (one to the left, one to the right, and one down the back), she was done.

Running to my mother's room to put the oil and comb back, I got a glimpse of myself in the mirror. The poorly lit hallway was ablaze as the lights reflected off my head. I hurried, hoping I'd have time for breakfast.

Third grade was boring for me. Not only was I past my multiples, I was reading books bigger than some of my classmates' arms. I sat next to my best friend, Nimesh, who also came to school with a shiny head. He was still in the multiples of nine and was reading *The Witches*.

The bell rang for class to start and my fellow students shuffled in and took their seats, one of them being Anh. She was one of my two arch foes, the other was Robbie, but I didn't have to deal with him this year. He got stuck with Mr. _____. I shuddered. The thought of that man would make any kid run for cover. He was known to have hit children. I witnessed him once choking a boy because he couldn't read properly. Good thing I have Mrs. Todd, the perkiest and nicest teacher I've come across in my five years of education.

"Mrs. Todd, Mrs. Todd," Anh hissed, her arm flapping in the air.

"Yes, Anh," Mrs. Todd replied.

"Why do Nimesh and Chetan have shiny heads?"

"I don't know, Anh. Maybe we should ask them." All students' eyes fell on the two of us. I became nervous and didn't want to talk. What if they make fun of me? I hated Anh. She always had to say something to bother me. Well, this time she wasn't going to get away with it! This time, I was going to let her have it. Watch, today at lunch, she's—

"I put baby oil in my hair," Nimesh announced without hesitation.

"What about you, Chetan?" Anh asked, her eyes taunting me. What she really wanted me to say was that I use baby oil. She wanted me to be humiliated in front of the class. I wasn't going to let her have the pleasure.

"I used water," I lied.

"And it gets that shiny?" Mrs. Todd asked, frowning.

"Yup." Mrs. Todd stared at me, trying to pry the truth out of me.

After a pause, she started, "Today in class, we'll learn about..."

* * *

Sixth grade started. Because of orientation, I was one of the few kids from Beach Elementary who knew their way around Ockley Green Middle School.

A group of 6th graders stood outside the cafeteria, aching for the new school year to begin. I was one of them. I knew a few of the faces around me, including one of my old four-square buds, Michael.

"Doesn't your brother go here?" he asked, his eyes bulging out of his glasses.

"Yeah," I said coolly.

"Why are you hanging around me? What if someone tried to beat you up? What if some..." Michael's endless babbling annoyed me. Once you got him started, nothing could stop him. "And what if someone tries to beat you up? Huh? What are you goin—"

"Wait, Michael, I think I see someone calling me." I walked to the other cafeteria door and thankfully Michael didn't follow. The bell rang, and the 6th grade began.

"Chetan! Why don't you ever comb your hair?" Jeremy asked, placing a french fry into his mouth.

"I do, but the wind messed it up." I looked at the people around me. Jeremy sat across from me and Nimesh to my right. Adam, an old friend from grade school, sat to my left and Michael completed our circle. Everyone was dressed in the latest fashions, except me. I wore a white T-shirt, blue jeans and a pair of imitation Nikes from K-mart. They had crusty hair, from the gel and hair spray they used every morning. Even Nimesh had left the baby oil behind in elementary school.

* * *

"Chetan! Come here with the baby oil and comb!" my mother shouted. I stood in front of the bathroom mirror. I squirted out my brother's LA Looks gel and ran it through my hair. It shined as much as it did with baby oil, but was a hundred times thicker. I picked up my brother's brush in disgust. The tangled hairs and white flakes that dotted the blue brush didn't look too inviting. The strong bristles scratched my head, burning my scalp as I ran it through my hair. I tried to mold my hair like his, ending up with something that could be called a hairstyle.

I marched to school and held my head up high in Ockley Green's crowded hallways. No one noticed my new do, of course, not even Nimesh, Jeremy, Michael, or Adam. But that didn't matter, I was happy with my hair's new shape.

Goodwill Jay

by Chrysanthius Lathan

I did it. I had finally punked Jay. I spoke up for every Goodwill-going, ghetto child and parent at Sabin Elementary. The chuckles, elbows, and snicker-sneers from my friends in line in the freshly waxed hallway told me so. So did the facial expression somewhere between pity and indigestion on Mr. Rodriguez' face when he turned to him and said, "That's karma, Jay, that's karma."

If there was a syndrome called "Teasing Tourette's," Jay Johansen had it. He was, by far, the most diabolical, merciless 4th grader known to don Air Jordans—albeit scuffed and as white as snow being left to die in an NYC street, they were Jordans nonetheless. So I already knew what 5th grade had in store well before this sunny September day.

It all began August 23. That was supposed to be my birthday. But NOOOOOOO. It was "school shopping" day at the "mall." The local Goodwill got the updated name from my brother Emanuel and me, 'specially to piss off Mom, who did not find it piss-off-worthy at all. We grew up pretty poor, although we would never know by the mountains of barbecued and fried chicken paired with the yams, potato salad, greens, minty-fresh sweet tea, and hunks of buttery cornbread that constituted our weekly Sunday meals. Laughter was how Emanuel and I coped with the frequent adult realities we faced as young kids. Mama held it together by whatever means necessary, even when it meant buying school clothes at the Goodwill—a serious mid-'80s infraction, not just a, but THE, fashion faux pas of the decade. The only thing I ever wondered was—how did we have a 1988 brand-spankin'-new, candy apple red, never-violated Olds Cutlass, and not enough to get clothes that still had virginity? "You got a job? Well, get one or shut up," was her final reply for anything involving cash. And she never forgot to read us our rights about six blocks from the store. "If y'all act right, you can pick out one thing you want. Otherwise, don't touch nothin', and Emanuel, leave folks alone!"

Anyway, we walked into the cave of a Goodwill in pursuit of that balm called laughter, and caught a whiff of the air. It smelled familiar—a wet dog inside of my Grandaddy's motor home that he's had since the '60s. "PEEEEEYOOOOOOUUU!" he yelled, seconds before Mama nearly snatched his arm out of its socket. "Do it again, I'll knock those lips down your throat," she said between clenched teeth. And with the threat of life, off we went. Emanuel and I had a dark, secret, fetish-like desire of going to the Goodwill with Mama. Heck, it was just plain fun! Where else could you go and try on too-big men's sportscoats with the patches on the elbows, play with toys that nobody cared if they got broken, find a Walkman, and wolf down a double-bacon cheeseburger, fries, and Coke—all in one cahoot? We had to face it—Goodwill was a kid's mecca. As long as you didn't buy your clothes from there. See, this had been a ritual on or near my birthday, year after year. But this one was the Grand Poobah of all wake-up calls.

"What'choo gon' look for this time?" Emanuel asked me while wearing a pot on his head.

"I don't know. Keds," I replied. "Not white, though. Mama will wash 'em and they'll get that yellow bleach ring around the rubber. Everybody'll know they're not new," I explained as an expert on disguising no-name clothes. "I'll get red. Or blue. No white, no yellow ring."

"Well," he added, "why do you care about yellow rings? Your teeth are yellow."

"Skip you, punk!"

"I really want some Jordans."

"Ooh, they have them one shoes that look just like Jordans at Volume's," I further advised. "They're kinda fresh, they just have two Velcro straps and the shoelaces are skinny." Just then, a golden light shone from the heavens, so blinding I took a pair of old blue-blockers from the shelf and put them on, turning toward the shoe racks. A pair of Jordans.

I don't know who got there first out of Emanuel and me, or what method of transportation we used to get there (he thought it was teleportation), but we were at the shoe racks in a matter of a millisecond. Revolving clothing racks and old mannequins did not stop us from getting there, either. We simply knocked them over. Emanuel tried them on. Too big. "Get 'em anyway," I said.

"Dummy!" he called me so fluently. "By the time I grow into 'em, a new kind will come out. Plus, Mama said nothing over $5.00."

I scoffed. "Whatever. They scuffed anyway." It was about then that I saw Jay at the burger counter with a very pretty woman. She wiped mustard from his white polo, fussing uncontrollably, so it seemed. "I told you not to wear this shirt anyway. Now I gotta come back here next month and get you some more clothes. Boys are so messy. Dang."

I ducked behind a hanging-off fitting room door and snuck off to the electronics, thinking blankly about seeing Jay. There was no way I was saying "Hi." We ended the trip on a pretty good note. I got some overalls out of it. Sure, they were too small. "That's what scissors are for," said Mama. "Make 'em into shorts." And though they may not have known it, I had those same overall shorts to thank—for they would lead me to victory weeks later.

As Mr. Rodriguez led the class back inside from the first gym class of the school year, the funk of fallen Gingko nuts was like noxious poison. Keela pushed Jay, and Jay pushed me, making me push Adriane. "Dang, Jay, MOVE!" Keela yelled.

"If Chrissy would use her Pro-Wings to fly out of the way, I could move," he jabbed, illegally popping his bubblegum. "Go fly with your family, the seagulls, Chris."

"L-l-leave me alone." I was the youngest of four siblings, unused to defending myself. This just made him jab quicker and harder. "L-l-l-l-l-l-l-l-l-l-l-l-l-l-l-shut up!" he teased. "L-l-l-l-l-l-l-llll…." Folks' giggles rose from the rear of the line like Thriller zombies, and I began to shrink, shrivel, look for a storm drain for me to dissolve, melt, and slip away into eternity. See, generally, as a career tease-ee, I make it a point to stand in line nearest the front, where I had teacher immunity and protection from the tease-er. I had to tie my shoe at the whistle and ran out of luck. Jay kept it up. "That's why you got those overalls from the Goodwill—"

It was then that I began to fill up and charge with a fluid that felt like a combination of pride, Kryptonite, jet fuel, and mustard. I looked at the ground. And there, with the same scuff on the same left shoe—was the same pair of ashy-butt-looking Jordans Emanuel put back on the rack. I magnified in on the white polo collar with a faint yellow stain that showed under his sweater. And when I opened my mouth, this is what fell out:

"Oh, I KNOW you ain't talkin', Jay. You didn't see ME at the Goodwill. I saw YOU and hid behind the mannequins from yo' ugly scary mama, who licked the mustard off yo' shirt you have on now, from that dirty old-people cheeseburger you ate! Y'all think I'm lyin'? Turn your left Jordan, Jay. A scuff. That's cause those are the Jordans MY big bro threw away, and he's gon use 'em to kick yo' butt for tryin' to sting on ME! NOW WHAT?"

And that was the day I punked Jay Johansen. As he painfully looked up the line, one face at a time, the faces staring back rendered no love. Just laughter. And the undigested pity of Mr. Rod. This was a day picked-on kids around the world would envy for life. So why did I feel so small when I saw the tear stream down the right side of his face and land on that mustard-stained collar? It reminded me of the times I had been at the burger counter with MY mother.

The moral of this story is: Everybody shops at the Goodwill. Everybody.

The author is a teacher in Portland Public Schools.

The Mochida family, 1942, on their way to an internment camp.

Bettmann Archive/CORBIS

Writing for Justice

Acting in solidarity with others is a learned skill, but not one taught in most schools. I want students to understand that change doesn't just happen: People work for change, whether ending slavery, fighting for the rights of women, stocking grocery shelves with produce from local farms, or creating schools where all students, regardless of their ethnicity or their parents' income, receive a rigorous, engaging curriculum. I designed this lesson to help students uncover those moments in their lives when they participated in an act of injustice, and then to use those narratives to rehearse acting in solidarity with others to change the situation.

Ally, Target, Perpetrator, Bystander

I begin the work of learning how to write and act for justice by defining key terms we use in our classroom throughout the year as we discuss issues of justice and injustice—target, ally, perpetrator, and bystander. (I borrowed these terms from the British Columbia Teachers Union.) I distribute the "Acting for Justice" chart (p. 91), so students can take notes on their papers while I write on the overhead. Before I begin the definitions, I let students know that people are complex. At any point in a day, we move in and out of these roles. Our behavior determines the role; we are not born perpetrators or targets. We might stand up for our sister at dinner and fall silent when we witness an injustice in the grocery store. This initial defining helps students get the gist of the terms, but the definitions become fuller as

I designed this lesson to help students uncover those moments in their lives when they participated in an act of injustice, and then to use those narratives to rehearse acting in solidarity with others to change the situation.

we read historical memoirs, pieces of literature, and talk about our own stories.

I tell students, "Allies are people who stand up for someone when they face injustice. They intervene when someone is mistreated; they don't stand by and watch; they don't participate in the injustice, and they don't run away when someone else is suffering. A target is the person who is the target of injustice." I use the term "target" instead of "victim" because victim implies passivity, as if the person cannot or does not act on his or her own behalf. I also tell students, "The target can be an individual, but can also be a group. For example, Japanese Americans were targets of injustice when the U.S. government forced them out of their homes and imprisoned them in internment camps during World War II. We might feel an injustice personally, but it is important to think about the possibility that we might be targets of injustice because of our gender, race, age, country of origin, religion, or sexual orientation."

This is obviously a quick gloss for a huge concept. Again, the terms begin to breathe as we read and study historical, literary, and personal incidents. I continue with the definitions, "The perpetrator commits the act of injustice. Again, this is complicated. The perpetrator can be a person, or a group of people, or even a law. And finally, the bystander is a person who observes the act of injustice, but who does nothing to intervene, nothing to stop the injustice."

Once students have a basic understanding of the terms, I pass out "On Cracking White City," James Farmer Jr.'s story of integrating Jack Spratt Coffeehouse in Chicago in 1941. (See p. 92.) Farmer was one of the founders of the Committee of Racial Equality, which later became the Congress of Racial Equality (CORE). (Students may remember him as the youngest scholar, played by Denzel Whitaker, in the film *The Great Debaters*.) In the interview, Farmer discusses some of CORE's early activities in the 1940s using Gandhi's nonviolent strategies. In addition to clarifying the terms, this piece gives me an opportunity to talk about finding our "moral ancestors," those people in history and our lives who crossed lines to make alliances for justice. To find moral ancestors, we look for people who embody characteristics we want to claim in our heritage. In "On Cracking White City," both the CORE members as well as the white customers who refuse to eat until the CORE members are served, earn the title.

As we read the memoir out loud, I stop along the way and engage students as participants in the story. I stop the first time after the waitress has served the white customers, but refused to serve the black customers. This is an important point in the story. Farmer noted, "By this time the other customers who were in there were aware of what was going on and were watching, and most of these were university people, University of Chicago, who were more or less sympathetic with us. And they stopped eating and the two people at the counter she had served and those whites in the booth she had served were not eating.... There were no seats available. So she walked over to two of the whites at the counter and said, "We served you. Why don't you eat and get out?""

I tell the students, "I am going to play the waitress, and I want you to be the white University of Chicago students." I pick a sassy student who I know will play along, and I say, "I served you your food. Will you please eat and get out." Typically, the student says, "No." So I go to another student and say the same thing. By this time the students are getting into it. More and more talk back. I egg them on, "Come on, people. You can see I have a situation on my hands here. Please just eat, so I can serve the others who are waiting."

The students shoot back, "You haven't served our friends. When you serve them we will eat." Students love the white customers who aren't part of the sit-in, but who act as spontaneous allies refusing to leave their seats or eat. They chuckle at the ingenuity of the allies' answer when they, too, are asked to "eat and get out." In the story, the university students answer, "Well, madam, we don't think it would be polite for us to begin eating our food before our friends here have also been served."

As we continue to read the interview, I ask students to answer the restaurant personnel as if they are CORE members. "The restaurant says they will serve the blacks in the basement. How do you answer them?" The students yell, "No. We won't be served in the basement." I come back at them with the restaurant's next proposal. "The restaurant says they will serve the blacks at the two booths in the back of the restaurant. How do you answer them?" The students yell, "No. We won't be served in the back of the restaurant." Again, I push them, "This is so unfair. Of all of the restaurants, why did you pick on us? Please, I'll serve you in the basement." The students won't have anything to do with this. At this point, they see through every strategy I come up with. While this sounds playful, and it is, this performance acts as a rehearsal for students learning to talk back to injustice, to see how others who have come before them have dared to "act for justice."

After we've finished reading "On Cracking White City," I ask students to go back to their chart and identify

Jack Moebes/CORBIS

Four African American college students sit in protest at a whites-only lunch counter during the second day of peaceful protest at a Woolworth's in Greensboro, N.C. From left: Joseph McNeil, Franklin McCain, Billy Smith, and Clarence Henderson.

who was the target of injustice, the perpetrator of injustice, the ally, and the bystander in the story. Sometimes students get confused. They think the restaurant is the target because that is where the sit-in took place, so I make it clear that we are looking at the target of injustice. Let me just say, no one ever agrees. Students argue, and this is good because they have to go back to the text to justify their answer. Most everyone agrees that the CORE members, and African Americans in general, are the targets of injustice because they aren't allowed to eat in the restaurant. Students all agree that the white University of Chicago students are allies. Some students also point out that the CORE members are allies for one another. Yes!

Then, it gets tricky. Are the police allies because they don't arrest the CORE members? Some students argue that the police are allies for this reason and because they winked. Other students argue that the police are bystanders, at best, because according to the law they should have forced the restaurant to serve them. They point back to the passage in the text where Farmer said, "We called the police department and told them what we were going to do. In fact, we read the state civil rights law to them. They weren't familiar with that. [Laughs] They assured us that if we followed the pattern which we outlined to them over the phone, there was nothing they could do to arrest us. They'd have no grounds for making an arrest because we were within our rights to insist upon service. And we asked them if they would see that we were served as they were obligated to do by law, but this they would not do. No, they wouldn't do that, but they wouldn't arrest us."

Students also argue about the role of the waitress. Is she a perpetrator because she doesn't serve the CORE members? Is she a bystander because she is "just following orders?" Great moral question. And not one I answer. I don't end by "telling" students the right answer, I just help clarify the roles. Most students place the whites who come, stand around, and leave as the bystanders.

We follow this complicated reading with a much more straightforward story, "The Music Lesson," written by my former student Sarah Stucki. (I include Sarah's story with this lesson although I originally included it in *Reading, Writing, and Rising Up* because it provides the clearest example of how bystanders can intervene when we move into the "Acting for Justice" section of this lesson.) In this story, Mr. Dunn, a music teacher, humiliates Mark Hubble, a Native American student in class. Mark never returned to class—or school—after that incident. And no one intervenes. Because a student wrote the story, "The Music Lesson" provides a clear, accessible model. We return to the categories, and students discuss each character's role in Sarah's story. Another story, "Member of the Club," written by Davis P. Heard, a Portland Public School teacher, demonstrates a perpetrator's guilt and remorse, and also provides an accessible model. It helps students remember those frozen moments when they observe an injustice, but look away, not wanting to get involved.

Before we move to charting our own stories, we read my student Josh Langworthy's story, "When I Was Young," about the physical abuse in his home, and the time he fought back. On the day Josh shared this story in class, there wasn't a dry eye. In one of the toughest classes I faced over my years in teaching, Josh's honesty broke the barrier between past failures many students experienced and the realization that their stories deserved to be written and heard and discussed. His narrative opened up other students to share similar incidents from their lives. Josh is one of the true heroes from my teaching career, not just because of his incredible honesty, but because he helped others in every way. Many students in his class struggled with literacy, and Josh was like a second teacher, helping them sort through memories, pushing them to get to work when they played. These stories are first draft stories, even though they appear in this book. They were written in a whoosh, and I left them as they are because this prompt, for me, is more about the stories than the polished product.

Charting Our Stories

Once students have been steeped in historical and literary descriptions of ally behavior, we return to their "Acting for Justice" charts. I begin by telling stories about times I was a target of injustice or discrimination. I start with typical and easy sibling stories that many students can relate to. I use specific details as I tell about how my older sister, Tina, used to force me to go to the little store on the corner to buy her cigarettes and ice cream sandwiches. She wrote notes to the store clerk, "Please give Linda one pack of Marlboros" and signed my mother's name. Now anyone could tell this was my sister's handwriting by looking at the big loops. She also prefaced my forced errands with the statement, "You best be making your break for the store before I…" I move to another "family" story about the time my first husband beat me in front of the Catholic Church in downtown Eureka and no one stopped to intervene.

Now let me pause and say I tell this story every year because I want students to know it's OK to write about stories that matter, to write about painful, personal topics. I was a battered woman who escaped one night after my husband beat me until he broke my nose, blackened my eyes, and tore out chunks of my hair. When he fell into a drunken sleep, I ran, bloody and half-clothed in a swimsuit and a fisherman's sweater, to a neighbor's house where I called a taxi to take me to a cheap hotel on the edge of town. I fell asleep on the floor, looking under the crack of the door, so I could see if his car pulled into the lot. I feared for the safety of my mother and the rest of my family, so I left my hometown the following day and found

a new home and new life in Portland. I tell this story because I want students to know that they can and should leave abusive situations. I want them to know that many of us have these stories, and there is no shame in telling them, no shame in leaving. And, every year, my story opens the floodgates for student stories. I also distribute information about shelters for battered women and children. After I tell my story, I ask students to list times they were targets of injustice. I ask a few students to share. I also say, "Don't worry if you don't have something in every category. Sometimes ideas for stories will come later."

As I move to my next story in the target category of the Acting for Justice chart, I tell students, "Sometimes we are targets of injustice as an individual, and other times we are targets because of our race, class, ethnicity, language, gender, or sexual orientation." I share how my 9th-grade teacher targeted me because of my class background when

I tell students, "Sometimes we are targets of injustice as an individual, and other times we are targets because of our race, class, ethnicity, language, gender, or sexual orientation."

she made me stand and pronounce words and conjugate verbs as an example of how not to talk. Then she called on the girl whose parents owned most of the restaurants in town to demonstrate how to pronounce words and conjugate verbs correctly. While I tell my stories, students fill out their "target" column on the Acting for Justice charts, and they talk about their stories. "As your classmates share, jot down any new memories that surface on your chart." I'm not concerned if students fill these charts completely; the activity provides a way for them to get quiet, so they can collect detailed memories.

We pause after each category—target, ally, perpetrator, and bystander—and I encourage students to share their incidents. I never rush this sharing or story-catching time because this narrative takes students to some of the most significant stories they will share all year. If I don't allow adequate time to prepare students to engage seriously, and I don't create in the classroom a willingness to be open and take risks with this story, students may never dare to write the honest stories that need to be written. Over the years I've discovered that students share based on their life histories, their own comfort with the class, and their willingness to talk about joyful and painful issues in their lives.

Let me pause. Some teachers will say this is "touchy-feely" stuff. Not rigorous. Not academic. Not part of school. I disagree. The best literature is the most honest; it doesn't gloss over the hard parts. It's why we love and hate Troy Maxson in August Wilson's *Fences*. He isn't nice. He's been injured, and he strikes back at his wife, his friend, his sons. It's why John Steinbeck's *Grapes of Wrath* continues to haunt us. Who can forget Ma Joad standing with the frying pan threatening her men to stand up and be men? Honesty in writing is hard to come by, but when it comes, it should be celebrated. And we need to make room for this kind of real work in the classroom.

Guided Visualization, Drafting, Sharing

After students have shared stories from their charts, I lead them in a guided visualization as I described in some detail in "Teaching Narrative Writing: Why It Matters." I encourage students to include a description of where the story takes place, a description of the people involved, and the dialogue of what was said during the incident the way Josh and Sarah did in the narratives I described earlier. I also encourage them to use interior monologues as a way of telling how they felt during this act of injustice and whether or not they were changed by the events.

I open the day of the read-around by talking about the importance of being present as students share their stories. As always, in every read-around, I ask students to take notes as people share their narratives. "Today, your class-mates are reading important stories from their lives. Some of these stories are painful. Some will be about times when they didn't act, but wish they would have. Others will share about times they did act. Your job today is to be hungry listeners. Be compassionate listeners. I want you to listen with your head and your heart. I want you to take notes on the topics, to note details that make the writing come to life, and to find honest feedback to share with each writer. I also want you to think about what conditions allowed peo-ple to act for justice, how people felt when they didn't act."

As students read their stories to the rest of the class, we listen, take notes, and talk to the writer. There is no arti-fice in this feedback. Students respond naturally. "That's hard, man," I remember CJ saying after Josh read his story. These stories lend themselves less to discussing liter-ary theory and more to discussing life.

After students have read and shared, I ask them to write a paragraph or two, using specific examples from

Spencer Jones/GETTY IMAGES

their classmates' stories: How do people feel when they are the targets of injustice? When they are laughed at? Excluded? How do they feel when they gather the courage to stand up for someone else, when they fight back against ignorance and hate? Why didn't some of us act even when we felt immoral standing by as a witness to injustice? After students write their collective text, we discuss their observations.

Acting for Justice: Rehearsing the Future

As my students shared incidents of injustice in their lives, I realized that they didn't know how to act differently. They felt stuck, backed into a corner, frozen. Most stu-dents identified themselves as bystanders or perpetrators of injustice, not targets, not allies. Students felt conflicted and unhappy about their roles in hurting others, and I knew that I needed to help them figure out ways to inter-vene, when appropriate. Instead of ending the lesson with the writing and sharing, I started using stories to rehearse strategies for interrupting these incidents of injustice.

Students felt conflicted and unhappy about their roles in hurting others, and I knew that I needed to help them figure out ways to intervene, when appropriate.

In the opening of this narrative lesson, students played the white University of Chicago students who, in solidar-ity with the CORE members, refused to move. They also played the CORE members who refused inferior seating in the restaurant. To demonstrate to students how to "Act for Justice," I return to Sarah Stucki's story, "The Music Lesson." Davis P. Heard's story "Member of the Club" also works for this exercise because it provides an opportunity for bystanders to intervene in an unjust situation. We reread Sarah's story together as a class. Then I say, "I want to act this story out like we did with 'Cracking White City.' I will play the teacher. I want one of you to play Mark. The rest of you are the class." We act the story out exactly as it happened.

Then I say, "OK. This time you have to figure out how to keep Mark in class. You all let this boy get humiliated. He never came back to class. Together, you have a lot of power. Figure out how you can intervene using your collective wisdom. I want you to channel James Farmer Jr. and CORE. I am going to walk out of the room. When I come back in, we will play the scene through again, but this time you help Mark. Talk together and come up with a strategy. You might have a back-up strategy, too."

I leave the class for about five minutes, walking into the hallway outside of the room. When I return, we replay the scene, but this time, students stand up for Mark. Over the years, they have employed two or three strategies. One is what I call the Spartacus approach. When I call Mark up, a number of students say, "I was the one who laughed." I say, "No, I heard Mark." But students don't back down. "I laughed."

Another strategy students have used over the years is collective action. When I make Mark come to the front of the class, they either start singing with him, or they walk to the front of the room and stand next to him. After they return to their seats, I say, "How did it feel to stand up for someone?" Even in a "rehearsal" for justice, students gather courage as well as ideas for how to intervene.

For the final piece of this lesson, they return to their stories to find ways to act for change. Before students move into small groups to share their narratives, I give them directions. "As you read these stories, I want you to select one where the group can intervene and change the outcome. If no one acted for justice in real life, figure out how you can take action this time to make sure that someone does just like we did with Mark." These scenarios provide the class with opportunities to discuss how they can make a difference on their own.

Each group acts out their scene and we discuss their intervention. Would it work? Is there another way that might work better? I also ask students how it felt to act as an ally. If a student was a target of injustice, I ask how it felt to have someone intervene.

After participating in this unit, two of my junior students told me about how they took these strategies to their choir class. According to Valentina, several girls had been laughing at one autistic boy all year. Apparently, he flapped his arms in an odd manner when he sang. The girls mimicked his movements, laughing until they intentionally fell off the risers in escalating fits of laughter. Valentina and Desiree confronted the other girls on the boy's behalf, telling them they didn't find it humorous. They were worried that the girls would attack them, but after a brief exchange, the girls stopped their harassment of the boy. Other students discussed how they banded together to confront a teacher's unfair grading practices.

Students need tools to confront injustice; they need to hear our approval that intervention is not only appropriate and acceptable, but heroic. Acting in solidarity with others is a learned skill—one I hope more of us will teach. ■

Acting for Justice

TARGET	ALLY

BYSTANDER	PERPETRATOR

On Cracking White City

The following oral history, recounted by James Farmer Jr., explains how the Committee of Racial Equality (which later became the Congress of Racial Equality) successfully integrated the Jack Spratt Coffeehouse in Chicago in 1941.

We went in with a group of about 20—this was a small place that seats 30 or 35 comfortably at the counter and in the booths—and occupied just about all of the available seats and waited for service. The woman was in charge again. She ordered the waitress to serve the whites who were seated in one booth, and she served them. She ordered the waitress to serve two whites who were seated at the counter, and she served them. Then she told the blacks, "I'm sorry, we can't serve you, you'll have to leave." And they, of course, declined to leave and continued to sit there. By this time the other customers who were in there were aware of what was going on and were watching, and most of these were university people, University of Chicago, who were more or less sympathetic with us. And they stopped eating and the two people at the counter she had served and those whites in the booth she had served were not eating. There was no turnover. People were coming in and standing around for a few minutes and walking out. There were no seats available.

So she walked over to two of the whites at the counter and said, "We served you. Why don't you eat and get out?" They said, "Well, madam, we don't think it would be polite for us to begin eating our food before our friends here have also been served." So a couple of minutes went by and she announced that she would serve the blacks, the Negroes, which was the term used then, in the basement. We, of course, declined and told her we were quite comfortable. She then said, "If all of the Negroes will occupy those two booths in the back we will serve you there." We declined again. She said, "I'll call the police."

The Gandhian Motif

Then I said to her, "Fine, I think that might be the appropriate step." By the way, we, still following the Gandhian motif, had called the police in advance, being completely open and above board, everything, in notifying the authorities. We called the police department and told them what we were going to do. In fact, we read the state civil rights law to them. They weren't familiar with that. [Laughs] They assured us that if we followed the pattern which we outlined to them over the phone, there was nothing they could do to arrest us. They'd have no grounds for making an arrest because we were within our rights to insist upon service. And we asked them if they would see that we were served as they were obligated to do by law, but this they would not do. No, they wouldn't do that, but they wouldn't arrest us.

Police Arrive

So we said, "Perhaps you should call the police." She did. Two cops came a few minutes later, looked the situation over, said, "Why, lady, what did you call us for? I don't see anybody here disturbing the peace. Everything seems to be peaceful." She said, "Won't you throw these people out on the grounds that we reserve the right to seat our patrons and would serve some of them in the basement?" The cop didn't know. He went to a telephone booth and made a call. I guess he was calling headquarters to see if they could do that. He came out and said, "Nope, sorry, lady, there's nothing in the law that allows us to do that. You must either serve them or solve the problem yourself." And the cops then walked out. On the way out they turned around and winked at us. [Laughs]

We stayed there until closing time and then got up and left and went back the next day, a little bit earlier, and stayed until closing time. And so on. They then tried again to negotiate—without success. We went back in, oh, several more times and tied up the whole afternoon, tied up all the seats. They were doing no business at all.

Finally they cracked. The next time we went in, they served everybody. And accepted money. Did not overcharge us. We then sent an interracial group, a smaller group, in the next day. Everyone was served. We then sent an all-black group in and they were served. We waited a week and sent another black group in, and they were all served. We sent individual blacks in and they were all served without any problem. So we then wrote them a letter thanking them for their change in policy.

"Prelude," from My Soul Is Rested *by Howell Raines, copyright © 1977 Howell Raines. Used by permission of G.P. Putnam's Sons, a division of Penguin Group (USA) Inc.*

The Music Lesson

by Sarah Stucki

I don't remember the words that were spoken, or if there were any, but I'll always remember his face. His tears. His sobs.

The choir room was extraordinarily noisy. The excitement of a new day was rushing through everyone. There was so much energy in the air. Enough to make lights shine and fires to start miraculously on their own. It was the perfect day for a complete disaster.

Mr. Dunn, the bald, squatty man, lined us up how we sang. The good ones were in the middle, bad ones on the sides, and, of course, his star, his daughter, Brittany, right in front even though she was tall and made it difficult for anyone to be seen behind her.

"All right, class, quiet down." He spoke in his fake, confident voice, the voice that made people squirm and their blood boil.

"Let's begin with scales. Ready and…" He tapped his baton on the music stand. He gripped it as though it held all the power in the world, his power that decided our self-esteem.

"La la la la la la la la la." We were running through the non-thought-containing notes. Clearing our throats to reach the high ones. Quietly bowing our heads for the low ones. Laughing when we made a mistake because we knew we were horrible. So did Mr. Dunn.

"Ha ha ha ha." Loud laughter burst from someone to the left of me. I turned to look and see who it was. My face turned red. It was Mark. My crush on him was given away by my bright face. Suddenly, a loud tapping. I whirled around to look at Mr. Dunn pounding on the music stand for us to stop with our scales.

"Who was laughing just now?" His veins stuck out of his stubby neck. Silence. "Who was it?" He struck the stand with his baton. His eyes searched the risers for the guilty party. The person for whom the lecture would be worthy.

I felt his eyes pass over me. I was afraid for Mark because I just knew that Mr. Dunn would figure out it was him. I guess it didn't help much that 59 out of 60 choir students were staring straight at Mark.

"Mark Hubble." His voice boomed throughout the auditorium. "What was so funny, Mr. Hubble? Why don't you share it with the class?" He stared at Mark with a smirk on his face. Mark just stared at his feet. "Excuse me, Mark, are you deaf? What was so funny?"

A mumble came from Mark's serious face. "Nothing," he said.

"Nothing, huh? Well, if it was just nothing, then why don't you come and show us how well you can sing?" He made this statement as though he were a god. "Come on, Mark. Stand here and sing your scales for the class." He pointed to a part in front of the music stand.

Mark was a good guy. He obeyed his teachers. He was never mean at all. He was "fortunate" to be at our school because he was from a reservation in Arizona. So, of course, he went to the music stand and stood before his peers. Us.

"You may begin now," Mr. Dunn spoke bluntly. The piano player began the run through the notes as Mark whispered the scale. "Sing louder, Mark, we can't hear you." Mark sang a little louder. Tears began to fall from his eyes. "Mark, you can sing louder. We heard you loudly before when you were laughing." Mark was crying harder now. Sobs began escaping from him.

He was very embarrassed, and I didn't blame him for crying. I would have too if Mr. Dunn had treated me like Mark, and I feel today that the only reason he was so mean to Mark was because Mark was Native American.

Mark never finished those scales that day, and he never came back again. I don't blame him for that either.

A Summer Night

by Jennifer Overman

"You lost it for us!" He was yelling. My father was. His face flushed with anger. He directed his anger at my mom, throwing things across our homey living room. Sure he was mad, but none of us could have seen what was coming next.

We were at a softball game, my parents' softball game. It was supposed to be fun, a good time, not to be taken seriously. It was supposed to be a time to catch up, relax, enjoy the nice summer evening. What could go wrong?

In the seventh inning, the game was tied. My mom was up to bat. She walked to the plate in her gray and black pin-striped shorts and t-shirt, bat in hand. There was a runner on third, a base hit would win the game, but with two outs, she was under a lot of pressure. And pain. In the fifth inning, she tweaked her ankle.

First pitch. Ball one. Second pitch. Ball two. So far so good.

"Good eye, Cindy," the team chanted. "Good eye."

Third pitch. Strike one. Fourth pitch. Whack! Line drive right over the first baseman. She ran. She was almost there, but she fell. Her ankle gave out. Third out, extra innings. Mom's and Dad's team lost the game in the eighth inning by two runs.

"Pizza at Pietro's," yelled the team captain.

My parents loaded the four kids into the truck and headed out. That's when it started, the verbal abuse. In that five minute drive to Pietro's, I never heard so many cuss words in my life. Dad parked the car and helped my mom out, slamming the door behind her. We all jumped.

When we walked into Pietro's, we all put fake smiles on our faces, pretending to be that "perfect American family" everyone dreams about. My father walked in that pizza bar like he was a god, with his unhappy trophy wife and his four picture-perfect children. What a lucky guy.

After two hours of pizza, soda, video games, and lots of chatter, we headed home. My father helped my mom into the truck, with yet again another slammed door behind her. The abuse started up once more. We should have been receiving Academy Awards for being such fabulous little actors instead of his verbal abuse.

My chubby little brother, only two, was sitting on my mom's lap being rocked to sleep when my father pulled her out of the chair. We were stunned, but what could we do? Little Andrew went flying. My mom flung her arms, saving my baby brother from cracking his head open on the television. She tucked him in close to her stomach just before the first punch. His verbal abuse cooked itself to physical abuse.

"Stop it," my older brother yelled. "Stop it!"

He wouldn't. It continued for a couple of minutes, him tossing my poor mom around the room. When the nightmare ended, his handprints were bruised around her biceps.

Thirty seconds hadn't passed before she packed our clothes and we stood by the door. We were going to my grandparents' house. My father urged, begged, and pleaded for us to stay.

"Mom will be fine by herself," he argued.

But how could we trust, let alone stay with a man who not only hurt my mom, but who could have potentially been my brother's murderer? We wouldn't, we couldn't, and we didn't.

Member of the Club

by Davis P. Heard

The loud clanging bell of East End School let out a whoop, scream and holler of children. They were the entire spectrum of a chocolate rainbow: caramel, coffee water, butter pecan, vanilla chocolate, all the colors of brown that anyone could imagine, tumbling and running and falling and jumping to get to the swings, merry-go-round whatever, because wasting time at recess was unthinkable.

But another group of girls, 3rd graders all herded over to the concrete covered swimming pool. The pool had been covered over for as long as anyone could remember, probably from the days of when it was a white Catholic school. According to Stickleg, the neighborhood wino tramp, "Soon as dey [the school board] 'cided they was gon let colored chirren have dis here ol school after they bought it from dem nuns they come in and full it up with concrete."

I told Mrs. King what Stickleg said and she said, "Terry, don't listen to Mr. Augustus." (That was his real name; Mrs. King never called anybody by a nickname.) "I have told you children over and over again that these neighborhood legends, stories and fables are not grounded in truth." I decided that I would ask Miss Thomas on Sunday cause Mrs. King didn't grow up in Haines.

Anyway, my 3rd grade friends were all excited about my newest idea for our latest club. I had passed a note to my best friend Joanne Gibson during reading. "I got a idea for a new club." She turned her head just a little and whispered, "What?"

Mrs. King was bent over our latest spelling test. She never looked up but said in her stern southern voice, "I know two people in this room if they don't close their mouth and get to their work they will be feeling the end of my strap when that recess bell rings." So we shut up with a quickness. Details would have to wait.

"OK, what's the name of this club?" Delores Jefferson was always the one who tried to be the boss of our class. She was tall and skinny with really long legs. Everybody always got caught when she was the runner in duck, duck, goose. The other girls that showed up was Ruthie, Mattie, Precious, Joanne, Diana, and Estherine.

Ruthie Coles was sitting on the edge of the pool looking at her leg. I knew what she was getting ready to do. Ruthie's legs were the nastiest things you ever wanted to see. She stayed outside late in the evening in the summer playing with her brothers so they were the main course for the Mississippi river birds (mosquitoes). She would scratch those mosquito bites until they bled. Then they would get these hard, black scabs that had a dot of red in the middle. Then she would pick at them until they bled. They would almost heal and then she would start picking at them all over again. She was intently picking at one of her bites and talking a mile a minute.

"Yeah, is we gon let Miss Mitchell girls in our club this time? I thank we oughta jus let it be us. They don ever come up with nuthin on they own. They always copying offa us. Las time when we had a party they didn't bring nothing to eat but two bags of 10 cent tater chips and dem old hard two for a penny cookies from Mr. Chan's."

"Hush, Ruthie," I said, "we only got a few minutes and I wanna get started. The name of the club is the Long Hair Club." Everybody was silent for a split second and then we all started talking at the same time.

"Oooh, that's a good name!" Mattie said. "Well, that takes out a lot of people." We all bust out laughing and looked at Diana Turner at the same time. Diana had hair so short you could smell her brains.

"I got long hair," she said as she turned her nose up and rolled her big eyes.

"Yeah, on the days yo Mama pin that horse tail on the back of yo scalp," Mattie said. She had stood up to adjust her slip. It was always hanging. We were falling over each other laughing.

Diana stood up to face Mattie. When she got mad, nervous, or scared she would sweat like she was a leaking faucet, and she was gushing like Old Faithful right about now.

"Well, at least it don't look like no kukaburr patch like yours." Mattie lunged for Diana and Delores jumped up and stood between them.

"Y'all stop!! We gon waste all our time with y'all talking bout each other. Terry, what's the rules for our club since you got the idea?"

I didn't have any rules. I never thought Diana would want to be in our club. She was in Miss Stone's room and the only reason she came over was because she saw a group of us huddled together. She always was nosy like that.

Estherine Reynolds hadn't said much the whole time we were sitting and talking. She was a really nice girl but not many people played with her a lot cause she stuttered. Not all the time but just enough to make some people who are impatient not want to stand and take the time to wait for her to get out what she had to say. She had the softest hair I had ever saw or felt on anyone. It had this light wispy texture that gave way to fat thick braids that would bounce when you put a barrette on the end. Because of her stutter she wouldn't always play with everybody else. Lots of times she would just get in a swing, stand up and pump way up high all by herself until recess was over. A few times, in between all the club making up that I would do, I would swing with Estherine and tell her how I wished I could go as high as she would. She would smile her big toothy smile and shout, "All you gotta do is just pump your legs!!"

All eyes were on Estherine. They really didn't want her in the club because then it would mean that we would have to wait and be patient and listen to her when she had a stuttering fit, but I knew if I said it was OK they would say it was OK.

The funny thing about this whole situation was that I could not stand Diana Turner. None of us could, but because she was rich and her mother always gave really nice gifts to everybody at Christmas and bought the most food whenever we had class parties, we knew that we could count on having a feast even though she would brag about how much her mother paid for everything she bought. I liked Estherine, but just not enough to let her be in our club and have all my other friends mad at me. Besides she wasn't as popular as the rest of us. We were all known for something we did really well. Joanne was good at arithmetic. Delores, of course, was the runner. Precious had the best handwriting. Diana wore the prettiest clothes, Mattie could sing and always led devotion at the beginning of class in weekly assembly, and Ruthie's mama did laundry for Miss Stone in exchange for piano lessons. Her and Ruthie were always going to churches singing and playing at programs and the 5th Sunday singing unions.

Estherine said, her voice beginning to hesitate, "But I gggggot long hair."

Diana spoke up taking control of the situation. She wanted to be in this group and she decided to help me out by saying, "Estherine, you ain't as popular as the rest of us. Everybody at school know us but don't nobody know you." The others nodded in agreement with Diana.

"Bbbbbut Terry said it was the Llllllong Hair Club and I ggggot long hair."

Diana's brash, take-charge personality gave me the courage to speak up: "Estherine we gon be doing a awful lot of talking in this club, and you talk too slow. Maybe you can be in our next club." Everyone agreed with my coldly blunt statement.

Estherine made one last effort to get me to change my mind. "Well, you said this was the Lllllllong Hair Club. Diana ain't got no llllllong hair."

Her truthful statement seared my mind and pricked at the walls of my usually tender heart. But because I knew they really did not want Estherine in the club also, I ignored what I knew was right and instead said, "Well, we just decided that we only want six girls from Miz King's class."

Estherine had a bewildered look on her face. I could not look her in the eye because I knew that she knew that we just didn't want her in our club. I saw her look deep into my eyes and say to my soul, "Remember the fun on the swings, how I helped you, how I included you. Didn't I show you how to go higher? Wasn't I your friend that day?"

She walked away, but it wasn't a sad departure. It was a "what a bunch of silly girls I really don't care if you don't want me in your dumb old club" departure. She went to the swings and did what she was best at, swinging higher than anyone else on the playground and not being afraid to do it.

The rest of the girls immediately began to chatter and make plans about things we would do, like wear red socks on Friday, two ponytails on Wednesdays, that kind of stuff. Their voices seemed far away, a backdrop to the painful truth of Estherine's statement rattling around in my empty, immature childish mind.

The Long Hair Club lasted about three weeks, give or take a few fights with Diana, the Thanksgiving program, after-school practices, and us just plain forgetting to "meet."

Even after the Long Hair Club met its demise things were never quite the same between Estherine and me. I would race to the swings and try to get the one next to her. She was always nice and would still encourage me to "pump hard," but I could tell that she no longer thought of me as special, as the person who was known as the one that was always nice to everybody.

A hard rain came up the summer before we went to 4th grade. Kids would sometimes go swimming in the city ditches. That summer before 4th grade, Estherine drowned in a city ditch near her house.

I remember the last time I tried to get a swing beside Estherine, but another girl got there before me. I remember her looking at me and saying with her eyes. "Well, how does it feel when it happens to you?" I see her, wind blowing back those wispy thick ponytails, her legs pumping, pumping, and pumping. Her eyes looking, searching deep into my soul.

The author is a teacher in Portland Public Schools.

When I Was Young

by Josh Langworthy

When I was young, I thought that I was the hardest shit ever. Nothing could hurt me. If anyone messed with me or mine, I'd just beat their ass. It didn't matter who they were because I could mess up anyone; anyone except him. I was terrified of him. He was big and strong and always hurt my mom. He didn't care if she begged him to stop; he enjoyed it, hitting a woman. It made him feel strong and powerful. He liked scaring a woman and two young children. We were scared, and he knew it. He could hit her over and over, and after each beating, she would promise me that it would never happen again, that she was done seeing him.

Then a few days later he would pop up with flowers and tears. He would cry, and then they would be back together. Within a few weeks it would be back to hitting.

This cycle would continue for years and years. This so-called man could pull a good sob story; shit, sometimes he would even convince me. Then the hitting would start. He would never hit me, but sometimes I wished he would, just so my mom could get a break; but she never did. He would hit her and hit her; she would beg for him to stop, but he never would. I would beg him to stop, but he just told me to "shut the f___ up." I wanted to stop him; I wanted to make him beg. I wanted to hear his cries for help. I just couldn't do it; he was too big, too strong. But I couldn't do it; I couldn't stop him. If only my body would move, I could end the begging. Why wouldn't it move? I was scared stiff.

Each time I would get closer to moving, but I never could. Then one day I came home from school, and my mom had fresh bruises. He was back. I was furious!

"What's wrong with your eye?" I demanded of my mom, even though I already knew. She didn't answer with words; she just started crying. I was scared, but this time I could move. This was it; it was finally time to be a man. Even though I was only 11, I was ready.

I sprinted up the stairs to my brother's closet. I grabbed his bat and was back downstairs. There he was, standing there like nothing was wrong. "Get the f___ out!" I yelled as I confronted him with the bat. I was ready to swing; I wasn't going to wait for another story. This was it. It was finally his turn to beg. And he was going to beg, beg for his life. I swung the bat with all I had. It soared through the air, but it never reached his face; he had moved. I could tell by the look in his eyes that he was scared. "Stop, please stop!" But it wasn't his voice, it was my mom's. I pushed her voice out of my head. I didn't want her to beg. It was his cries that I wanted to hear.

I swung again, another miss. Why couldn't I hit him? He was just too fast, but he couldn't keep running forever. Sooner or later he'd have to stop and fight, and that's what I wanted: a fight. I went to swing again, but the bat wouldn't move. "Impossible," I thought. "He's in front of me. He can't have it." Then it hit me. It was my mom trying to help him. But why help him, the man who had caused us so much pain? Then her voice came back. "Stop, Josh, stop! You're going to hurt him. F___ing stop!" It was her voice all right, but she didn't sound sad; she was pissed. Pissed at me for trying to protect her, for trying to make the man that had hurt her feel pain. I was confused.

Then all of a sudden the bat was out of my hands. She was yelling something and pointing at the door, but I didn't care. I couldn't hear her anymore. I was off to the kitchen for a knife. The bat hadn't worked, but this time he was going to die. I grabbed a knife and headed back to the living room. But there she was, standing in the doorway yelling at me. Her voice came back into focus. "You want to stab someone? Stab me." I was confused; I was scared. Why did she want me to hurt her? My body was frozen again. "Out!" she yelled, pointing at the back door.

How could she choose him over me? F___ it, I didn't care anymore. It was time for me to leave.

Alan Wieder

Trolling for Stories: Lessons from Our Lives

In 1982, during an interview with Kay Bonetti about her work, Toni Cade Bambara said, "When I look back at my work with any little distance the two characteristics that jump out at me is one, the tremendous capacity for laughter, but also a tremendous capacity for rage." Both sentiments come across in stories from her collection *Gorilla, My Love.* Her narrators are typically sassy, young African American girls whose insights about what it means to be black and poor in U.S. society offer the reader laughter, but also seethe with a quiet rage that such inequality can exist in a country that promises justice. I originally taught Toni Cade Bambara's story "The Lesson" to help my junior and senior students at Jefferson uncover and write about lessons they've learned about race, class, gender, and sexual identity, but when I taught it to a group of freshmen in Jefferson's Young Men's Academy, I learned to shift and adjust the lesson as I listened to their sto-

This "lesson" is about what I taught, but also what I learned from these young men about what it means to grow up male in our society.

ries. So this "lesson" is about what I taught, but also what I learned from these young men about what it means to grow up male in our society.

In this story an educated neighbor, Miss Moore, gathers up the neighborhood children, including Sylvia, the sharp, wisecracking black girl who narrates the story, and takes them on field trips. Miss Moore had been to college and "said it was only right that she should take responsibility for the young ones' education...." In this story, Miss Moore takes Sylvia and the other children to an FAO Schwarz toy store on Fifth Avenue in New York City. Sylvia learns a lesson about money—who has it and who doesn't. The children resent Miss Moore for disturbing their summer vacation with her education plans. "And she was always planning these boring-ass things for us to do, us being my cousins, mostly, who lived on the block cause we all moved North the same time and to the same apartment then spread out gradual to breathe." The children arrive at the store and marvel that someone could pay $1,000 for a toy sailboat or $35 for a clown, which gets Sylvia thinking:

> Thirty-five dollars could buy new bunk beds for Junior and Gretchen's boy. Thirty-five dollars and the whole household could visit Grandaddy Nelson in the country. Thirty-five dollars would pay for the rent and the piano bill too. Who are these people that spend that much for performing clowns and $1,000 for toy sailboats? What kinda work they do and how they live and how come we ain't in on it? Where we are is who we are, Miss Moore always pointin out. But it don't necessarily have to be that way, she always adds then waits for somebody to say that poor people have to wake up and demand their share of the pie and don't none of us know what kind of pie she talkin about in the first damn place.

Miss Moore provides the kind of education that happens when students confront real-world issues. When the curriculum, instead of sanitizing the past and excluding the present, holds a mirror to students' lives so that the inequality and injustice students experience starts to breathe in the classroom, students wake up. Bayard Rustin, the architect of the 1963 March on Washington, looked for places of friction to expose the racism in our society to the public. This narrative assignment searches for those places in students' lives where pain and rage seethe, so that they can be discussed instead of suppressed or denied.

Reading "The Lesson" and Finding Stories

I taught this narrative assignment in Darryl Miles' class in Jefferson's Young Men's Academy, a group of freshman boys, mostly African American, with one Latino, one Asian, and two white boys mixed in. Before students read the story, I told them about a few lessons I've learned over the years. And while I was trying to get to big ideas—the places of friction—I started off weak. Plus, I was a white woman, a guest teacher who visits their class. In my initial list, I clumsily attempted to demonstrate that we constantly learn lessons that we file away without even realizing it, but every lesson we learn started with an experience that we could tell a story about. "I learned not to touch hot stoves, not to brake too hard going down steep hills on my bike, and I learned to stay away from my father when he was drinking. Take a few minutes to think about lessons you have learned over the years and make a quick list."

The students' initial list of lessons mimicked mine, sounding like aphorisms that they had pulled out for the guest teacher.

My list was thin and off-point, and their initial list of lessons mimicked mine, sounding like aphorisms that they had rehearsed and pulled out for the guest teacher. A few went deeper and made me want to hear the story behind the headline: Trust your gut instinct. Wear a helmet. Listen to elders. Think before you speak. Parents always win. Don't expect money, earn it. Some things you want, never just fall in your hands. Don't ride your bike fast down a brick road. Always say "excuse me" when you pass someone, especially my dad. Never lie to your parents when you might get caught.

Before we started reading the story out loud, I asked them to think about Bambara's title. "Why did the author call this 'The Lesson'? What lessons do the characters learn and who or what teaches them?" After we finished reading, I asked students to write about the lessons Sylvia learned in the story. Students struggled to come up with a response. Josh said, "Never go on a field trip with Ms. Moore," which was funny, but clearly not where I was trying to go. Another student said, "Sylvia learned not to judge a book by its cover." Another maxim. "What does that mean?" I asked. He shook his head. Hmmm. No one had his hand up. Kris broke the awkward silence, "She learned how to act in public." They were trying to please me, and this wasn't working.

"What does she learn about money?" Clearly, I was going to have to steer the conversation more. But this was turning out like one of those painful teaching moments where the teacher has the answers, and the students are reluctantly trying to save her by guessing wildly in an attempt to end the humiliation.

Josh said, "She learns that some people have enough money to buy fancy boats while other people don't have enough money to feed their kids."

"Does she think that's right?" I asked the class.

"No, but some people work harder than others, so some people have more money than others," Mitchell added. The boys went on in this fashion. If you work hard, you get ahead.

I knew these students didn't believe that all the inequality they'd seen and experienced could simply be explained away with a "some people work harder than others," but I'd come about this in the wrong direction.

"Let me ask you this. Public education is the right of every student in Oregon, isn't it? But when I go around to different schools in the suburbs, it doesn't look equal. One school I visit regularly has computers and couches in the library; there are computers lining the hallways. They are open and available for all students to use. Is that true here?"

"No. Jefferson never gets treated right." Once I hit on an area where students experienced prejudice, they started talking. "If we tell someone we go to Jefferson, their faces change, and they move away or say stuff to us." The conversation shifted away from inequality too quickly, and talking about popular perceptions of Jefferson was a non sequitur, but students were animated. I pursued this conversation because I thought it might lead back to lessons and stories about inequality.

"And why is that?" I asked.

"Because people think that we are gang members. And they believe all the rumors."

"People look at Jeff as a lower-class school. I feel like I have to prove that I'm smart," Josh said. This riled the boys up. Clearly, all of them shared this experience.

"What other lessons have you learned like that?"

"I learned that some kids treat me differently because I am biracial. My dad's black and my mom's white, and kids say things," Dylan said.

"I get followed around in stores. They always think boys steal," Mark added.

"Is there a place in the story about people not being treated fairly?"

D'Anthony said, "Yeah, where she talks about democracy. When Sugar says, '[T]his is not much of a democracy if you ask me. Equal chance to pursue happiness means an equal crack at the dough.' See, not everyone has the same choices." Right.

The idea of "class" was too far removed from the boys; they lived it, but they didn't see it. And, especially in the wake of Barack Obama's inauguration, these students had been hearing nonstop that, "Everyone can make it if you work hard and just believe." "Yes we can!" everyone heard over and over. They needed more than one story to grasp the concept of social class, but they did understand inequality based on school and race.

I tried to shift the assignment to race because I thought I might get more traction. "Let me tell a story about when I learned about race. My black neighbors in Eureka, California, had to get written permission from every neighbor in order to buy their house. It's called redlining, and it happened in Portland, too." Blank stares. The gates on the Laurelhurst community here, that barred families of color, must have seemed as distant as slavery. My story didn't elicit any response from students.

Adding Student Models: "Lessons from Outdoor School" and "Moment in Time"

I decided to get to the idea of digging up the stories behind the "lessons" we carry with us, instead of focusing on specific lessons about race and class—to come at the big idea of the lesson through their stories first. I read Khalilah Joseph's story, "Lessons from Outdoor School," (see p. 111) aloud to them because it provides an accessible model for students as they begin thinking about lessons they've learned. Every 6th-grade student in the Portland area spends a week at Outdoor School, an environmental education program located at a variety of residential campsites on the Sandy River near Mt. Hood. High school sophomores, juniors, and seniors return as "student leaders," and after a short but intense training, become soil, water, or animal experts for their 6th-grade campers. And they miss a week of school. (Unless they are super-campers like my daughter Gretchen who returned as a student leader twice a year during her sophomore, junior, and senior years.) The majority of student leaders are white. So when Khalilah and Romla, two African American students, entered the forest as student leaders, they felt like outsiders. Khalilah's skillful retelling of how that changed is a delightful, playful testimony to our ability to overcome difference.

Jim Whitney

Kirkland Allen ponders his revision.

I asked the young men what lesson Khalilah learned, and Mark came back with, "Don't judge a book by its cover." Hmmm. "What does that mean?"

"She thought all white people were the same, and she didn't want to be with them. When she had fun with them, she stopped judging them," Josh said.

"OK, has that happened to you? Have you ever been judged by someone or judged someone else? Think about that. Khalilah wrote this as her lesson story when she was a student at Jefferson. Start making a list of stories you could write."

Fortunately, the bell rang, and I remembered a story written by my student Kirk Allen about a time when he was walking down the same side of the street as a white woman. It was around midnight, and Kirk was returning home from a party that had been turned out by the police. The woman stepped onto Kirk's front porch, not knowing it was his house, and pulled out pepper spray and a knife. She told him to stop following her; she threatened to call the police; she accused him of blending into the dark. Kirk ends his story, "There are targets. No, scratch that. There are young, black male targets." I had a video clip of Kirk reading the story followed by his classmates sharing similar events. When I showed the clip the next day, students finally found their stories.

This experience of trolling for stories reminded me about the importance of prompts, but also about the importance of sticking with kids until they find their stories. Had I pushed for students to write too early in this process, they would not have found their passion, that place of rage and laughter that Bambara talked about in her interview. Each of the models showed students how a writer told the story of their "lesson." These young men just needed a story that unlocked theirs.

Josh said, "I know what he's talking about. There was a fight brewing at school between these two kids. Everyone decided to take it off the school grounds to a park, but as soon as the fight started, some man driving by called the police. As soon as the police came, everyone took off running. I wasn't involved in the fight, so my friend and I just walked over to the bus stop and waited for the bus. There was a crowd of white students there too. The police pushed my friend and me up against the wall and searched us. We were the targets because we were black." In my years at Jefferson, how many times had I heard stories like this from black students? Post-racial America? Not yet.

Had I pushed for students to write too early in this process, they would not have found their passion, that place of rage and laughter that Bambara talked about in her interview.

This led to a flurry of stories along similar lines. Ultimately, they did write about lessons, which fell into two categories: Think-before-you-speak-or-act stories and what Dylan labeled as "This society is jacked" stories. I was impressed by the young men's honesty and their willingness to be vulnerable. I attribute this to the narratives we read and our conversations, but also to Darryl Miles, their teacher, who models these attributes when he shares his own stories with them. Their writing raised issues that demanded attention beyond revising for narrative elements—although students did write and revise their stories.

After students discovered a vein of stories to mine, I distributed the Narrative Criteria sheet (p. 113) and colored highlighters. Students highlighted Khalilah's dialogue, blocking, and character and setting description, so they got the gist of what to include in their stories. Then we moved into a guided visualization, which provided a passageway to quiet writing time.

Writing and Revising and Learning Together

When we started the read-around, I asked students to listen for the lesson each writer learned. Josh wrote about a time he did something "stupid" to fit in. "[My former school] was a hard school to fit into. I was in between two groups and trying to be somebody I wasn't. At the time I would do just about anything to get into a certain group." He went on to relate a story about bringing knives to school, getting arrested, and paying the price. "After it was all over, I owed my parents $1,000 for court fees. That was the worst mistake of my life. I made my mom cry, and if you've done that, then you know how bad the feeling is."

After his classmates talked about what they liked about Josh's story, they identified his lesson as learning the cost of betraying himself in order to fit in. When I asked them if any of them had ever done something they regretted in order to belong, most of them raised their hands. Jay's story provided a similar content. A friend asked him to steal a sweater for him from Macy's, and Jay did. When a security guard tackled Jay, wrestled him to the ground, and handcuffed him, Jay's friend walked past as if he didn't know him. Like Josh, Jay acknowledged that he was trying to be someone he wasn't, and he paid the price for that mistake, but he learned a valuable lesson about stealing, and also about trusting his own instincts instead of trying to belong.

Kirk's story sparked Dylan and Tony's, especially the last line about "young, black male targets." They told stories of learning that the rules are different for whites and blacks. Dylan told of a jubilant night after winning a basketball game, staying up late with friends, playing "crackhead race," where they spin around about 25 times and then try to race down the street. The opening to his story included humorous details and youthful exhilaration, and the ending was all rage—Bambara's twin emotions:

When we are getting to the end of the block, the cops pulled up and I'm thinking to myself, this is gonna be trouble. When a cop, a white cop at that, sees two black teenagers wobbling down the street, that's a bad start from the get go. The cops stepped out of the car, walked up to us, and asked if we knew what time it was.

I said, "Yes, it's 11:45." I was reaching into my pocket to get my I.D. Without hesitation, the cop pulls out his gun and puts it to my head. At this point, I don't know what to do. I'm just frozen. I'm speechless.

My friends are yelling at the cop, saying, "What are you doing?" The cop cusses at them. Tears of anger come out of my eyes and burn my face....

After the cop leaves, I stomp down the street armed with my anger, and as I turn the corner, I bumped into one of John's neighbors. When I look at him, I picture the cop, and I go off. I punched him two times until he drops. Johnny came and got me off him. I didn't sleep that night.

And the lesson? Unequal treatment for blacks? Black males as targets? Or as Dylan wrote, "This society is jacked"? As Dylan read his story, I thought about what it meant to be 15 and to have someone with the authority of a police officer put a gun against your head, and a society that allows this story to be repeated again and again. I thought about the coldness, the roundness of that metal against this boy's beautiful temple. I thought about Dylan's justified anger, misdirected against a neighbor. I thought about the suspension and expulsion rates of students of color, and Daniel Beaty's poem about the "lost brilliance of the black men who crowd these [prison] cells" (see p. 37). And I knew that one lesson I take away is my moral obligation to tap into this injustice, this birthplace of anger and rage, to expose it and validate students' experiences. But if I unleash this kind of rage and pain, I also have a moral obligation to teach students how to navigate a society that discriminates against them and to teach them how people have worked to change these injustices. ■

Moment in Time

by Amianne Wight

It was one of those mornings where us kids woke up at the break of dawn. The thought of opening presents tied acidic knots in our bellies. Mom, always one step ahead, was in the kitchen preparing the traditional breakfast: cinnamon rolls, scrambled eggs, ham, and cranberry juice to wash it down. Bruce and I shut off all of the lights and plugged in the Christmas tree, watching each blink lead in the dance with the ornaments. I was so off in my own world I barely heard the knock at the front door.

By this time my father was up. Curious to see who would visit at such a peculiar moment, he answered the door. Three men stood on the porch with boxes of wrapped gifts, clothing, and food. Dad invited them to come in. They dropped over 10 boxes on the kitchen table and floor. One of the burly guys said, "There's still more out in the van."

"Amianne, go help unload the rest of the stuff." My dad was the prizewinner for volunteering my services. His commanding way was rather annoying. At this point I was confused. Our family had plenty of food, clothing, and presents. Why would our church friends go out of their way to bring us things we already had?

While I was in the van, grabbing a box filled with oranges, I overheard the two men talking, "I'm sure glad we could help that family."

"Yeah, it must be hard being handicapped and raising two kids."

I have never felt as much of a charity case as I did at that moment. It was then that I realized all of this was pity from a church that assumed we couldn't handle Christmas by ourselves. I got offended because for the first time I saw my parents as handicapped. I never before had a problem with accepting my parents' disabilities until that moment. This incident opened the door to a rude awakening.

I was on my way to becoming a big 6th grader. The goals for these years are to find true identity, have cool friends, and gain acceptance from everyone. I started to feel embarrassed of my parents because they walked and talked differently. I became more and more self-conscious. When Mom answered the phone with a shaky hello, my friends would ask me later if that was my grandmother or apologized for waking my mother up. Every time I went through the ritual of telling them what it means to have cerebral palsy. I was tired of the explanations.

Ignorant kids in our stinging fights would say, "At least my mama don't break dance when she walks." Or the good ole, "At least my daddy ain't no Jerry's kid." Little comments like these kept filling the gunpowder into my rocket bottle which I was soon to light.

I never invited my parents to parent-teacher conference night. I was afraid of the laughter, comments, stares, and questions. I feared humiliation the most, and this was the first sign of my domestication into adolescence. I only thought of Amianne and never my parents. Their thoughts of being rejected and hurt came to me when I was about 13. I realized the love and understanding they gave me enough to put my own fears of rejection aside. I didn't care anymore about what others thought.

When someone eases their way into a conversation about my parents with a, "So, your parents are handicapped..." I butt in with, "No, they're handi*capable*."

Lessons from Outdoor School

by Khalilah Joseph

The minute I sat down on the bus with the Sandy River sign, I knew it was going to be a long weekend, and I was stuck, stuck like Chuck. Don't get me wrong. I was on my way to be trained as an Outdoor School counselor, something I'd wanted to be since I'd gone to Outdoor School in the 6th grade. But being surrounded by a mass of strange white faces was giving me second thoughts.

Rolling her eyes, Romla, my friend from school and the only other African American on the bus, frumped down into the seat behind mine. "Uh uh, Khalilah."

"Man, I already know. Why couldn't we go to the camp with people like us?"

Romla and I scanned the bus. A sea of white faces clouded our eyes. Everybody seemed to be white and way too damn happy. They were all natural with their blond and brown untamed heads. There was no escape. They were everywhere. Shouts of "awesome" and "radical" polluted the air. Putting on her shades, Romla pulled her hood down low and maneuvered her body into a semi-comfortable position on the hard, ugly green seat. Irritated, I just hummed the chorus to "Thug Passion," hoping Tupac would keep me sane.

The bus rumbled and bounced on. I peered out the window, feeling relaxed by the grazing cows and peaceful farm scenes, but still unsure of what would happen once I reached my destination. After about 45 minutes, we reached the Sandy River camp site. I felt uneasy as the bus twisted down the winding road into camp. A sign reading Sandy River greeted us. We were in the middle of nowhere! A big log cabin sat in the middle of a huge field, looking more like a dried-out football field than a park. Smaller cabins were littered throughout and trees surrounded the whole mess.

Romla peered from under her dark shades, wrinkling her face into a frown. The sight was none too inviting.

"I wanna go home now."

"I feel you. We could walk."

Instead of hitting the road, we dumped our bags into the already forming mound and trudged across the field to the main cabin for dinner. We found an empty table in the back corner and sat there with our plates heaped high with dry, unseasoned chicken, limp lettuce salad, lumpy mashed potatoes, and watery gravy.

It could have just been me feeling self-conscious, but I can swear that every time I said something, someone was looking in my mouth. "I must look better than I think," I told Romla, "because a lot of people sure are staring."

"No, that's not it at all. People just have staring problems."

We snapped our heads to the side as a girl with a blondish-colored head plopped down next to us. We were not feeling too friendly, and Romla had started rolling her eyes before we realized it was Djamila, another student from Jefferson High School.

"Djamila, what are you doing here?"

With her blue eyes looking tired, she glanced around the room. Her expression suggested she was feeling the same way we were. "I had to come, the other camp was too full. I'm glad you two are here. These people are so snotty."

After dinner we learned a song about a yellow duck. If we were in better spirits, we might have loved it, but since our spirits were low, we just mumbled miserably, "Quack, quack, quack, quack, quack, quack."

Now it was time to break off in groups. Groups were supposed to inform us of our counselor duties and get us better acquainted with the other kids. Djamila, Romla, and I were all put into different groups. If I wasn't so old, I swear I might have cried when we parted.

Everyone in my group acted as if they'd rather be somewhere else, so our group leader suggested we make posters of what a troublemaker might look like. Every poster except the one my group made ended up looking like the kids who live in my neighborhood. I asked sarcastically, "Oh, I guess all bad kids are named Jerome or Kesha. Are there no bad kids in Beverly Hills?"

Nobody answered me. They just laughed uncomfortably, but I wasn't playing. I was ready to get the hell out of Pine Valley.

Group was over, so it was time to meet back at the main cabin. Everyone filed out into the cool, dark night. We were all clumsy in the dark, since the trail was new to us. A tall redheaded basketball player from St. Mary's tripped on a tree stump which sent her tumbling into me, and in turn, I spiraled into a mousy brown-haired girl who looked as if she'd just stepped out of a Gap advertisement.

I still had an attitude, but damn, that was funny. We looked liked something out of a Three Stooges movie. We all looked at each other unsure of what to do. In an instant, we were laughing hysterically as we helped each other up from the dirt mound we'd landed in. Nursing our bruises, we managed to make it back the main cabin.

"Let's sit together," Cassie, the Gap girl, suggested, and we agreed. I searched the room, looking for Romla and Djamila. They sat at the same table we had earlier, but this time with new friends who an hour earlier had been complete strangers.

With my new friends in tow, I headed for the table. Rubbing the knot that was beginning to form on my forehead, I laughed at how something so painful had turned my whole weekend around. When it was time to be dismissed, my table sang at the top of our lungs, "Quack, quack, quack, quack, quack, waddle, waddle, waddle, waddle, waddle."

Narrative Criteria

Mark each of these literary elements on your draft. If you have highlighters or colored pencils, color each of the elements with a different color. If not, put the number of the element in the margin of your paper. For example, every time you use dialogue put #1 in the margin next to it. (The elements marked * are not essential, but give your writing more depth.)

____ **1. Dialogue:** Use your characters' words, pacing, and language.
- Let the reader "hear" your characters speak.
- Make your characters sound different. People have fingerprints and "voice-prints." Grandmothers and 7-year-olds use different words, longer or shorter sentences. Make sure your characters sound real.

____ **2. Blocking:** Provide stage directions for your characters.
- Use it with dialogue to help the reader see your characters in action.
- Show what the characters are doing while they are talking: Leaning against a wall? Tossing a ball in the air? Looking out the window? Jingling change in their coat pocket?

____ **3. Character Description:** Make your characters come to life.
- Use physical details: Clothing, age, smells, hair color and style.
- Show the character in action: Is the character bossy? Shy? Rowdy?

____ **4. Setting Description:** Give sensory details—sights, smells, sounds.
- Where does the story take place?
- Walk the reader through the place where the story happened.
- Use names of streets, parks, buildings. Be specific.

___***5. Figurative Language:** Use imaginative language to sharpen descriptions.
- Use metaphors and similes when describing characters or setting.
- Try personification—give human qualities to nonhumans.

___***6. Interior Monologue:** Let us hear your character's thoughts.
- What is going on inside the character's head?
- What is the character thinking while the action is happening?

___***7. Flashback:** Provide the character's "back story" through a scene from the past.
- Give the reader background information by having characters remember or tell stories from their past.

Narrative Openings

Read the following openings by student writers. Think about the best opening for your story. Sometimes the hardest sentence to write is the first one. Use these writers to jumpstart your writing.

SNAPSHOT

This opening creates a picture, a "snapshot," for the reader. Usually the snapshot is a silent photo—one that describes the setting. This one comes from "Porch Story" by student writer Dana Young:

Like a dying animal with no hope, the lazy sun finally gave in. Shooting out its last rays of light, it cast a shower of pinks and purples across the canvas sky. The air wasn't hot, but rather moist and sticky. I sat there in this mild steam bath stretched out like a cat on my lawn chair. It was a quiet evening in Cranbury, New Jersey, but then it always was. That was the only good thing about staying in a retirement community. There was all the quiet you would ever need. So if you can get past the smell of death and the people who never stopped complaining, Cranbury is definitely your place.

This opening comes from "Super Soaker War" by student writer Bobby Bowden. Notice how the description of the weather sets the scene. Also, Bobby names the street, which anchors the "place" as well:

It was a hot day on Mississippi Street. The sun was blaring down like a heat lamp, and the sky offered no protection with clouds or smog. My older brother and Roxie our dog were on the porch. The dog's tongue was hanging out of his mouth like a pink slug.

CHARACTER

This opening puts the character in focus. This piece, "Grandma's Kitchen," comes from student writer Alisha Moreland. Notice how the description of Grandma's kitchen as well as her actions and words helps us know more about her character:

We gathered together in Grandma's kitchen. We gathered in the name of food. In Grandma's domain, she was the director and we were the employees. Grandma would lift her chubby hands, one on her hip, the other in the air—"I want you to get da eggs fo' the co'nbread. Alisha, I want you to make the macaroni." We all moved and were guided by THE HAND, Grandma's hand. There was a melody in her kitchen; it kept us moving. Her kitchen contained a rhythm that made our souls dance.

"Them black-eyed peas soaked and ready to go, Grandma."

Grandma turned and gracefully swayed her finger. "Put 'em in that there pot with the ham hocks." The kitchen soon filled with the delicious scents of soul food.

In this opening paragraph from "The Pains of Third Grade," student writer Chetan Patel writes in first person, so we learn about his character through his narration of the events. We can tell he is a little cocky:

We were about to correct our test. I was full of confidence. I had never missed more than one problem on a math test. Math was my subject. Back then, my schoolmates considered me a god in mathematics. While they were learning 2 times 3, I was figuring out 12 times 11. When they were doing 8 divided by 2, I was discovering the troubles of long division. Yep. I knew it all back then. And this simple test on the multiples of 3 was like child's work. I laughed at it, ha, ha!

SHOCKING OPENING

This opening puts us in the story and makes us want to know more about what's happening. It comes from "Death's Corner" by student writer DeShawn Holden.

It was a misty, dark night at half past eleven. The moonlight pierced the darkness with its rays. The shadowy moon hid itself behind the trees on the corner of Fifteenth and Prescott, the corner where drugs and violence reigned, the corner where death sat on its throne.

The night was cold and peculiar. The corner was desolate. Stores were closed and people were locked in their homes. Fear sat by their sides. They didn't dare walk on this lifeless ground. The corner was known for its many deaths, killings, and drug busts. There was an invisible warning sign that read: Do Not Enter.

DIALOGUE/SCENE

In this opening, student writer Pam Clegg jumps right into the scene, landing the reader in the middle of a movie. This excerpt is from her narrative, "My Nerves Wasn't All She Got On."

"Pamela!"
What she want now? Dog, every time I start watching TV she always wants to call.
"Pamela, git up here now!" Mama yelled down the steps.
I knew it. She always gots to go upstairs in our room.
"Ma'am?" I said when I entered the room.
"Didn't I tell you to clean this closet and this room? It look like a pig sty. How can you live in this mess?"
"Mama, this ain't my stuff. It's Tracy's. I cleaned my part of the room."
"Girl, how you gon' tell me this is Tracy's stuff when I'm looking at the clothes I bought you scattered around this room and thrown in this closet?"
"Mama, that's not..."

Tightening Writing

Take out one of the pieces that you like, but you think might need some work.

1. Read the piece silently, then read it out loud. Are there spots where you stumble when you read? These areas might need revision.

2. Do you have too many abstract words like love, honor, glory, or friendship? Often abstract nouns like these are ghost words—people can't see them. Give the ghost some clothes. If you love playing basketball, let us hear the ball, see the hoop, feel the snap of a pass.

3. Remember, lists work in any piece: fiction, essay, or poetry. Use them to quicken the pace by listing one-syllable words, quick words: run, jump, shoot. If you want to slow the writing down, extend the verbs into phrases, like Quincy Troupe does:

> you double-pump *through human trees*
> hang *in place*
> slip *the ball into your left hand*
> then deal it *like a las vegas card dealer off squared glass*

Notice Scott Russell Sanders' list in his essay "The Men We Carry in Our Minds":

> When I was a boy, the men I knew labored with their bodies. They were marginal farmers, just scraping by, or welders, steelworkers, carpenters; they swept floors, dug ditches, mined coal, or drove trucks, their forearms ropy with muscle; they trained horses, stoked furnaces, built tires, stood on assembly lines wrestling parts onto cars and refrigerators.

If you are telling reasons why you love skiing, go for it, like Kyle Fish does in this list:

> I love the turns, the jumps, the rails, and the black diamond runs.

Add as many items to your list as you can think of. You can weed later. Get them all down now.

4. Get active! Highlight every *is, was,* and *were* you find in your piece, then go back and determine if you can rearrange the line or sentence.

Here's an example from a student essay:

Original: Logan's decision to buy two mules was a shock to Janie.
Revision: Logan's decision to buy two mules shocked Janie.

Make the verb the workhorse of your sentence. Find strong verbs. Notice Judith Ortiz Cofer's verbs: "I do remember the way the water pipes banged and rattled, startling all of us out of sleep until we got so used to the sound that we automatically shut it out or raised our voices above the racket. The hiss from the valve punctuated my sleep like a ... dragon sleeping at the entrance of my childhood."

5. Watch out for too many adjective noun combinations. Remember, W.H. Auden said, "Adjectives are the potbelly of poetry." See how tired the expressions below sound. "Gray head" and "tired hands" sound like the words have been together for too long.

The wrinkled old woman
held her gray head
in her tired hands.

Use nontraditional combinations to startle the reader to attention. Surprise your readers. Try using metaphors or similes (make a comparison). If you have seen or heard a combination before, twist it for effect. Poet Elizabeth Woody wrote:

Our blind fingers
touch with the feet of birds...

Her crêped fingers,
teethmarked with red speckles,
held mine tight
as she showed our finger moons to me.

6. Get rid of the excess. Good writing is lean. Cut out fat—those little words that don't say anything.

a. For example, in essays there is no need for the phrases, "I think," "I believe," or "In my opinion."

b. Cut unnecessary words like *really, always,* and *very.*

c. Get rid of adverbs, like *slowly, quickly.* Make your verbs do the work.

7. Don't try to impress your reader with your large vocabulary. *Use everyday language.* Don't use big words if ordinary words will do. Look back at Ernest Hemingway, Toni Morrison, and Alice Walker.

8. Allow for surprises. This means tricking your editor into leaving the room. In first drafts, write fast and hard. Don't stop to think; go ahead and make mistakes, take risks. If you pre-plan everything, you probably won't have any "ahas" along the way.

9. Explode a detail: Take one image and keep moving in on it, adding more and more detail. Think of your pen as a camera that zooms in, gathering details. Jefferson student Mira Shimabukuro wrote, "I learned how to start with a detail and get smaller":

> *One thin-necked vase*
> *Pinwheel full…*
> *A photo, half hidden moon*
> *Rising in the half pane…*

10. See if you can mix up your sentence lengths. Add a list. A question. Toss two together with an "and" or a "but." Notice how sports writer Dave Zirin mixes up his sentences—using lists, questions, long and short sentences:

> I went to college in the Twin Cities, a refugee from the scowling confines of New Yawk. Minnesota was like another planet, a place I almost bolted after the first day when I was carded for trying to buy a lighter. But the people easily won me over. How could you not love a place that gave us Prince, Hulk Hogan, and cheese curds? The combination of fried dairy products, pro wrestling, and funk was just too much to resist. It's the kind of place where my buddy John would choose to relocate and raise a family despite having roots in La Jolla, California.

TEACHING FOR JOY AND JUSTICE
3: Writing Essays

Leni Feaomeoata
works on his essay.

Linda Christensen

Writing Wild Essays
from Hard Ground

"My Ebonics essay is fire," Grant High School student Ryan Halverson
told the Lewis & Clark College education students. "You really should read
it. I've never worked so hard on an essay." Jerrell, Ryan's classmate, contends
that his essay is also "fire," slang for not just great, but outrageously great.
Athena, Dennise, Denzell, James, Katie, and a number of other students from
the junior level African American Literature class I co-taught at Grant High
School want me to find a place to publish their pieces. A few days after students taught lessons about Ebonics at Lewis & Clark, Ryan told me, "This is
the first time I've stayed up all night to write
and revise an essay. It is my masterpiece.
I want to get it on a flash drive, so I can
save it."

**My most successful teaching stems from long-term
explorations of topics that ask big questions.**

When I asked students at the end of the Politics of Language unit what I
should keep and what I should ditch next time I teach it, Jerrell wrote, "Keep
the essay. Make students rewrite it until they get it right." He told me he has
never rewritten an essay so many times. All of the students rewrote their essay
at least twice; some rewrote it three or four times.

First, let me be clear, not every essay-writing assignment delivers such
devotion to writing; in fact, many flounder and leave students wailing that
they don't know what to write about or how to get started. When that happens
I know my teaching failed. But over the years, I've learned to create the conditions to help students to write "fire" essays more often.

So, how do we get students to care enough about their writing so that they stay up all night? How do we make them so proud of their work that they don't pitch their papers in the garbage can instead of treasuring them as masterpieces? I believe we must steep students in engaging work that connects to their lives; rehearse the essay throughout the unit by thinking, discussing, and arguing about big ideas; teach how essays work by examining models by student and professional writers; and *teach* them *how* to write by guiding them through the essay-writing process.

First Things First:
Embedding the Essay in Curriculum That Matters

Students write better essays when I spend big chunks of time on curriculum units so they can become knowledgeable about the subject matter. During these units I probe for their passion, exploring the link between the social context, the text, and the students' lives. I know my teaching is "fire" when students come back and talk about conversations with their parents, grandparents, or friends about the issues we're reading and writing about in class. My most successful teaching stems from long-term explorations of topics that ask big questions: The Politics of Language, the Struggle for Education, Native American Literature and History, Immigration: Past and Present, Men and Women in Literature and Society. I embed the teaching of essay writing as part of the course of study. Simply stated: To write great essays, students need to have something to write about.

Collecting Evidence Along the Way

Writing an essay starts on the first day of any curriculum project. Let me explain: From the moment I pass out the roles for the linguistic tea party or the novel, students begin gathering potential evidence and rehearsing the arguments for the essay they ultimately write a month or two later. Also, each of the curriculum units I've developed is an extended exploration—posing a question and developing evidence through multiple views of the topic. In my early years of teaching, I assigned essays *after* we read the novels or worked through a unit, but I didn't prepare students for a culminating essay by teaching them how to collect information along the way. So on essay writing day, they had to return to the novel or unit and start from scratch. Of course, we still return to the text, but we gather ideas and topics that interest as we move through the unit.

To get students to collect evidence during our curricular journey, I use a variety of techniques—and during a long unit, I typically use most of them:

- *Dialogue journals* (see p. 202) where students collect quotes, argue with the text(s), and make notes for themselves about their reading.

- *Character silhouettes* (see p. 177) where groups of students create life-size silhouettes of characters in a book or history and write relevant quotes and notes about their character's traits on the inside of the body and pertinent quotes and notes about society's impact on their character on the outside of the body.

- *Retrieval charts* (see p. 228) which generally help students gather information that may demonstrate patterns over a number of shorter pieces, movies, readings about a topic—for example, looking at cartoons for the stereotypes, by noting the race, class, and gender of the heroes, servants, and evildoers.

- *Short response papers* throughout the study which might include poems, interior monologues, or summaries or conversations with authors from a variety of readings. Students later use these materials as resources for the essays, places to mine for their earlier aha's or analysis, or just reminders of where to locate specific quotes they want to use in their essays.

I teach students specific methods of "retrieving" and "collecting" information from reading, media, and discussions, and I engage them in discussing the topic.

Through these various techniques, I teach students specific methods of "retrieving" and "collecting" information from reading, media, and discussions, and I engage them in discussing the topic. In any writing assignment, I attempt to teach for that assignment, but I'm also mindful of creating long-term templates for students, so that the work they do on one essay or narrative or poem builds knowledge for the next one. They accumulate strategies about how to take notes and create their own retrieval charts. I am transparent about this as well. I tell them, "These are all models that people use to collect evidence as they read. There's no magic in any one of them. The only magic is figuring out which method works for you."

Because many of my students have been organizationally challenged, I keep a work folder in the classroom or students keep a section of their binder where they store these pieces. At the end of the unit, students have dialogue journals, retrieval charts from a variety of readings, color-marked readings with marginal notes, poetry, and summaries in their folders that they can forage through as they build their essays.

Examining and Highlighting Model Essays

While I don't believe in formulaic essays, I do believe that essays have a framework that students need to be familiar with: introduction, thesis, body of evidence, and conclusion. Essay writers also employ tools that help the reader navigate the text, and students need to know how to use those tools as well: transitions, integrating quotes, and citing sources. In other words, essays have a set of conventions that most writers follow. Students need to be explicitly taught those conventions, so they can enter the academic world and feel comfortable there. I don't expect that students, whatever age they might be, know those conventions when they enter my class. So I never just assign essays, I *teach* students how to write a variety of essays, so they gain experience using these writing tools and can navigate new terrain with confidence.

Essay writers also employ tools that help the reader navigate the text, and students need to know how to use those tools as well.

Beyond that, I want students to understand that when they write essays, they should engage in the same kind of language play they use when they write poetry and narratives. While essays tend to be a more suit-and-tie style writing than what is typically referred to as "creative writing," they don't have to be stuffy.

Before we write more formal essays, I like to introduce students to "Essays with an Attitude" (See *Reading, Writing and Rising Up*), which use their own lives as evidence. We read brilliant essays by writers like Patricia Smith, Jimmy Santiago Baca, Tom Robbins, Barbara Ehrenreich, Leonard Pitts Jr., Dave Zirin, and Howard Zinn. These writers demonstrate how to dance with language while they tackle tough issues. They certainly don't write five-paragraph essays. They write essays using historical events, current news, as well as examples from their owns lives, which is what I want my students to learn to do.

Students need to have models that demonstrate what the essay looks like. Honestly, I, too, still need models

Linda Christensen

when I write—especially if I'm writing for a new magazine or writing in a format that I don't encounter as often, like a grant proposal. In order to teach students how to write, I get them to take model essays apart, tinker with them, and learn how the parts work together.

When I was in Mexico, I learned that the Zapatistas save heirloom seeds to make sure that their children will have ancestral corn seeds that haven't been infected by genetically modified seeds. They have "safe houses" where they store their seeds. Over the years, like the Zapatistas, I have saved files and files of my former students' papers, so that I can share them with my current students, passing the wisdom of one year's students to the next year's crop.

Before students begin writing their essays, I drag out my files and select an essay or two for them to examine, so they know what I want their papers to look like. These essays don't have to be error- or problem-free, but they need to demonstrate how a literary analysis works or show how an essay can weave together multiple sources of information. I try to find essays that do more than tread old water. If I can't find an appropriate model, I write one. Sometimes I might just use a paragraph or two from these heirloom essays—a sassy introduction, a great use of transitions and analysis, or a conclusion that demonstrates a different way to wrap up the paper.

Marking up and highlighting these essays takes a full period in class. First, I distribute multiple colors of highlighters (or colored pencils or crayons). The students and I read samples of the kind of essay they will write (literary analysis, song or poetry reviews, "essays with attitude," proposals, synthesis essays which bring together multiple resources), and we notice how the writer put the essay together. We read through the entire essay first and talk about the writer's thesis and what kind of evidence the writer used for support. Then we go back and examine the essay paragraph by paragraph and talk about the function of each, starting with the introduction. We highlight each type of paragraph with different colored markers: Introduction, evidence paragraphs, and conclusion. We look for the thesis statement. For example, we read Anna Hereford's introduction to her *Beloved* essay and talk about her opening, her thesis, and her promise to the reader:

> Toni Morrison says, "The best art is political and you ought to be able to make it unquestionably political and irrevocably beautiful at the same time." In her novel, *Beloved*, Morrison demonstrates her ability to produce the "best art." She creates horrifying images of slavery so vividly they stay with the reader forever. Her imagery is terribly beautiful, searingly beautiful, painfully beautiful.

We note that her thesis is that Toni Morrison creates horrifying images of slavery. "What is Anna going to have to prove in her essay? What are the key words in Anna's thesis?" Students mostly agree that the key words are images or imagery and slavery. We underline that promise: horrifying images of slavery.

I ask students to notice the transitions in Anna's essay and highlight those in another color. I say, "Note how the key word 'image/imagery' appears in her transitions and helps her pull the essay forward." We read the first transition, "One of the images Morrison embeds in the reader's mind is the tree on Sethe's back." At this point I often draw a picture of a train on the blackboard. I mark the introduction/thesis as the engine, the connectors between the cars as the transitions, the cars as the evidence paragraphs, and the caboose as the conclusion. I point out that the links/transitions connect the essay and refer back to the thesis.

If the essay has embedded or block quotes, we notice how the writer slipped the quotes in. "Circle or highlight the punctuation. See how that block quote is preceded by a colon? Mark that. What else do you notice about how Anna punctuated or used quotes?" I tell students, "Write marginal notes or arrows to remind yourselves how the quote is indented, how it is introduced, how it is analyzed. You can't just drop a quote in to plump up the essay." We highlight and mark up the essay, so that students can

refer back to it as a guide when they get stuck on their essay writing.

From this close reading of model essays, students generate a list of what their essay should include. This list becomes the essay criteria sheet. (See p. 145.) Most of the criteria remain the same from essay to essay—introduction, body of evidence, transitions, conclusions. However, the *kind* of evidence depends on the type of essay. In a literary analysis, students need to include evidence from the texts, so they need to use block and embedded quotes and analysis of the quotes. Other types of essays may need historical details, anecdotes from their lives, or facts and statistics.

Finding Essay Topics

I don't assign specific essay topics. I want students to find their own passion. When I control the topic, I take a huge chunk of learning away from students. One of the most difficult tasks in writing is winnowing down our ideas to find the heart of what we want to say about a topic. When students write for the teacher instead of writing out of a compelling need to speak out, the writing is often tedious, not worth writing, and not worth reading.

When students write for the teacher instead of writing out of a compelling need to speak out, the writing is often tedious, not worth writing, and not worth reading.

On the day we actually start working on the essay, students and I brainstorm topics for most of a 55-minute period; often, this is recollection because throughout the unit when they argue or question or emotionally connect to a reading or an issue, I say, "Put that in your notes. That would make a great essay topic." Sometimes we collect these ideas on a large piece of paper or a corner of the blackboard as we move through the unit.

For example, at the end of the Politics of Language unit, I said, "As we've been studying language and power, what moved you? What was important about this unit? What interested you? What do you want to tell other people about?" And the list begins—or continues: Jayme, James, and Katie were interested in assimilation; Job, Dee, and Molly wanted to write about Native American boarding schools; Annie was intrigued by the Soweto uprising; Dennise wanted to write about student resistance; and the majority of students chose to explore Ebonics. When students brainstormed essay topics for *Their Eyes Were Watching God,* they listed the role of gossip in the novel and our lives, an exploration of color—from Mrs. Turner to Grant High School, an interrogation into the physical abuse between Tea Cake and Janie, and a talkback to Richard Wright's critique of the novel. They also come up with topics that won't go too far, but we list them anyway because when we begin listing evidence, they will see the idea wither.

Brainstorming Evidence

Once the topic list is on the board (and on their papers), we discuss each topic, I say, "Where could you find evidence for this? Let's list it." Students refer back to the articles, memoirs, movies, and metaphorical drawings we studied and create a reference log of potential evidence on the board under each topic. For example, under assimilation, students listed Joe Suina's piece about boarding schools, Molly Craig's experiences in *Rabbit Proof Fence,* and Kenyan activist Wangari Maathai's memoir. This procedure allows us to share our collective memory of what we've studied, but the class talk also provides an opportunity to place our readings into categories, to sort through the material and figure out what we know and what we need to find out.

Thinking about audience means that there is a real reason and purpose for this piece of writing, beyond a classroom grade.

This is the place where I push students to create links to their own lives. I tell them, "Look, you can use incidents from your own life as evidence as well. If you have had experiences with language that this unit tapped into, put those in the paper." In the language essay, Dennise discussed how speaking Farsi with her grandmother ties her to her culture and history. Another student, Lamont, wrote about how boarding schools created a feeling of homelessness for children because they were taken from their homes and taught contempt of their language and culture. They weren't comfortable at home or in the schools. He shared a story about his elementary classmates teasing him because he is adopted. "I felt like those kids in the boarding schools. Kids at school would say, 'No one loves you. Your mom gave you up for adoption, and your new fam-

ily had to take you.' I know what it feels like to not feel at home anywhere." He used this in his essay.

We also discuss audience: Who needs to know about this? Because as students approach their topics, their audience will determine language choice, examples, and tone. Thinking about audience means that there is a real reason and purpose for this piece of writing, beyond a classroom grade. "Who do you want to read this? Who are you trying to convince? Could this be published? Would the local newspaper publish it? A neighborhood newspaper? The library? *Rethinking Schools* magazine? Teachers at this school?" Of course, many essays do not go beyond the classroom, but the more often we can supply a real audience, the better the writing becomes, even when the audience is the class in a read-around.

Once I turn students loose on the essay, I ask them to commit to a topic and brainstorm more detailed information. (I also let them know that discarding a topic that shrivels is a time-honored writing tradition.) During some essay-writing sessions, I gather students with similar topics into small groups and encourage them to share their ideas, quotes, page numbers, and pieces they think will work as evidence for their topic.

Once students begin writing, they discover the gaps in their knowledge—as Donald said, "I wasn't paying attention during that part." For example, Anne needed more background information for her essay on the Soweto Uprising to fill out her understanding of the conditions in South Africa that led students to walk out of school in protest over the imposition of Afrikaans. Sometimes students start in one direction and discover an interesting path they want to pursue. Dee wrote about Native American boarding schools, but he wanted to include contemporary information about the current Native American language restoration efforts, so he read an article on Bud Lane's work on the Siletz Reservation in Oregon.

As students noisily work through this process, they are in different places: some need more articles; some need to return to the book; others need to think about the points they want to make and the stories that will help them; others have commitment issues; and one or two confess to not paying attention during the unit. We do a lot of this work in class, and it is messy.

Wall of Thesis Statements

For years, I pushed students to write their thesis statements before they collected their evidence. This was a mistake. Their thesis didn't fit their facts. It sounded great,

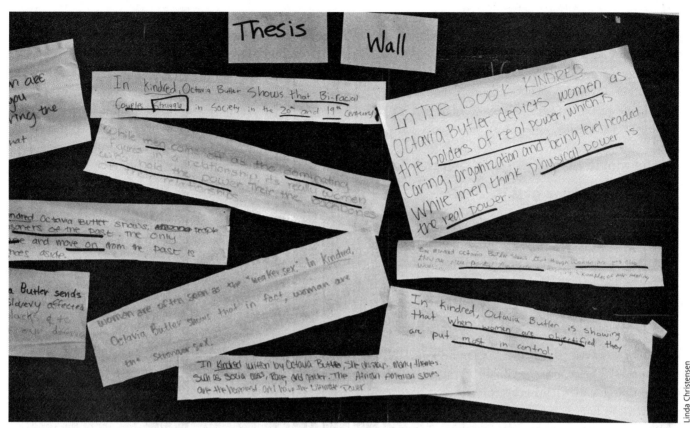

Thesis statement wall.

Linda Christensen

but couldn't find any purchase once they started writing. Now, I wait until after students collect information to work on developing a thesis statement.

I explain that a strong thesis statement is essential for writing a strong essay because:

- It provides a roadmap for the writer by stating what the essay will prove. It answers the question: What is this essay about?

- The thesis statement is more than a statement of the topic—language and power; it *defines the writer's interpretation* of a specific aspect of language and power, for example, how language played out in Native American boarding schools and what the student thinks about that;

- A strong thesis helps the writer *shape* the essay by clarifying its topic and its stance: What do you think about language and power? What is your perspective on the topic? It also helps the writer weed evidence: It clarifies what the essay is not about and what evidence is not relevant.

I also point out that the thesis statement is typically somewhere in the first paragraph of the essay and clues the reader in on the point of the essay and that it can be stated explicitly or implicitly. I don't get rule-driven about this, telling students that it must include three parts or certain kinds of phrasing. I want them to get the gist of a thesis statement. I used to get too technical, and I lost students and myself. And, as a writer, I frequently have a working thesis or direction, then adapt and change it along the way. I write my way to understanding. I bring in drafts of my writing and hang them on the wall to demonstrate this.

After we go over the mission of the thesis statement, I tell students to write one or two drafts of potential statements for their essay. Once most students have at least one statement, I tell them, "Share your thesis statements with a partner. I want you to think about what your friend is trying to prove. Is it clear? Is there evidence for it? Once you've helped each other, revise your sentence if your partner was confused. Then select your 'best' statement and write it on this strip of paper or blackboard." During this time, I travel furiously around the room, noting great sentences, and some that provide teaching points—too broad, too narrow, not enough evidence.

After all students have their thesis statements (without names) on the wall, we walk around the room discussing each statement. Now, even if I had a document projector or a working overhead with transparencies, I would still use this method as least once or twice a year. I get students out of their chairs. We walk around the room in a huddle of humanity as we discuss thesis statements. I start by saying, "As you know, I don't spell everything correctly and neither do other people, so there's no need to point out when someone has misspelled a word or two. We're looking for clarification about thesis statements, not spell-

Unlike movie teaching, I don't teach a lesson once and everyone gets it.

ing and grammar." I herd them to a couple of promising statements, pause, and ask questions. For example, in the thesis statement, "When it came to the character Janie in Hurston's novel *Their Eyes Were Watching God*, skin color did not matter." I ask, "What has the writer promised to prove?" As students make suggestions, I underline the key phrases. For this statement, the writer has to prove that skin color did not matter to Janie. "Can the writer back up this thesis? What evidence would you suggest?" After students discuss Mrs. Turner's "color struck" attitude and compare it to Janie's attitude, we decide that the writer has enough evidence. I also ask, "Can this statement be improved? How?" It is not necessary to visit every thesis, but we visit enough for students to gain clarity about what promises they've made in their statements.

I never humiliate students in this process. When I see very weak thesis statements, I note them so I can work with those students individually. I do find problematic or overstated thesis statements to discuss because I want students to learn how to narrow or refocus. Sometimes these statements help students clarify their understandings or misunderstandings of the novel or unit. Take, for example, this statement: "Janie, in *Their Eyes Were Watching God*, is fascinated by wealth and power in her youth, and later finds that it truly cannot make up for a deficiency in passion." The first part seemed off to me, so I asked the class, "Is Janie fascinated by wealth and power? Where do you see that? I don't see Janie as fascinated. Her grandmother believes property and wealth is necessary to help black women, but Janie is concerned about passion and love." The class argued. Michael disagreed. He found the quote about Janie's first vision of Joe as proof that she was struck by the way he dressed. "It was a citified, stylish dressed man with his hat set at an angle that didn't belong in these parts. His coat was over his arm, but he didn't need it to represent his clothes. The shirt with the silk sleevehold-ers was dazzling enough for the world." These conversa-tions push students (and me) to return to the text, to make sure they can prove their points, but also to see that they need to convince the reader with evidence. When students return to their seats, I ask them to revise their thesis statements.

I type up a few of the best thesis statements at the end of the day to distribute so students have models if they get stuck. I use this method once or twice during the year to help students develop a solid thesis, but any strategy needs follow-up. Unlike movie teaching, I don't teach a lesson once and everyone gets it. I circle back, re-teach in one-on-one sessions, and figure out a different way to approach it and re-teach it again later in the year. Sometimes the cloudy thesis is not a problem with writing, it is a problem with thinking. The student lacks clarity on the topic and needs to talk or write more to gain a clearer understanding of the points they want to make.

Introductions

My favorite part of teaching the art of essay writing is showing students how to write introductions. Because students are witty and playful, introductions provide a great jumping-off place for helping them get out of the strait-jacket of formulaic essays.

I show students how to write introductions using quotes, anecdotes, questions, and surprise (or "knock-you-upside-the-head") introductions. For example, when teaching literary analysis, I share five or six sample intro-ductions, including Ime Udoka's opening which uses a quote from *Their Eyes Were Watching God:*

> "So the white man throw down de load and tell de black man tuh pick it up. He pick it up because he have to, but he don't tote it. He hand it to his women folks." Quotes that stereotype black men as lazy are typical in Zora Neale Hurston's *Their Eyes Were Watching God,* but Tea Cake breaks that stereotype. In fact, Tea Cake proves to be a role model for how men should act.

When students are writing a synthesis essay, I share dif-ferent, more general models of introductions. For exam-ple, Hannah Miller's opening demonstrates how to use a pithy quote to punch straight into the language essay:

> "Ebonics is no more lazy English than Italian is lazy Latin," states John Rickford, Stanford linguistics pro-fessor, in his essay, "Suite for Ebony and Phonics." Many people believe that Ebonics is just slang or poor grammar, but they're wrong: Ebonics is a language.

Like Hannah's opening, Ryan Halvorsen's question introduction to his essay, "'Bout Dem Ebonics," doesn't hem and haw on the sidelines, it dances on the page, chin up, fists balled, ready to tackle doubters:

> Lazy? Wrong? Improper? Stupid? "Some slang shit," as Lamont "Big L" Coleman says in his rap "Ebonics"? To correct Big L and others, Ebonics is way more than slang.

After we read each introduction, I ask students the same questions we asked when we visited the wall of thesis statements, "What does Ime promise the reader? How about Hannah? What does the writer to have to prove? What evidence will the writer use? Can the writer make this essay work?" Of course, the introduction does not necessarily lay out what the writer has to prove. It could just provoke and tease, but this exercise gives me another opportunity to hit thesis and support as well as effective introductions.

After I've gone through a few models, students wave me off, impatient to write their own and share. (See p. 141 for more examples.) Because I use student models all the time, students point out their classmates' papers as models during our sharing time, "Oh, you need to save Destiny's introduction for next year." Each student's paper ups the ante for the next. When students share their snappy openings, they feed off each other, and their playful shout-outs of admiration and applause benefit both the nimble writers who found a way into their essays quickly as well as the struggling writers, who sometimes need a few more examples to get started. It's not uncommon for students to return the next day with a new opening they want to share with the class.

Writing Evidence Paragraphs

As I discussed earlier, we highlight model essays to demonstrate how to write evidence paragraphs, noting transitions, embedded quotes, block quotes, and summaries. After we write the thesis and introduction, I teach a quick craft lesson at the beginning of the period on writing evidence paragraphs. When we discussed how to embed quotes from experts into their language and power essays, Katie Chickadonz asked about how to include the survey she conducted. Katie took the research question that John Rickford discusses in his essay about the use of "bin." Rickford wrote:

> Years ago, I presented the Ebonics sentence "She bin married" to 25 whites and 25 African Americans from various parts of the United States and asked them if they understood the speaker to be still married or not. While 23 of the African Americans said yes, only 8 of the whites gave the correct answer.

Katie used the same example as she surveyed students at Grant for background research for her essay. Katie discovered that all of the African American students at Grant High School answered correctly, and no white students knew the answer. She wrote, "Of all students interviewed only one was able to produce a simple and succinct definition of Ebonics, 'The vernacular English spoken by African Americans.'" She goes on to ask, "Why is Ebonics so foggy in people's minds? What in the history of this dialect has caused it to remain so misunderstood, even today?"

For other students, the question is how to condense a story or use a quote from a passage to prove a point. I return to student models to demonstrate the process. I give students a handout indicating specific strategies—introducing quotes, embedding quotes, talking about quotes. This is an excerpt from a handout:

> *Notice the great use of embedded quotes from Annie Oldani. She weaves them into her paragraph:*
>
> They marched out into the streets, singing songs and waving anti-Afrikaans signs with slogans such as "Down with Afrikaans" and attacking Prime Minister B.J.

Taryn Wright-Ramirez writes during Daniel Beaty's workshop.

At Carlisle Indian School, Pennsylvania, a group of Native American girls with their teachers, early 1900s.

Vorster and his government with sayings like, "If we must do Afrikaans, Vorster must do Zulu." The young protesters were stopped by road barricades and police. "Then it became really a torrent, a sea of young, black faces. Masses of students, I mean, we'd never seen such a demonstration in many, many years. And at that point, the police tried to stop the protest from going on to Orlando Stadium," recounts observer Nthato Motlana. Mkhabela, too, remembers the strong police presence, saying, "I've never seen that many police. And you didn't only have police at the time, you had the Defense Force too, so you had the Army."

Notice the smart "talk" in Dante Jones' essay. He introduces the author, then summarizes Suina's point, then he analyzes Suina's experience in his own words:

Joseph Suina, in his essay "And Then I Went to School," discussed how Native American schools erased his and his people's identity. As a younger boy he witnessed the school's trademark, "Leave your Indian at home." If accidentally caught speaking his home language, he received a dirty look or a slap with a ruler. As he attended school longer, he started to oppose his grandmother's house and the environment she lived in. He became ashamed of where he came from. He felt lonely and forgotten, no longer part of his ancestors."

Conclusions

When performance poet and playwright Daniel Beaty visited Grant High School, he taught students to "button" the end of their poems—to end them on a powerful note. He said, "Button the end. Make your audience want to stand up and shout when you finish." He was speaking of performance poetry, but the same principle holds true when writing essay conclusions. Too often, student essays limp to an end; they peter out rather than pump up. I realized that I needed to teach them to "button" their essays with the same excitement with which they start them, so I began noticing and collecting types of conclusions that writers use in the same way that I focused on openings years ago: Circle back to the beginning, pose a possible solution, restate and emphasize thesis, provoke further questions. (See handout, p. 143.)

I use the same lesson plan for teaching introductions and conclusions: Examine and discuss models, practice writing a few, share a few. Jayme Causey uses a question ending on his essay on language assimilation. He also provokes the reader by pushing beyond language to the larger idea of cultural identity:

So is everyone supposed to be the same? Or is our uniqueness what makes the world such an interesting and diverse place? If assimilation was an acceptable tactic, we would all end up just alike: Same name, same hairstyle, same language, same lifestyle, same culture. Each individual's cultural identity makes them who they are. Their language, clothes, beliefs affect their everyday life. Now what fun would it be if we had a world full of John and Suzies instead of Lakeeshas, Jaymes, and Josés?

Erika Miller's essay explores how the media—from cartoons to *Seventeen* magazine—contributed to her anorexia and obsession with body image. Her conclusion points out a potential solution:

We need to change the way people think about women. We don't need to be sex objects who live to please men. Times have changed. We must no longer be dominated by male fantasies of what a woman should be because we are all intelligent, wonderful people who have a lot more to offer than a slim body and a pretty face.

Mahala Ritcherson's essay, "Battle to Change the Color Line," tackles the daily racism that occurs in schools:

> There must be a required class dealing with these issues, a time when we can get together with students of other cultures and really talk.... Racism can be right in the open and people choose to ignore it. Between classes I pass a locker with the words, "Go Back to Japan" written on it. As I look back, a boy speaking Vietnamese is turning the lock. We are not always brilliant with our prejudice, but it still hurts.

Mahala's conclusion reemphasizes the need for schools to take racism seriously:

> Schools are where we learn to make it in this society, and in order for us to make it, we cannot be afraid of each other. We need to open our eyes and make respecting our fellow students more important than any P.E. or Career Education class. The school system needs to wake up and start working to end this racism before we all slip away or explode.

In his essay on *Their Eyes Were Watching God*, Kirk Allen defended his thesis that Logan was Janie's best husband. The rest of the class disagreed with him, but that actually pushed him to write a better essay, countering their arguments. His conclusion sums up his points:

> Logan was Janie's best husband. He's the only one who really took care of Janie. Logan was more of a grandfather to Janie. He provided for her and showed her the ropes, taught her how the world worked. He never pushed her around or put his hands on her the way Joe and Tea Cake did. He was a real husband. He had to teach her that her place was not where she chose to be, but where he told her to be. She was too young and her hormones were raging. She could have been set with Logan, but she left a dependable Honda for a Lamborghini, choosing flashy instead of dependable.

While I totally disagree with Kirk, I love his ending metaphor.

Frankly, I find conclusions hard, too. Models help us find our way, but so does a sense of purpose. In my experience, when students write essays out of a passionate desire to communicate with others, their conclusions demonstrate a drive, a call to action that helps "button" the ending.

Responding and Conferencing: Essay Revision 101

Once students start writing, they need to power through a draft. But some students get stuck or confused along the way, and I don't want to wait until I collect a pile of papers to get them back on course. They need immediate intervention. I moved to in-class conferencing as a way of troubleshooting drafts while they are *in process*.

When I work with students during class, I can intervene while they write, instead of waiting until after they have written.

These days I spend more time working on the essay during class time. While students write or collect more evidence over these three- or four-day work sessions, I hold mini-conferences with them, quickly reading over their drafts or the first chunk of their writing during writing time, asking questions, suggesting other places to look for evidence, noting where they slid off track,

Linda Christensen conferencing with Jayme Causey.

129

Antoinette Sithole, sister of Hector Pieterson who was murdered by South African police in 1976, stands beside Sam Nzima's photograph at the Hector Pieterson Memorial in Soweto 30 years later.

Gideon Mendel/CORBIS

returning them to the model essay to point out how to embed or analyze quotes. Yes, this takes class time, but teaching students how to write is my job, and I honor the complexity of this difficult task by taking the time to do it right. When I work with students during class, I can intervene while they write, instead of waiting until after they have written.

Also, as I read the drafts *in process,* I usually notice patterns of errors students are making in their writing and prepare a 10-minute lesson for the beginning of the next day's class to address these issues. Sometimes these errors are typical mistakes students encounter. For example, when students write literary analysis, unless the essay is tethered to a strong thesis statement, they have a tendency to retell the story rather than analyze it. So I type up a short demonstration on retelling versus analysis and remind them to use their transitions to link their essay forward. Another typical mistake students make is to stick in a series of quotes without properly introducing them or analyzing them, so I pull paragraphs from the work-in-progress of a student who has correct attribution and share that model.

In the language essay, my common refrain is "story" the essay. In other words, too often students make assertions without providing evidence: "Native American boarding schools made children feel ashamed of their homes and language." Rather than always finding a quote as evidence, I want them to use the stories from Native American memoirs and biographies we study in class—Ernest White

Thunder or Joseph Suina—to help the reader both see and feel the shame that they endured at boarding schools. Michael Moser added both stories to his paragraph:

By not feeling comfortable in either environment, kids became defenseless at school or at home. Some kids bought into the system and came home speaking English. The banter they received at school like "Kill the Indian, save the man," or "Leave your Indian at home," made them feel psychologically less important. Some tried to stand up for themselves. Rose was a teenager at a boarding school who decided she was going to speak her language no matter what. The teacher beat her until her hands bled. Afterwards she proclaimed, "I'm going to speak Indian when I go home." Others, like Joseph Suina, learned to be ashamed of his home from his school experiences.

I used Michael's paper to model what I mean by "story it" during our opening revision lessons.

Usually, some students in my class are proficient writers who need a quick chat—asking questions about sections that lack clarity or making suggestions to move them to their next draft, but they understand the language of writing, so my conferences with them are quick, sometimes via email. These writers also have access to computers at home, whereas, most of my students use the computers in the school or public library. I embed my remarks in bold directly in the text of these students' essays and do a quick verbal check-in with them to make sure they understood my remarks. Their "errors" might be the use of passive voice or bland writing that needs to gain some energy by cutting fat language. Sometimes I point out additional resources or remind them of a story they could include. I print off a copy of their papers for them to work on during class. For example, Annie Oldani wrote a strong essay on the Soweto Uprising, that I quote above; I was able to email a response to her, so she could work on a revision during class. My remarks are bracketed:

> Children pour into the streets. They sing songs in their native tongue [Xhosa] and link arms to show their unity. [Good opening: I like the visual image. I also like the strong verbs—pour and sing and march.] They march in protest of the South African apartheid government and the oppression of their culture that comes from it. They refuse to accept the Afrikaans language they are being told they must speak because it represents more assimilation by their rulers, and tries to squeeze the native culture and tradition out of the African people. [See if you can tighten this sentence. Restructure to get rid of passive—"are being told."] These children recognize that life under white rulers is something that their parents have begun to accept, but they refuse to allow it to go any further. They had tolerated many of the things that had been changed and taken away from their communities, but they would draw the line at taking away their language. [I would include a brief history of Apartheid in South Africa: Colonized by the Dutch and English. Give a one-paragraph background on it. I will bring a book, but you can look it up as well.]

Another chunk of the class are writers who struggle, but who have an idea about how to write essays and who have a good topic. I spend most of my class time with this group of students, in side-by-side conferences. Their essays need shaping, pruning, and reorganizing. They might have the wrong quote to illustrate a point or their quotes might lack an introduction or analysis. When I conferenced with Dee, for example, I said, "You have an incredible understanding of boarding schools, but your language is general. You need to story it. What stories could you use to show how boarding schools took away language and culture? You can use quotes or you can tell the story, briefly, but you have to have some proof here."

Another section of my class are students who either lack writing skills or who missed a big chunk of the curriculum. They need longer periods of intervention than I can give them during class. I meet with them at lunch or at the beginning or end of the day, and I schedule a small-group meeting because I need to slow down and go back over the basics.

Students work on their essays during this extra time, mapping out the topic and support, writing a thesis and introduction, for example. We also discuss which chunks of the writing they can work on during class the following day. I sometimes show them how their classmates approached embedding quotes or using transitions. Students gain traction during these sessions, and we often continue these meetings throughout the year. After a while, my intervention is marginal, but focused time with an adult nearby helps them complete the task.

Teaching essay writing requires a nonnegotiable belief that students can write, and that they have something important to say.

Teachers ask how I get students to come to these voluntary, small-group sessions. The answer: I tell them to come. If they don't come, I call them at home or on their cell phone. I find that students want to learn, but struggling writers would rather look like they *don't want* to work than look like they *can't* do the work. Creating a safe place to ask questions and get help provides them the time they need to catch up with their peers. In an ideal world, I would have an extra period to work with struggling students because they don't lack capacity, they lack skills.

Don't get me wrong, students still have to take their essays home to work on them more or type them up, but taking the time *during* class while the writing is hot, is the way to work on revisions.

Creating Writers

I used to complain that my students were lazy. "They don't take the time to write good essays," I'd tell my colleagues. "They don't want to revise." Now, whenever I start blaming students, I force myself to take a hard look at my practice. If my students aren't writing "fire" essays, then there's a good chance that I'm not teaching with fire.

Good writing takes time. After working in the Oregon Writing Project with teachers for over 20 years and as an editor for *Rethinking Schools* for most of two decades as well, I know that writing is hard for students *and* for teachers. We can dumb it down and script it so that students write passing essays for the state test. They might all sound alike, but, heck, they have the formula down.

If we believe that we are *teaching* writing instead of *assigning* writing, then we must focus on the progress students make from draft to draft rather than focus on the final product. The best writing instruction happens *during* the writing, not after. The *teachable moments* emerge when we make space in the classroom for writing and conferencing as part of the class. This means constructing class time so that students get feedback and instruction while they are working on a draft. And believe me when I say that in my classroom, those are some noisy, chaotic, but necessary days.

Teaching essay writing requires a nonnegotiable belief that students can write, and that they have something important to say; it requires an understanding that good writing takes both time and multiple drafts. Teaching students to write with power and passion means first immersing them in curriculum that matters, getting them fired up about the content so that they care about their writing, and then letting them go. Given the right conditions, students will write wild essays, blooming up from the hard ground of their lives; their arguments will swoop and surprise. They will own their ideas, speak from their own authority, dare to break out of five paragraphs, mow over transitions, delight readers with their wit and wisdom and common sense, and invent language that laughs or struts across the page. ■

From Checkerboards to Roosters: The Power of Imagery

by Anna Hereford

Toni Morrison says, "The best art is political and you ought to be able to make it unquestionably political and irrevocably beautiful at the same time." In her novel *Beloved*, Morrison demonstrates her ability to produce the "best art." She creates horrifying images of slavery so vividly they stay with the reader forever. Her imagery is terribly beautiful, searingly beautiful, painfully beautiful.

One of the images Morrison embeds in the reader's mind is the tree on Sethe's back. The tree was planted on Sethe's back by her master's nephews. Why? Because she fought back while they stole her breast milk after raping her. Amy describes the scars on Sethe's back to her:

> It's a tree, Lu. A chokecherry tree. See, here's the trunk—it's red and split wide open, full of sap, and this here's the parting for the branches. You got a mighty lot of branches. Leaves, too, look like, and dern if these ain't blossoms. Tiny little cherry blossoms, just as white. Your back got a whole tree on it. In bloom. What God have in mind, I wonder. I had me some whippings, but I don't remember nothing like this.

Morrison doesn't say, "Slavery is a terrible thing." She imprints the beatings into the reader's mind, shows the puss-filled scars. The reader feels the aching pain as Amy touches Sethe's back from the trunk to the blossoms.

Morrison's image of black families as checkers on a checkerboard evoked sadness. Slaves were objects and the whites didn't care who went where.

> ...in all of Baby's life, as well as Sethe's own, men and women were moved around like checkers. Anybody Baby Suggs knew, let alone loved, who hadn't run off or been hanged, got rented out, loaned out, bought up, brought back, stored up, mortgaged, won, stolen or seized. So Baby's eight children had six fathers. What she called the nastiness of life was the shock she received upon learning that nobody stopped playing checkers just because the pieces included her children.

A child the bet in a poker game? A slaveowner deciding a child's worth in dollars? How did slaves survive knowing they were seen as objects without feelings, without voices? Morrison portrays the feeling of diminished self-worth as the slaves at Sweet Home's ownership is transferred to their master's brother-in-law. He reminds them of their value, nothing, every day. His actions scream at them that even the farm animals deserve better than the slaves do.

Paul D remembers sitting by the tree chained up with an iron bit in his mouth. Five roosters walked by staring at him. The "king" rooster walked by after the first five. Paul D helped the king rooster out of his shell; he saved his life. That rooster grew up hateful, despising everything in the yard. That day, he sat on the tub and stared at Paul D, his beak in a smile. "[H]e looked so...free. Better than me. Stronger, tougher. Son a bitch couldn't even get out the shell by hisself but he was still king and I was..." Morrison's picture of a rooster crowing over a chained man with a bit in his mouth is one that doesn't fade.

The most powerful scene in the novel is Sethe cutting off her daughter's head with a handsaw. Not because her daughter was an unwanted child. Sethe saved her from a life of slavery like she had. Her master came to collect Sethe and her children. In a lovesick frenzy, Sethe attempted to murder all her children before he could put his hands on any of them. Beloved was the only one she successfully saved. She explains the situation to Paul D:

> "I stopped him," she said, staring at the place where the fence used to be. "I took and put my babies where they'd be safe."...
>
> "Your love is too thick," he said, thinking, That bitch is looking at me; she is right over my head looking down through the floor at me.
>
> "Too thick?" she said, thinking of the Clearing where Baby Suggs' commands knocked the pods off horse chestnuts. "Love is or it ain't. Thin love ain't love at all."
>
> "Yeah. It didn't work, did it? Did it work?" he asked.
>
> "It worked," she said.
>
> "How? Your boys gone you don't know where. One girl dead, the other won't leave the yard. How did it work?"
>
> "They ain't at Sweet Home. Schoolteacher ain't got em."

Sethe's willingness to murder her children to keep them from bondage answers the question: How evil is slavery?

Toni Morrison found the answer when she discovered a newspaper clipping about a mother who chopped her child's head off in order to save it from a life of slavery. From that one clipping, one image, she was able to compile enough rage to fill a whole book.

'Bout Dem Ebonics

by Ryan Halverson

Lazy? Wrong? Improper? Stupid? "Some slang shit," as Lamont "Big L" Coleman said? To correct Big L and others, Ebonics is way more than slang.

One of the myths about Ebonics is that it is lazy English. As John Rickford, Stanford linguistics professor, wrote in his essay, "Suite for Ebony and Phonics":

> Ebonics was variously described as "lazy English," "bastardized English," "poor grammar," and "fractured slang." Oakland's decision to recognize Ebonics and use it to facilitate mastery of Standard English [SE] also elicited superlatives of negativity: "ridiculous, ludicrous," "VERY, VERY STUPID," "a terrible mistake." Linguists—the scientists who carefully study the sounds, words, and grammars of languages and dialects—were less rhapsodic about Ebonics than the novelists, but much more positive than most of the media and the general public. At their January 1997 annual meeting, members of the Linguistic Society of America [LSA] unanimously approved a resolution describing Ebonics as "systematic and rule-governed like all natural speech varieties," and referring to the Oakland resolution as "linguistically and pedagogically sound."

Rapper Lamont "Big L" Coleman is a perfect example of the myth that Ebonics is slang when in truth it has nothing to do with slang. Big L's song "Ebonics" is nothing but slang. He used words like "jake" which means police and "key" which refers to cocaine. Ebonics, on the other hand, is rule-governed. Rickford shows Ebonics' rules in the following sentences:

Present perfect progressive: He bin runnin (=SE "He has been running")
Present perfect progressive with remote inception: He BIN runnin (=SE "He has been running for a long time, and still is")

Professor Rickford explains that Ebonics is a dialect of English, which has "some pretty distinctive features of its own." Ebonics has a reputation for being "lazy" as if people didn't care enough to use "proper English." But what makes a language a language in the first place? If a language has no rules or guidelines to follow, it is not a language; it is only slang. A language must have rules in order to be considered a language. Ebonics speakers follow certain rules when they speak their language. If Ebonics has rules, it is as much a language as any other language. Some of the rules that Rickford and Linguistics Professor Geneva Smitherman list are as follows:

1. Absence of third person singular present-tense *s*. I go, you go, we go.
2. Absence of possessive *'s*. Jacoa came over to that girl house.

3. Zero copula which is an absence of *is* or *are*: Denzell crazy.
4. Invariant *be*. For this one I have to use Rickford's words from *Spoken Soul*:

> This invariant habitual be is probably the best-known but least understood of AAVE's grammatical signposts. Many outsiders to Spoken Soul believe that black folk replace Standard English is and are with invariant be all the time, as in, "He be talkin' to her right now." But AAVE is actually more discriminating. For one thing, invariant habitual be describes only an event that is performed regularly or habitually, as in "He be talkin' with his lady every day." Contrast this habitual sense with "He Ø talkin' to her right now"—which is what a speaker of Spoken Soul might say when describing an event taking place at the moment of speech, without any implication that it happens regularly. (113)

Who speaks Ebonics? Is Ebonics only used by African Americans? The answer is no. Although Ebonics is strongly used in the black population. Rickford writes that Ebonics is mainly used in the working class African American homes and with adolescents, but it is also used by whites, especially in southern states because of the large numbers of African Americans who live in the South.

Some people say that speaking in this language means that the speaker is uneducated or not intelligent. Of course, this is a complete misconception. Some of the most intelligent people speak this language, from writers and doctors to lawyers on an occasional basis when with their family or friends. It is the "home" language of African Americans as Geneva Smitherman says.

Ebonics is a hidden language because of how little is known about it by so many people, but people who know it and use it, love it, like author Toni Morrison said in an interview, "The Language Must Not Sweat":

> The language, the only language.... It's the thing black people love so much—the saying of words, holding them on the tongue, experimenting with them, playing with them. It's a love, a passion. Its function is like a preacher's: to make you stand up out of your seat, make you lose yourself and hear yourself. The worst of all possible things that could happen would be to lose that language. There are certain things I cannot say without recourse to my language.

Morrison's quote speaks to what Ebonics really is—my language. It is part of me, my character, who I am. Ebonics is here to stay and shows no signs of fading away in either the black or white communities. In the words of Ebonics: It's BIN here and it's bouts ta stay.

Politics and Their Eyes Were Watching God

by Amanda Wheeler-Kay

"[T]he story of Janie Crawford was a wasted one. It did nothing to wake the country up to inequality. Zora's characters were too simple. They eat and laugh and cry and kill." Richard Wright's criticism of Zora Neale Hurston's acclaimed novel *Their Eyes Were Watching God* is wrong. He might as well have said that worms have legs or that women belong in the kitchen.

Wright regarded writing as a political tool; yet, he only looked at one political issue—racial inequality. Although this is an important issue that the world—and especially this country—needs to recognize and change, we can't forget about or simply write off other issues like sexism or homophobia that are also political and important. Hurston's novel deals with a political issue—women's roles in society.

Through Janie Crawford, the main character, Hurston points out struggles that women have growing up and trying to find a place in this society. Often, other people's values and concepts hinder this process.

Janie's first ideas about women were shaped by her grandmother, who raised her. Nanny thought a woman needed a man's protection and that the best men were the ones who provided the most. When Janie "got her womanhood on her," Nanny pushed Janie into the waiting arms of Logan Killicks, who reflected Granny's ideals—a man with a house and property and the "onliest piano in town."

Janie soon found out that Killicks' 60 acres were fine for him, but they had little to do with her. He obtained them before she came, and they would remain his after she left. As she stated, "Ah ain't takin' dat old land tuh heart neither. Ah could throw ten acres of it over de fence every day and never look back to see where it fell." Furthermore, she didn't love Logan; she didn't even like him, and they had nothing in common. This was the first time that Janie realized, despite what Nanny believed, that being married didn't bring love or protection. "She knew now that marriage didn't make love. Janie's first dream was dead, so she became a woman."

When Joe Starks came along, Janie found someone to talk to and dream with. Her soul began to wake up, so she left Logan and traveled with Joe to begin the search for her place. She soon discovered though that life with Starks meant she became who he wanted her to be, not who she wanted to become. "[H]e told her to dress up and stand in [his] store all evening…he didn't mean for nobody's wife to rank with her." When he told her, "Ah told you in de very first beginnin' dat Ah aimed tuh be a big voice. You oughta be glad 'cause dat makes uh big woman outa you." Instead of joy, "coldness and fear took hold of her. She felt far away from things and lonely." During the twenty years of their marriage, Janie's soul went into hibernation. Jody's death brought the first decision she made in her years of marriage to him: "[S]he burnt up every one of her headrags" that he made her wear.

In the weeks and months following Jody's death, Janie set about re-awakening her dreams and began to put pieces of herself back together to build an identity free of a husband. "[S]he'd lie awake in bed asking lonesomeness some questions" and discovered things about herself she had kept buried before she hadn't known those things were important:

[S]he had been whipped like a cur dog, and run off down a back road after things.... Some people could look at a mud-puddle and see an ocean with ships. But Nanny belonged to that other kind that loved to deal with scraps. Here Nanny had taken the biggest thing God ever made, the horizon—for no matter how far a person can go the horizon is still way beyond you—and pinched it in to such a little bit of a thing that she could tie it about her granddaughter's neck tight enough to choke her. She hated the old woman who had twisted her so in the name of love.... She had found a jewel down inside herself and she had wanted to walk where people could see her and gleam it around. But she had been set in the market-place to sell. Been set for still-bait. When God had made The Man, he made him out of stuff that sung all the time and glittered all over. Then after some angels got jealous and chopped him into millions of pieces, but still he glittered and hummed. So they beat him down to nothing but sparks but each little spark had a shine and a song. So they covered each one over with mud. And the lonesomeness in the sparks make them hunt for one another, but the mud is deaf and dumb. Like all the other tumbling mud-balls, Janie had tried to show her shine.

Although she had many suitors during this time, they didn't represent the horizon. "She had already experienced them through Logan and Joe." As she told her friend Pheoby, "Ah jus' loves dis freedom."

During this time of self-realization, Tea Cake came along. He didn't try to form Janie. In fact, he taught her things she didn't know she was capable of, like how to shoot a gun and how to play checkers. Janie married Tea Cake, moved down to the muck and wore overalls. Together, "they made a lot of laughter out of nothing." With Tea Cake, "[Janie's] soul crawled out from its hiding place."

Women's roles in society have always been dictated by men like Logan and Jody, who care more about their own wants, needs, and reputations, than they do about the women they married. The world needs more men like Tea Cake who can love a woman without suppressing her individuality. This novel "wakes people up" to women's needs.

As to Wright's claim that the characters are too simple, isn't each of the items he mentioned a part of life? People do eat. They do laugh. They do cry. And that's what makes characters real. In order to get a message or learn from a story, people must be able to relate to it. The best technique is to make the message touch the audience. This is why Richard Wright's statement is so wrong. He doesn't understand that *Their Eyes Were Watching God* is a book about life.

Filling the Emptiness

by Ayesha Davis

I was raised in a home of five children, six including myself. My father was an alcoholic and a drug addict. My mother was on her way to the same behavior. She hid my father's problem for many years until our home was falling apart. My father was a lady's man, sharing himself with others while my mother said nothing, pretending everything was all right. He would come home drunk, and they would fight and he would move out for periods of time, and return again. My mother continued to take him back and tried to keep the marriage and family as one.

Reading *Yellow Raft on Blue Water*, by Michael Dorris, I found the character Christine reminded me of my mother. Christine married a man named Elgin Taylor. Like my father, he ran in and out of her life. And Christine, the lonely, alcoholic woman, who wasn't complete without a man in her life, obviously loved this man. He was supposed to be a husband and father, but he didn't live up to either title.

She filled the hole in her heart with Elgin the night they met. She was depressed about her brother Lee who was in the army, so she pushed her hurt on Elgin and decided she needed him:

> "I have a brother," I said. "Lee. I just heard that he's a MIA." I watched him from his reaction I would know what soldiers knew about MIA's, know how bad it was....
>
> "He'll be fine, your brother. They get lost all the time, then they get found. You wait. You're going to get a telegram delivered under your door saying he's OK."
>
> It was what I wanted to hear.... He was just what I needed.

She stuffed how she felt inside for the pleasure of a man's body close to hers, thinking it would change reality. Her happiness was based on Elgin's presence. She even believed his guarantee that her brother Lee was alive would bring him back in one piece. Christine told him her secrets, changed her personality and appearance to please him. Elgin, always late for dates came home with sex on his mind and alcohol on his breath. This was all he gave, and Christine loved him even more.

Elgin became an addiction for her. She got pregnant hoping a baby would make Elgin stay, but his absences became even more frequent. When he wasn't around, she took pills or drank. When her daughter, Rayona, called her an alcoholic, she denied it:

> In school they had taught her all this crap about drinking and how bad it was for you, smoking too, and she was convinced that I used more than I did, that I was an alcoholic. Sometimes I found myself sneaking around my own apartment like some kid, hiding a bottle of V.O. in a shoebox and dreaming up excuses to satisfy her.

She couldn't shake her dependence on Elgin. She accepted his moods, his free style of living, his infidelities. She even tried giving him her car to keep him around. Christine's way of trapping Elgin in her love net soon ran out.

Rayona, Christine and Elgin's daughter, grew to dislike her father's unkept promises and his absences. She saw her mother's desperate need for him and resented it. When her father visited Christine in the hospital, Rayona thinks, "I try to imagine what Mom is so upset about. She and Dad never live together for more than a week before they start picking on each other and talking divorce. But they never go through with it. Being married never stops either one of them from doing what they want. It doesn't interfere."

I know what Rayona felt, and I knew how hopeless her family situation was. She knew her father wasn't any good for her mother. Just as I, too, realized my father wasn't fit for my mom. I held on to all of his unkept promises and to the hope of keeping my father around even as he continued to wreck our lives each time Mom took him back.

Watching my mother struggle with her marriage and knowing how she believed she could make it work has stuck with me. I have been involved with relationships that led me nowhere, as I tried to fix what was broken from the start.

From our mothers' examples, Rayona and I were more aware of this cycle of dependence. We didn't have to wait until we were grown women to face the shock of what our mothers dealt with. We can train ourselves to deal with relationships differently. We can talk to counselors about how to deal with loving ourselves instead of filling our emptiness with alcohol and drugs or an unhealthy man.

Introductions

Here are a few samples from students to make your pen a willing instrument. As you read these openings, think about what each writer promises the reader. Also, notice how these writers include the author and title of the book in their openings.

The Anecdote Opening: The anecdote is a small story writers use to illustrate the topic of the essay. This introduction provides a strong launch for your essay. However, the anecdote is a tricky lead because sometimes people get so wrapped up in their story, their essay gets lost. Notice how Jenelle pulls the reader in with her personal story, then ties it to the novel.

"Men are dogs!" Kesha said when I walked in the door.

"Sure are," Vonda replied. "Did you hear what Leroy did to Kenya when he was supposedly going out with Bonnie?"

"No, girl, what did he do?" Kesha leaned in to get the gossip.

Every time I walk into a room or go somewhere, I hear girls talking about how men are dogs, and how they always cheat on their women. Zora Neale Hurston, in the novel *Their Eyes Were Watching God,* does nothing to dispel the myth that men, especially African American men, are bad news. In fact, it seems that her book encourages that myth.

—*Jenelle Yarbrough*

Quote: The quote is a classic opening, pairing a quote from the book or about the book with the thesis statement.

According to Toni Morrison, Zora Neale Hurston's gift in *Their Eyes Were Watching God* is language. She celebrates the language of everyday black people through porch stories, big lies, folk sayings, metaphors, and the use of black vernacular.

—*Chetan Patel*

"So the white man throw down de load and tell de black man tuh pick it up. He pick it up because he have to, but he don't tote it. He hand it to his women folks." Quotes that stereotype black men as lazy are typical in Zora Neale Hurston's *Their Eyes Were Watching God,* but Tea Cake breaks that stereotype. In fact, Tea Cake proves to be a role model for how men should act.

—*Ime Udoka*

ASSIGNMENT: Literary Analysis Essays

Questions: As Chelsea, DeShawn and Daniel skillfully illustrate, the question opening engages the reader through a series of questions meant to pique the reader's interest. Then they tie those questions to the novel.

What makes a woman a woman? Is it a man? Is it raising children? Must girls have a full-time mother to become a "true" woman? Do young women let society shape them to fit what it wants them to be? In the novel *Their Eyes Were Watching God* by Zora Neale Hurston, Janie Crawford, the main character, is shaped by her need for a man to "pollinate her" so that she could bear fruit and grow past Nanny. Because she wants a man to define her womanhood, Janie "wait[s] for the world to be made" instead of making it herself.

—Chelsea Henrichs

How does a girl learn to become a woman? Is it through the relationship of men? Do parents teach their daughters through advice or example how to become a woman or does it come naturally? In the book *Their Eyes Were Watching God* by Zora Neale Hurston, Janie Crawford, the main character, learned to become a woman through her relationships with men.

—DeShawn Holden

Should people be treated differently depending on their race or class? Do rich people deserve more respect than poor people? If a person makes $200,000 a year, should the rest of us bow down? Should poor people open the doors for the rich? In the play *Pygmalion*, by George Bernard Shaw, upper-class people are given respect, while lower-class people are constantly disrespected.

—Daniel Collins

Bold Statement Opening: This is the opening for writers who want to start with a punch and hit the reader upside their head with their point. As Ime demonstrates, this opening doesn't waste any time letting the reader know the issues he will explore in his literary essay.

In order to be successful, a man has to make his mark on the world. While women may be able to get by on their looks, men must succeed financially. In the book *Their Eyes Were Watching God,* by Zora Neale Hurston, a man is considered successful if he has money, a decent job, or land. Those who do not possess these qualities are frowned on by everyone except the main character, Janie.

—Ime Etuk

Conclusions

Jefferson High School students wrote the following conclusions. While these conclusions only represent a few of the ways to end an essay, reading them might help you end yours.

Circle Back to the Beginning

With this conclusion, the writer returns to the introduction. For example, in her essay "Banding Together," Michelle Burch discusses the demise of Jefferson's music program. Her piece opens with a scene of chaos in the band room and ends with those same students at a concert:

> We blasted out "The Lion King." The clarinets got lost. The trumpets played louder, as if to cover up their mistakes. The freshmen drummers were overtaken by an uncharacteristic shyness and seemed hesitant to make even a sound. And on the last note, when Mr. Briglia gave the final downbeat, I played loudly. I was the only one. A moment later, the rest of the group struggled to join, but by that time Mr. Briglia had given the cut-off. A clarinet squeaked. A cymbal crashed. And then, silence. Hesitant applause began. Mr. Briglia put down his baton and beamed. He waved us up to stand for our recognition and the applause grew. I looked around at the other band members. Their heads were down, a soft flush rising on their cheeks. I knew what they felt. Proud, for getting up on that stage; embarrassed for each mistake that had contributed to the mess; warm, in the generous and unconditional applause from friends and relatives; and sad, at the miserable state of the Jefferson music program. We knew that ten dedicated musicians and their supportive families could not build a great music program. It takes a whole school and a whole community's support, and that was something we didn't have.

In his essay "African American English: Slang, Dialect, or Language?" Milton McCullough discusses the Ann Arbor Decision, where the court ruled that there was a possible relationship between black students' low reading scores and the failure of the school to take into account the home language of the children. The judge ordered the school district to find a way to identify black English speakers in the schools and to "use that knowledge in teaching such students how to read standard English." In his conclusion, Milton returns the reader to his original question about African American English/Ebonics as a legitimate language:

> Although the Ann Arbor decision was made in 1977, in 1994, students are still being told their home language is wrong, incorrect, inferior, nonstandard. In order to compensate for what they've been denied, African Americans must be taught the history of their own tongue.

Possible Solution

With this conclusion, the writer proposes a solution to the problem outlined in the introduction. For example, Erika Miller's essay explores how the media—from cartoons to *Seventeen* magazine—contributed to her anorexia and women's obsession with body image. Her conclusion points out a potential solution:

> We need to change the way people think about women. We don't need to be sex objects who live to please men. Times have changed. We must no longer be dominated by male fantasies of what a woman should be because we are all intelligent, wonderful people who have a lot more to offer than a slim body and a pretty face.

Restate and Emphasize Thesis

Mahala Ritcherson's essay "Battle to Change the Color Line" tackles the daily racism that occurs in schools. In her opening, she wrote: "There must be a required class dealing with these issues, a time when we can get together with students of other cultures and really talk.... Racism can be right in the open and people choose to ignore it. Between classes I passed a locker with the words "Go Back to Japan" written on it. As I looked back, a boy speaking Vietnamese was turning the lock. We are not always brilliant with our prejudice, but it still hurts." Her conclusion reemphasizes the need for schools to take racism seriously:

> Schools are where we learn to make it in this society, and in order for us to make it, we cannot be afraid of each other. We need to open our eyes and make respecting our fellow students and their cultures more important than any P.E. or Career Education class. The school system needs to wake up and start working to end this racism before we all slip away or explode.

Further Questions

In this conclusion, the writer poses questions that remain unanswered and prompts the reader to continue thinking. In his essay "Standard English," Andrew Loso struggled with the issue of Standard English. As a young white man in a predominantly African American school, he left his reader with questions about Standard English:

> If having a "standard" English can cause people to quarrel or cause loss of culture or divide people into groups, why do we have it? It causes an uproar between urban youth and their teachers. It builds walls between races. We need to throw away the term "standard" English. Without it people would be free to speak, write, and sing with their own particular style and character, and not be pressured by society into speaking one "standard" dialect. To break down the walls in society between different groups, we must first examine the foundation on which we built them.

Essay Criteria

Write an essay that clearly states your opinion on the novel you read. Support your opinion using evidence from the novel. In this essay, also focus on tightening your sentences and using active verbs.

Attach this sheet to your essay. Color-highlight each of the following elements of an essay:

____ 1. **Thesis Statement:** Stated or implied. Write it in the space below. Highlight it on your paper.

____ 2a. **Introduction:** What kind of introduction did you use?
   Anecdote
   Quote
   Question
   Bold Statement

____ 2b. **Book Title** (underlined or italicized) and author.

____ 3. **Transitions:** Refer back to your thesis. Keep your essay moving.

____ 4. **Evidence:** Prove your point with specific examples from the novel. *On your essay, mark each of the ways you used examples from the text.*
   Block quotes using the text for proof
   Embedded quotes using the text for proof
   Paraphrase of incidents, language, characterization
   Analysis — why this evidence proves your point

____ 5. **Conclusion:** What kind of conclusion did you use?
   Summary
   Circle back to the beginning
   Possible solution
   Restate and emphasize thesis
   Further questions to think about

____ 6. **Tight Writing:**
   Active verbs
   Lean language
   Metaphorical language
   Sentence variety

____ 7. **Grammar, punctuation, spelling checked and corrected.**

On the back of this page, describe what you need to do to revise this essay.

Peer Response: A Letter

Your name: _____

Partner's name: _____

Today, find a partner. Swap papers. You will write at least a two-page letter in response to your partner's paper.

In order to keep writing, writers need to know what they are doing right, as well as what they need to revise. What is delightful, memorable, outstanding about this piece? What can you say to keep this writer writing? Make this your first paragraph.

1. Help your partner keep what's working:

- What essay criteria — introduction, thesis, transitions, evidence, analysis — are included in this essay?

- Discuss each one. Tell what worked in the essay.

- You might include what you learned from the essay. What new insights did your partner discuss?

- Also point out specific sentences you liked, what got you thinking. For example, you might say, "When I read your opening line, I thought I might want to add more to my paragraph about the history of Ebonics." OR: "I loved the way you said ..." OR: "The quotes you chose helped me understand how boarding schools contributed to the destruction of languages."

In other words: *Be specific.*

2. Help your partner revise:

- You might note if you got confused anywhere and needed more information. Sometimes writers leave out important information. Again, *be specific* about what confused you.

- What was missing from the essay? For example, you might say, "You put in quotes, but you never talked about the quotes. Perhaps you could explain in more detail."

- What needs to be added? For example: "If you used transitions, it would help the reader follow your essay."

- Point out where to get information: "You didn't talk about how Wangari Mathaai, the woman from Kenya, talked about the way the nuns humiliated the girls if they spoke their native language."

Alan Wieder

Honoring Our Ancestors: Building Profile Essays

Neither my parents nor my grandparents are famous. Their names won't be found in any history textbooks. Their modest graves are not national historic sites. My paternal grandfather fished for salmon in the Pacific Ocean. My maternal grandfather ran a dairy farm. My father owned a rough-and-tumble fisherman's bar, and my mother kept track of their children and their money. But every day of their lives they were heroic. They created homes for their families, full of love and tradition. Through their daily lives, stories, laughter, and punishment, my parents taught me how to become a moral citizen of the world.

Unfortunately, their lessons and stories never made their way into my education. Where I came from and who I came from were never part of the lesson plan. Students can pass through years of school without ever seeing anyone who looks like them in the school-house—either on the walls or in the books. What students don't see in their education can make as big of an impression as what

Students of all backgrounds should see themselves represented in the school curriculum.

they do see. Our choices say who counts and who doesn't, whose stories are important and whose aren't. Students of all backgrounds should see them-selves represented in the school curriculum. If the "official" curriculum does not include them, the "unofficial" curriculum must. I teach the Honoring Our Ancestors essay to invite my students' families into our classroom.

I teach this essay at the opening of the year so students can begin look-ing for heroes with a small "h" who emerge from our study of our lives, as well as our study of literature and history. We celebrate Daniel Collins' grandmother, Pastor Mary H. Smith, who helped people who were left homeless after Hurricane Katrina; we pay tribute to Gina's mother, Leanne Grabel, who started a poetry café, as well as Donnie McPherson, a wrestling coach, who "saved" one of my students from the streets. As the year progresses, students also recognize characters from literature, like Eliza Doolittle from George Bernard Shaw's *Pygmalion*, who wants to learn to "talk right," but who refuses to change her essential character in order to fit in, and Celie, from *The Color Purple*, who learns how to stand up for herself.

Teaching the Profile: Building Evidence with Anecdotes

Because my students need many opportunities to practice their literacy skills, every task, even ones that build community and connections in my class, must also develop their reading and writing habits. This assignment is a profile essay, which students can return to again and again. It is a beginner's essay, a way for students to slide into essay writing without the additional weight of analyzing a novel. When students are learning the craft of essay writing, I like them to work first with familiar material.

During this lesson, I teach students how to use anecdotes, or small stories, as evidence in an essay. The writing also plays double duty with juniors and seniors because a variation of this assignment is on the common college application every year—to write about a person who

It is a beginner's essay, a way for students to slide into essay writing without the additional weight of analyzing a novel.

has had an influence on you and describe that influence. Whether students use this essay for applications or not, the assignment helps them understand how to construct a response. (See "Writing the College Essay: Creating a Vision of Possibility," in *Reading, Writing, and Rising Up*.)

Telling Stories

To shift students into writing about their "ancestors," I tell them about my mother. I put her name, Lena Christensen, on the overhead, and I talk about specific stories that demonstrate how she took care of our family. My niece Kelly has Tourette's syndrome, and school was painful for her. Mom picked Kelly up daily, took her for walks on the beach, patiently worked with her on her multiplication

tables, and created a place where Kelly felt safe and loved. When my brother, Billy, divorced, Mom made sure that his children, Dina, Troy, and Chet, spent vacations with us. She wanted them to understand that they were still part of our family after the divorce. My mother came up every summer when my daughters were young and took care of them while I taught the Writing Project. She took them to swimming lessons at Grant Park, and she had dinner ready when I came home from work. As I tell my students, "These stories—or anecdotes or vignettes, as they are sometimes called—will help build my essay. If my thesis is that my mother's life work was to knit a family together, to make everyone feel connected and responsible for one another, then I need to prove that. These stories *show* my reader how she did that."

I also tell stories about other people who influenced me, in case students don't want to write about family members: Mr. Cetina, the principal of my elementary school; Ms. Carr, my junior English teacher; and Mrs. Johansen, my speech and debate teacher. To cast the net wide enough to bring in a diverse range of influences, I discuss my moral ancestors from literature and history.

Then I ask students to make lists of people they might want to write about. "Make a list of people who you would like to honor. Think about categories: family members, coaches, teachers, a person in your church or summer camp. You can also include people who have blazed the path for you to follow." After students create their lists, we share to spark new ideas.

Developing Writers' Eyes

Before I tell students how to construct a profile essay, I ask them to examine a few profiles with a writer's eyes, to figure out how this piece of writing is structured. While essays use a common framework—introduction, thesis, body of evidence, and conclusion, they don't all use the same kinds of evidence. A literary analysis, for example, examines and analyzes a piece of literature, so the evidence includes quotes from the novel, poem, or story.

The profile essay is a word portrait developed through anecdotes and descriptions of an individual. I immerse students in examples of profiles, so they begin to sort out the kinds of paragraphs writers use in developing their essays. I find models everywhere: sports pages—especially Dave Zirin's columns—obituaries, former student essays, the portrait of the inventor in John Berendt's *Midnight in the Garden of Good and Evil*, and the many fine profiles of exterminators and rat catchers in *Rats* by Robert Sullivan.

These models help students understand how other writers wove anecdotes and description into their essays to paint their portraits.

As we read a few models out loud together, I say, "Let's figure out how these writers designed their essays. What do you notice? Look at the function of each paragraph. What kind of work is it doing? What is its purpose?" While professional models demonstrate the breadth of the profile, student essays about their "ancestors" provide leaner and often more accessible models. The skeleton of the essay is more visible. Students point out the detailed description of Brenda Bufalino in Neena Marks' college essay. Neena chose to write about Bufalino because she is a tap pioneer, an "ancestor" for Neena, who used the essay in her successful application to New York University's School of Performing Arts:

American Tap Dance Foundation

Brenda Bufalino

Brenda Bufalino is as wild as her name. She bursts in the room laughing, her bell bottoms rippling and flowing from the draft she creates as the reckless door slams abruptly behind her. Bam. My attention is fixed on the slim, shapely body defined in black shiny spandex. Her shoes, black, witchlike, teeter at three inches with a pointed toe. She storms across the room. Her dynamics in walking alone almost knock me over. She sits. I begin to check the legend out more closely. Her slightly aged face is framed by an exotic, busily-bright, multicolored turban with fringe. She jingles. Her bracelets, rings, and necklaces clang together as she slips her witch shoes off and pulls out a pair of multicolored gray taps that resemble my grandfather's golf shoes.... She is a pioneer. The first woman to put on a pair of flat tap shoes and still the only woman considered a master.

Jessica Knutson's description of "Holt," her middle school math teacher, is shorter, but still demonstrates the idea of creating a "portrait," using both physical details as well as actions that help us see her teacher:

Just looking at Holt made you think "math teacher." He had grayish hair, parted and combed over to one side. Big, thick glasses covered half of his face. When he was happy, a big smile covered the other half.

Holt was happy frequently. When a student answered a question correctly, he rewarded them with a loud, "YES," as he pumped his fist in the air and lifted his knee. Math jokes made Holt roar with laughter, the notes of his voice bouncing off the walls.

Larry Johnson's description of his wrestling coach is concise but metaphorical. "Coach McPherson is about 5 foot 8 and weighs about 185 pounds. He is short and looks like a pit bull with a big head. He has a small body, but a strong heart. His voice is loud and squeaky like a train."

We continue to examine the profiles to ferret out the work or function of other paragraphs. "OK. We've noticed that writers describe the person they're writing about. What else do you notice about the models? What kinds of work do other paragraphs perform?" Students observe the way writers—students as well as professionals—use stories to illustrate the individual's personality or traits they admire. Neena Marks' profile about tap master Bufalino uses an anecdote to show us her "ancestor" at work:

"Are you ready to hoof?" she belts out in her deep, gruff voice. We gather around. She begins warming up our feet. She calls it a scale—taking the foot through a full range of sounds by hitting different parts of the taps. Suddenly, I feel like a musician, orchestrating precise and intricate rhythms. "Make your feet sing," she smiles as she exposes her nicotine-stained teeth. Her voice, worn from years of smoking, captures me. She begins to sing the quality of the taps: Gung ga ge go cac-ta-cha. The rhythm internalizes. I am possessed as I start singing to myself.

Neena's scene helps the reader see and hear Bufalino, moving her from icon to teacher as she taps and calls out instructions. She also weaves in a piece of Bufalino's background history.

Most of the models I select also include some reflection, which students may or may not notice, but I always point out. Jessica's reflection on "Holt" examines what she learned from her time with him:

Now that I have moved to a different school and different math teachers, I realize what a big impact Holt had on me. His willingness to work through a problem with me no matter how long it took was unique. If I had trouble with something, he explained it to me in as many different ways as he could until I understood.

He came in a little early or stayed a little late to make sure I was totally clear with whatever problem I had difficulty with.

Later in her essay, she reflects on how his math lessons influenced her piano playing: "Holt's techniques helped me artistically too. I found that I learned Bach fugues more easily on the piano because of Holt's teachings about patterns and logic. Fugues have a logical progression from chord to chord."

I want students to learn how to scrutinize models so when they leave my class, they will know how to navigate unfamiliar writing territory.

Obviously, class would move along more quickly if I just told students upfront to write an essay about a person that includes description, scene, reflection, and a thesis that unifies the essay; however, my teaching point is broader than this one essay. I want students to learn how to scrutinize models so when they leave my class, they will know how to navigate unfamiliar writing territory.

Getting Specific

Too often, when students write about their parents or grandparents, or others, they lapse into vague generalizations, piling on phrases like, "She was always there for me. She had my back." They don't get specific. To prevent that from happening, I put the phrase, "She was there for me" on the overhead. I say, "Imagine that someone wrote this about your person; what examples could you give me so I believed you?" Students shout out examples: She came to my games. She made dinner every night. She read to me when I was little. She hugs me when I'm sad. He showed me how to throw a football. I didn't believe I could do math, but my 8th-grade math teacher showed me that I could. The discussion provides a basin for students to catch ideas while they brainstorm.

To segue into the students' list of examples, I play "Hey, Mama," from Kanye West's CD *Late Registration*. West's beautiful song is a tribute to his mother. After listening to the song and reading the lyrics, students discussed specific examples from his song: She made him chicken soup, never put a man over him, taught him to ride a bike:

Late December, harsh winter gave me a cold
You fixed me up something that was good for my soul

Famous homemade chicken soup, can I have another bowl?
You work late nights just to keep on the lights
Mommy got me training wheels so I could keep on my bike
And you would give anything in this world

West's song helps illustrate my point that, even in lyrics, the writer has to provide specific evidence.

Moving into Writing

Once I have frontloaded the assignment by developing criteria and examining models, I ask students to list their heroes on their charts and we share them with the class. After students have selected their heroes, I ask them to write a description of these people. I tell them, "You can write a physical description: What does the person look like? What stands out about the person? Does he wear a sweater? Does she wear hats to church? Give us enough details so we can see your person, so we could pick him or her out of a crowd. Let us hear your ancestor talk or give advice." In essays, I repeat the write-and-share pattern I use with both poetry and narrative. Those who found a way into their description give ideas to writers who are stuck.

Once students have a handle on description, I tell them, "Create a scene where you show us your person in action. This story should illustrate *why* you want to honor this person. Think about Neena's story about Brenda Bufalino in action, how she taught students to tap. A scene may include dialogue as well. Remember Kanye West sang about how his mother made him chicken soup and helped him learn to ride a bike. What scene would help the reader understand your person? Ask yourself this: What is it that you admire about this person? Can you show it? Go into detail. Get specific. You can cut back later, but write big now. If you get stuck, move to another story. You can write more than one."

After students write scenes and share them, I encourage them to add some history of the person—some background information that helps us understand this person as Neena did. I also remind them to add a reflection. "What did you learn from your ancestor that you will take with you into your future?"

What's Your Thesis?

What makes something an essay and not simply a profile is that there is a point—that the descriptions and anecdotes are "evidence" that support a key statement about an individual. I raise this initially when I discuss the example about my mom knitting the family together.

Andrea London/GETTY IMAGES

I return to the thesis now that students have gathered evidence—descriptions and examples about their "ancestor." I tell students, "The thesis drives the essay. You have an infinite number of stories to tell about some characters, but your thesis will determine which stories you choose and which ones you leave out. When we started this essay, I talked about my mother knitting our family together. Knowing my thesis means that I select stories that show my mother in that role. Without a thesis about her role in the family or in my life, I would have no way of knowing which stories fit in my essay—are 'evidence'—and which fall outside my thesis. For example, my mom also loved to bake pies. That could fit in, but I'd have to tell a story about how her pie-baking was symbolic of her love, knowing that Lee loves blackberry, I love lemon meringue, and Kelly loves apple. But the story about the morning she slipped on the ice on the back porch doesn't fit in. Think about your individual. What do you want to honor about this person?"

We read back through a couple of sample essays to find the writer's thesis. Many of the thesis statements in these essays are not spelled out; they are implied through the stories. I ask students to write out their thesis statements and put these at the top of their papers, so they can remind themselves which stories "fit" their essays and which ones need to be discarded.

Writing the Introduction

When students have written the core chunks of their paper—thesis, description, scene, background history, and reflection—we work on writing the opening for their essay. I share a few of my past students' openings to get them to move beyond the dull, "My hero is…" Kirkland Allen's introduction to his essay about his grandmother demonstrates an essay opening, but also the use of metaphor:

> How did it happen? How was I blessed with a hero who bails me out of trouble and guides me to the right roads in life? She is my own GPS. My grandmother is with me like my shadow, except she stays by my side even in dark situations.

Neena Marks used a description of Bufalino as an opening for her essay. Chelsea Hendricks, on the other hand, opens with dialogue from the dance teacher she chose to honor:

> "If I came to see you, I'd ask for my money back! I've paid. Give me something to watch! If you're going to dance, dance," the tiny, dark woman says over the banging of the piano. We all laugh, but I take what she says and store it away. Her words make me push myself harder.

Larry opened his essay with a scene that demonstrates why he needed Donnie McPherson's help:

> Standing on the corner before football practice, I saw Bruce coming down the street, so I started beating him up for no reason. I was already late for football practice. Then I saw Donnie McPherson, one of the football coaches, coming my way. He saw me and said, "Man, what the hell are you doing? You're always grabbing or hitting on somebody. You need to put that energy to use on the wrestling mat." I thought he was joking, but he wasn't. That started my wrestling career.

I share an anecdotal opening from the book *Freedom Riders: John Lewis and Jim Zwerg on the Front Lines of the Civil Rights Movement*. The book tells about how John Lewis rode the bus as a "Freedom Rider":

> Young John Robert Lewis wanted to get out of Alabama in the worst way. He wanted to leave behind the state that placed limits on his life just because of the color of his skin. Lewis and his cousin, Della Mae, planned the perfect escape. The children agreed to saw down one of the towering pine trees by their homes and fashion it into a bus. "We were gonna make a bus, and we were gonna roll out of Alabama," recalls the

grown Lewis, smiling. Lewis and his cousin knew that "somehow we needed to get out. If we could just make this bus ... we'd be all right."

Arranging and Revising the Essay

After students have written the "parts" of the essay, I encourage them to move the parts around to find the best way to tell the story of their ancestor. "There is no one way to write this. You might choose to open with a description, move to a scene and end with a reflection. Read your paper over and play with the order. What works best?"

Revising is, of course, the key to good writing; however, it doesn't happen without a push and some feedback. I distribute the Profile Essay Criteria (p. 157) to students and ask them to color-highlight their essay and determine if they have included each of the categories. If they haven't, I encourage them to add the pieces that are missing so they can have a stronger paper. While it might seem juvenile to color-highlight essays as well as narratives, I have discovered that students benefit from the concrete reminder of the expectations. When they leave my class, I want them to have internalized the criteria, so that writing becomes intuitive, and they don't panic at each new assignment.

Too often, schools ask students to drop their identities at the door. We fill them up with algebraic formulas, periodic tables, grammar and punctuation rules. But the classroom becomes richer when students connect our lessons to the lessons they learn at home, in church, or on the wrestling mat. When we honor where our students come from, we honor who they are. We tell them that they matter. And then, the learning can begin. ■

Brenda Bufalino

by Neena Marks

Brenda Bufalino is as wild as her name. She bursts in the room laughing, her bell bottoms rippling and flowing from the draft she creates as the reckless door slams abruptly behind her. Bam. My attention is fixed on the slim, shapely body defined in black shiny spandex. Her shoes, black, witchlike, teeter at three inches with a pointed toe. She storms across the room. Her dynamics in walking alone almost knock me over. She sits.

I begin to check the legend out more closely. Her slightly aged face is framed by an exotic, busily-bright, multicolored turban with fringe. She jingles. Her bracelets, rings, and necklaces clang together as she slips her witch shoes off and pulls out a pair of gray taps that resemble my grandfather's golf shoes. She is sly. I can tell just by the precision and intensity she has in tying her shoes. She is a pioneer. The first woman to put on a pair of flat tap shoes and still the only woman considered a master.

She stands. She is there for us. No rank or status involved, just rhythm. Purely rhythm. She shakes her right foot over the floor and five billion perfectly clear, even taps echo across the room and penetrate my already intimidated mind. She shakes the left perfectly.

"Are you ready to hoof?" she belts out in her deep, gruff voice. We gather around. She begins warming up our feet. She calls it a scale—taking the foot through a full range of sounds by hitting different parts of the taps. Suddenly, I feel like a musician, orchestrating precise and intricate rhythms.

"Make your feet sing," she smiles as she exposes her nicotine-stained teeth. Her voice, worn from years of smoking, captures me. She begins to sing the quality of the taps: Gung ga ge go cac-ta-cha. The rhythm internalizes. I am possessed as I start singing to myself.

Wow. I am tapping, making sounds so clear and precise, as if each tap ignited a light that carried through my center and out each extremity, filling the room with a warm, yellow light, giving me security to let go of my fears, my intimidations, my doubts. I feel myself tapping as my feet supply the music. Never before has my tapping, my dancing felt so integrated. I glance to catch Brenda's enormous encouraging smile; we share the emanation and clarity in the room as the dancers light their taps and burn free of inhibitions.

"Now you're tapping," the baritone voice explodes with raw inspiration, shaking the walls of Jefferson's "Dungeon" dance studio. The four walls contain my light. My inspiration integrates with the sound of Brenda's voice and pours openly into a new place for me—a place where dance and life have no boundaries.

Donnie McPherson

by Larry Johnson

Standing on the corner before football practice, I saw Bruce coming down the street, so I started beating him up for no reason. I was already late for football practice. Then I saw Donnie McPherson, one of the football coaches, coming my way. He saw me and said, "Man, what the hell are you doing? You're always grabbing or hitting on somebody. You need to put that energy to use on the wrestling mat." I thought he was joking, but he wasn't. That started my wrestling career.

Coach McPherson is about 5 foot 8 inches and weighs about 185 pounds. He is short and looks like a pit bull with a big head. He has a small body, but a strong heart. His voice is loud and squeaky like a train.

McPherson has a reputation for helping people, especially young men. He helped me directly. He sat me down and gave me the "Coach McPherson" talk. "You can straighten out your act now. You know you can do better than you are doing. Don't follow in your brother's footsteps."

Coach McPherson is the best out of all of the coaches I've known. He teaches me more than wrestling skills. He teaches me how to survive. He comes into the room with a joking look on his face. When it is time to practice, he is as serious as a heart attack. When I started wrestling, it was hard. I wanted to quit, but he told me that I was tighter than that and made me stay.

How can I become a positive influence to someone else? I feel that I can be an influence to others in the same way Coach McPherson was to me. I have already practiced the skills of helping others inside of Peninsula Wrestling Club. I work with young kids, coaching them and helping them with their problems like Coach McPherson helped me.

Mario Tama/GETTY IMAGES

Hurricane Katrina and Everyday Heroes

When Hurricane Katrina exploded across the South, tearing up levees, drowning people who couldn't afford to escape her wrath, and exposing the way the United States government treats the poor, especially those who are black and poor, I figured I would have to put my curriculum plans on hold. It didn't feel right to watch this destruction on the nightly news and turn away from it during school hours. As I said earlier, our curricular choices say who counts and who doesn't—whose stories are important and whose aren't. To ignore this tragedy would have said their lives didn't matter.

I wanted to honor people whose lives had been interrupted, and I wanted my students to see past the images of the hurricane blowing down buildings and to question how our country could allow this devastation to occur. I wanted students to learn to

Our curricular choices say who counts and who doesn't— whose stories are important and whose aren't. To ignore this tragedy would have said their lives didn't matter.

find and analyze facts about contemporary tragedies, to ferret out patterns of actions that continue to produce injustice and inequality.

But injustice wasn't the only story that surfaced. Through the chaos and the crisis, through the lies and the deaths, a counter-narrative emerged: the story of how everyday people worked together to help each other when their government failed. To link this breaking news to my curriculum, I asked students to think about their everyday heroes and write profiles as a way to make a connection between their lives and the heroes who emerged during the hurricane.

My student Daniel Collins wrote, "Pastor Mary H. Smith, also known as my grandmother, is the greatest person alive today." Daniel included a physical description: "She has gold teeth, wears glasses, is a good dresser, keeps her hair whipped." Daniel's tribute to his grandmother integrated an anecdote that came back to our discussions of New Orleans:

> After Hurricane Katrina struck in and around the New Orleans area, [Grandma] sold our vacation home in Phoenix, Arizona. With the money that came from the vacation home and the money from her bank account, she rented hotels and apartments for about ten families she was going to bring from New Orleans and small towns around that area. After their arrival, she supplied the ones that didn't have food stamps with food.

Daniel's grandmother and her church raised money to help those left homeless in the wake of Katrina's devastation and the government's inept response.

Josh Langworthy's tribute to his foster mother, Michelle McCallister, doesn't use a physical description; instead he describes her work:

> Michelle used to work at Department of Human Services as a systems manager. Her job was to make sure that the caseworkers were getting what they needed to help the foster kids on their case loads. Then she wrote the contracts to get the appropriate funding for the needed services. One day she was going over a case that spoke out to her. She decided to ask the caseworker about the two boys that the case belonged to. Those two boys just so happened to be my brother and me. After a few hours of convincing, my caseworker managed to get Michelle to open her home to my brother and me. I was very happy to be moving anywhere because we were living in a hellhole at the time.

As sometimes happens when the writing gets good and honest, Josh Langworthy's essay cracked my junior class open. Josh acted hard; he got angry easily, and he constantly tapped something—fingers, toes, pencils, stapler—but Josh risked his tough-guy image when he shared his essay with the class:

> Freshman year was one heck of a year. Almost every day I got a new discipline referral. I don't know what Michelle was thinking, but she put up with me. That year, Mr. Chetard, the vice principal, had my home number on speed dial. And even though I was always in trouble, Michelle decided to take my brother and me to Disneyland for the first time. We had never been there before because in a childhood like ours, you don't even daydream about going someplace like that. Michelle and Rick (my foster dad) paid for the whole thing out of their own pockets.

Josh's openness encouraged others to share honestly. His essay provided the break that moved us from an English class to a safe place where we could talk about real problems and real issues. But his piece also demonstrated how to use vignettes to build an essay.

No doubt, there will be more Katrinas, more injustice, more opportunities for us to drop our curriculum and read the news. But as we do that, I hope we couple those critical readings with lessons that celebrate the unlikely heroes in our students' lives and allow students time to practice working together and constructing a community. ∎

Profile Essay Criteria

____ **1. Thesis Statement:** Stated or implied. Write it in the space below.

____ **2. Introduction:** What kind of introduction did you use?
Question
Quote
Anecdote (story)
Metaphor
Description

____ **3. Evidence:** Tell the reader about your ancestor.
Anecdotes (stories that prove your point)
Descriptions: Physical appearance, habits, struggles, history
Reflection

____ **4. Conclusion:** What kind of conclusion did you use?
Summary
Circle back to the beginning
Reflection

____ **5. Tight Writing:**
Active verbs
Lean language
Metaphorical language
Sentence variety

____ **6. Grammar, punctuation, spelling checked and corrected.**

On the back of this page, describe what you need to do to revise this essay.

Help: A Tribute to Michelle McAllister

by Josh Langworthy

"How was your day?" is the question I hear on a daily basis when I come home from school. The person who says this is my foster mom, Michelle McAllister. I've known her for coming up on three years. I've lived with her the whole time. Michelle has helped me tremendously in such a short period of time.

Michelle used to work at Department of Human Services as a systems manager. Her job was to make sure that the caseworkers were getting what they needed to help the foster kids on their case loads. Then she wrote the contracts to get the appropriate funding for the needed services. One day she was going over a case that spoke out to her. She decided to ask the caseworker about the two boys that the case belonged to. Those two boys just so happened to be my brother and me. After a few hours of convincing, my caseworker managed to get Michelle to open her home to my brother and me. I was very happy to be moving anywhere because we were living in a hellhole at the time.

I moved into Michelle's house in 8th grade. I had only been living there for a month or so when the school I was attending finally got tired of my attitude and was going to expel me. They called my mom (Michelle), and she came to the school and talked to the principal. Since I lived out of the district, my mom (Michelle) convinced the principal to transfer me to a school in my neighborhood, so that I didn't have to go to an alternative school and got to stay at a regular school.

I transferred school districts and started to adjust to the new school. Even though I met a lot of new people, I still spent a lot of my weekends at home. Michelle decided to go and buy my brother and me brand new bikes. This was a big shock to me because for my whole life no one had just bought me something because they wanted to. The bike made it easier for me to do things with my newfound friends and some of the old ones. Over time, I put that bike to good use. I rode it everywhere and popped way too many tires to count.

Freshman year was one heck of a year. Almost every day I got a new discipline referral. I don't know what Michelle was thinking, but she put up with me. That year, Mr. Chetard, the vice principal, had my home phone number on speed dial. And even though I was always in trouble, Michelle decided to take my brother and me to Disneyland for the first time. We had never been there before because with a childhood like ours, you don't even daydream about going somewhere like that. Michelle and Rick, my foster dad, paid for the whole thing out of their pockets, which wasn't cheap. We stayed there for about a week and had a blast.

Michelle knew that I was really into skateboarding, so she bought my brother and me both brand new snowboards before we'd ever been up on the mountain. This was a big risk that she took but it turned out good in the long run. I am an avid snowboarder although I have only been snowboarding for a year or so. She has driven my brother and me up to Mt. Hood so many times, so that we could snowboard. This year she is going to try to get my caseworker to pay for me to get on the snowboard team, and if the state doesn't cover all of the costs, she said that she and Rick will cover the difference.

Michelle helped me turn my life around. I don't think that she fully realizes how much she has impacted my life. If she would not have opened her house to me, I would not be graduating from high school, I would not be going to college, I would not be going to end up as a fireman. I would have ended up in jail. All I have left to say is: Thank you.

TEACHING FOR JOY AND JUSTICE
4: Literature in Context

Curtina Pittman
reads *Kindred*.

Dylan Leeman

Beyond Anthologies: Why Teacher Choice and Judgment Matter

I was sitting at an outdoor café on North Mississippi Street in Portland when I overheard a young woman talking on a cell phone about teaching high school language arts. "Part of having a set curriculum is not a bad deal in a lot of ways," she told her caller. "There's no creativity, but I don't have to make up lessons. Part of me felt guilty last year for not working as hard as the other teachers, for just taking other people's lessons and using them in my class. I know it's not great, but I don't have to think about what I'm teaching." Later, as I took my teapot back inside, I watched her perusing a huge anthology.

This teacher's comments made me sad for her and for her students because in giving over the content of her class to an anthology, she gave away her power and her creativity. My artistry as a teacher is discovering a story or a book that helps my students see themselves as capable of overcoming social barriers, or finding the poem that inspires them to write celebratory or probing poems about their lives, or creating a curriculum unit that connects them to the burning issues of the day.

I consider teaching a craft. And as a social justice teacher, I understand that my choice of stories is critical as I encourage students to imagine a more humane, democratic world in my 55-minute class periods.

I consider teaching a craft. And as a social justice teacher, I understand that my choice of stories is critical as I encourage students to imagine a more humane, democratic world in my 55-minute class periods. Stories can shape students' beliefs about how we treat each other, how we work together, how we live on our land, what's important, and what's worth working for. In her autobiography, *Unbowed*, Kenyan activist Wangari Maathai writes about how the stories told around the fire before dinner both entertained and educated children. "Because Kikuyu culture was oral, refined methods had been developed of passing knowledge to, and shaping the values of, future generations through, among other activities, stories." The need for stories that pass knowledge and shape values persists today, but too often in our society we have given over the transmission of stories to television, Hollywood movies, and textbook companies. As a result, the lessons our students are taught have more to do with consumption and individual success than with how to live a life that connects us to our community and land.

I found an analogy to these different models of teaching—one constructed by teachers and one constructed by textbook companies—when I read *The Omnivore's Dilemma*. The author, Michael Pollan, contrasts a "grass farmer" and an industrial farmer. Joel Salatin, the grass farmer, is an artist, a scientist. He studies his land and his animals. He has a fierce commitment to raising food that is in harmony with the land. He "practices complexity" by choreographing the daily movement of cows, chickens, and pigs, "each of which has been allowed to behave and eat as it evolved to....[H]e has little need for machinery, fertilizer, and, most strikingly, chemicals....This is perhaps the greatest efficiency of a farm treated as a biological system: health."

On the other hand, George Naylor grows corn on an industrial farm. He coaxes acres and acres of the hybrid number 2 field corn into high yields with "technology, machinery, chemicals, hybrid genetics, and sheer skill." As Pollan points out, "Most of the efficiencies in an industrial system are achieved through simplification: doing lots of the same thing over and over." Naylor's farming degrades the land, pollutes the water, and "depletes the federal treasury which now spends up to $5 billion a year subsidizing cheap corn." Although industrial farmers receive a subsidy check, they aren't getting rich. The real beneficiaries of industrial farming are huge corporations like Cargill and ADM who "provide the pesticide and fertilizer to the farmers; operate most of America's grain elevators; broker and ship most of the exports; perform the wet and dry milling; feed the livestock and slaughter the corn-fattened animals; distill the ethanol; and manufacture the high-fructose corn syrup....Oh, yes—and help write many of the rules that govern this whole game, for Cargill and ADM exert considerable influence over the U.S. agricultural policies....Cargill is the biggest privately held corporation in the world."

For teachers, think of the textbook and testing industry, which are now located in the hands of fewer and fewer companies. Think about the deskilling of teachers that accompanies the packaged curriculum arriving in our bookrooms. Someone else selected the pieces of literature, someone else created the writing assignments, someone else wrote the guiding questions—someone else, more interested in profit than in nurturing a critical, empowered citizenry. Where is the skill and artistry in that? Naylor's farming lacks both the artistry and the deep knowledge of Salatin's farming. As Pollan writes, "[P]lanting corn feels less like planting, or even driving, than stitching an interminable cloak, or covering a page with the same sentence over and over again."

The Texts I Choose and Why

Real teaching is like grass farming, not industrial farming. Teaching is an art and a science. It requires complexity, not simplicity. It requires deep content knowledge, as well as what Pollan calls "local knowledge"—in our case, knowledge of the students in the classroom and the community. Choreographing the growth of students as readers, writers, and thinkers is every bit as complicated as farming in harmony with the land. "Grass farming with skill involves so many variables, and so much local knowledge, that it is difficult to systematize. As faithful to the logic of biology as a carefully grazed pasture is, it meshes poorly with the logic of industry, which has no use for anything that it cannot bend to its wheels and bottom line, and at least for the time being, it is the logic of industry that rules."

At one point, Salatin gets Pollan on the ground to really examine the grass. Reading that passage made me think of teachers, on the ground, watching students with the same kind of rapt attention. How do we systematize the teaching of literature when every student, every class, every school, every community has its own logic? How do we bend the class to fit the system? What kind of logic demands all teachers read the same story on the same day? Even when I teach the same class two periods in a row, I'm apt to change the lesson slightly.

Teaching literature involves complicated variables: Time of year, student skill level, contemporary issues, local issues, students' lives, as well as the broader goal of teaching students to read the script of their lives against the backdrop of contemporary U.S. society: war, poverty, rampant materialism, and the daily barrage of media-driven escape. I'm thinking that corporate textbook companies aren't that interested in getting my students to scrutinize the world that way.

When choosing literature, I try to pay attention to students, the conditions of their lives, and the events unfolding in the world in the same way Salatin examines his grass. I pore over student papers; I observe students as they write, read, talk, listen. I ask questions as I watch them in class: Why does Alex sit for so long before writing? Is he thinking or is he stuck? Is this a pattern? Lucy's eyes aren't on the page. She's pretending to read, not reading, just turning the page every once in a while. I know her brother's in prison for sex abuse. Would she read *The Color Purple*? Would it help her with what's happening at home?

It's a foolish culture that entrusts the education of its children to corporate textbooks that teach students the same way that industrial farmers plant corn.

Hurricane Katrina is devastating New Orleans: How do I bring that story to class, to get students to read the race and class issues that are unfolding on the nightly news? Who is rescued? Who is turned away? What about the war? What piece of literature will arm them with the right questions when a military recruiter approaches them in the hallway? How can I give them enough background knowledge to ask questions about the president's latest speech? I analyze contemporary local, national, and world issues students need to understand in order to develop as real citizens of the world, who know more than how to read and write, who also know how to analyze and talk back.

Joel Salatin says, "It's a foolish culture that entrusts its food supply to simpletons." And I would add, it's a foolish culture that entrusts the education of its children to corporate textbooks that teach students the same way that industrial farmers plant corn: "covering a page with the same sentence over and over again."

Rethinking the Classics, Asking "Whose Classics?"

As an English major, I was taught to bow at the feet of the masters who crafted the classics we studied. My high school English teacher told us, "Classics are the pieces of literature that have stood the test of time." I didn't question their value, their place as masterpieces, or the social

messages they imparted. I didn't ask who chose them as classics. I dissected them to find themes, symbols, tone, figurative language; we rolled passages around in our mouths, like precious pearls. In college, I read similar classics, adding the clank of each title like a champion weightlifter adds weights on a barbell.

For a number of years, I passed on the knowledge I learned in my graduate literature classes to my students. After all, older, wiser, and more well-read professors passed this knowledge on to me during literature seminars. In order to help my students become culturally literate, I chose from this esteemed lot of literature and served them like gems. I turned my class, full of struggling students, into mini-graduate literature seminars. I never asked what my students needed, what books reflected their lives, what stories or poems would connect them to the world or each other.

Don't get me wrong, some of these are great books, but I was consuming them and teaching them without raising the basic question: Why are these books classic and

Charlie Waite/GETTY IMAGES

why am I reading them and teaching them? Much later I learned to ask questions that fundamentally changed my choices: What do I want students to learn from these books? Whose classics are these? Why are these books classics? Why these authors? Who chose them? And what does the choice indicate about who counts in our society? Whose gender, race, language, and country of origin do these books reflect?

In Jimmy Santiago Baca's essay "Coming into Language," he illustrates this point poetically:

> One night my eye was caught by a familiar-looking word on the spine of a book. The title was *450 Years of Chicano History in Pictures*. On the cover were black and white photos: Padre Hidalgo exhorting Mexican peasants to revolt against the Spanish dictators; Anglo vigilantes hanging two Mexicans from a tree; a young Mexican woman with rifle and ammunition belts crisscrossing her breast; César Chávez and field workers marching for fair wages; Chicano railroad workers laying creosote ties; Chicanas laboring at machines in textile factories; Chicanas picketing and hoisting boycott signs.
>
> From the time I was seven, teachers had been punishing me for not knowing my lessons by making me stick my nose in a circle chalked on the blackboard. Ashamed of not understanding and fearful of asking questions, I dropped out of school in the ninth grade. At seventeen I still didn't know how to read, but those pictures confirmed my identity....Back at the boardinghouse, I showed the book to friends. All of us were amazed; this book told us we were alive. We, too, had defended ourselves with our fists against hostile Anglos, grasping for breath in fights with the policemen who outnumbered us. The book reflected back to us our struggle in a way that made us proud.

As a teacher of language arts, I can choose texts that tell my students that they are alive, that they matter, that teach lessons about human connections, about building a civil society. Students' rebellion—mute or vocalized—against literature that excludes them or makes them invisible is a rational decision. Even when our principals, school districts, or superintendents hand us huge anthologies, we can choose the stories and poems, or bring in podcasts or our own stories and read them in a way that honors our students and our profession.

Literature serves multiple purposes. And I use the term "literature" loosely; a better term is "text," because while I teach novels, stories, poetry, and plays, I also bring in biography, essay, nonfiction, and nonprint texts. Certainly, I want students to understand literary genres,

literary tools, but because literature is a social artifact, when I choose texts for my students to read, I choose pieces that help them peel back the layers to examine the way that people of color, gays and lesbians, or the poor are portrayed. I choose books and units that provide examples of ways that people organize for change; I find stories where characters put aside selfish interests for the greater good. I look for literature that helps us clarify our own lives and the choices we make. I select pieces that provoke us to think big thoughts, to argue about ideas that matter, to look at our lives and our choices, to help us understand why things are the way they are and to imagine how they could be different.

Conscious Choosing: Literature About the World

At one point, Joel Salatin, the grass farmer, says, "The way I produce a chicken is an extension of my worldview." Exactly. What I teach and how I teach is an extension of my belief about the capacity of humans to grow and change, my understanding that while students might enter my classroom without skills, they don't enter my classroom without knowledge or talent or potential. Although we live in a world scarred by racism and imperialism, where the "[n]ormalization of the unthinkable comes easily when money, status, power, and jobs are at stake," as Edward S. Herman wrote in his article "The Banality of Evil," I can create a curriculum that intentionally scrutinizes literature and history to help students see through the way race and class have worked to privilege some and marginalize others. But I also select literature that highlights the resistance of the oppressed, rather than their defeat.

We live in a time where the gap between the haves and have-nots exists not just in test scores, but in access to health care, homes free from lead, and food free from toxins. At a time when some of my students' parents must choose between paying the rent and buying food, when health insurance is a luxury, reading literature as a word search for literary terms seems indulgent at best, and an extraordinary waste of an opportunity to help students make sense of why these gaps exist and how to change them.

Sometimes that means selecting pieces of literature that help students understand the contemporary political landscape, including local struggles. While history texts can give students facts about treaties and laws, literature provides the backstory about who benefited from those agreements and who lost. Bill Bigelow and I chose Portland-based writer Craig Lesley's novels *Winterkill*

Native Americans fishing for salmon at Celilo Falls on the Columbia River, 1941.

and later *River Song* when we team-taught Literature and U.S. History. Both of these books are set on the Columbia River and use local history to tell how the building of the Dalles Dam "drowned" Celilo Falls, an ancient salmon fishing spot on the Columbia River; they also describe the contemporary fight for native fishing rights, which continues today. The novels evoke the broken treaties, the displacement of Native Americans, and the theft of their land and resources. Lesley's novels also wrestle with the fractured relationship between a father and son. Both *Winterkill* and *River Song* show how the loss of land and tradition devastated the River People and how that historic loss continues to wreak havoc in the present.

Our teaching intersected with the trial of David Sohappy, a Yakama spiritual leader, who was sentenced to a five-year prison term for selling 317 salmon out of season. Sohappy defended his ancestral right to fish according to the 1855 treaty with Indian nations, which guaranteed the Columbia River tribes the right to fish at "all usual and accustomed places." We paired Lesley's historical fiction with the powerful poetry of Elizabeth Woody and short fiction of Ed Edmo, both local Native American authors. Because this story takes place in the Portland area, we were able to bring authors as well as David Sohappy's attorney to our class.

We took students to Horsethief Lake to see the pictographs and walk in the landscape Lesley describes in this novel. Looking out over the flat water behind the Dalles Dam, we showed pictures of Native Americans dip fishing at Celilo Falls and read the passage about the day the Army Corps of Engineers "drowned" the

falls—we listened to the language of loss. On the same trip, we read the narrative on the walls of the Army Corps of Engineers visitor's center at the Dalles Dam, which spoke of the "trade offs." Bill and I had a great time with students engaging in a hunt for passive language at the museum: How do we disguise history through passive language? Bigelow wrote about our unit in "Talking Back to Columbus: Teaching for Justice and Hope" in *Rethinking Columbus*:

> The museum is a Corps of Engineers house of propaganda. Native people are portrayed as relics of a distant past, associated solely with archaeological digs. The exhibit texts' passive and muddy prose hides any human responsibility for the sabotage of river Indians' lives. The museumspeak acknowledges that changes occurred, but masks the choices preceding these changes, who made them and why. Linda and I encouraged students to take notes on the exhibits and, through poetry and essay, to write about the day.

The Celilo Falls/Dalles Dam unit—including novels, poetry, articles, and court cases—is one that I revisited for years in my teaching because it helped students see beyond setting as a "local color" aspect of literature. Again, the choice is critical. In order to understand the current fight over water for irrigation, native salmon rights, and the breaching of dams, students need to understand the history of the land and people where they live. The literature I teach should feature folks like David Sohappy, who fought for his rights and the rights of his grandchildren to live on their ancestral land. Students need to read the treaty, to learn that Native American history didn't end with some battle on the plains; it is a continuing story.

Reading for Hope, Courage, and Transformation

When I choose books or other texts for students, I also try to connect students to historical and fictional characters who work for justice, who see themselves as activists, who become "warriors" because of their circumstances, or who "awaken" to social issues. I want students to feel hopeful about tackling tough issues, to know that others who came before them saw problems and rolled up their sleeves to work on them. I want to counter the consumer-driven images that portray the American dream as mansions and luxury cars with images of the joy and satisfaction that come with working with other people on issues that matter.

Melba Pattillo Beals' memoir, *Warriors Don't Cry,* helps students see the desegregation movement from the perspective of a person their age. The story of the Little Rock Nine is an epic tale of high school students who put their lives on the line when they challenged the segregated and unequal education system in Arkansas and ultimately the United States. Beals' story details how young people struggled to gain access to education, but through her story—and the role play I developed around the *Brown v. Board* case—students also understand that all members of the African American community paid a price through loss of jobs, violence, or threats on their lives and security. I set *Warriors Don't Cry* in an education unit within the context of the larger Civil Rights Movement, including an emphasis on the development of Citizenship Schools, Freedom Schools, and the local struggles to desegregate and work for equity in Portland Public Schools. (See p. 169.)

Ultimately, I want students to understand what Roy DeBerry wrote about his work with the Student Nonviolent Coordinating Committee (SNCC):

> The movement shaped me in a way that I wouldn't have been shaped otherwise. I look at some of my classmates that went through school the same time I did. While some of them may have made it materially and have "good jobs," making fairly decent salaries or in their own business, I get a sense, when I sit around and talk to them, that there's a space there. There's a void, a kind of emptiness.... Other experience was important, but not equivalent to the movement that I was engaged in from '62 through '65. It's almost as if everything else is a footnote. There was a sense of mission, a

sense of correctness, a sense of change. Not only were we transforming ourselves and our lives, but we were also transforming the lives of our parents.... It's because of those changes. It's because of the risks people took.

DeBerry's voice is one of many in Ellen Levine's *Freedom's Children,* a collection of first-person stories by young activists who participated in the Civil Rights Movement. Like Beals and DeBerry, these students describe that feeling of joy, and lifelong commitment to justice, that came from participating in the movement. Their voices provide the kind of mythic stories I want students to carry with them from my class.

Overcoming Difficult Situations in Our Lives: *The Color Purple* and *Deadly Unna*

As a reader, I know that literature helped me locate characters who faced and overcame the circumstances I confronted. Their struggles helped me find a way out of my difficult times. I can still remember the day I found *The Color Purple.* I read all night. I wept. Although my circumstances were not as severe as Celie's, I had lived with an alcoholic father and an abusive husband. The dinner scene where Celie stands up to Mister is one of the all-time great scenes in literature: "I'm poor, black, I might even be ugly, but dear God, I'm here. I'm here."

So when I select texts, I also look for pieces of literature that "speak" to students about overcoming difficult situations. I look for characters who have grappled with

Linda Christensen

Katie Chickadonz reading in class.

loss, divorce, poverty, who have struggled with their conscience. Not all students have suffered the same conditions, so while some students find comfort in characters whose circumstances resonate with them, other students might read to develop empathy. For example, in *Deadly Unna,* an Australian coming-of-age novel by Phillip Gwynne, the main character is forced to choose between

When I select texts, I also look for pieces of literature that "speak" to students about overcoming difficult situations.

going along with the racist attitudes exhibited by the white community towards the indigenous community or disrupting those patterns by crossing racial barriers. He chooses to disrupt the pattern. Some students of color were stunned by the similarities between the racial oppression in Australia and the United States. Morgan, who is African American, writes about the racism in the story and how the main character tries to fight it. Joy writes about the physical abuse: "Physical abuse occurs in many families, and it is not contained by continents. Blacky in the novel *Deadly Unna,* by Phillip Gwynne, was abused by his father. He is a lot like my friend, 'Rose,' whose father hits her when he drinks. She doesn't have a good relationship with her father and neither does Blacky."

Taking Back Our Classrooms

The young teacher at the outdoor café on North Mississippi Street is a victim of our current education system that brings in anthologies and experts, and "inservices" her in a large room with other teachers, where she dutifully takes notes while the textbook representative talks about how "easy" this new book is to use, how much time it will save her. They've done all of the work: selected the literature, searched for the stories and poems, written the questions and essay assignments. It must be hard for her to imagine how teaching could be different, how it could be joyful. She doesn't understand how that work, like Joel Salatin's study of his land, is what teaching is about.

Although she teaches in another school district, I picture her standing in my old room at Jefferson High School, looking out at Mt. Hood and wondering what she's going to teach tomorrow. I imagine that Andy Kulak, Anne Novinger, Gloria Canson, Russ Peterson, Pam Hooten, Danica Fierman, Theresa Quinn, Dianne Leahy—past and present language arts teachers at Jefferson—file into her room and start talking about Michael Eric Dyson's essay on Ebonics in his latest book or the just-right vignette about poverty from Sherman Alexie's book *The Absolutely True Diary of a Part-Time Indian.* I see her becoming part of a creative community, building curriculum together. And her classes are electric because they are learning about something that matters. ■

Elizabeth Eckford was turned away from Little Rock's Central High School by National Guardsmen under orders from Gov. Orval Faubus.

Francis Miller/GETTY IMAGES

Warriors Don't Cry: Connecting History, Literature, and Our Lives

In her memoir, *Warriors Don't Cry,* Melba Pattillo Beals walks students into the events of Central High School and makes them feel the sting of physical and emotional abuse the Little Rock Nine suffered as they lived the history of the *Brown v. Board of Education* decision. Beals' book tells the story of young people who became accidental heroes when their lives intersected a movement for justice in education, and they made the choice to join the movement instead of taking an easier path.

Because the book is written about Melba's high school experience, it hits close to home for students. They wonder how she kept going. And while they admire Grandma India, they think it's unfair when Melba isn't allowed to attend the school's wrestling matches. They feel Melba's pain when her friends don't attend her birthday party and they applaud Minniejean for dumping chili on the boy who harassed her. They discuss the horrors that the students faced—the mobs, the daily acts of violence—and wonder how the Little Rock Nine persevered. These conversations open the door for us to talk about how Melba and her family see her actions as a part of a collective struggle for African Americans, not just an act for Melba's self-improvement. Through the story of the Little Rock Nine, students can see that at points in history, people have the power to reshape the course of events.

Through the story of the Little Rock Nine, students can see that at most points in history, people have the power to reshape the course of events.

Beals' memoir also underscores how hard African Americans have worked to get an "equal" education in this country, how much they have sacrificed— including their lives—for the right to learn. *Warriors Don't Cry* is a home-run book with students: They not only read it, they get passionate about it. In Portland, students read *Warriors* in many untracked 9th-grade academies that integrate language arts, social studies, and science classes. I taught this memoir in the junior year when I taught a combined Literature and U.S. History class. In fact, the book can be taught from 5th grade on up.

Overview of the Unit

I start with a role play to give students background knowledge of the historical context of segregation and the struggle for civil rights. After the role play, students write a "Writing for Justice" narrative about an incident from their lives. (See p. 85.) Then students engage in a literary tea party as they meet key players in the book. While students read, they keep a dialogue journal where they keep track of their insights and questions. They also identify targets and perpetrators of injustice as well as allies and bystanders. During the unit, students write an essay, poetry, and interior monologues. They draw literary postcards, engage in improvisations, and create character silhouettes to collect evidence for their essay. I interlace footage from the videos *Eyes on the Prize* and *Standing on My Sisters' Shoulders* so students can see and hear events described in the memoir. The videos and other texts from the time period help students understand that the story of the Little Rock Nine was part of a larger movement to reshape U.S. society. The book also provides a jumping-off point for a study of schooling—including personal connections, and local and national education struggles for education.

A Historical Framework

Instead of leaping into Beals' memoir as an unproblematic celebration of *Brown*, I give students a sense of the discussions that might have happened over dinner tables, in barbershops, or at church socials as Little Rock community members argued about integrating Central High School. I wrote a role play to make sure that even before starting the book, students could understand how different groups in the city might have responded to integration. I opened the role play with the question: Should Central High School be integrated? To be honest, as a literature major, I was appallingly ignorant about much of U.S. history. However, my lack of knowledge helped me understand the gaps in historical information that students might have. For example, I didn't know that some African Americans did not want to integrate schools for a variety of reasons, including a fundamental distrust in a government that had

George E. C. Hayes, Thurgood Marshall, and James Nabrit Jr., who argued the case against school segregation, stand in front of the U.S. Supreme Court Building.

never taken their well-being into account. I didn't really know the history of the struggle. I knew the big stuff. I had a basic understanding of the Supreme Court decision and Thurgood Marshall's role, and I had the visual images of one of the Nine, Elizabeth Eckford, hounded by the mob; but to teach this book effectively, I needed details. I read, I researched, and I wrote the roles.

The year is 1957. In the role play I play the Little Rock School Board, and I invite five groups, who hold a variety of opinions on integration, to a meeting to make suggestions about how to proceed with desegregating Little Rock's schools following the *Brown* decision. Each group has an opportunity to persuade the school board— me—to agree with their resolution and to question their opponents.

After informing students of their responsibilities, I divide them into the five groups: Families of the Little Rock Nine, African Americans Opposing Integration, Governor Orval Faubus, Local Business Owners, and the NAACP. Then I give students a menu of resolutions to present to the school board—or the choice to create their own:

- Central High School should be immediately opened up for any African American who wants to attend.

- A handful of African American honors students may attend Central High School as a test case to determine whether or not integration will work.

- Instead of integrating Central High School, the state should increase funding for a segregated black school, so that "separate but equal" means just that.

- Arkansas should create a voluntary integration program for white and black students at a neutral site—a new school that would iron out the problems and create a map for future integration.

- There should be no integration. Central High School should remain segregated and black-only Paul Lawrence Dunbar High School should also remain segregated.

After discussing the resolutions, students read their roles and discover information about their group's position that they share with the rest of the class later during presentations and deal-making. For example, the Families of the Little Rock Nine role helps students understand the huge sacrifices these students and their families made because they dreamed for a better future:

> You understand that the segregation laws that keep blacks and whites separate and unequal must be broken. You and your children know that they are the intellectual equals to white students who attend the school. There is no reason except racism for black students to attend poorly funded schools. It may be rough going for a while, but nothing in life comes easy. In the long run, your families' sacrifices will benefit all African Americans and the country as a whole. (See the full roles on pp. 180-185.)

The roles also alert students to the social issues and pressures at work in Little Rock. The African Americans Opposing Integration role raises issues of funding and violence, but also questions whether white teachers at Central will care about black students:

> You aren't sure that putting your children in a school with white children is going to make them better educated. Dunbar Senior High School is the only high school for blacks in Little Rock. Students come from throughout the state to attend Dunbar in order to get what many consider the best education. Dunbar is known for its remarkable student body and faculty. You know these teachers have your children's best interests at heart. You worry that if integration is successful, it will ultimately lead to the defunding of Dunbar High School because white students will not transfer to black schools. As enrollment decreases, outstanding black teachers may lose their jobs. They will most likely not be hired at Central High School.

Interior Monologues

After students read over their roles, they write interior monologues—the thoughts and feelings from their characters' points of view. I use interior monologues throughout my units as a way for students to develop an understanding and appreciation for how a literary or historical character might feel at a critical point in a novel or historical event. I've discovered that writing helps students get into the heads of historical characters, to imagine the hopes and fears behind the choices that people confronted. Students use information from their role as they write their interior monologue. For example, an African American parent who opposes integration might discuss her fears for her child's safety in an integrated school, but also write about her despair over Jim Crow laws. I usually give a few models to students so they can see how someone else approached this writing task.

For this particular interior monologue, I encourage students to create identities—name themselves, name their children. The more they inhabit the role, the more effectively they will be able to participate in the role play from their group's standpoint. A small business owner, for example, might name the business and tell a little about it, but also discuss their perspective on the question of integration and back it up with information from their role. To get students started, I say, "Read over your role. Think about how your group will address the question: Should Central High School be integrated? Give yourself a name. Name your children. Using ideas from your role, write your character's thoughts and feelings about integrating Central High School. Write as if you are this person thinking about the question. Use the word 'I.'"

After writing for 10 to 15 minutes, students share their monologues with their group members. This helps clarify their understanding of their groups' concerns as well as their positions. Alisha, a student in Sandra Childs' class at Franklin High School in Portland, wrote in part:

> My name is Cyd. I'm 32. I'm a single mother and I own a bookstore. I have two kids, Robert and Ann. They both go to Dunbar Senior High School. I want my children to get the best education they can. I know and trust that my kids will get what they deserve. Integration will only cause trouble. Things will get violent, I know, I've heard white kids talk. I've heard what they say. I don't want my kids to get shot. I believe that everything should stay the way it is because nothing good will come of this.

After sharing their writing, the group reads over the menu of resolutions and decides which resolution best represents their feelings about integration. At this point, the group either chooses one of the resolutions or creates a resolution to present to the school board. I tell them, "After you decide on your resolution, think about your arguments. Go back to your roles and interior monologues and list your reasons. Everyone in the group needs the list of arguments because you will all need to be able to explain your position." Then they are ready to meet the other groups—to find allies and to uncover their opponents' arguments on the topic.

Alliance-Building

Prior to the actual role play, students engage in an alliance-building session. This activity helps them find others who support their position. I tell them, "Choose half your group as 'travelers' who will move to the four other groups and attempt to find allies—people who support your point of view. The more allies you have when you go before the school board, the better chance you have of determining the decision on integrating Central High. You may have to slightly change your resolution to win allies, but you don't want to change so much that you are no longer consistent with your group's perspective. Half of your group will 'stay at home' and receive visitors and share your perspective and attempt to gain allies as well."

This session often whips students up. They might be ho-hum about the assignment until this point. They gain clarity about their position as they argue with other groups. As students try to persuade others to support their resolution, they hone their arguments, compromise with their allies, and sniff out their opponents' perspectives. While students roam the room or entertain guests, I listen in on the groups. If a group member or a group strays too far from their role's position, like Gov. Faubus immediately opening all Little Rock high schools to blacks, I may intervene. I also stir the pot by pointing out their differences.

After students reconvene in their small groups, they write up a "statement" to be delivered at the school board meeting about their position on integrating Central High School. In this statement they must identify their group, state their resolution, and use solid reasons to convince the school board to support their position. I encourage them to return to their roles and their interior monologues as they build their arguments.

"Everyone in your group needs to contribute to this statement, and everyone needs to have a copy because you are all responsible for speaking at some point during the meeting. You might choose one or two group members to give your statement and then choose one or two group members to answer questions or cross-examine other groups." I award points to each speaker: If every member of the group speaks, then each group member earns double credit. This encourages the loquacious to give up some airtime to their shy or reluctant classmates.

The Role Play

The students and I arrange the room in a circle. Each group sits together with a placard displaying its name— Little Rock Nine, NAACP, etc. I pound the gavel (or stapler) to open the Little Rock School Board meeting; I announce the order in which I will hear their testimony; I pair pro and con in my speaking list to encourage spirited debate—for example, Business Owners and NAACP. Before beginning my role as School Board Chair, I tell students, "Take notes during each group's testimony, so you can ask questions and point out flaws in your opponents' logic or information. Think about what information you have that will counter their arguments." If students aren't pointing out problems with each other's resolutions, I will ask a question or two to model the process. For example, I might ask the parents supporting integration, "Aren't you worried about what will happen to your children when those doors close? Have you seen what happened when Autherine Lucy, an African American student, was admitted to the University of Alabama? White students and residents rioted. You put all of our lives in danger."

After each group has had an opportunity to share their statement and argue, I cut off the arguments. I learned over the years to stop while they are still passionate instead of waiting until they are tired of the question.

After the Role Play

At the end of the role play, I ask students to lay their group role aside and write about what they think happened in real life. How do they know? Typically, students write that those who supported integration won because students from diverse racial backgrounds go to school together.

Then we discuss which resolution they think should have been made at the time. Students rarely choose the historically "accurate" resolution; their history and perspectives play into their decisions. Typically, at Jefferson, a predominantly black school, students believe that Central High School should be opened up immediately for any African American. Theresa Quinn and Heidi Tolentino,

Integrating Central High
School, Little Rock, Arkansas.

two 9th-grade language arts teachers, use this role play at a predominantly white school across town, where students usually decide that a neutral site should be chosen for voluntary integration.

As students grapple with the issues of segregation, integration, and injustice, argue with their classmates, and give impassioned speeches to convince me, as the head of the school board, of their position, they also learn some key background knowledge that helps them better understand Melba Pattillo Beals' story. Perhaps more importantly, they see that there was nothing inevitable about integration.

For example, after participating in the role play, when students begin reading *Warriors Don't Cry*, they understand why Melba's family is angry that she signed up to integrate Central without telling them. The African Americans Opposed to Integration group talks about the threat of violence that will be aimed at the entire community over integration. They've witnessed the violence aimed at blacks in other states who attempted to integrate buses and lunch counters. So students understand Melba's family's reaction when she writes in *Warriors Don't Cry*:

> We all stood like statues as the newsman talked about Little Rock's segregationists, who were determined to stop our children from entering white schools at any cost.... By then Mother was pale, her lips drawn tight as she glared at me. All of them circled around me. With horrified expressions they looked at me as though I had lied or sassed Grandma.... When had I planned on telling them? Why did I sign my name to the paper saying I lived near Central and wanted to go, without

asking their permission? Did I consider that my decision might endanger our family?

Throughout the book, Melba shows readers both the economic hardship and the violence wreaked on the black community because of the Supreme Court decision. By the time we finish the role play, most students are beginning to understand that the narrative behind the still photos of historic moments are filled with complicated choices and heroic actions of ordinary people who worked together to bring about change.

Writing for Justice Narrative

As students read *Warriors Don't Cry*, they examine the methods used by civil rights groups to crack school segregation. While this is Melba's story, it is also the story of an alliance of groups that came together over decades to end the apartheid conditions of blacks in the United States. Because I want students to understand how people working together can create change, I ask them to write a narrative about a time when they acted as an ally, perpetrator, target, or bystander. (See "Writing for Justice," p. 85.) Writing the narrative before reading Melba's story roots the terminology and themes in their own lives first, so they can more readily identify those roles during their reading.

The Tea Party: Discovering Characters and Themes

In this tea party, students become one of five characters in the book: Melba Pattillo Beals, one of the Little Rock Nine; Daisy Bates, a member of the Little Rock

173

NAACP; Grandma India, Melba's maternal, gun-toting, Bible-quoting grandma; Danny, a soldier in the 101st Airborne; or Link, a white senior at Central High School. Each role gives students information about the character's relationship to Melba, and hints at larger issues in the book—from President Eisenhower sending in troops to the NAACP organizing to help the students.

After students read their roles, I say, "Underline key facts about your character. The key facts are: Who are you? What is your relationship to Melba? What is your perspective on integration? Also, underline any interesting fact or piece of information you think others might want to know. After you have underlined, turn your card over and list those key facts. Doing both of these activities will help you remember your role, but also, if you forget, you can look down and see those facts."

Grandma India's role, for example, gives students a sense of her feistiness as well as her connection to Melba and her ideas about integration:

> You are going to love me. I am a tough love kind of Grandma. You might find me sitting in a rocking chair, but instead of knitting and crocheting, I'll have my rifle on my lap. My grandbaby Melba is integrating that high school to make things better for African Americans, but as Frederick Douglass said, "Freedom does not come without a struggle." No one is going to make this easy. So I've got my gun ready in case anyone plans on troubling us. I am highly religious, but I am highly practical as well. Don't mess with my grandbaby.

Students note that she's Melba's grandmother, that she understands the need to sacrifice for the greater good of her people, and they love that she's got her gun on her lap as she sits in her rocking chair.

Prior to the tea party, I demonstrate how to "become the character." As students begin the tea party, I tell them, "Your goal is to meet four other characters from the autobiography. Find out as much as you can about each character and write down this character's relationship to Melba, their perspective on integration, and other details. Do not read each other's cards. You must introduce yourselves. Talk. You can't sit down and yell for other characters to come to you. You can't just hand your card to someone else and say, 'Here, read this.' You must mingle. This is a 'get up and move around' activity." Once students have introduced themselves two or three times to their classmates, they are comfortable presenting the information about their character. They don't need to look at the card anymore.

The Little Rock Nine pose in Daisy Bates' living room, 1957. From top left, Jefferson Thomas, Melba Pattillo, Terrance Roberts, Carlotta Walls, Daisy Bates, Ernest Green, and from left bottom, Thelma Mothershed, Minniejean Brown, Elizabeth Eckford, and Gloria Ray.

After students have met the four other characters, I ask them to write down three questions and three predictions they have about the book. I also ask them to draw a diagram or picture that explains the relationship of the characters. "This is important work," I tell them, "because your mind is making connections now that will help you as you read. Figure out how these characters are related now to avoid confusion later. Also, good readers automatically begin asking questions and making predictions as they read. These are reading habits that keep you engaged as you read."

Students' questions have included: Will Grandma shoot someone? Will Melba get hurt when she goes to school? Their predictions often follow typical romance novels: Melba will fall in love with a white boy and get married. But others are more serious: Someone will get hurt or die before the end of the book. Melba's mother will lose her job. I often write these on the blackboard or overhead so we can return to them as we read the book.

Although it may seem redundant to use both a role play and a tea party prior to reading this book, these activities cover different territory. The role play provides historical background. The tea party introduces characters in the book.

Warriors' Dialogue Journal: Allies, Perpetrators, Targets, and Bystanders

Warriors Don't Cry provides students with role models of ordinary people who became extraordinary when they chose to act against the injustice they experienced. Before students read the book, I remind students of the terms they encountered in the Writing for Justice narrative: Ally, perpetrator, target and bystander. (See p. 86 for definitions.) I tell students, "These roles aren't static. As a result of personal relationships and education, people who are perpetrators can become allies. Think about your own lives. There might have been times when you stood by and watched something happen, then you made a decision to act. In this book, I want you to keep track of Melba's allies and perpetrators, but I also want you to watch for those times when people changed roles. What happened that allowed them to act? What changed for them?"

I use students' dialogue journal notes and questions about allies, perpetrators, targets and bystanders as discussion prompts. At the beginning of the period, students share their questions and notes in small groups. I ask each group to write a question on the board. Students wrote: Was Link really an ally? He helped Melba to safety, but he never renounced his friends' activities. When Minniejean wanted to sing, were the rest of the Little Rock Nine allies to her? Who in the community helped Melba's mother when her job was threatened? And what about the teachers in the school? Who made the classroom safe? Who didn't? What strategies could the community have used to help the Little Rock Nine?

Over the years, students have noted different forms of allies—from the NAACP leaders who fought for integration through the courts; to Grace Lorch, who led Elizabeth Eckford to safety on the first day of integration; to Melba's white classmate, Link, who called each night to let her know which halls to avoid, and who helped her escape torture on numerous occasions. (See p. 202 for a dialogue journal model.)

Strategies for Deepening Conversation and Bringing Students Back to Class

I don't give reading quizzes or tests. If I engage students daily in the content of the book by taking them back to the text through drawings, photographs, improvisations, discussions, and poetry, I keep students mentally and physically engaged in the class. As we read a book, I try to vary the work, both to keep students interested and also to make the work more academically rigorous. Some days, students meet in small groups of four or five students to share their dialogue journals and engage in a discussion. Groups select a quote and a question for the class to discuss, and these become the jumping-off point for our day's discussion.

Over the years, I designed strategies to immerse students more thoroughly in our readings. I discovered that these also catch up stragglers who have come back to class after absences or students who have entered class midway through a unit. If we think of a unit as a journey, then we're stopping at cafés, reading historical plaques in rest areas, and walking by the ocean as we move forward. We pause throughout to debate, draw, make connections, write, talk, and listen as we examine texts more closely. These activities aren't make-work designed to keep students busy; they fulfill vital functions. As students replay

Through engagement in these activities, I want students to find places that ignite their passion for learning while I bring students who have fallen behind back into the class.

key scenes during an improvisation or sketch a metaphorical drawing, they rehearse arguments for their essays, develop stronger reading skills, and explore tough issues that affect their lives. Through engagement in these learning activities, I want students to find places that ignite their passion for learning while I bring students who have fallen behind back into the class.

Improvisations: Returning to Key Scenes

Improvisations are short scenes that students act out. Sometimes these are straight from the book we're reading, and students act out the scene, so we can discuss the characters' actions or think about alternative decisions characters could have made. I also use them to put students in the shoes of historical or literary characters who had to make tough choices. I use them to provoke discussions about the tender, tense places where interesting issues erupt.

After arguing whether Melba was right to sign up to integrate Central High School without her parents' consent, students who have disengaged from the unit or reading can get hooked back into the book. Improvisations provide an opportunity to catch up because students need to reread key sections and talk with classmates about the text. Students also see chunks of the book acted out, so they get the gist of what they've missed. And, in complete

Thurgood Marshall and civil rights activist Daisy Bates with several of the Little Rock Nine, 1958.

honesty, for struggling readers, they don't have to reread the entire text in order to be pulled back into the class.

About halfway through *Warriors*, I say, "Write down what you believe are the five pivotal scenes from the memoir so far—times when people made key decisions, when people were confronted with tough choices." As students share their lists, I write them on the board and add ones that I think are important. Even creating the lists produces interesting discussion as students explain or defend their choices. I divide the class into groups and assign each group a scene to act out.

I tell the class, "First, reread the section you will act out. Read it aloud or to yourselves and then discuss it. After you read, figure out how you will act out the scene and designate which character each of your group members will play." Because I've taught teenagers long enough to know almost every way they can undermine my lesson through adolescent silliness, I also say, "If you don't take this seriously, you will have to redo the scene." The more fully I articulate my expectations, the more seriously my students take the assignment.

As students rehearse the scenes in the classroom and in the hallway, I rearrange the desks so there is room for an acting space. I also move from group to group, listening in on their conversations, prodding them when needed, helping them get in character, reminding them that they are not reading from the book, they are acting out the scene. They needn't memorize the exact language from the text—it's an improvisation, not a scripted play.

When it's show time, I say, "Introduce the scene. Give us a brief overview and tell us which character each of you is playing." Because I am shy and I know how hard it can be to get up in front of their peers, I also tell students, "This can be awkward. It's hard to see our classmates acting in an unfamiliar role. We might be tempted to laugh at the incongruity, but we don't laugh at people attempting to work, nor do we laugh at the painful scenes humans have had to endure." To encourage thoughtful participation, I ask students to take notes on each scene. "Listen for the lines you love. Sometimes in the moments of these unrehearsed scenes, your classmates deliver incredible lines. Write them down. You will write an interior monologue from one of the characters' points of view, so steal some lines along the way. You will also ask questions about character motivation and actions. Take notes so you will be prepared."

After each improvisation, I ask students to stay "on stage" and in character, so the rest of the class and I can ask them questions. For example, we might ask Danny, the soldier from the 101st Airborne, how he felt when he saw Melba attacked during the assembly. Or we might ask Grandma India why she wanted Melba to stay at Central High School when the threats to their lives escalated.

Improvisations prompt students to reread the text for nuanced understanding. They discuss contentious issues—Should the Little Rock Nine have stayed at Central or returned to Dunbar High School?—and argue them from multiple perspectives. As students probe these charged situations through questions, they move into more complex understandings of the material. The arguments and discussions prompted by these skits help students become better readers, better thinkers, as well as inform their essays at the end of the unit. But they also bring back into class the students who have strayed or fallen behind.

Literary Postcards

Cynthia MacLeod, my daughter Anna's 5th-grade teacher and co-director of the Portland Writing Project for many years, introduced me to literary postcards. In this activity, students draw postcards of significant scenes from the book and then write poetry, letters, messages from one character to another, interior monologues, or diary entries explaining what's happening in their lives at that moment.

Together the class brainstorms significant events out of the chapters we've read up to that point in the same way we do with the improvisations. I list the scenes on the board while students find the page numbers. For example, students listed the day Melba burned her books in the backyard, Grandma India sitting in her rocker with her embroidery and her gun after Melba received threatening phone calls, Minnijean dumping chili on the boy's head in the cafeteria, Melba waiting for her friends to come to her birthday party.

Most students enjoy a day of crayons and drawing, and a quiet descends on the class as they search their books or draw. However, some students feel challenged by their drawing talent. I tell them, "I am not worried about your artistic ability. I want you to draw the scene in any way that is comfortable for you. You can draw stick figures. You can use colors to express the tone. Don't get hung up on the artwork. However, I would like you to write the line or passage that inspired your drawing."

Once students draw the picture on the front of the card, I give them choices about what to write on the back. I say, "You can choose what you want to write on the back. You can write a letter from one character to another expressing their thoughts or feelings at that moment or describing where they are and what's happening. Melba keeps a diary, so you can write a diary entry from Melba's voice. I don't want a recitation of events. I want you to write from the character's feelings rather than just tell what's happening. You might choose to write a poem from the character's point of view or an interior monologue that helps show us what the character is thinking or feeling about this situation."

Again, the pause to go deeper into the book, to slow it down, benefits both students who rip through novels as well as the ones who struggle to find their way in. Sharing the postcards and letters or poems also opens up opportunities for discussions about our different understandings and interpretations of big moments in the book.

Character Silhouette

The character silhouette is a playful, joyful activity for most students. Students spread across the floor of the classroom and into the hallway, tracing a classmate's body on big rolls of paper, searching for quotes and page numbers, and arguing about a character's influences as they work on their silhouette. Like the improvisation and literary postcard, this activity takes students back to the text and provides time for them to talk about the book or unit with a small group of students. I assign this activity about two thirds of the way through a novel or play; then we come back to the posters again at the end of the book.

I begin by asking students to name the book's main characters. In *Warriors*, students name Melba, Grandma India,

Link, and Danny. Sometimes students include Melba's mother. In most classes, I need seven or eight groups because ideally each group has four students. I let students choose their groups. If no group chooses to work on a character, I don't fuss about it. I might end up with four groups creating silhouettes for Melba and four for Link, their favorite characters. The point isn't coverage, it's pushing students to have more in-depth conversations about the character.

Each group spreads a body-sized sheet of construction paper on the floor and outlines the body of one of their classmates. I remind students to take their dialogue journals to the work group, so they can more easily locate their

The pause to go deeper into the book, to slow it down, benefits both students who rip through novels as well as the ones who struggle to find their way in.

notes as well as find the page numbers and references as they work. On the inside of the body, they list the character's traits and goals, then they find quotes or actions that illustrate those traits. They note the page numbers next to the quote. On the outside of the body, they write key influences on the character, including laws, historical events, and race and/or class restrictions that shaped this person. For example, with Melba, students would write *Brown v. Board* as an outside influence because this Supreme Court decision plays a key role in the story. They would cite instances and quotes about the struggle for integration around the outside of Melba's silhouette. On the inside, they might put "hardworking" and "smart" as well as other character traits with passages and page numbers.

At the end of the period, each group tapes their silhouette to the classroom or hallway wall and shares highlights from their poster. The posters provide quick references for students, reminding them of page numbers or important events as we discuss the book over the course of the unit. For the struggling student, the small-group work provides a place to catch up on the book; for other students, the character silhouette creates a pause point to ruminate on a character, exchange ideas with classmates, percolate ideas for essay topics, and gather evidence.

Each of these activities serves multiple purposes. They deepen student reading and understanding of the book by constructing opportunities for students to reread the text numerous times and with a critical and historical lens. They present opportunities for students to create inter-

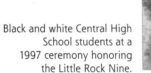

Black and white Central High School students at a 1997 ceremony honoring the Little Rock Nine.

Cynthia Johnson/GETTY IMAGES

pretations of the text—as a poem, interior monologue, improvisation, drawing. They also provide context and material for student writing. As often as possible, I try to make student work in class a "performance" instead of merely an assignment that students turn in to me, because when there is a larger audience for their work, students tend to be more engaged, and frankly, they take more time and care in their writing when they write for their peers.

Eyes on the Prize

After we've read through the third chapter, we watch the first segment of *Eyes on the Prize: Fighting Back: 1957-1962*. This segment of the documentary about the Civil Rights Movement focuses on the integration of Central High School; it prepares students to understand the background and climate that Melba and the other eight students entered. The segment opens with a preacher quoting scripture to justify segregation: "Desegregation is against the Bible." Mississippi's Sen. James Eastland states that, "All the people of the South are in favor of segregation. Supreme Court or no Supreme Court, we are going to maintain segregation down in Dixie." The documentary shows white students shouting, "Two, four, six, eight. We don't want to integrate!" in scenes of riots that occurred when Autherine Lucy was admitted to the all-white University of Alabama.

At the end of chapter three of *Warriors Don't Cry*, Melba is preparing to go to school. As the family listens to the news, they learn that Gov. Faubus has called in the Arkansas National Guard and people are gathering at the school. Melba hears on the news, "Hundreds of Little Rock citizens are gathered in front of Central High School awaiting the arrival of the Negro children. We're told people have come from as far away as Mississippi, Louisiana, and Georgia to join forces to halt integration."

As we watch *Eyes on the Prize*, Gov. Faubus' threat in the role play to bring in the National Guard to stop integration turns into visual images of the Little Rock students attempting to get past the guards. My students watch Elizabeth Eckford try to enter Central High School that first day, and see the subtle movement of the guards twitching their batons, as they follow the governor's orders to allow only white students to enter. They later read this passage from *Warriors*:

> The anger of that huge crowd was directed toward Elizabeth Eckford as she stood alone, in front of Central High, facing the long line of soldiers, with a huge crowd of white people screeching at her back. Barely five feet tall, Elizabeth cradled her books in her arms as she desperately searched for the right place to enter. Soldiers in uniforms and helmets, cradling their rifles, towered over her. Slowly she walked first to one and then another opening in their line. Each time she approached, the soldiers closed ranks, shutting her out. As she turned towards us, her eyes hidden by dark glasses, we could see how erect and proud she stood despite the fear she must have been feeling.

I call students' attention to the white woman, Grace Lorch, who rescues Elizabeth, takes her to the bus, and rides with her because she is a great example of an ally. I stop the video at this point and return to the book.

Grace and her husband, we discover in chapter four, organize tutoring sessions for the Little Rock Nine, so they can keep up on their lessons during the time they are denied entrance to Central High. We read chapters four, five, and six, where Melba discusses the struggle between Gov. Faubus and President Eisenhower over whether states have the right to refuse to obey a federal law. Then we resume watching the rest of the segment. We watch "the face of resistance" as an unruly mob attempts to get at the Little Rock Nine. We watch as the crowd goes after two African American reporters, hitting one on the head with a brick. Finally, we watch as Eisenhower calls in the 101st Airborne to protect the black students. I end the video after Gov. Faubus and other governors close down schools across the South rather than integrate—about 30 minutes into the *Eyes on the Prize* segment.

Students then write a poem or interior monologue. We brainstorm moments in the video to write from: Thurgood Marshall when he's asked about gradualism, Elizabeth Eckford when she's surrounded by the white crowd, Grace Lorch when she gets ready to board the bus, the brick that hits the black reporter, Minnijean when she dumps the chili on the head of the boy who hassled her, the African American cafeteria workers who applauded Minnijean's actions.

Writing the Essay

As I discuss in "Writing Wild Essays from Hard Ground," I don't assign specific essay topics. Students generate these along the way. When students hit on an idea during discussion, I might say, "Write that down. That would make a great essay." As we move to the end of the book, I ask students, "We've been reading *Warriors Don't Cry,* studying integration and ally behavior. What moved you? What interests you? Make a list."

After about five to 10 minutes, I begin collecting their ideas on the board: Sandra wanted to write about Grandma India's role in sustaining Melba's spirit; Travis and John were intrigued by the whites who act as allies in the book and in the *Eyes on the Prize* video; Damon wanted to look at the larger context of school integration by connecting Little Rock with the earlier case Thurgood Marshall argued in *Westminster v. Mendez*; Carl chose to examine the effects of Melba's decision to integrate on the rest of her family. In other words, students choose topics based on their interest. My only condition is that they use material in the book as part of their evidence.

Once we have a strong list of potential topics on the board, we brainstorm evidence, referring back to sections of *Warriors* as well as other videos and articles we read during the unit. When we discuss evidence, I encourage students to think about incidents from their own education. We also discuss potential audiences for the essay. Who needs to read about this period of history?

The battle to end segregation and the battle to win equal access to a rigorous and relevant public education continue today.

After the group collectively develops evidence, students return to their own topic and their dialogue journals to gather quotes and page numbers, remind themselves of scenes. On a follow-up day, I move students to topic-alike groups to share ideas and evidence. While these groups work, I pull the stragglers together and work with them on generating topics, giving them sections to reread, and making dates to show parts of the videos again.

Moving Beyond *Brown*

The battle to end segregation and the battle to win equal access to a rigorous and relevant public education continue today. As Melba Pattillo Beals writes in the introduction to a new edition of her book printed after the 50th anniversary of *Brown v. Board,* "I am grateful for this time of celebration but I don't want it to obstruct all our perceptions of the fact that there is still a lot of work to be done.... The first round of this battle was never about integration, in my opinion. It was always about access—access to opportunity, to resources, to freedom. The enemy was more visible, the battle lines drawn in plain sight.... Until I am welcomed everywhere as an equal simply because I am human, I remain a warrior on the battlefield that I must not leave. I continue to be a warrior who does not cry, but who instead takes action."

After reading *Warriors Don't Cry,* I want students to celebrate the hard work and sacrifices of Melba Pattillo Beals and the Little Rock Nine, but I also want them to understand that the battle isn't over. I end the unit with an education research project that helps students place this decision in the larger context of both the history of education as well as our current struggles for racial equality. (See "Final Project: Education Unit," p. 188.) ■

Should Central High School Be Integrated?

MENU OF RESOLUTIONS

- Central High School should be immediately opened up for any African American who wants to attend.
- A handful of African American honors students may attend Central High School as a test case to determine whether or not integration will work.
- Instead of integrating Central High School, the state should increase funding for a segregated black school, so that "separate, but equal" means just that.
- Arkansas should create a voluntary integration program for white and black students at a neutral site—a new school that would iron out the problems and create a map for future integration.
- There should be no integration. Central High School should remain segregated and black-only Paul Lawrence Dunbar High School should also remain segregated.

GROUP DIRECTIONS

Your group will attend a meeting of the School Board. The question before the Board is: Should Central High School be integrated? Your group's job is to convince the school board to agree to your resolution. You will do this in two ways—by writing convincing arguments to persuade the Board and by finding allies who support your resolution. Remember there is strength in numbers.

1. Your group may choose one of the resolutions listed above or craft one of your own. After you have a resolution, state your reasons for supporting this action. Use evidence from your role.

2. You will choose half of your group as "travelers" who will move to the four other groups and attempt to find allies—people who support your point of view. The more allies you have when you go before the School Board, the better chance you have of determining the decision on integrating Central High. You may have to slightly change your resolution to win allies, but you don't want to change so much that you are no longer consistent with your group's perspective.

3. Half of the group will "stay at home" and receive visitors and share your perspective and attempt to gain allies as well.

4. After you have determined who your allies are, your group will reconvene and write up a statement to be delivered at the school board meeting. In this statement you want to:
   - State who you are—your group's name.
   - State what you want to happen—your resolution.
   - Give solid reasons for your resolution.

You also want to determine who is going to speak and who is going to answer questions from other groups.

African American Families Opposing Integration

SHOULD CENTRAL HIGH SCHOOL BE INTEGRATED?

Let's get one thing straight: You are opposed to segregation and to the Jim Crow laws—written and unwritten—that keep African Americans from gaining true equal rights under the law.

But you aren't sure that putting your children in a school with white children is going to make them better educated. Dunbar Senior High School is the only high school for blacks in Little Rock. Students come from around the state to attend Dunbar in order to get what many consider the best education. Dunbar is known for its remarkable student body and faculty. You know these teachers have your children's best interests at heart.

You worry that if integration is successful, it will ultimately lead to the defunding of Dunbar High School because white students will not transfer to black schools. As enrollment decreases, outstanding black teachers and principals may lose their jobs. They will most likely not be hired at Central High School.

You are also concerned about the outbreak of violence that is accompanying integration throughout the South. In 1956, a young African American woman's presence on campus set off rioting at the University of Alabama and the University's authorities forced her withdrawal.

In the past, the jobs, the homes, and the lives of African Americans have been at stake when big changes have been proposed. You see the handwriting on the wall: Those who attempt to integrate are going to be the targets of segregationists. You want change, but you are unwilling to sacrifice your children.

Local Business Owners

SHOULD CENTRAL HIGH SCHOOL BE INTEGRATED?

The Supreme Court ruled during the famous court case *Brown v. Board of Education* that segregation in the public schools was unconstitutional. As they stated, "separate schools are inherently unequal." They also said that offending states must desegregate schools with "all deliberate speed."

You are worried about what the Supreme Court decision to desegregate is going to do to your business. It's fine for some judges to say that whites and blacks should go to school together, but you know how much citizens value their children's education. If Central High School is desegregated, white parents are going to take their children and their business to towns where desegregation isn't happening. Who is going to move in? Who will buy or build new homes? This just isn't smart business.

You don't get why the NAACP is picking on Little Rock when there is an outstanding black high school—Dunbar Senior High School. Is there really a need to integrate in Little Rock?

You've always gotten along with everyone in town. But you are concerned about the violence that might spring up when people are forced to do something they don't want to do.

Businesspeople value stability above all else. This is a radical, unprecedented change and there's no telling what protest and turmoil this integration could bring to Little Rock. Your businesses and communities will suffer.

Governor Orval Faubus

SHOULD CENTRAL HIGH SCHOOL BE INTEGRATED?

You are up for re-election. In the last election you beat an all-out segregationist at the polls. You've earned a reputation as a moderate. But then the Supreme Court integrated schools with *Brown v. Board of Education,* stating that "separate schools are inherently unequal." They also said that offending states must desegregate schools with "all deliberate speed."

Folks are mad. Your state was one of the targets of that court decision. The federal government is telling you and the people of your state that you cannot continue to have separate schools for white and black children.

It's true that Arkansas, including Little Rock, integrated buses, but lots of folks in your state want segregation to continue. They did not want to integrate buses, lunch counters, bathrooms, pools, or drinking fountains. But they especially do not want to integrate schools. Nor do they want the court system to tell them how to educate their children.

These folks who elected you are furious. You have a tough situation on your hands. The local NAACP (National Association for the Advancement of Colored People) is pressuring local school boards to desegregate schools with "all deliberate speed." Nine African American students plan to integrate Central High School in Little Rock.

You have said repeatedly that you will not desegregate schools.

Families of the "Little Rock Nine"

SHOULD CENTRAL HIGH SCHOOL BE INTEGRATED?

The Supreme Court ruled during the famous court case *Brown v. Board of Education* that segregation in the public schools was unconstitutional. As they stated, "separate schools are inherently unequal." They also said that offending states must desegregate schools with "all deliberate speed."

Your children have been chosen by the NAACP (National Association for the Advancement of Colored People) to integrate Central High School. In fact, they volunteered to integrate and because of their outstanding academic performance, they were the nine students accepted. All of your families are hardworking, church-going people who expect your children to earn good grades.

While you know that the African American teachers at Dunbar High School are excellent and have high expectations for your children, you also know that Central High School has the money to offer more classes and newer books. They have well-equipped science laboratories.

But more than that, you consider this an action for the recognition of equal rights for African Americans. As one student chosen to integrate wrote, "I hope that if schools open to my people, I will also get access to other opportunities I have been denied.... Our people are stretching out to knock down the fences of segregation.... I read in the newspaper that one of our people, a woman named Rosa Parks, had refused to give up her seat to a white man on an Alabama bus. Her willingness to be arrested rather than give in one more time led to the Montgomery, Alabama bus boycott. I felt such a surge of pride when I thought about how my people had banded together to force a change."

In addition, you understand that the segregation laws that keep blacks and whites separate and unequal must be broken. You and your children know that they are the intellectual equals to the white students who attend the school. There is no reason except racism for black students to attend poorly funded schools.

It may be rough going for a while, but nothing in life comes easy. In the long run, your families' sacrifices will benefit all African Americans and the country as a whole.

NAACP (National Association for the Advancement of Colored People)

SHOULD CENTRAL HIGH SCHOOL BE INTEGRATED?

You celebrated the victory of *Brown v. Board of Education* when the Supreme Court ruled that public school segregation was unconstitutional. As they stated, "separate schools are inherently unequal." They also said that offending states must desegregate schools with "all deliberate speed."

The victory was sweet, not because it immediately desegregated the Jim Crow schools, but because it gave you the prize you had been seeking for 58 years — since the Supreme Court upheld segregation in the *Plessy v. Ferguson* decision.

Before this you had the moral conviction that these schools were wrong and contrary to the guarantees of American citizenship. You were forced to go to back doors. You were forced to live in hollows and alleys and back streets. You were forced to step off sidewalks and remove your hats and call anyone white "Sir" or "Ma'am." If schools were provided, your children went to shanties while whites went to real schools. Your children used hand-me-down books and school supplies. You rode in the rear seats of buses and trolleys and in the dirty, dangerous front end of train coaches. You could not vote. You were beaten, shot, and burned, and no man was punished for the crime.

Slowly in this 58 years, you have wiped out lynching. You knocked out the strongest barriers to voting. Men and women are working at more and better jobs and at better and better wages.

Now, your children at long last will have equality in education. You recognize that you must use the law to push for integration as swiftly as possible in every community where segregated schools still exist. The law is now on your side. This generation of children will receive the education they deserve.

Tea Party

Melba Pattillo Beals: This book is my autobiography. I wrote it because I was involved in a major historic event in United States history. I was one of the Little Rock Nine—one of the nine African American students chosen to integrate Central High School in Little Rock, Arkansas, in the 1950s. Let me tell you, I had some hard times. People kicked me, spit on me, tried to kill me, but I survived. I wrote this book to tell my story and to ease my pain.

....

Grandma India: You are going to love me. I am a tough love kind of Grandma. You might find me sitting in a rocking chair, but instead of knitting and crocheting, I'll have my rifle on my lap. My grandbaby Melba is integrating that high school to make things better for African Americans, but as Frederick Douglass said, "Freedom does not come without a struggle." No one is going to make this easy. So I've got my gun ready in case anyone plans on troubling us. I am highly religious, but I am highly practical as well. Don't mess with my grandbaby.

....

Link: It's true that I'm white, and it's true that my friends wrote up cards saying things like, "Two, four, six, eight, we don't want to integrate." I am a witness to all of the terror that Central High students caused the Little Rock Nine. It's true that they chased Melba and urinated in Ernest Green's gym locker, but I'm not like them. I see beyond skin color. I saved Melba's life.

....

Danny: I'm the one who told Melba that warriors don't cry. She was on the battlefield in that high school. She was a soldier in the war against segregation, and I helped her. President Eisenhower sent in the 101st Airborne to stop the violence against the black students who attempted to integrate Central High School. I had Melba's back.

....

Daisy Bates: I work with the local National Association for the Advancement of Colored People (NAACP). I own and write for a local black newspaper. I am a longtime activist who understands the sacrifices we need to make to better the conditions of blacks in the United States. I took these nine children under my wing because I knew how hard they were going to have to struggle in order to make change.

....

Tea Party

Write about each of the other four characters you meet at the tea party.

Character name: _____

Description: _____

_____

_____

_____

Character name: _____

Description: _____

_____

_____

_____

Character name: _____

Description: _____

_____

_____

_____

Character name: _____

Description: _____

_____

_____

_____

On the back of this paper:

1. Write four questions that you have about the characters or the book.

2. Write three predictions about the book or the characters.

Final Project

EDUCATION UNIT

For your final project on the study of education, you may choose any of the following research project options or create one of your own, with my approval. The outreach component of this project will take place in fourth quarter: for example, a field trip to teach a lesson at a school or college, or a presentation for Grant's administration or faculty. So as you begin your project, think about your audience.

Research History of Tubman Middle School

If you choose to research the history of Harriet Tubman Middle School, you will want to read past news articles about the Black United Front's demands and the boycotts that ended in the creation of Tubman Middle School. You will want to discover why leaders in the African American community wanted a middle school in the community. What prompted the BUF's demands? You may want to interview people who were around at that time, especially Ron Herndon. You could write this as a piece of historical fiction or you could write it as a journalist reporting on Tubman now and then.

Research the History of Desegregation in Portland and/or Oregon

If you choose to research the history of desegregation in Portland and/or Oregon, you will want to find past articles about the history of segregated schools. There are a number of avenues to pursue on this topic. You may choose to look at the first case of segregation and research the story of how William Brown pressured the Portland School District to provide education for his children in 1867. Or you may want to look at the Portland Public Schools desegregation plan. After *Brown v. Board of Education,* how did Portland plan for integration? Again, you may choose to write up your research as historical fiction, a traditional research paper, or a proposal to the Portland School Board.

Research the Freedom Schools or Citizenship Schools

The Freedom Schools and Citizenship Schools were two education projects developed during the Civil Rights Movement. Both operated in the Deep South. Thousands of volunteers, mostly college students, taught black children about black history and their civil rights and also taught them reading and math. The Citizenship Schools registered black voters and taught basic literacy skills to adults who hadn't had opportunities to attend school. These are two of my favorite education stories. The people involved—especially Ella Baker, Septima Clark, and Bob Moses—are my heroes. The stories of each of these education projects would make great historical fiction. You might also choose to develop a literary scrapbook. Bob Moses is still alive and still teaching. You could try to contact him about his work.

Research Education and Race at Grant High School

If you choose to research and analyze a race issue at Grant, you may write up your research and present it as a proposal to Grant administrators or teachers. There are particular "indicators" that researchers study when they look at issues of race and justice in schools—for example, level of classes, dropout rates, grades, attendance, and failure rates. You might look at the number of African American students in clubs, honor society, or AP classes. If African Americans are represented in the same proportion in these activities and classes as they are in the school's population as a whole, write up your results along with your thoughts about what other schools might have to learn from Grant. On the other hand, if you discover that Grant needs to work more on a certain issue, write a proposal about how to create a change in the school.

Descendants of fugitive slaves attended this historic local school in Buxton, Ontario, Canada, an Underground Railroad village. Shown here is the class of 1909/1910.

Reuters/CORBIS

Literature Circles:
Slavery and Resistance

Too often, textbook images and stories portray the history of enslaved African Americans as victims, shackled to their fate. These books highlight the horrors of slavery—chains and whippings—instead of focusing on the daily struggle and resistance of the enslaved. Slavery is certainly the story of greed, of an economic system that put profits before humanity. But this period of history—and its reflection in literature—also offers the parallel story of resistance. I developed this literature circle to demonstrate the resilience, intelligence, resourcefulness, and creativity of a people who overcame tremendous hardship to survive.

For years, I taught this unit using *Kindred* or *Beloved* as a central text. Since I moved to literature circles, I have used a number of books: *Kindred*, by Octavia Butler, *Beloved*, by Toni Morrison, *47*, by Walter Mosley, *Incidents in the Life of a Slave Girl*, by Linda Brent, *I, Tituba, Black Witch of Salem*, by Maryse Conde, *Middle Passage*, by Charles Johnson, and Frederick Douglass' *Narrative of the Life of Frederick Douglass, An American Slave*. The books reveal different aspects of slavery and provide a wide range of reading levels as well as genres and time periods, so students have choice.

I developed this literature circle to demonstrate the resilience, intelligence, resourcefulness, and creativity of a people who overcame tremendous hardship to survive.

As a teacher, a chorus of voices gives me constant, and sometimes conflicting, advice. One voice urges me to give students choice—and I do. Students choose their topics in narratives, poetry, and essays; they choose

189

their outreach audiences, topics, and genres. But another, equally loud voice reminds me that students need guidance and grounding in history in order to develop critical consciousness. If I allowed Seth and Michael their choice, fantasy and video games would be the outcome. I need to be a friend of my students' minds, to paraphrase Toni Morrison, pushing them to think about the world, past and present. While I believe that student interest and questions must direct our discussions, I can't relinquish my duty as an informed guide and teacher.

When I first learned about literature circles at a conference, I led open-choice circles where students chose from a selection of unrelated books—historical fiction, science fiction, mysteries, classics, etc. I quickly abandoned this practice in favor of themed literature circles. I have too little time with students, so every book we read needs to contribute to developing both literary and critical capacities. I love to teach themed literature circles because I have the best of both worlds—students get choice and I still get to bring the class together for discussions and writing prompts. When my students read books around a common historical period or topic, we have richer conversations than we had when students chose random books.

Some of my students have urgent skill deficits that I must tackle, so every lesson in every unit must work on multiple levels, addressing critical reading, historical and/or literary background information, and writing instruction. While students read their literature circle books, I provide additional readings on the themes, including poetry, short stories, films, primary source documents, as well as history texts to enrich the class talk. The common readings and writings allow me both flexibility and control in teaching the literature circle. Some days students work in small groups; other days, I call the class together for a read-around of interior monologues, poetry, and other imaginative and personal writing. Some days, students take over as teachers, creating assignments from their books. I continue the trajectory of teaching a unit while building students' writing and analytic skills on a book of their choice.

Introducing the Books: A Slightly Different Tea Party

To introduce the students to the books, I begin with a tea party peopled with the main character from each of the books. During this time, students have an opportunity to learn about the characters and situations, as well as the genre of the novel. Students meet:

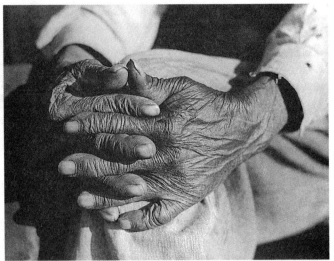

The work-weathered hands of Henry Brooks, a former slave from Greene County, Georgia, May 1941.

Jack Delano/Bettmann/CORBIS

- Dana, from *Kindred*, an African American from the 20th century who travels to the past to save her white ancestor;
- Frederick Douglass, from his autobiography, who writes about his life in slavery and his escape, as well as his analysis of the horrors of slavery;
- Rutherford Calhoun, from *Middle Passage*, a womanizing, alcoholic freed slave, who ends up on a slave cargo ship heading back to Africa where he learns firsthand about the slave trade;
- Linda Brent, from the autobiography *Incidents in the Life of a Slave Girl*, who describes her life in slavery and her escape;
- Sethe, from *Beloved*, who escaped from slavery, but whose love of her children forced her to commit unthinkable acts to keep them from returning to slavery;
- Tituba, from *I, Tituba, Black Witch of Salem*, who was hanged during the Salem witch trials; and
- 47, a teenaged boy from Walter Mosley's book *47*, who discovers the mystical Tall John and learns about the beauty of his people and the mental shackles that slavery imprints. (See pp. 204-205 for the tea party roles.)

When I wrote these roles, I tried to capture a sense of the main character and the book. I gave the main character's name, the book title, and any awards a book had won. Sethe, from *Beloved*, addresses the critical question of the novel: How far would you go to keep your children out of slavery? Because some of these books are sexually explicit or use language considered inappropriate to the classroom, I also issue a "warning" for some of the books:

> Sethe (*Beloved*—Winner of the Pulitzer Prize for Fiction): I escaped from slavery, but I am haunted by the chains of its memory. My life is choked by the past. I am a woman who has lost too much—a husband, a child, friends. I found a new man to love, but the ghosts of our past keep tearing us apart. Ask yourself the question: Would you rather your children live in slavery or die so they don't suffer the abuse you suffered? (*This book contains mature themes and language.*)

After the tea party, I give a short talk about each book and read a gripping passage so students can get a sense of the language. I spread copies of all the books out on a table, so students can thumb through them, look at their size, and the difficulty of the text. Sometimes I steer students towards or away from a particular book. I love *Beloved*, but it is a difficult book for many students. In an untracked class, some students are up for the challenge and some will find it frustrating. Many students read and love *Kindred*, which has elements of science fiction and mystery. After students have an opportunity to meet the four or five main characters from the books, they make a preliminary choice.

Because students sometimes select books that they don't love, I give them a five-day grace period to change books and groups with the caveat that they have to catch up with their new group. One year, I couldn't get several of my young men who either struggled as readers or struggled as students to read any book; they picked up and abandoned book after book. I discovered Walter Mosley's *47*, and finally, they buckled down and read. They loved the fantasy aspects of the novel.

Establishing the Dialogue Journal

I tell students, "The enslaved did not sit back, put their wrists out waiting for shackles. They fought back. They resisted. As you read your books, record acts of resistance in your dialogue journal, both large—running away, fighting back, inciting rebellion—as well as small—breaking tools, working slowly, learning to read and write. I want you to keep track of the ways the enslaved survived. In other words, how did they keep their sanity, community, and spirituality intact during these terrible times? Plantation owners sold their children, their husbands, their mothers. How did enslaved people get up each day in the face of so much pain?"

To prepare students to keep their dialogue journals, we read "Fight, and If You Can't Fight, Kick" together as a class before students begin reading their books. In this powerful oral testimony, a woman who had been enslaved tells about her mother's refusal to surrender her humanity to slavery, clearly showing the resistance I want students to find in their books:

> The one doctrine of my mother's teaching which was branded upon my senses was that I should never let anyone abuse me. "I'll kill you, gal, if you don't stand up for yourself," she would say. "Fight, and if you can't fight, kick; if you can't kick, then bite." Ma was generally willing to work, but if she didn't feel like doing something, none could make her do it. At least, the Jennings couldn't make, or didn't make her.

The narrator tells the story of the time she saw her mother's doctrine in action. Mistress Jennings struck her mother, Fannie, with a stick. Fannie fought back, beating her mistress and nearly tearing her clothes off. When asked why she struck her mistress, she answered, "Why, I'll kill her, I'll kill her dead if she ever strikes me again." Fannie doesn't stop there. When the master tells her she will have to be whipped by law, she fights back even harder:

> Two mornings afterward, two men came in at the big gate, one with a long lash in his hand. I was in the yard and I hoped they couldn't find Ma. To my surprise, I saw her running around the house, straight in the direction of the men. She must have seen them coming. I should have known that she wouldn't hide. She knew what they were coming for, and she intended to meet them halfway. She swooped upon them like a hawk on chicken. I believe they were afraid of her or thought she was crazy. One man had a long beard which she grabbed with one hand, and the lash with the other. Her body was made strong with madness. She was a good match for them. Mr. Jennings came and pulled her away. I don't know what would have happened if he hadn't come at that moment, for one man had already pulled his gun out. Ma did not see the gun until Mr. Jennings came up. On catching sight of it, she said, "Use your gun, use it and blow my brains out if you will."

In her response to the piece, my student Carliss connected to Fannie's fighting spirit and saw herself in the portrait: "This scene made me think about how some slaves would do whatever it took to keep themselves whole. I think it takes courage and strength to decide you are not going to take it. I believe if I lived back in those days, I would have been like this lady in the story. I'm glad to see that slaves weren't afraid of man or death. To some, fighting was all they could do. I like the line, '…the black mother and exemplary worker who was both feared and respected by her masters and who, by her courage and militancy, imposed certain restrictions upon them.'"

I also work to help students understand the history of this time period because the actions of the characters in each book are constrained by the repressive laws and violence of the time. I ask them to keep track of laws and institutionalized practices, formal and informal: Buying and selling people out of slavery; teaching slaves to read and write; marriage; work situations; physical abuse; the role of free blacks; children born into slavery; and the relationships between master and slave. Jennifer pointed out the law that slave masters own the children by citing the passage where Mistress Jennings tells Fannie, "You can't take the baby, Fannie, Aunt Mary can keep it with the other children." Later, when the narrator's father and mother were taken from her, Jennifer also noted,

As a white teacher, I understand the need to construct "moral ancestors," to connect students to those whites who acted for justice and humanity during a time when many did not.

"According to law, families can be broken apart."

Students also noticed the ingenuity and talents that enslaved people possessed. Jasmine wrote, "Slaves had a ton of skills" in the margin beside the list of jobs Fannie's husband performed: "Pa was also a sower of all seeds. He was a yardman, houseman, plowman, gardener, blacksmith, carpenter, keysmith, and anything else they chose him to be." (See "Slavery and Resistance Dialogue Journal," p. 202.)

As a white teacher, I understand the need to construct "moral ancestors," to connect students to those whites who acted for justice and humanity during a time when many did not. Over the years my white students have been vocal about this. I learned the importance of including this piece of history when Justine said, "Didn't we ever do anything right?" When I talk with students, I say, "Look. I'm white. But I don't feel guilt over the past. Instead I identify with those whites who fought for justice. I take Lucretia Coffin Mott and John Brown as my moral ancestors, but Ella Baker and Septima Clark, two African American civil

rights workers, also feel like family." So I also encourage students to identify whites who acted as allies with African Americans in their novels.

Resistance, laws, historical evidence, and allies are part of the overarching themes I ask students to record, but students also take notes on ideas and passages that percolate for them. Jennifer, who read *I, Tituba, Black Witch of Salem*, kept track of how Tituba's need for love drove her into desperate situations. Seth, who read *47*, kept track of the ways Tall John taught 47 about the beauty and intelligence of black people.

Students' dialogue journals provide the content for group as well as class discussions. On the day we discuss laws, I might say, "In your reading group today, talk about laws, written or unwritten, and how they affected your characters. Bring a passage and question from your book to discuss when we convene back together as a large class." Each group writes these on the board, on an overhead or on a large piece of paper, so we can refer to the questions and passages during our class discussion. These guide our discussion about both history and historical fiction: "Was it a law that slave masters could beat their slaves? If masters killed people who were enslaved did they have to go to prison? Why couldn't enslaved people learn to read? Was that a law? Why?" Sometimes their questions prompt me to bring in additional movie clips or historical documents to address their questions.

In case it sounds like I orchestrate every move, let me say that students discuss their own passions and insights in their literature circles. The young women who read *I, Tituba, Black Witch of Salem* had great discussions about whether love made you a captive, if love was another form of slavery. The students who read *Kindred* argued about the effectiveness of the time travel. Justin thought it didn't work. Melvin thought it did. Also, some days, students run the class discussions. For example, one year the group that read *Kindred* brought the following assignment to class: "On page 97, Dana worries that she and her husband, Kevin, are becoming accustomed to slavery and their roles in it. On p. 99, Dana says, 'My god, why can't we go home. This place is diseased.' Imagine that two people from 2098 arrive in Portland in 2008. What would they think is diseased about our society? Share with your small group. Designate someone from your small group as a recorder to make a list of your 'diseases' to share with the large group." When we have enough time, students also collect their own narrative writing assignments and challenge the class to write. For example, the Frederick Douglass group

Frederick Douglass.

gave the following assignment: "Douglass described someone who helped him learn to read and write. Write about a person who helped you."

Literature circles require a balancing act. My trick is to give students enough time to work on their own and with their groups, so they can discuss their ideas, while interspersing whole-class instruction that informs their reading with historical facts, poetry, and articles that offer insight into the theme. (See "Slavery and Resistance Calendar," p. 203.)

Writing Narratives: Frederick Douglass Stands Up

As I have stated previously, students write poetry, a narrative, and an essay in almost every unit I teach. In this literature circle, students write about a time they stood up or wish they had—a prompt I borrowed from Bill Bigelow.

Before we move into writing, I distribute Frederick Douglass' account of his fight with his temporary "master," Mr. Covey. This compelling piece of Douglass' autobiography (chapter 10) provides a parallel story to Fannie's in "Fight, and If You Can't Fight, Kick." After Mr. Covey unfairly beats Douglass, Douglass attempts to get his master, Mr. Thomas, to intervene. Instead of intervening, Mr. Thomas "ridiculed the idea that there was any danger of Mr. Covey's killing me, and said that he knew Mr. Covey; that he was a good man." When

Douglass returned to Covey's farm, Covey attempted to beat Douglass again. But this time Douglass stood up and fought back. Covey never beat him again. Douglass reflected on the impact the fight had on his life:

> This battle with Mr. Covey was the turning point in my career as a slave. It rekindled the few expiring embers of freedom, and revived within me a sense of my own manhood. It recalled the departed self-confidence, and inspired me again with a determination to be free. The gratification afforded by the triumph was a full compensation for whatever else might follow, even death itself. He only can understand the deep satisfaction which I experienced, who has himself repelled by force the bloody arm of slavery. I felt as I never felt before. It was a glorious resurrection, from the tomb of slavery, to the heaven of freedom. My long-crushed spirit rose, cowardice departed, bold defiance took its place; and I now resolved that, however long I might remain a slave in form, the day had passed forever when I could be a slave in fact. I did not hesitate to let it be known of me, that the white man who expected to succeed in whipping, must also succeed in killing me.

I ask students to look at the circumstances that allowed Douglass to stand up and fight back this time when he hadn't before. What triggered his resistance? What factors contributed to his ability to fight back this time? I remind them of Fannie in the "Fight, and If You Can't Fight, Kick" narrative: "How are Fannie's and Douglass' situations the same? Look at the language they use to describe their unwillingness to be beat again. Douglass says, "[H]owever long I might remain a slave in form, the day had passed forever when I could be a slave in fact. I did not hesitate to let it be known of me, that the white man who expected to succeed in whipping, must also succeed in killing me." Fannie says, "I'll go to hell or anywhere else, but I won't be whipped." I don't know the answer to this question, but it provokes good discussion. Is it because they have nothing left to lose? Frederick doesn't have family, but Fannie does. I encourage students to add to our discussion with passages or stories of resistance from their books.

To move into the writing, I ask students, "Think back over your own life to a time when you stood up for something you believed in. It could be a time when, like the mother in 'Fight, and If You Can't Fight, Kick,' you felt you actually had to get into a physical fight. It could be a time when you had to argue with someone older or more experienced than you. Perhaps you took an unpopular stand that went against your peer group. You might also

193

write about a time when you wished you had stood up, but you didn't. List as many events as you can remember."

Once students list events, I ask a few students to share their ideas to help those students who are stuck. Randi talked about standing up to an older sister who always pushed her around; Jessica confronted her father about cheating on her mother; James told his father not to call him any more after he failed to show up one too many times; Rhonda challenged a teacher who gave her a lower grade on a test than she felt she deserved; Alex said he didn't stand up when his middle school counselor told him to change his behavior, even though he felt that he had to put on a white mask when he entered school.

The stories from this prompt lend themselves to a powerful read-around because the narratives come from defining moments in students' lives.

Once most students have an idea for their story, I give them a list of questions to think about as they write. I say: "You don't have to answer every question. This is a narrative, not a short answer quiz. But as you write this narrative and tell the story about what happened, I also want you to step back from the incident and explore what gave you the confidence to stand up this time. Or if you didn't stand up, why not and how do you feel about that? Here are some questions to think about: What happened? Where were you? Who else was there? What was said? Write the description so that a reader can see and hear what's happening. Explain why you felt you had to stand up for what was right. What were the risks you were taking in making a stand for what you believed in? What was the outcome of your action? How do you feel about your action as you look back on it in time?"

The stories from this prompt lend themselves to a powerful read-around because the narratives, like the ones in the "Writing for Change" narrative, come from defining moments in students' lives. Some tell about the times they found the courage to stand up or talk back for the first time; others share the moments when they wish they had but didn't—stories we can all tell. The collective text from this lesson mirrors the questions we discussed after reading Douglass' narrative: What circumstances allowed your classmates to stand up and fight back this time when they hadn't before? What triggered the resistance? What factors contributed to our ability to fight back this time? If we

didn't fight back, what circumstances held us back? How did we feel about the situation afterwards?

What I hope students take away from this assignment is that we all have the power to take charge of our lives, to determine how we are going to live and on what terms. These stories give us courage to imagine ourselves as capable of fighting injustice, as Carliss Holland did when she wrote, "I believe if I lived back in those days, I would have been like this lady in the story." (See "Teaching Narrative Writing: Why It Matters" for a full description of teaching narratives, p. 60.)

Writing Poetry: Deepening Understanding and Prompting Discussion

Writing poetry about the historical novels pushes students back to the text to re-read and talk about the book, to find visual imagery and strong language that they might use in their poetry. The distillation of a scene from literature into a visual image creates a context for students to produce their own literature. Our read-around of these pieces provides class time for students to share those understandings with their classmates.

Using the poetry formats I discuss in "Writing Poetry from History and Literature" (p. 50), students develop ideas together in their small groups. I ask them: "Whose point of view can you write from? What scenes make the best poetry? Is there an inanimate object that might 'see' what's happening?" I share my former student Sam Jackson's poem "Iron" as a model of using an inanimate object to tell the story of slavery:

> I am just an iron,
> forged of molten steel,
> formed
> into a stamp,
> the stamp of ownership.
> I am put
> in raging fires,
> red hot,
> hot as hell.
> Pushed onto a black man's
> back,
> leg,
> or face
> to show he is property.
> Property,
> like me.
> It hurts me just
> as much as it hurts them.

But they don't forget the pain
and humiliation.
They don't forget.
I do,
because I am
just an iron.

I use poetry from published poets as well as from my former students to prompt new poems. In the poem, "at the cemetery, walnut grove plantation, south carolina, 1989," Lucille Clifton meditates on the nameless enslaved people whose work is evident at the cemetery, but whose names are not. Clifton writes to these people:

nobody mentioned slaves
and yet the curious tools
shine with your fingerprints.
nobody mentioned slaves
but somebody did this work
who had no guide, no stone,
who moulders under rock.
tell me your names,
tell me your bashful names
and I will testify.

Clifton's poetic meditation and direct address provide one way for students to enter a poem about their book or slavery. We look at the physical details Clifton uses from her visit to the plantation: rocks, tools, fingerprints. I encourage students to use physical details in their poems. We note her lines: "tell me your names/tell me your bashful names/and I will testify." I ask, "Who can you write your poem to? Who can you 'testify' for? Whose history can you restore in your poem?"

Students write their poems or interior monologues on their own and share them in a class read-around. As students read, we pause not only to praise, but to discuss how the poem illuminates the condition of slavery, the suffering of enslaved people, as well as their resistance and courage.

Weaving in History: Howard Zinn

To help students understand the larger historical context of this time period, we read "Slavery Without Submission, Emancipation Without Freedom," a chapter from Howard Zinn's *A People's History of the United States*. Depending on the skill level of the class, I distribute the chapter and ask students to read for specific information or we read the chapter out loud together. I tell students, "Look, this is a history textbook that most colleges use. I have complete faith that you can read this too."

The home of the American Quaker and abolitionist Levi Coffin (1798–1877). Located in Cincinnati, it functioned as a stop on the Underground Railroad.

I admit, it might seem odd to read a history book in an English class, but in this literature circle, students are reading historical fiction or memoir. It is essential for them to understand historical references—names of historical figures, laws. But I also want them to get a sense of the sweep of resistance as well as the pressure to maintain slavery that was happening throughout the country. Zinn's work informs them about the various ways that individuals and groups fought to end slavery—from armed insurrection, to education through newspapers and speaking tours, to the Underground Railroad.

As students read Zinn's chapter, I ask them to find the following abolitionists and to describe each person's plan to end slavery: David Walker, Denmark Vesey, John Brown, Nat Turner, Frederick Douglass, Harriet Tubman, William Lloyd Garrison, and J. W. Loguen. "Also, find out if this person worked alone or if they were part of a movement. I want you to think about which plan to end slavery you would join if you lived during these times."

Students create a chart of the abolitionists, their methods, and their allies, as they read the chapter. They note whether or not they see any of these methods reflected in their books. In a brief "in the midst" persuasive essay, students make a case for the strategy they believe works the best and defend it during a class discussion. Some years this section expands to a post-literature-circle research paper or children's book for outreach to neighborhood elementary schools.

To help students understand the complex relationship between blacks and poor whites, students read Zinn's explanation and also examine their own books. Zinn does a great job discussing how people in power kept natural allies from getting together. Zinn writes, "The instances where poor whites helped slaves were not frequent, but sufficient to sow the need for setting one group against the other. [Eugene Genovese, in his comprehensive study of slavery, *Roll, Jordon, Roll,*] says:

> The slaveholders...suspected that non-slaveholders would encourage slave disobedience and even rebellion, not so much out of sympathy for the blacks as out of hatred for the rich planters and resentment of their own poverty. White men sometimes were linked to slave insurrectionary plots, and each such incident rekindled fears.

As Zinn notes, "This helps explain the stern police measures against whites who fraternized with blacks. In return, blacks helped whites in need. One black runaway told of a slave woman who had received fifty lashes of the whip for giving food to a white neighbor who was poor and sick."

The description of the strength of the black community resonated for many of my students, personally as well as in their books.

As students read Zinn, I keep returning them to their books. "Where do you see this? How did the author use this historical information?" The buying and selling of families runs like a current through all of the books students read. According to Zinn, the interviews conducted by the Federal Writers Project in the 1930s demonstrated the capacity of blacks to endure even the most difficult circumstances and transform that pain into actions to save their community. Zinn quotes George Rawick's book *From Sundown to Sunup:*

> The slave community acted like a generalized extended kinship system in which all adults looked after all children and there was little division between "my children for whom I'm responsible" and "your children for whom you're responsible."... It was part and parcel, as we shall see, of the social process out of which came black pride, black identity, black culture, the black community, and black rebellion in America.

This description of the strength of the black community resonated for many of my students, personally as well as in their books, where they find many examples of the extended family structure described in the chapter.

Students also pointed out that although these family separations may have developed alternative family systems, they also caused pain. As evidence, the *Beloved* group shared Toni Morrison's image of enslaved people as checkers on a checkerboard, moved at the will of the master:

> It made sense for a lot of reasons because in all of Baby's life, as well as Sethe's own, men and women were moved around like checkers. Anybody Baby Suggs knew, let alone loved, who hadn't run off or been hanged, got rented out, loaned out, bought up, brought back, stored up, mortgaged, won, stolen, or seized. So Baby's eight children had six fathers. What she called the nastiness of life was the shock she received upon learning that nobody stopped playing checkers just because the pieces included her children. Halle she was able to keep the longest. Twenty years. A lifetime. Given to her, no doubt, to make up for hearing that her two girls, neither of whom had their adult teeth, were sold and gone and she had not been able to wave goodbye. To make up for coupling with a straw boss for four months in exchange for keeping her third child, a boy, with her—only to have him traded for lumber in the spring of the next year and to find herself pregnant by the man who promised not to and did. That child she could not love and the rest she would not. "God take what He would," she said. And He did, and He did, and He did and then gave her Halle who gave her freedom when it didn't mean a thing.

Morrison's writing demonstrates that the pairing of story and history makes for powerful, unforgettable literature.

Writing the Essay—Metaphor and More

As always, students choose their topic and their path as they generate essays from these texts. (See "Writing Wild Essays from Hard Ground," p. 120.) I structure help along the way, so they don't arrive at the end of our journey without ideas or evidence. A number of the dialogue journal topics and class discussions help students locate evidence for potential essays: Scenes of resistance and rebellion, passages that demonstrate allies and hope, as well as laws and social conventions of the time. The character silhouette and the quick persuasive essay on the abolition movement can also lead to essays.

Sometimes, I take students through a metaphor exercise to help them think about one of their characters more deeply, but students can also use the metaphor as a frame for their essay. I tell them, "Create a metaphor for one of the characters in your book. For example, Rufus in *Kindred* was a street corner bully. Alice was a bruised orchid. Then draw your metaphor." Once students have drawn their metaphors, I ask them to write an explanation and share them in their groups. "Explain your metaphor. For example, if I write that Rufus is a street corner bully, I might say, he always thinks he can get his way. If his words don't convince people, he uses force to beat them into submitting to him." The drawings and explanations evoke good discussions about the characters in students' small groups.

After students share their explanations, I ask them to list examples from their texts to prove their point, including the page number and a summary of the passage. This draws students back to the book to search for evidence. "What actions prove that Rufus is a bully? You can't just say that someone is a bully. You have to prove it. Make a list of the times he bullied Alice, his mother, or Dana. Then find the examples and note the page numbers. Also, as you re-read the section, see if there are any great quotes that you might want to pull out." This exercise works well in literature circle groups because students have the gift of many minds and many dialogue journals to help them collect evidence. The extended metaphor provides a strong frame, particularly for struggling writers, as they write their essays.

We spend most of two weeks drafting and revising these essays. We move back and forth between whole-group work and small-group work. I bring the entire class together to brainstorm topics that might work for any book—resistance, families, allies—then students move to their book groups to add more topics and help each other with evidence. We come back together to develop thesis statements and write introductions and share them in the large group, but students also check in with their classmates. The book groups make great response groups for first drafts.

Slavery, Resistance, and Lessons About Struggle

As teachers, our choices in literature signal our beliefs about the world. I want my choice in this unit to signal that change is possible, but that we must work for it to happen. I hope my students, of all races, walk away with the knowledge that they stand on the shoulders of men and women who fought injustice. I also hope they understand that their daily choices contribute to continuing that legacy or undermining it. As Frederick Douglass said, "If there is no struggle there is no progress. Those who profess to favor freedom and yet depreciate agitation...want crops without plowing up the ground, they want rain without thunder and lightning. They want the ocean without the awful roar of its many waters.... Power concedes nothing without a demand. It never did and it never will." ■

Fight, And If You Can't Fight, Kick

by Ophelia Settle Egypt

The following oral testimony of a former slave provides a vivid character sketch of a type of slave frequently depicted in slave narratives and primary sources—the black mother and exemplary worker who was both feared and respected by her masters and who, by her courage and militancy, imposed certain restrictions upon them.

The narrator was born and lived in a small town in Tennessee. Her narrative is of great interest also because it describes conditions on a small farm, where the master and his family lived in close intimacy with four families of slaves. In this account one catches fascinating glimpses of the complex relationship of masters and slaves, and one can get a sense of the daily interaction, affection, hatred, and conflict which must have characterized life under slavery for both races. Historical accounts of slavery based on laws, plantation overseers' records and the observations of travelers fail to convey this lively reality.

— Gerda Lerner

My mother was the smartest black woman in Eden. She was as quick as a flash of lightning, and whatever she did could not be done better. She could do anything. She cooked, washed, ironed, spun, nursed and labored in the field. She made as good a field hand as she did a cook. I have heard Master Jennings say to his wife, "Fannie has her faults, but she can outwork any [slave] in the country. I'd bet my life on that."

My mother certainly had her faults as a slave. She was very different in nature from Aunt Caroline. Ma fussed, fought, and kicked all the time. I tell you, she was a demon. She said that she wouldn't be whipped, and when she fussed, all Eden must have known it. She was loud and boisterous, and it seemed to me that you could hear her a mile away. Father was often the prey of her high temper. With all her ability for work, she did not make a good slave. She was too high-spirited and independent. I tell you, she was a captain.

The one doctrine of my mother's teaching which was branded upon my senses was that I should never let anyone abuse me. "I'll kill you, gal, if you don't stand up for yourself," she would say. "Fight, and if you can't fight, kick; if you can't kick, then bite." Ma was generally willing to work, but if she didn't feel like doing something, none could make her do it. At least, the Jennings couldn't make, or didn't make her.

"Bob, I don't want no sorry [slave] around me. I can't tolerate you if you ain't got no backbone." Such constant warning to my father had its effect. My mother's unrest and fear of abuse spread gradually to my father. He seemed to have been made after the timid kind. He would never fuss back at my mother, or if he did, he couldn't be heard above her shouting. Pa was also a sower of all seeds. He was a yardman, houseman, plowman, gardener, blacksmith, carpenter, keysmith, and anything else they chose him to be.

I was the oldest child. My mother had three other children by the time I was about six years old. It was at this age that I remember the almost daily talks of my mother on the cruelty of slavery. I would say nothing to her, but I was thinking all the time that slavery did not seem so cruel. Master and Mistress Jennings were not mean to my mother. It was she who was mean to them.

Master Jennings allowed his slaves to earn any money they could for their own use. My father had a garden of his own around his little cabin, and he also had some chickens. Mr. Dodge, who was my master's uncle, and who owned the hotel in Eden, was Pa's regular customer. He would buy anything my pa brought to him; and many times he was buying his own stuff, or his nephew's stuff. I have seen Pa go out at night with a big sack and come back with it full. He'd bring sweet potatoes, watermelons, chickens and turkeys. We were fond of pig roast and sweet potatoes, and the only way to have pig roast was for Pa to go out on one of his hunting trips. Where he went, I cannot say, but he brought the booty home. The floor of our cabin was covered with planks. Pa had raised up two planks, and dug a hole. This was our storehouse. Every Sunday, Master Jennings would let Pa take the wagon to carry watermelons, cider and ginger cookies to Spring Hill, where the Baptist church was located. The Jennings were Baptists. The white folks would buy from him as well as the free Negroes of Trenton, Tennessee. Sometimes these free Negroes would steal to our cabin at a specified time to buy a chicken or barbecue dinner. Mr. Dodge's slaves always had money and came to buy from us. Pa was allowed to keep the money he made at Spring Hill, and of course Master Jennings didn't know about the little restaurant we had in our cabin.

One day my mother's temper ran wild. For some reason Mistress Jennings struck her with a stick. Ma struck back and a fight followed. Mr. Jennings was not at home and the children became frightened and ran upstairs. For half an hour they wrestled in the kitchen. Mistress, seeing that she could not get the better of Ma, ran out in the road, with Ma right on her heels. In the road, my mother flew into her again. The thought seemed to race across my mother's mind to tear mistress' clothing off her body. She suddenly began to tear Mistress Jennings' clothes off. She caught hold, pulled, ripped and tore. Poor mistress was nearly naked when the storekeeper got to them and pulled Ma off.

"Why, Fannie, what do mean by that?" he asked.

"Why, I'll kill her, I'll kill her dead if she ever strikes me again."

I have never been able to find out the way of the whole thing....

Pa heard Mr. Jennings say that Fannie would have to be whipped by law. He told Ma. Two mornings afterward, two men came in at the big gate, one with a long lash in his hand. I was in the yard and I hoped they couldn't find Ma. To my surprise, I saw her running around the house, straight in the direction of the men. She must have seen them coming. I should have known that she wouldn't hide. She knew what they were coming for, and she intended to meet them halfway. She swooped upon them like a hawk on chicken. I believe they were afraid of her or thought she was crazy. One man had a long beard which she grabbed with one hand, and the lash with the other. Her body was made strong with madness. She was a good match for them. Mr. Jennings came and pulled her away. I don't know what would have happened if he hadn't come at that moment, for one man had already pulled his gun out. Ma did not see the gun until Mr. Jennings came up. On catching sight of it, she said, "Use your gun, use it and blow my brains out if you will."…

That evening Mistress Jennings came down to the cabin.

"Well, Fannie," she said, "I'll have to send you away. You won't be whipped, and I'm afraid you'll get killed."…

"I'll go to hell or anywhere else, but I won't be whipped," she answered.

"You can't take the baby, Fannie, Aunt Mary can keep it with the other children."

Mother said nothing at this. That night, Ma and Pa sat up late, talking over things, I guess. Pa loved Ma, and I heard him say, "I'm going too, Fannie." About a week later, she called me and told me that she and Pa were going to leave me the next day, that they were going to Memphis. She didn't know for how long.

"But don't be abused, Puss." She always called me Puss. My right name was Cornelia. I cannot tell in words the feeling I had at that time. My sorrow knew no bound. My very soul seemed to cry out, "gone, gone, gone forever." I cried until my eyes looked like balls of fire. I felt for the first time in my life that I had been abused. How cruel it was to take my mother and father from me, I thought. My mother had been right. Slavery was cruel, so very cruel.

Thus my mother and father were hired to Tennessee. The next morning they were to leave. I saw Ma working around with the baby under her arms as if it had been a bundle of some kind. Pa came up to the cabin with an old mare for Ma to ride, and an old mule for himself. Mr. Jennings was with him.

"Fannie, leave the baby with Aunt Mary," said Mr. Jennings very quietly.

At this, Ma took the baby by its feet, a foot in each hand, and with the baby's head swinging downward, she vowed to smash its brains out before she'd leave it. Tears were streaming down her face. It was seldom that Ma cried, and everyone knew that she meant every word. Ma took her baby with her.…

An uneventful year passed. I was destined to be happily surprised by the return of my mother and father. They came one day, and found me sitting by the roadside in a sort of trance.…

"Puss, we've come back, me and Pa, and we've come to stay."…

She and Pa embraced and caressed me for a long time. We went to the cabin, and Master Jennings was there nearly as soon as we were.

"Hello, Fannie. How did you get along?" he asked.

"Why, Mr. Jennings, you know that I know how to get along," she answered.

"Well, I'm glad to hear that, Fannie."

Ma had on new clothes and a pair of beautiful earrings. She told Aunt Mary that she stayed in Memphis one year without a whipping or a cross word.

Pa had learned to drink more liquor than ever, it seemed. At least, he was able to get more of it, for there were many disagreements between Pa and Ma about his drinking. Drinkers will drink together, and Mr. Jennings was no exception. Pa would have the excuse that Master Jennings offered him liquor, and of course he wouldn't take it from anybody else. It was common to see them together, half drunk, with arms locked, walking around and around the old barn. Then Pa would put his hands behind him and let out a big whoop which could be heard all over Eden....

Our family was increased by the arrival of a baby girl. Ma was very sick, and she never did get well after that. She was cooking for Mistress Jennings one day when she came home and went to bed. She never got up. I guess Ma was sick about six months. During that time she never hit a tap of work. She said she had brought five children in the world for the Jennings, and that was enough; that she didn't intend to work when she felt bad.

On the day my mother died, she called Pa and said...."Go tell Master Jennings to come in, and get all the slaves too."

Pa went and returned in five minutes with old master.

"Fannie, are you any worse?" said old master.

"No, no, Master Jennings, no worse. But I'm going to leave you at eight o'clock."

"Where are you going, Fannie," Master Jennings asked as if he didn't know that Ma was talking about dying.

Ma shook her head slowly and answered, "I'm going where there ain't no fighting and cussing and damning."

"Is there anything that you want me to do for you, Fannie?"

Ma told him that she reckoned there wasn't much of anything that anybody could do for her now. "But I would like for you to take Puss and hire her out among ladies, so she can be raised right. She will never be any good here, Master Jennings."

A funny look came over Master Jennings' face, and he bowed his head up and down. All the hands had come in and were standing around with him.

My mother died at just about eight o'clock.

Ophelia Settle Egypt, J. Msouka, Charles S. Johnson, "Fight, And If You Can't Fight, Kick." Black Women in White America: Documentary History. *Ed. Gerda Lerner. New York: Vintage Books, 1973. 34-40.*

Dialogue Journal

You will discuss your novel with your group and the class several times a week. You will also write an essay about your novel. It is important that you keep track of the page numbers for your quotes, facts, and observations as you read. This will prepare you for your literature circle group meetings as well as help you when you write your essay.

For every "chunk" you read:

- Write *at least* two questions that you want to discuss with your group and/or the class.

- Write *at least* two "ahas"—surprises or new knowledge.

- Keep track of ways the enslaved resisted:
  - Running away
  - Breaking tools
  - Fighting back

- Keep track of historical facts about slavery:
  - Buying people out of slavery
  - Teaching slaves to read and write
  - Marriage between slaves
  - Work situations
  - Physical abuse
  - Role of free blacks
  - Children born into slavery
  - Relationships between slave owner and slave

- Keep track of ways the enslaved survived. In other words, how did they keep their sanity, community, and spirituality intact?

- Keep track of any people who crossed race or class lines to act as allies with African Americans in your novels.

Calendar

Monday	Tuesday	Wednesday	Thursday	Friday
Read: "Fight, And If You Can't Fight, Kick" Dialogue journal work Discussion	Tea Party Book Talk Choose book Set reading dates	Literature Circles: Questions, statements, and quotes Read in class. *Reading Homework:*	Literature Circles: Questions, statements, and quotes Read in class. *Reading Homework:*	Read "Slavery Without Submission, Emancipation Without Freedom," Zinn *Reading Homework:*
Literature Circles: List key scenes—any focus on resistance/ rebellion. Discuss w/Zinn.	Literature Circles: Questions, statements, and quotes Read in class. *Reading Homework:*	Literature Circles: Find key passages that demonstrate allies, hope. Discussion *Reading Homework:*	Literature Circles: List 5 key scenes. Draw a scene. Write a poem, letter, interior monologue. *Reading Homework:*	Share scenes and poetry. Read in class. *Reading Homework:*
Watch *Sankofa* or *Roots*. Take notes. *Reading Homework:*	Watch *Sankofa* or *Roots*. Take notes. *Reading Homework:*	Read Lucille Clifton. Write poetry from movie. Share. *Reading Homework:*	Literature Circles: Questions, statements, and quotes Read in class. *Reading Homework:*	**Narrative: Write about a time you stood up/resisted.** *Reading Homework:*
Read-around narratives *Reading Homework:*	**Metaphor Poem/Essay: Create metaphor. Draw metaphor. Explain metaphor. List examples from text to prove point.** *Reading Homework:*	Essay Overview: Class brainstorm key topics Literature circles: Discuss essay topics. Accumulate evidence for topics. Share quotes, evidence. *Reading Homework:*	Write a tentative thesis, list support; write introduction. Share in class.	Work on essay. *Homework: Write Essay*
Essay Draft #1 Due Essay Response Groups	*Essay revision work* Conferences w/teacher	*Essay revision work* Conferences w/teacher	*Essay revision work* Conferences w/teacher	**Essay Revisions Due Poetry Reading #2**

Tea Party

Sethe (*Beloved*—Winner of the Pulitzer Prize for Fiction): I escaped from slavery, but I am haunted by the chains of its memory. My life is choked by the past. I am a woman who has lost too much—a husband, a child, friends. I found a new man to love, but the ghosts of our past keep tearing us apart. Ask yourself the question: Would you rather your children live in slavery or die so they don't suffer the abuse you suffered? (*This book contains mature themes and language.*)

....

Dana (*Kindred*): OK, what's up with this? Here I am a 26-year-old black woman in the year 1976, and I keep getting called into the past to save a white man who turns out to be my ancestor. If that's not bad enough, not weird enough, the past is during slavery times and as a black woman, those white ancestors of mine mistake me for a slave. Nothing in my education or knowledge of the future helped me escape slavery.

....

Frederick Douglass (*Narrative of the Life of Frederick Douglass, An American Slave*): Although many know me as a statesman, writer, and diplomat, I began life enslaved. I was a slave to many masters. A turning point of my life came when I became a house slave to a wealthy family in Baltimore. It was there that I tricked white children to teach me to read. This changed my life forever. My many slave experiences helped me become the person I am today. I once fought and beat a white man and learned a valuable lesson about life. This book is my story, the narrative of a slave's life. Perhaps the most famous line from my narrative is, "You have seen how a man was made a slave; now you will see how a slave was made a man."

....

47 (*47*): I am a young slave boy. My name, the one branded on my arm, is 47 because I am the 47th slave on a 19th-century plantation in Georgia. The master didn't see fit to give me a real name, which only begins to tell you about the troubles I've seen. Yes, I witness injustices—family members sold away, whippings, and the daily grind of hard work. But a strange being named Tall John, who appears to be a runaway slave boy, comes into my life and changes my destiny. Tall John is part science fiction and part old slave myth taken from High John the Conqueror, a spirit from Africa who comes to free all of the slaves. He teaches me a crucial lesson: Neither a slave nor a master be.

....

Rutherford Calhoun (*Middle Passage*—winner of the National Book Award): The year is 1830. I am a freed slave, an ardent womanizer, and a self-confessed liar and thief. I was forced to flee New Orleans because of bad debts and bad romance. But my bad luck got me into even more trouble. The ship I stowed away on was the slave ship *The Republic* on its way to pick up human cargo in Africa. The ship's captain lives on the borderline between genius and madness, the crew members are seafaring scum, and the slaves eventually packed into the hold belong to an ancient tribe of magicians. This book is the story of my journey. *(This book contains mature themes and language.)*

....

Linda Brent (*Incidents in the Life of a Slave Girl*): Most of the slave narratives are by men, but this is the story of my journey from slavery to freedom. Old Dr. Flint's daughter owned me, but it was Dr. Flint who made my life miserable. "My master met me at every turn, reminding me that I belong to him, and swearing by heaven and earth that he would compel me to submit to him. If I went out for a breath of fresh air, after a day of [hard work,] his footsteps dogged me. If I knelt by my mother's grave, his dark shadow fell on me even there." In other words, the man hounded me, tried to rape me, and refused to let me marry the man I loved—even when this man scraped together enough money to buy my freedom.

....

Tituba (*I, Tituba, Black Witch of Salem*): You will find my name in the history books of the Salem witch trials. This novel takes what little piece of history was given to a black woman and makes me come back to life. At the age of 7, I watched as my mother was hanged for fighting back when a plantation owner tried to rape her. I was raised by Mama Yaya, who taught me the secrets of healing and magic. Her secrets brought me joy and pain during my life. Unfortunately, like too many women, I fell in love with the wrong man—John Indian. I followed him into slavery, and into Salem, Massachusetts, where the "good citizens" hanged witches—or anyone different. This is my story—part true and part invented. *(This book contains mature themes and language.)*

....

5: Language and Power

Steve Liss/GETTY IMAGES

Uncovering the Legacy of Language and Power

"You will never teach a child a new language by scorning and ridiculing and forcibly erasing his first language."　　　　　—June Jordan

Lamont's sketch was stick-figure simple: A red schoolhouse with brown students entering one door and exiting as white students at the other end of the building. Kahlia's illustration depicted a more elaborate metaphor: She drew a map of Africa hanging from a tree; tightly closed red lips cover the heart of the map. A U.S. map flies over the tree, and sentences swirl around it: "I cannot speak my language. My identity is gone. My African language is gone. The language I grew up with has been taken from me."

In the classroom, according to my students who study the linguistic history of the colonized, too often the job of the teacher is to "whitewash" students of color or students who are linguistically diverse.

Over the years, students have drawn mouths sewn shut, tongues nailed to the ground, languages squeezed out or buried under stacks of English grammar books, a Spanish voice box removed, graveyards for indigenous languages, a mouth rubbed out by an eraser with the word English written across the top, and language trees with the withered leaves of Korean, Spanish, Russian, African languages dropping off while the red, ripe English fruit flourished. As my students' drawings depicted over and over in a variety of ways, schools and societies erase language and culture.

Our schools do not have linguistic genocide as their mission. In fact, most schools and school boards fashion mission statements about "embracing diversity." Multilingual banners welcome visitors in Spanish, Russian, Vietnamese on the hallway walls of most school buildings these days, but in the classroom, according to my students who study the linguistic history of the colonized, too often the job of the teacher is to "whitewash" students of color or students who are linguistically diverse.

English Only laws in many states have banned Spanish and other languages from some classrooms. Ebonics was used as fodder for racist jokes after the Oakland School Board proposed teaching Ebonics. Native American languages were decimated in boarding schools during a time when "Kill the Indian, Save the Man" directives gave straightforward instructions to teachers. Although I intentionally invite and acknowledge the variety of languages and voices from our community into the classroom, I learned this wasn't enough. I can tell students to use their home language in their poems and narratives, and I can bring August Wilson's plays, Lois-Ann Yamanaka's stories, and Jimmy Santiago Baca's poetry into my class to validate the use of dialect and home language; but without examining the legacy of language supremacy, I maintain the old world order because I haven't explored why Standard English is the standard and how it came to power, and how that power is wielded to make some people feel welcome and others feel like outsiders.

After years of teaching and tinkering with this language unit, I finally realized that I needed to create a curriculum on language and power that examined the colonial roots of linguistic genocide and analyzed how schools continue to perpetuate the myths of inferiority or invisibility of some languages. I also discovered the need for stories of hope: stories of people's resistance to the loss of their mother tongues and stories about the growing movement to save indigenous languages from extinction.

Depending on how many pieces of the unit I include, this curriculum takes between five and 10 weeks. Students read literature, nonfiction texts, poetry, and watch films. They write narratives, poetry, and a culminating essay about language. For their final "exam," they create a "take-it-to-the-people" project that teaches their chosen audience an aspect of our language study that they think people need to know in order to understand contemporary language issues. The curriculum includes any of the following five segments: Naming as a Practice of Power; Language and Colonization; Dialect and Power; Ebonics; and Language Restoration.

Linguistic Genocide Through Colonization

Max Weinreich, a Yiddish linguist, wrote, "A language is a dialect with an army and a navy." In other words, it's about power. In order for students to understand how some languages came to be dominant, they need to understand how and why indigenous languages were wiped out or marginalized. According to the Living Tongues Institute for Endangered Languages, over half of the world's languages have become extinct in the last 500 years. In fact, David Harrison, a linguistics professor at Swarthmore, says, "the pace of their global extinction exceeds the pace of species extinction." Students need to understand how this invisible legacy that privileges some languages—and people—and excludes or decimates others continues to affect us today.

Teaching about language and power is huge and complex and messy because language policies and colonial practices played out in different ways across the globe. In some places, the languages died with the people who spoke them, as colonial powers took both the land and the lives of the people they "encountered." In some instances, indigenous groups were pitted against each other. In many places, colonists renamed every nook and cranny, banned native languages, and created governments, schools, and economic systems using the language of the colonizer's home country.

Today, language is still contested territory in many parts of the world. Because most political, educational, and commercial interactions take place in the language of the colonizer or the primary language, many indigenous languages have become marginalized or extinct. Parents are frequently forced to choose between teaching their children in their home language or pushing them to study the language of the dominant social groups. In a workshop in San Francisco, a teacher talked about how the educational and economic necessity of learning English pressed her to put her Vietnamese language aside. "I didn't feel like I had a choice." Ultimately, this forced choice causes a disconnect between generations of language speakers and a loss of family ties, traditions, and cultural memory.

Because of time, my classes didn't study each language situation in depth; instead, we looked for patterns across the stories. In many places, the colonizers taught people shame about their "primitive" or "backward" language and cultural practices. As Ngugi wa Thiong'o, a Kenyan teacher, novelist, essayist, and playwright, wrote in his essay "The Language of African Literature":

> The real aim of colonialism was to control the people's wealth ... [but] economic and political control can never be complete or effective without mental control. To control a people's culture is to control their tools of self-definition in relationship to others. For colonialism, this involved two aspects of the same process: the

destruction or the deliberate undervaluing of a people's culture, their art, dances, religions, history, geography, education, orature and literature, and the conscious elevation of the language of the colonizer. The domination of a people's language by the languages of the colonizing nations was crucial to the domination of the mental universe of the colonizers.

Ngugi stopped writing in English and started writing in his native tongue—Kikuyu—as a protest against the devaluing of his mother tongue, but also as a way to revive and celebrate literature in his language. This "conscious elevation of the language of the colonizer" and the parallel domination of the "mental universe" that Ngugi wa Thiong'o describes is echoed in stories from Kenya to Ireland to Australia to the United States.

I need to teach students how and why some languages have power and others don't.

The "domination of the mental universe of the colonizers" continues today in the daily interactions that "nonstandard" language speakers must negotiate when they enter the halls of power—schools, banks, government and employment offices. Whether it's the marking down of essays because of "poor" grammar or the conscious or unconscious way that lack of linguistic dexterity marks a speaker or writer as "unfit" for a position—a job, a college, or a scholarship—language inequality still exists. The power of the standard language is so pervasive and so invisible that students need to uncover what they take for granted and internalize as personal failure. But I also need to teach them how and why some languages have power and others don't.

The Linguistic Tea Party

To familiarize students with the context and characters they will meet during our journey into language and colonialism, I wrote a tea party to introduce the personalities and events they will encounter as we read stories or watch movie clips. The roles also alert students to the patterns that emerge in the unit—loss of languages, humiliation, shame, and beatings, as well as the heroic efforts to save dying tongues. I tried to make the tea party entice students into curiosity about language study—admittedly, not a subject that most students initially rate as the number one topic they want to learn about.

As George Bernard Shaw wrote in the preface to his play *Pygmalion*, which I typically teach as part of the unit,

"I wish to boast that Pygmalion has been an extremely successful play all over Europe and North America as well as at home. It is so intensely and deliberately didactic, and its subject is esteemed so dry, that I delight in throwing it at the heads of the wiseacres who repeat the parrot cry that art should never be didactic. It goes to prove my contention that art should never be anything else." Although I hesitate to crow like Shaw, the "dry" and "didactic" subject of language engages students because language is so closely tied to culture and home.

In constructing the tea party roles, I write in first person, so students feel more comfortable introducing themselves as the person. Bud Lane's role, for example, gives students a sense of the urgency around the issue of language preservation. Although Oregon was once among the most linguistically diverse places on earth, it is now infamous as a language-death hot spot according to the Living Tongues Institute for Endangered Languages, because there are few remaining first speakers—people who learned the language as children:

Some people already count my language as dead. I speak Oregon Coastal Athabaskan. At 50, I am one of the youngest speakers of my language. Here in the Northwest, we are a hot spot for language extinction. I'm hoping to change that. You see, I think that the language and the people are the same. I didn't grow up speaking my language either, but I found an elder Siletz woman who knew the words, but who never spoke them in public. She'd been taught shame of her native tongue by white society. But Nellie Orton found her voice and taught me my language. Now I teach our language at the local school, so that our children can save our native tongue.

Each character can answer at least one question on the tea party question sheet. (See p. 226.) For example, Lane's character answers the question, "Find someone who started or joined an organization to preserve his or her language. Who is the person? Why did the individual decide to take this action?" Most of the tea party questions can be answered by more than one person.

Students meet a spectrum of characters, including Distinguished Professor Geneva "Dr. G." Smitherman; Irish poet Gearóid Mac Lochlainn; Hawaiian writer Lois-Ann Yamanaka; Carmen Lomas Garza, a Mexican American artist; Hector Pieterson, a 12-year-old boy killed in the Soweto Uprising; and Neville Alexander, a South African linguist working to restore mother tongue literacy in Africa. (See pp. 218-225 for the full roles.)

After I distribute a role and tea party questions to students, I ask them to read the role and underline key facts that their classmates need to know: Where is this person from? What is his or her experience with language? I also tell them to highlight any piece of information they find particularly compelling. Then I tell them to turn the role sheet over and write those key facts on the back. Students are more likely to remember the facts if they read them, write them, and recite them. Once most students have completed these tasks, I demonstrate what I want them to do. I pretend I am one of the characters, say Esther Martinez, and I walk to a student across the room and say, "Hi, I'm Esther Martinez. I want to tell you a few things about myself." I ham it up, so they won't feel awkward pretending they are a character from our tea party. Students are stiff and unsure the first time they introduce themselves as their character, but after a few conversations, they own their role; they've become John Rickford or Hector Pieterson.

After the tea party, I ask students to write a paragraph about what they learned about language and power and then we talk. During our post-tea party discussion, Deandre said, "[The society] tried to take people from what they were raised to believe in, and I don't believe that was right." When I pressed him, "Who was one person you met who had something taken away from them?" he talked about his own character, Joe Suina. He said, "Well, myself. My name is Joe Suina. I am currently a professor of Curriculum and Instruction at University of New Mexico. I was punished at school for speaking my language, and they tried to teach me that my language was not right. They tried to turn me into what was the dominant culture. They tried to make me believe what everyone else believed in."

Reading the School Stories: Finding the Patterns

After the tea party, we dive into the readings and movies. I want to saturate students in the stories—memoirs and fiction—about language. We begin by examining five memoirs about language and boarding schools—two from the United States, one from Australia, one from Kenya, and one from Canada. These are short 2- or 3-page excerpts from longer pieces and two video clips. In addition to reacting to each piece about language and boarding schools through writing and discussion, students keep track of each person's experiences on a chart, including a description of the race and class of each main character. I tell them to record who is forced or encouraged to change their language, who doesn't have to change, and who forces the change. (See Story Retrieval charts on pp. 228-229.) Because the unit is long, the charts help them collect evidence over the span of the unit, so they can quickly go back and retrieve evidence for the culminating essay or project.

I begin by examining what happened to Native Americans. The video *In the White Man's Image*, a documentary about Native American boarding schools, shows the Carlisle Indian School established by Captain Richard Pratt, who attempted to assimilate Native American children into white society from 1879 to 1918. Today Pratt's mission is widely viewed as cultural genocide. Pratt's

Bettman Archive/CORBIS

(Left) Chiracahua Apaches as they looked upon their arrival at the Carlisle Indian School, an institution dedicated to inducing Native Americans to abandon their traditional ways. (Right) Chiracahua Apaches after four months at the Carlisle Indian School.

motto was, "Kill the Indian and save the man." In order to "kill the Indian," he punished children for practicing their religion and speaking their language. He renamed them, cut their hair and took away their clothes. Native students resisted Pratt's attempts to "deculturize" them as one of my students, Harold, put it. Many died, others ran away, few graduated, and ultimately, most maintained their Native American identity. Pratt used before and after photographs of the students to sell white audiences on the success of his school.

In the White Man's Image portrays the boarding school system at work, but doesn't focus as much on the individual stories, except for Ernest White Thunder, who resisted the campaign to take away his culture by running away

Dee said, "If you kill the Indian culture, you might as well kill the Indian because nothing about him is really him."

from the school and refusing to eat. Ultimately, he died. His resistance was a touchstone for some students who referenced White Thunder and later wanted to review his section of the video for their essays and projects. Dee said, "If you kill the Indian culture, you might as well kill the Indian because nothing about him is really him."

Joe Suina's essay, "And Then I Went to School: Memories of a Pueblo Childhood" (see p. 230), describes his experiences at a boarding school where he learned to be ashamed of his language and his home:

> My language, too, was questioned right from the beginning of my school career. "Leave your Indian at home!" was like a school trademark. Speaking it accidentally or otherwise was punishable by a dirty look or a whack with a ruler. This reprimand was for speaking the language of my people which meant so much to me. It was the language of my grandmother. . . . [I]t was difficult for me to comprehend why I had to part with my language. . . . I understood that everything that I had, and was part of, was not nearly as good as the whiteman's. School was determined to undo me in everything from my sheepskin bedding to the dances and ceremonies which I had learned to have faith in and cherish.

Because the video clips are only about 15 to 20 minutes each and the stories are short, we mostly read them aloud in class together, filling in the chart individually, then discussing each piece as a class, as we move through the

stories. The boarding school stories, videos, and discussion take about a week. As we read one story after another, students see the pattern of punishment and shame that permeate the stories. When I asked, "What do these stories have in common? What do you learn about language and power?" Josh said, "When people weren't allowed to speak their own language, and when they were punished for speaking it, people felt inferior and stupid. It crumbled the community."

After learning about language policies in Native American boarding schools, we look at similar practices in Australia and Africa. Molly Craig's experiences in Australia, recounted in the film *Rabbit Proof Fence*, parallel Suina's experience in Native American boarding schools. Molly was part of Australia's "stolen generation" of mixed-race children who were taken from the "bad influence" of their families and isolated in boarding schools where they were trained as maids and day laborers—another forced assimilation into the white society. Part of the process of merging "half-caste" children into white culture was separating them from their language as well as their religion. After watching a video clip from *Rabbit Proof Fence*, I asked students to respond to Molly's story in an interior monologue or poem. Throughout these stories, students connected with loss of culture and heritage, but they also connected with Molly's resistance. In the following poem, Jennifer Overman takes on Molly's point of view, expressing her resistance:

> Write that I was a half-caste,
> taken away from my family and my home
> to be cleansed of my aboriginality,
> to be a slave.
>
> When you speak of me,
> Say that I refused to be erased,
> That my blood would stay the same,
> That I would not serve my other half.

Maria succinctly captured this resistance to "whitewashing" in her piece from Molly's perspective when she wrote simply, "You can never wipe the brown from my skin."

In her memoir *Unbowed*, Wangari Maathai, who won the Nobel Peace Prize for her work on the Green Belt Movement in Kenya, describes the ongoing process of humiliation that caused students to abandon their language at school, at home, and later when they became part of the country's educated elite. Her words echo the pain heard in the other stories we read:

A common practice to ensure that students kept pressure on one another was to require those students who were found using a language other than English to wear a button known as a "monitor." It was sometimes inscribed with phrases in English such as "I am stupid, I was caught speaking my mother tongue." At the end of the day, whoever ended up with the button received a punishment, such as cutting grass, sweeping, or doing work in the garden. But the greater punishment was the embarrassment you felt because you had talked in your mother tongue. In retrospect I can see that this introduced us to the world of undermining our self-confidence.... The use of the monitor continues even today in Kenyan schools to ensure that students use only English. Now, as then, this contributes to the trivialization of anything African and lays the foundation for a deeper sense of self-doubt and an inferiority complex.

When I asked students to make connections between the stories, they pointed out both the enforced changes as well as the changes that students in the readings adopted to avoid embarrassment. Although students initially laughed at Denzell Weekly's comparison of the boarding schools to the movie *Men in Black*, ultimately, they agreed with his explanation. He said, "This is like the movie *Men in Black*. For anyone who's seen *Men in Black*, there is a flashlight. They're looking and they're flashing and they erase all of your memory. They tried to come in and just brainwash, basically take away their language and their culture." When students become passionate about a subject, this is what they do: search their own experiences to make original, unusual connections to the curriculum.

A number of students wrote their essays about assimilation. (See "Writing Wild Essays from Hard Ground" for a full description of the essay-writing process.) While some students merely summarized the series of events, Dennise Mofidi focused on children who resisted assimilation. "The children who did not fear punishment were the ones who fought for their culture. They were the ones who suffered horrible consequences, including the loss of their lives." She went on to relate this to her relationship with her grandmother and Farsi:

Today assimilation is still happening. Children go to school and see that everyone else is speaking English and feel different if they are the only one who does not speak English at home. My family came here from Iran and speaks both English and Farsi. My mother and father taught me to speak Farsi, and I do at home and when I'm with my family. My younger brothers, on the

April 1994, Soweto, South Africa — Members of a Soweto school drama group reenact the events of the 1976 Soweto student uprising.

other hand, do not speak Farsi. I asked them why and they told me, "I don't want people to know that I speak another language or ask me how to say a word in Farsi because then they will want me to talk in Farsi all the time and we live in America, not Iran." I couldn't believe that being different at school was so hard that they would not want to be able to talk to their family.... My grandmother and I talk all the time in Farsi. She tells me about Iran and what it is like there. She also shares stories of life when she was younger. I love talking with my grandmother and couldn't imagine being like my brothers and needing someone to translate.

In his final essay, Daunte Paschal wrote about Carmen Lomas Garza's experience in school. "In 'A Piece of My Heart/Pedacito de mi corazón,' Garza wrote about her life growing up as a full-blooded Chicana in a predominantly white school.... Because of those girls at her school making fun of her, she started to feel ashamed about her food that her mother had made. Garza was verbally assaulted, and she eventually felt as if she was born in the wrong race and wrong culture. Assimilation will do that to you."

Resistance: Soweto Uprising

On the day we studied the Soweto Uprising, I started class by projecting the image of Samuel Nzima's famous photograph of Mbuyisa Makhubu carrying the dead body of 12-year-old Hector Pieterson. I played "Nkosi Sikelel' iAfrika" (God Bless Africa) while students entered the classroom. Then we read and listened to a podcast about this historic event where thousands of students marched out of their schools in a mass demonstration against the use of Afrikaans as the language of instruction. Students refused to learn in the "oppressor's tongue." This protest against the education that blacks received in South

Africa was built on years of grievances against the Bantu Education Act established in 1953 as well as years of grievances against apartheid, racism, and exploitation. Black schools were overcrowded and underfunded, preparing students for a life in the mines, not the university. The imposition of Afrikaans pushed the radicalized student movement to action against the language as well as the government.

As students listened and read about the Soweto Uprising, I asked them to take notes in three columns: one column on the details for the demonstration, one on their reactions, and one on connections they made to the other pieces we had studied. A number of students admired that people their age "took matters in their own hands," as Kalia Haa Watts wrote. Annie Oldani, who wrote her essay on the uprising, noted that "[The students] felt so isolated from their culture and their families that they didn't think they would support their cause. The adult generation is resigned to taking their place in the society and not fighting the oppression of their people." Michael's reaction to the story of the uprising echoed the feelings expressed by a number of students:

> I know a lot of kids put their well-being on the line for their education, and I respect that more than anything because I don't know too many people who'd be so quick to stand up and plan the gathering of thousands of students and say this is what we need to do to create change and better opportunity. I like how they didn't tell their parents and were resourceful enough to band together and do what they had to do. A line that stood out to me was "the parents are immune to the yoke of oppression."

After gathering information about the Soweto Uprising, students wrote from the point of view of a witness to the day's events. I encouraged students to think of people, but also to think about inanimate objects. Their list included: rocks students threw, Hector Pieterson's sister (from the photograph), the school, a burned-out car, a student involved in the uprising. (See "Unleashing Sorrow and Joy: Writing Poetry from History and Literature," p. 50, for a full explanation of how I teach these poems.) Annie wrote from the point of view of a student who watched Hector Pieterson die:

> *We no longer march*
> *Now we fight*
> *Not just for our language*
> *Not anymore*
> *But for ourselves*

> *For Hector*
> *Who wanted to laugh*
> *Wanted to cry*
> *Wanted to speak the words of his family*
> *The words of his people*

Jayme's poem as Hector's classmate uses the "Write that I ..." frame (see p. 52) that helped some students move into their poems:

> *Write that I*
> *sang as loud as I could*
> *in unison with my brothers and sisters*
> *until a deafening "Nkosi Sikelel´ iAfrika"*
> *was all that could be heard.*
> *Write that I,*
> *along with my people,*
> *posed no threat to the police*
> *except for*
> *the threat of our knowledge*
> *the threat of our desire*
> *the threat of our power*
> *marching united and strong*
> *like a pack of lions.*

Students demonstrated both pain and outrage through their poetry and interior monologues, a fitting memorial to the children of Soweto. But their poetry is also an expression of their understanding of the events in a way that quizzes or discussions miss.

Metaphorical Drawings

Once we've read the memoirs about the boarding schools in the United States and Kenya, watched video clips from Australia and Ireland, and listened to and read about Soweto, I bring boxes of crayons and colored pencils and large pieces of blank paper to class. I ask students to create a visual representation of language and power, telling them, "Don't worry about your drawing ability. I'm looking for the quality of your ideas, your ability to work with all of that information you've collected over the last quarter." After the initial excitement of using crayons in a high school class and the initial groans that they can't think of a single metaphor, the ideas start rolling. We begin the conversation by recalling the definition of a metaphor and brainstorming a few examples. I walk a fine line of giving them enough models to jumpstart their imagination, but not so many that my ideas crowd out theirs. I show them a couple of drawings from former students, including stick figure sketches, so they can see a range of possibilities, but

also because I don't want their drawing skills to get in the way of their ideas. When they complete the drawing, they write a paragraph explaining their metaphor.

As I noted in the opening of the chapter, student metaphorical drawings of lips sewn shut, language coffins, and severed tongues are evocative. Michael Moser drew three boxes, each locked with a padlock. The writing on the first one said, "Freedom of thinking, knowledge, freedom of speech"; the second box had a heart with the words "family, name, culture, homeland" on the exterior; the third one said, "religion, soul, language, culture." Michael wrote:

> To assimilate someone you take way their mind, heart and soul. Their mind is the right to think and their freedom to speak their own language. To take away their heart is to take the things they love, like their family and their home. The third is how the boarding school kids were taken from their families and forced to adopt a new religion and new language. And to take someone's soul is to take everything they stand for.

Kirkland Allen drew a picture of a dark-skinned woman with her black hair pulled straight by a comb with the word "school" across it. On the side of his picture, he drew a series of cans and jars labeled "Proper English Magic Grease," "Plan B Insurance," and "After School Bands." The title on his drawing read, "If You Can't Achieve It, Weave It." He wrote:

> In this piece a nappy-headed woman is getting her hair done. Proper English Grease moisturizing it, a school comb working with the grease, forming it into a white version. After-school rubber bands hold the hair together, giving her the thought that going back is bad.

Deandre, a talented rapper, excels in assignments that call upon him to bring his gifts of rapping to bear on the content of our unit. He drew a stage with two flags, a U.S. flag and a flag with "Africa" written on it. A microphone stood in front of each flag. The U.S. mic was plugged in.

A hand unplugged the African microphone. He said, "It's about unplugging our voice."

When students shared their drawings with the class, I pushed them to fuller explanations. "What's that tell us about language and power? What's your explanation? What does your drawing illustrate?" While the student drawings demonstrated understanding, their discussion of their drawings bordered on generalizations, littered with indeterminate pronouns. For example, a number of students said, "They beat students for speaking their language." I pushed them to identify who "they" were, to name names. "Who beat them? Where did this happen? Locate it." At one point, I said, "Let's name them together. Whose languages and cultures were taken away? Who took them away? You need to be specific." This is an important part of the activity because too often students describe or recite events, but in the past I've failed to push them to analyze their drawings. Students know things in their bones, and the metaphorical drawings tap this "bone knowledge." But without pressing kids to precisely articulate their analysis, the brilliant insights revealed in their drawings may stay in their bones.

Although the drawings might seem like a day of child's play—and we do have fun on those days—they also serve a critical purpose: They help students rehearse the creation of a thesis and support for their upcoming essay. Even if the students do not use the drawings and metaphors in their language essays, creating an image that summarizes their understanding about language pushes them to think more deeply about the patterns they saw across the readings and to start articulating those understandings as they draw, as they write their explanation, and as they present their piece to their peers. This class-talk about the topic, the use of specific and varied examples, the building on each other's ideas, helps them later as they construct their essays.

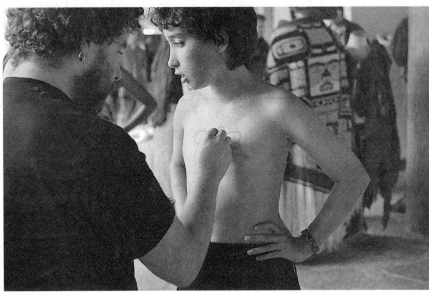

Farah Nosh/GETTY IMAGES

Brothers Gwaai (left) and Staas prepare to perform a Haida language play at the Haida Heritage Centre at Skidegate beach, Haida Gwaii, Canada. The language of the Haida is considered highly threatened with fewer than 70 fluent speakers left in the world.

Language Restoration

Because of time limitations, we never spend as much time on the language restoration movement as it deserves. But after all of the death and destruction, I want students to become familiar with some of the current work across the globe to save indigenous languages. Students need to critique, but they also need to learn how to build and rebuild. The inspiring stories of language preservation from Ireland to Kenya to South Africa to Hawaii and the Oregon Coast provide great models of how grassroots people—from grandmothers to youth activists—are creating language schools as well as lobbying for legislation to keep languages alive.

For example, Neville Alexander, Director of the Project for the Study of Alternative Education in South Africa (PRAESA), created the National Language project to bring "mother tongue" literacy back into the lives of African people across the continent. He recognized that because of colonization many people had become illiterate in two languages—their mother tongue and the colonial language. As the Language Plan of Africa states, "Colonial conquest, imperialism and globalization established a hierarchy of standard languages, which mirrors the power relations on the planet. The overall effect of this configuration has been to hasten the extinction of innumerable language varieties and to stigmatize and marginalize all but the most powerful languages." His organization promotes a culture of reading and writing in African languages, and works with publishers to develop a market for African language writing and literature. Alexander and others in his organization have also initiated programs with teachers to help develop materials and strategies to bring back mother tongue literacy in the schools.

In the United States, language activists, including Esther Martinez, pushed for legislation to keep the remaining 150 of the original indigenous languages alive. The Esther Martinez Native American Languages Preservation Act, H.R. 4766, was passed in 2006. This legislation provides money to support Native American language immersion programs: language nests, survival schools, and language restoration programs. As the website Cultural Survival points out:

> Native American languages are not disappearing because they are obsolete. They are disappearing because of a U.S. government policy to specifically terminate American Indian language. Under this program, which lasted until the 1950s, children were taken from their homes and forced into boarding schools where they were beaten and had their mouths washed out with blistering lye soap for speaking their language. With that background of brutality, they did not speak their language in their homes as adults, so their children never learned it—the chain was broken. But the remaining Native American languages can be saved. There are proven techniques that enable elders to pass on their languages to their children and grandchildren. Immersion schools surround Native youngsters with their own language and build fluency quickly and naturally. Native Hawaiians launched an immersion program in the 1980s, when there were fewer than 30 speakers of Hawaiian under the age of 18. Today there are 2,000 speakers in that age range.

Other tribes have set up similar schools, with similar results. Others are teaching Native languages to adult learners who will pass them on to their tribes' children.

To bring the point home, we read our local paper's article, "Last of the Siletz Speakers," about Bud Lane's work to keep the Oregon Coastal Athabaskan language alive by teaching at Siletz High School. He recorded the elders in the community and developed a dictionary for the language. Now he teaches the language to students at Siletz High School and works with researchers at the Living Tongues Institute in Salem, Ore., to preserve his language.

In retrospect, I should have spent more time on the incredibly exciting language preservation work, perhaps by assigning student groups different language projects to research and report on as part of the unit. Next time. ■

References and Recommended Background Information

Anzaldúa, Gloria. (1987). "How to tame a wild tongue." *Borderlands/La frontera: The new mestiza* (pp. 53-54). San Francisco: Spinsters/Aunt Lute.

Crawford, James. (1992). *Hold Your Tongue: Bilingualism and the Politics of "English Only."* New York: Addison-Wesley Publishing.

Delpit, Lisa, & Kilgour Dowdy, Joanne (Eds). (2002). *The Skin that We Speak: Thoughts on Language and Culture in the Classroom.* New York: The New Press.

Delpit, Lisa, & Perry, Theresa (Eds). (1998). *The Real Ebonics Debate: Power, Language, and the Education of African American Children.* Boston: Beacon.

Heape, Steven R. (Executive Producer) and Chip Ritchie (Director). (2008). *Our Spirits Don't Speak English: Indian Boarding School.* Dallas: Rich Heape Films. (Available at www.richheape.com.)

Lesiak, Chris (Writer and Director). (1988). "In the White Man's Image." *PBS: The American Experience* [Television Series, 17 February 1992 (Season 4, Episode 12)]. (Available from WGBH Education Foundation. http://shop.wgbh.org/product/show/8390)

Lippi-Green, Rosina. (1997). *English with an Accent: Language, ideology, and discrimination in the United States.* London: Routledge.

Martinez, E. (2004). *My Life in San Juan Pueblo.* Urbana: University of Illinois Press.

Mac Lochlainn, Gearóid. (2002). *Stream of Tongues: Sruth Teangacha.* Conamara, Ireland: Cló Iar-Chonnachta.

wa Thiongo, Ngugi. (2004). *Consciousness and African Renaissance: South Africa in the Black Imagination* [PDF document]. Retrieved Steve Biko Memorial Lecture online at: www.ukzn.ac.za/CCS/files/NGUGI-BIKO.pdf

Yamanaka, L. (undated). *The politics of Pidgin.* Promotional material. New York: Farrar, Straus & Giroux.

Tea Party

Hector Pieterson (Soweto, South Africa): I was 12 years old in 1976, when the South African police killed me on June 16. The colonial government decided that blacks would be educated in Afrikaans, the language of white Afrikaners in South Africa. It's a language that was used by the rulers, and black children hated Afrikaans. Most of our teachers didn't even know Afrikaans, so many of us failed our classes because we didn't understand the language. We didn't want to speak the language anyway because it was the language of the South African government, our oppressors. We became frustrated by our teachers' and parents' inability to change the system, so groups of students formed our own meetings in March 1976. We started slowdowns and class boycotts. On June 16, between 10,000 and 15,000 students left their schools and marched in the streets of Soweto, a black township near Johannesburg. We sang the song "Senzeni na?" ("What have we done?"), and carried signs that said, "Away with Afrikaans" as we made our way towards Orlando Stadium. Before we reached our destination, the police opened fire on us.

Damien O'Donovan (Ireland, *The Wind That Shakes the Barley*): In 1920, I watched one of my friends, Michael, get beaten to death by the British army for speaking Irish. After the British invaded Ireland and took over, we were forbidden to speak Irish in school. The teachers had a "tally stick," which they beat us with if they caught us speaking Irish. We didn't want to speak the language of the people who took over our country. We felt like traitors to our own history when we spoke English. In 1893 an organization called "Conradh na Gaeilge" (the Irish League) was formed to try to keep our language alive. Language is part of our identity. The Irish League wanted to preserve our literary culture as well as our language. They didn't succeed in stopping the decline of our language, but they instilled pride. "Within twenty years the Irish language was inextricably linked to the question of Irish independence. *'Ni tír gan teanga'* ('without a language you have no country') was the new battle cry of the men and women who fought for independence in 1916. When freedom finally came, the Irish language was designated the first official language of the new nation."

Gloria Anzaldúa (Texas, *Borderlands/La Frontera: The New Mestiza*): I am a Tejana Chicana. I grew up in Texas near the Mexican border. When I was a child, my teacher hit me when I spoke Spanish at recess. When I was a student at the Pan American University, I, and all Chicano students, were required to take two speech classes to get rid of our accents. Instead of giving up my language, I used my Chicano English to talk back. My language is my identity. Until I can be proud when I speak my language, I cannot take pride in myself. Until I am free to write bilingually and to code-switch without having always to translate, I cannot take pride in myself. I will no longer be made to feel ashamed for existing. I will have my voice: Indian, Spanish, white. I will have my serpent's tongue—my woman's voice, my sexual voice, my poet's voice. I will overcome the tradition of silence.

Joe Suina (New Mexico, "And Then I Went to School"): I am a professor in the department of Curriculum and Instruction at University of New Mexico. I grew up in a Pueblo home with my grandmother until I was 6. Then I was sent to school, which was a painful experience. I was told, "Leave your Indian at home." When I spoke the language that my grandmother and I sang and prayed in, I was punished with a dirty look or a whack with a ruler. In school I was taught that the way my grandmother spoke was not right. I learned that my people were not right. Unfortunately, I was taught to be ashamed of my language and my home. I was one of many indigenous people whose language and culture were stripped so we could assimilate into the dominant culture.

John Rickford (Stanford, "Suite for Ebony & Phonics"): I am a linguist at Stanford. My book, *Spoken Soul*, is about African American Vernacular English, otherwise known as Ebonics. And don't laugh when you say it. Ebonics came to be a joke with late-night comedians after the Oakland School Board approved a resolution recognizing it as the primary language of African American students. But it is no joke to linguists—or to African American writers. What some label a "lazy language" or a "slang language," James Baldwin called "this incredible music." Ebonics has a systematic, complex grammar structure that most linguists identify as originating in Africa. Of course, this debate mirrors similar debates across the globe. Like many linguists, I understand that linguistic identity is tied up in cultural identity. When our language is stigmatized by the broader society, children learn to be ashamed of their mother tongue.

Lois-Ann Yamanaka (Hawai'i, "Obituary"): I was raised in Pahala, a sugar plantation town on the Big Island of Hawai'i. I write my poems and stories in Pidgin instead of Standard English because I cherish the language, culture, and people I grew up with. With my stories, I fight back against the teachers who told me I would never make it if I spoke Pidgin. If I stopped speaking my language, I would be cutting my ties to my home and relatives, my family gatherings, the foods prepared and eaten by my people, and I would change my relationships to friends and neighbors. I grew up with the sound of Pidgin in my own mouth, in my own writing. When I spoke it and wrote it, I discovered the institutional racism so profound in generations of us here in Hawai'i that we cannot even smell it for what it is.

Ngugi wa Thiong'o (Kenya, "Consciousness and African Renaissance: South Africa in the Black Imagination"): I am a Kenyan writer of Kikuyu descent. I began a successful writing career writing in English before turning to work almost entirely in my native language, Kikuyu. I wrote several successful novels in English—*Weep Not, Child; A Grain of Wheat; The River Between*; and *Petals of Blood.* Then in 1986, I wrote *Decolonising the Mind*, my "farewell to English." For me, English in Africa is a "cultural bomb" that continues a process of erasing memories of precolonial cultures and history. Speaking or writing in English is a new form of colonialism—of taking away our cultural heritage and memories and replacing them with a language and view of the world that fails to honor our people's literature and culture. By writing in my mother tongue, I am not only honoring Kikuyu traditions and our past, I am acknowledging and communicating their present. African writers need to reclaim their mother tongues.

Gearóid Mac Lochlainn (Ireland, "I Am the Tongue"): I'm a Belfast poet who writes about the urban experience in Northern Ireland. My language shows the fragmented, shrapnel-strewn life I've lived in "north of Ireland." I write in a language—Irish—that is neither fashionable nor profitable. I believe that the outlawing of the Irish language was the main tool in the overall silencing of voices of dissent—just like with the American Indians. In fact, when I went to New York, I heard about native language restoration on the Pine Ridge Reservation. I left New York and went out to Pine Ridge because I'm working to set up Irish language programs in Belfast's schools.

Molly Craig (Australia, *Rabbit Proof Fence*): When I was 14 years old, my sister, my cousin, and I were stolen from our family in Jigalong, Australia, and taken to the Moore River Native Settlement—an internment camp for mixed-race Aboriginal children. Here, we were taught that our language, our culture, our religion, our parents were bad and everything British was good. Here, my native tongue—Mardujara—was beaten out of me. The government believed that "mixed" Aboriginal children were smarter than their darker relatives. They believed we should be taken from the bad influence of our families and should be isolated and trained as maids and day laborers. As one Australian official said, "We have power under the Act to take any child from its mother at any stage of its life....Are we going to have a population of one million blacks in the Commonwealth or are we going to merge them into our white community and eventually forget that there ever were any Aborigines in Australia?" I walked 1,000 miles home along the rabbit proof fence, carrying my little sister much of the way. Later, my children were stolen from me and taken to the Settlement. They were told they were orphans.

Neville Alexander (South Africa, "Feeling at Home with Literacy in the Mother Tongue"): I am the director of an organization in South Africa that brings "mother tongue" literacy back into our children's lives. For too many years, colonization and globalization have resulted in the "linguistic genocide" of African languages. Our organization is helping to inspire a sense of unity and a common African identity that was stripped away when European colonizers came to Africa. They not only took the natural resources of our land. They took our identity and our languages. In order to "succeed" we had to learn their languages. Over the centuries, many of our people have lost their languages. They have become illiterate in two languages—their mother tongue and the colonial language. I want African children to be read to and to read for themselves versions of the same stories in their mother tongue or in the language of their choice, so we are publishing children's books in African languages. Our organization is working to establish and promote a culture of reading and writing in African languages. We want to ensure that universities and other higher education institutions undertake and sustain the development of African languages. We are working to motivate and support publishers to develop a reading market in African languages.

Wangari Maathai (Kenya, *Unbowed*): I grew up in Kenya, a country in Africa. For most of my young childhood, I lived at home and spoke my native language. But when I went to school, my language was banned. In fact, if we were caught speaking our language, we had to wear a button known as a "monitor." The monitor had phrases stamped on it: "I am stupid, I was caught speaking my mother tongue." As I describe in my book, *Unbowed*, "At the end of the day, whoever ended up with the button received a punishment, such as cutting grass, sweeping, or doing work in the garden. But the greater punishment was the embarrassment you felt because you talked in your mother tongue. In retrospect, I can see that this introduced us to the world of undermining our self confidence." After a while, we just stopped talking our own language. "The use of the monitor continues even today [in 2007] in Kenyan schools to ensure that students use only English. Now, as then, this contributes to the trivialization of anything African and lays the foundation for a deeper sense of self-doubt and an inferiority complex." I won the Nobel Peace Prize in 2004 for my work on the Green Belt Movement in Kenya.

Bud Lane (Siletz, "Last of the Siletz Speakers"): Some people already count my language as dead. I speak Oregon Coastal Athabaskan. At 50, I am one of the youngest speakers of my language. Here in the Northwest, we are a hot spot for language extinction. I'm hoping to change that. You see, I think that the language and the people are the same. I didn't grow up speaking my language either, but I found an elder Siletz woman who knew the words, but who never spoke them in public. She'd been taught shame of her native tongue by white society. But Nellie Orton found her voice and taught me my language. Now I teach our language at the local school, so that our children can save our native tongue. "Once among the most linguistically diverse places on Earth, Oregon has drowned under the English tide. It now is infamous as a language-death hot spot. By Living Tongue's standards, hot spots are areas with a high concentration of different languages, few remaining first speakers—people who learned the language as children—and little language documentation."

Carmen Lomas Garza (Texas, *A Piece of My Heart/Pedacito de mi corazón*): I grew up in Texas in the 1950s. "When I was five years old my brother came home crying from the first grade in public school on the third day of classes because the teacher had punished him for speaking Spanish. She had made him hold out his hands, palms down, and then hit him with a ruler across the top of his hands." I was afraid to go to school because I didn't want to be beaten for speaking my language. Later, I was punished or ridiculed for my accent and made to feel ashamed. I wondered why white students were praised for learning a new language and practicing their Spanish in the halls, but Mexican American students were punished for doing the same. "By the time I graduated from high school I was confused, depressed, introverted, and quite angry."

Dr. Geneva Smitherman (*aka "Dr. G.," Talkin and Testifyin*): I am Distinguished Professor of English at Michigan State University and Director of the African American Language and Literacy Program. As a linguist and educational activist, I have been at the forefront of the struggle for language rights for over 25 years. As a writer, I forged a writing style that combines academic discourse and African American Language that has become widely celebrated for efficacy in making the medium the message. I have written many books including *Talkin and Testifyin: The Language of Black America, Black Talk: Words and Phrases from the Hood to the Amen Corner,* and *Talkin That Talk: Language, Culture and Education in African America.* I am considered a leading authority on Black English, also known as Ebonics and African American English.

Esther Martinez, also known as P'oe Tsawa, Blue Water (New Mexico, "Protecting Native American Languages and Culture"): I was a storyteller and Native Language teacher. I fought for years to preserve the Tewa language, the language of my people of the Northern Pueblos of New Mexico. I created Tewa dictionaries for each of the pueblos. Until my death, I continued to tell the stories of my people. For too many years the United States government's policies of termination, relocation, and assimilation of Native American tribes resulted in the loss of our land and our language. I am proud of the Esther Martinez Native American Language Preservation Act created in my name to give money to tribes to create programs to prevent the loss of their heritage and culture.

Aileen Figueroa (Klamath River, "Speak It Good and Strong"): I was one of the last fluent speakers of the Yurok language, the native language of the Yurok people who live on the Klamath River in Northern California. I was born on the Lower Klamath River in 1912, and I attended elementary school in Klamath until I was forced to attend the boarding school in Hoopa, which forbid students from speaking their native languages. I ran away from the school and made it to Redwood Creek, where I was caught by a truant officer. Because I went home to Klamath instead of staying at the boarding school, I kept my language and culture. You see, language is shaped by the landscape, the culture, and the people who speak it. For example, there are "two different Yurok words to describe dogwood—one used when the plant is in bloom, the other when it is not. The words sound nothing alike. But encoded within the words is a small story about the natural systems in which the Yurok lived. By the time the dogwood bloomed each year…the great green sturgeon that still inhabit pockets of the Klamath were no longer in the river. That meant it was safe to swim without fear of ripping yourself open on the gigantic creature's ferocious spikes." I worked with a linguist to create a written form of our language, and I taught it for 60 years. Before my death, I started the Yurok Elder Wisdom Preservation Project, and I participated at the American Indian Academy at McKinleyville High School.

Andrew Windy Boy (Chippewa/Cree, North Dakota, *Our Spirits Don't Speak English*): "I did two boarding schools in North and South Dakota in the mid-60s to the early 70s. I wasn't allowed to talk my native tongue or practice my native ways. They cut my hair. They put a dunce cap on me and made me wear it when I talked my native tongue. Kids laughed at me. They punished me for talking my first language. Whenever I talked, Cree would come out, and they hit me. I got hit so much I lost my native tongue. The only thing I remember is my Indian name. I hope nobody has to go through this. We have to have our own language. How else can we talk to our spirits? They don't understand English." (From *Our Spirits Don't Speak English: Indian Boarding School.*)

Momodou Sarr (The Gambia, "The Symbol"): The "Symbol" referred to several objects used to stop children at my elementary school in The Gambia from speaking our language at school. The teachers made us wear either a dead cow skull or a chain of empty little milk cans stringed together to form a necklace if they caught us speaking in our home language from the moment the school bell rang to the end of the school day. Almost all of us spoke the majority dialect, Mandinka. The language of instruction at school was English. As soon as we crossed the invisible boundary between school, village and community, we spoke English. The "Symbol" made you visible to the rest of the student body. It also isolated you from your friends, and worst of all, it took away your dignity and self-esteem. Once you assume the burden of wearing the "Symbol," you become the hunter, lurking in corners hoping to catch someone speaking in the local dialect. The hunted knew that the hunter hid in corners, yelling out names during recess hoping to catch fellow students by surprise. The hunted also knew that the hunter hid in the bathroom, sitting on top of the toilet bowl to avoid detection.

Tea Party

1. Find someone who was forced to speak another language. Who is the person? How did this affect the person?

2. Find someone who lives on a different continent than you do. Who is the person? How is his or her experience with language similar to your experience? How is it different?

3. Find someone who is resisting having another language imposed on him or her. Who is the person? How is the person resisting?

4. Find someone who started or joined an organization to preserve his or her language. Who is the person? Why did the individual decide to take this action?

5. Find someone who was punished or penalized if the person spoke his or her native language. Who is the person? How exactly was this person treated? Who did this to the person?

6. Find someone who has an example about the importance of his or her traditional language? Who is the person? Why is his or her language important to him or her?

7. Find someone who was humiliated or shamed for speaking his or her language. Who is the person? What country is this person from? How did he or she feel about the experience?

8. Find someone who said farewell to English and writes only in his mother tongue. What is this mother tongue? Why doesn't this person want to write in English? What country is the person from?

Reflection: Whose story touched you? Who would you like to know more about?

Collective text: Write a paragraph about language and power. What do the people who are forced to change their language have in common? How do they feel about their language? What are your thoughts about this? Give specific examples.

Story Retrieval

In the chart below, keep track of stories as we read or watch them. Questions to keep in mind: Who has to change their language? Who doesn't? What does each group have in common? Use one sheet for each story and note page numbers or quotes you want to return to later.

Character/ Story	
Race/Ethnicity Details	
Social Class Details	
Change Language? Details	
Notes, Questions and Points to Remember	

Story Retrieval

In the chart below, keep track of the patterns in the stories as we read or watch them. Questions to keep in mind: Who has to change their language? Who doesn't? What does each group have in common? Note page numbers or quotes you want to return to later.

Character/ Story				
Race/Ethnicity Details				
Social Class Details				
Change Language? Details				
Notes, Questions and Points to Remember				

And Then I Went to School

by Joe Suina

I lived with my grandmother when I was 5 through 9 years of age. It was the early 1950s when electricity had not yet entered our Pueblo homes. The village day school and health clinic were first to have it, and to the unsuspecting Cochiti, this was the approach of a new era in their uncomplicated lives.

Transportation was simple. Two good horses and a sturdy wagon met the daily needs of a villager. Only five, maybe six individuals possessed an automobile in the Pueblo of four hundred. A flatbed truck fixed with side rails and a canvas top made the usual Saturday morning trip to Santa Fe. It was always loaded beyond capacity with people and their wares headed for town for a few staples. The straining old truck with its escort of a dozen barking dogs made a noisy exit, northbound from the village.

A Sense of Closeness

During those years, grandmother and I lived beside the plaza in a one-room house. Inside, we had a traditional fireplace, a makeshift cabinet for our few tin cups and bowls, and a wooden crate carried our two buckets of all-purpose water. At the innermost part of the room were two rolls of bedding—thick quilts, sheepskin, and assorted—which we used as comfortable sitting couches by day and unrolled for sleeping by night. A wooden pole the length of one side of the room was suspended about ten inches from the vigas and draped with a modest collection of colorful shawls, blankets, and sashes, making this part of the room most interesting. In one corner sat a bulky metal trunk for our ceremonial wear and a few valuables. A dresser which was traded for her well-known pottery held the few articles of clothing we owned and the "goody bag"—an old flour sack Grandma always kept filled with brown candy, store-bought cookies, and Fig Newtons. These were saturated with a sharp odor of moth balls. Nevertheless, they made a fine snack with coffee before we turned in for the night. Tucked securely beneath my blankets, I listened to one of her stories about how it was when she was a little girl. These accounts appeared so old fashioned compared to the way we lived. Sometimes she softly sang a song from a ceremony. In this way, I went off to sleep each night.

Earlier in the evening we would make our way to a relative's house if someone had not already come to visit us. There, I'd play with the children while the adults caught up on all the latest news. Ten-cent comic books were finding their way into the Pueblo homes. Exchanging "old" comics for "new" ones was a serious matter that involved adults as well. Adults favored mystery and romance stories. For us children these were the first links to the world beyond the Pueblo. We enjoyed looking at them and role-playing our favorite hero rounding up the villains. Grandmother once made me a cape to leap tall buildings with. It seems everyone preferred being a cowboy rather than an Indian since cowboys were always victorious. Sometimes stories were related to both children and adults at these get-togethers. They were highlighted by refreshments of coffee and sweet bread or fruit pies baked in the outdoor oven. Winter months would most likely include roasted piñon nuts and dried deer meat for all to share. These evening gatherings and the sense of closeness diminished as radios and televisions increased over the following years. It was never to be the same again.

The winter months are among my fondest memories. A warm fire crackled and danced brightly in the fireplace, and the aroma of delicious stew filled our one-room house. The thick adobe walls wrapped around the two of us protectingly during the long freezing nights. To me, the house was just right. Grandmother's affection completed the warmth and security I will always remember.

Being the only child at grandmother's, I had lots of attention and plenty of reasons to feel good about myself. As a preschooler, I already had chores of chopping firewood and hauling in fresh water each day. After "heavy work" I would run to her and flex what I was convinced were my gigantic biceps. Grandmother would state that at the rate I was going I would soon attain the status of a man like the adult males in the village. Her shower of praise made me feel like the Mr. Indian Universe of all time. At age 5, I suppose I was as close to that concept of myself as anyone.

In spite of her many years, grandmother was highly active in the village ceremonial setting. She was a member of an important women's society and attended every traditional function, taking me along to many of them. I'd wear one of my colorful shirts she made by hand for just such occasions. Grandmother taught me appropriate behavior at these events. Through modeling she showed me how to pray properly. Barefooted, I greeted the sun each morning with a handful of cornmeal. At night I'd look to the stars in wonderment and let a prayer slip through my lips. On meeting someone, grandmother would say, "Smile and greet. Grunt if you must, but don't pretend they're not there." On food and material things, she would say, "There is enough for everyone to share and it all comes from above, my child." I learned to appreciate cooperation in nature and with my fellow men early in life. I felt very much a part of the world and our way of life. I knew I had a place in it, and I felt good about it.

And Then I Went to School

At age 6, like the rest of the Cochiti 6-year-olds that year, I had to begin my schooling. It was a new and bewildering experience—one I will not forget. The strange surrounding, new ideas about time and expectations, and the foreign tongue were at times overwhelming to us beginners. It took some effort to return the second day and many times thereafter.

To begin with, unlike my grandmother, the teacher did not have pretty brown skin and a colorful dress. She wasn't plump and friendly. Her clothes were of one color and drab. Her pale and skinny form made me worry that she was very ill. In the village, being more pale than usual was a sure sign of an oncoming fever or some such disorder. I thought that explained why she didn't have time just for me and the disappointed looks and orders she seemed always to direct my way. I didn't think she was so smart since she couldn't understand my language. "Surely that was why we had to leave our 'Indian' at home." But then I didn't feel so bright either. All I could say in her language was "Yes, teacher," "My name is Joseph Henry," and "When is lunch?" The teacher's odor took some getting used to also. In fact, many times it made me sick right before lunch. Later I learned from the girls this smell was something she wore called perfume.

An Artificial Classroom

The classroom, too, had its odd characteristics. It was terribly huge and smelled of medicine like the village clinic I feared so much. The walls and ceiling were artificial and uncaring. They were too far from me and I felt naked. Those fluorescent light tubes made an eerie drone and blinked suspiciously over me, quite a contrast to the fire and sunlight my eyes were accustomed to. I thought maybe the lighting did not seem right because it was man-made, and it wasn't natural. Our confinement to rows of desks was another unnatural demand made on our active little bodies. We had to sit at these hard things for what seemed like forever before relief (recess) came midway through the morning and afternoon. Running carefree in the village and fields was but a sweet memory of days gone by. We all went home for lunch since we lived a short walk from school. It took coaxing, and sometimes bribing, to get me to return and complete the remainder of the school day.

School was a painful experience during those early years. The English language and the new set of values caused me much anxiety and embarrassment. I couldn't comprehend everything that was happening, but I could understand very well when I messed up or wasn't doing so well. Negative messages were communicated too effectively and I became more and more unsure of myself. How I wished I could understand other things in school just as well.

The conflict was not only in school performance but in many other areas of my life as well. For example, many of us students had a problem with head lice due to the "unsanitary conditions in our homes." Consequently, we received a harsh shampooing which was rough on both the scalp and the ego. Cleanliness was crucial, and a washing of this sort indicated to the class that one came from a home setting which was not healthy. I recall one such treatment and afterwards being humiliated before my peers with a statement that I had "She'na" (lice) so tough that I must have been born with them. Needless to say, my Super Indian self-image was no longer intact.

"Leave Your Indian at Home"

My language, too, was questioned right from the beginning of my school career. "Leave your Indian at home!" was like a school trademark. Speaking it accidentally or otherwise was punishable by a dirty look or a whack with a ruler. This reprimand was for speaking the language of my people which meant so much to me. It was the language of my grandmother, and I spoke it well. With it, I sang beautiful songs and prayed from my heart. At that young and tender age, it was most difficult for me to comprehend why I had to part with my language. And yet at home I was encouraged to attend school so that I might have a better life in the future. I knew I had a good village life already, but this awareness dwindled each day I was in school.

As the weeks turned to months, I learned English more and more. It may appear that comprehension would be easier. It got easier to understand, all right. I understood that everything I had, and was a part of, was not nearly as good as the whiteman's. School was determined to undo me in everything from my sheepskin bedding to the dances and ceremonies which I had learned to have faith in and cherish. One day I dozed off in class after a sacred all-night ceremony. I was startled awake by a sharp jerk on my ear, and informed coldly, "That ought to teach you to attend 'those things' again." Later, all alone, I cried. I couldn't understand why or what I was caught up in. I was receiving two very different messages; both were intended for my welfare.

Values in lifestyle were dictated in various ways. The Dick and Jane reading series in the primary grades presented me pictures of a home with a pitched roof, straight walls, and sidewalks. I could not identify with these from my Pueblo world. However, it was clear I didn't have these things, and what I did have did not measure up. At night, long after grandmother went to sleep, I would lie awake staring at our crooked adobe walls casting uneven shadows from the light of the fireplace. The walls were no longer just right for me. My life was no longer just right. I was ashamed of being who I was, and I wanted to change right then and there. Somehow it became very important to have straight walls, clean hair and teeth, and a spotted dog to chase after. I even became critical of, and hateful toward, my bony, fleabag of a dog. I loved the familiar and cozy environment at grandmother's house, but now I imagined it could be a heck of a lot better if only I had a whiteman's house with a bed, a nice couch, and a clock. In school books, all the child characters ever did was run at leisure after the dog or kite. They were always happy. As for me, all I seemed to do at home was go for buckets of water and cut up sticks for a lousy fire. Didn't the teacher say drinking coffee would stunt my growth? Why couldn't I have nice tall glasses of milk so I could have strong bones and white teeth like those kids in the books? Did my grandmother really care about my well-being?

Torn Away

I had to leave my beloved village of Cochiti for my education beyond 6. I left to attend a Bureau of Indian Affairs (BIA) boarding school 30 miles from home. Shined shoes and pressed shirt and pants were the order of the day. I managed to adjust to this just as I had to most of the things the school shoved at me or took away from me. Adjusting to leaving home and the village was tough enough. It seemed the older I got, the further I got from the ways I was so much a part of. Since my parents did not own an automobile, I saw them only once a month when they came in the community truck. They never failed to come supplied with "eats" for me. I enjoyed the outdoor oven bread, dried meat, and tamales they usually brought. It took a while to get accustomed to the diet of the school. Being in town with strange tribes under one roof was frightening and often very lonely. I longed for my grandmother and my younger brothers and sisters. I longed for my house. I longed to take part in a Buffalo Dance. I longed to be free.

I came home for the four-day Thanksgiving break. At first, home did not feel right anymore. It was much too small and stuffy. The lack of running water and bathroom facilities was too inconvenient. Everything got dusty so quickly, and hardly anyone spoke English. It occurred to me then that I was beginning to take on the whiteman's ways that belittled my own. However, it didn't take long to "get back with it." Once I reestablished my relationships with family, relatives, and friends, I knew I was where I came from. I knew where I belonged.

Leaving for the boarding school the following Sunday evening was one of the saddest events in my entire life. Although I had enjoyed myself immensely the last few days, I realized then that life would never be the same again. I could not turn back the time just as I could not do away with school and the ways of the whiteman. They were here to stay and would creep more and more into my life. The effort to make sense of both worlds together was painful, and I had no choice but to do so. The schools, television, automobiles, and many other outside ways and values had chipped away at the simple cooperative life I began to grow in. The people of Cochiti were changing. The winter evening gatherings, the exchanging of stories, and even the performing of certain ceremonies were already only a memory that someone commented about now and then. Still, the two worlds were very different and the demands of both were ever present. The whiteman's was flashy, less personal, but very comfortable. The Cochiti were both attracted and pushed toward these new ways which they had little to say about. There was no choice left but to compete with the whiteman on his terms for survival. To do that I knew I had to give up part of my life.

Joseph Suina retired from the University of New Mexico faculty in 2006. He now devotes himself to farming, family, and the Cochiti tribal council. This article originally appeared in the New Mexico Journal of Reading, *Winter 1985. Used by permission of the author.*

Speak It Good and Strong

by Hank Sims

Yurok Youth Vow to Bring Back the Language of Their Ancestors

This is how it used to be. For no one knows how long—at least 700 years, probably many more, maybe back as far as the creation of the world—all the people who lived between Little River and the Klamath River on the coast, and inland up the Klamath to Weitchpec, were Yurok, and they spoke their own language. Having been born of the area, the language was minutely attuned to the landscape and the seasons, so that the very words and sentences reflected the rhythm of the place.

By 1950—100 years after settlers began arriving at the North Coast of California in great numbers—the Yurok language was all but gone, as were the languages indigenous to Humboldt County: Hupa, Wiyot, Tolowa, Karuk, Mattole, and Chilula, among others. The children of the Yurok were taken away from their families and sent to boarding schools, where they were beaten for using their native tongue. Parents spoke English to their children when they came home, and grandparents got old and passed away. People were made to feel ashamed of their language. It dwindled away almost to nothing.

But a couple of weeks ago, when Archie Thompson arrived in Arcata a little bit late to a meeting and spotted Jimmie James, the two men, both in their nineties, joyously clasped hands and suddenly the old language was pouring out of them, each strange syllable following unhurriedly upon the last. They spoke with the unconscious confidence that people have when expressing themselves in their first language—the confidence that is the most difficult thing to acquire when learning someone else's. For a moment, listening to them, you could almost imagine what it used to sound like hundreds of years ago, up the coast and along the lower Klamath.

Few of the 35 or so people who were attending that day's strategy session at Potawot Village, which had been convened by the Yurok Elder Wisdom Preservation Project, would have been able to understand precisely what Thompson and James said to each other in their greeting. They'd all heard such conversations before, between two people who'd grown up with the language, and even the best speakers among them knew that they had a long way to go before approaching Thompson's and James' fluency.

And no one objected—no one would dare object—when, for the second time that day, James hijacked the microphone to gently admonish the assembled students of the Yurok language, most of them the grandchildren and great-grandchildren of the people of his generation. A kindly gentleman with a sharp sense of humor, James told them that the Yurok they spoke just didn't have the "ring" of the language that the old Indians spoke.

"All of us here, we know how to talk, and we know what it sounds like," he said, indicating himself, Thompson, Aileen Figueroa, and Georgiana Trull, the four elders who were able to attend the strategy session. "I hope I'm not discouraging you, but what you need to get hold of is the real word, and what the language really means."

The words were mostly there, but the younger generation was missing the most important aspect of the language: its soul.

"You got to speak it good and strong," James continued a moment later. "There's a lot of you folks out there interested in learning. But it ain't getting to you. And it's our fault. And it's your fault."

What James was saying, everybody already knew it. But it helped them to hear it again, from the mouth of a respected elder. Because all of the people there were determined, from those who have been studying Yurok for 20 years to the high school students who have just started to pick up the language. They made a promise to themselves, to their elders, and to the generations to come. They're going to bring it back. James' words served as a reminder that more was at stake than grammar lessons, and it made them want to work harder.

The Elder Hammer

Kathleen Vigil, a 62-year-old resident of Westhaven, founded the Yurok Elder Wisdom Preservation Project a couple of years ago because she knew that time was running short. Vigil is the daughter of Aileen Figueroa, one of the oldest members of the Yurok Tribe and a master speaker of the language. The project was born of a terrible realization—that people of her mother's generation, the last generation to have any contact with the old Yurok ways, would not be around forever.

"There was a gathering in Klamath for the Yurok language, and a cry came out," Vigil said last week. "My mother was 91 or 92 at that time, and we really needed to do some documentation on her."

Figueroa is one of the Yurok people's treasure troves of information, of the old stories and history of the tribe. But most important to her mother's heart, Vigil said, was the language. The idea that the language would someday die with her and the few surviving speakers was a great weight on Figueroa's heart, Vigil said.

And the language preservation programs in place at the time weren't doing enough, Vigil felt. People weren't learning quickly enough. Not enough people were prepared to devote the amount of time necessary to truly understand it. Classes would cover the basics, then people would drop out. The elders would have to start over with a whole new class, once again teaching students how to say hello, goodbye, man, woman.

"The language would get at a point, and it would stop and no one would do anything with it anymore," Vigil said. "It was like—we don't want to hurt your feelings."

Vigil decided that the passing of the language to the younger generation needed to be intensified—more people needed to devote more time to language preservation, and they needed to study it more deeply.

Leo Canez, a 30-year-old Eureka resident and a special projects coordinator for the Arcata-based Seventh Generation Fund, now sits on the board of the Elder Wisdom Preservation Project and helped organize and coordinate the language strategy session at Potawot Village. He had his own tale to tell about how he came to realize that he had to work to restore the language.

A little over a year ago, he was talking with Georgiana Trull—of the elders who attended the strategy session—and telling her all the things that he was involved with in his work with the Seventh Generation Fund. He was telling her about the interesting, empowering work that various Native American groups were doing around the country, and how he felt honored to play some role supporting their efforts. Trull was nonplussed, he said.

Instead, she pointed at him and said, "And what are you doing for your people?"

Canez has a name for this type of moment. He calls it "The Elder Hammer."

A few weeks later, he said, he was sitting around with some friends. There were a few elders at the table, and they began talking to each other in the old language. As Canez tells it, he and his friends all looked at each other, and they all had the same thought: Why can't we understand what they are saying?

That's when he decided to attend language classes, and to devote himself to bringing Yurok back.

Novice Speakers

Early on in the strategy session, 26-year-old Kishan Lara, who is taking her doctorate in linguistics and education at Arizona State University, told everyone that there are people out there, respected linguists, who are saying that Yurok is already an all-but-dead language, that it will be gone in 10 years, when most of the people who grew up with it will be gone. But Lara only brought up what these linguists had to say because she was sure they were wrong.

"People are going to be speaking this language out in the community in 10 years," she said. "And I hope Aileen and Jimmie know this, because it is our promise to them."

Maybe half of the people at the two-day Potawot Village strategy session were around Lara's age, and all of them were as determined as she was. Many of the young people in the room studied at the several weekly community classes held around the

Yurok Reservation and in Arcata. Some of them—teenagers or recent high school graduates—had studied at Hoopa High School, where Yurok has been offered as a "foreign language" option for a few years now. Others were students at the brand-new American Indian Academy charter school in McKinleyville, where Figueroa and Vigil lead a daily class in the language for students.

At the meeting, many of the young speakers talked about what the language has given them in the time they've been studying it. Skip Lowry, a 25-year-old who does work at the reconstructed Su'meg Village, a Yurok site in present-day Patrick's Point State Park, said that he has found it easier to pray once he became able to do so in Yurok. "I feel like the physical side of our culture has been preserved somewhat, and now I see the spiritual side coming back," he said.

One of Georgiana Trull's grandsons, 25-year-old Frankie Joe Myers, said that one of the positive things about living in this day and age is the wider American culture no longer pressures people to give up their roots, as it did in the past. "In my father's generation, it wasn't looked on as positive to be Indian," he said. "In a way, it's become popular. It's become cool to be Indian." Learning the language went along with the rebirth of traditional dances—the Brush Dance, the World Renewal Ceremony—over the past few decades, and these ceremonies, together with the language, strengthened his identity as a Yurok, he said.

But many of the young people also talked realistically about their frustrations in learning Yurok. Virginia Myers, Frankie Joe's sister, recently took a semester off from her studies at UCLA to care for her grandmother and to study the language with her. Myers said that she originally thought that after three months or so, she would be reasonably fluent. In fact, it is taking much longer than that. As Virginia recounted to the group, Trull would at times become frustrated with her granddaughter, telling her, "You're not thinking Indian! You've got to think Indian!"

Part of the problem, everyone realized, was that too often they were still thinking in English then translating their thoughts into Yurok. That, plus the fact that few people had been able to accurately capture the rhythm of their elders' speech. Carole Lewis, a 54-year-old Hoopa resident who has been studying the language for some 20 years, apologized to the elders present on behalf of everyone. "I can see the sorrow they have for their language, because in a way we're murdering it." She exhorted her fellow students, those just starting out, to listen more closely to the audio recordings made by the elders. "We're going to lose some of it anyway," she said, "but if we don't pay attention we're going to lose a lot more."

But like almost everyone there, Kishan Lara remained confident.

"The Yurok are a resilient people," she said. "We've been through a lot of hardships, and we came back. And the language is going to be no different."

Aiy-yu-kwee´

From the Yurok point of view, the language has always been there—it was given to the people by the Creator, along with the Yurok lands. That's what the old stories teach, and any questions are pretty much settled there. Although linguists and anthropologists not brought up in the Yurok tradition raise a number of interesting questions about where the language came from, they don't have a much better answer about how it got to the North Coast.

Like Wiyot, the language of the people that lived around Humboldt Bay, Yurok belongs to a family of Native American languages called "Algic" languages, meaning they are distantly related to certain languages of the Midwest, such as Cheyenne, Blackfoot, and Cree, and to others of the Northeast, like Massachusett, Micmac and Narragansett. But Yurok and Wiyot are the only Algic languages spoken west of the Rocky Mountains—the myriad other languages spoken in the West before contact belong to some other language family, or, like Karuk, have no apparent relation to any other language at all. The academics are not exactly sure how a language from the east came to be spoken in coastal northern California.

But throughout the centuries, the language clearly became deeply intertwined with this land. A couple of days after the strategy session, Canez gave an example. There are two different Yurok words to describe dogwood—one used when the plant is in bloom, the other when it is not. The words sound nothing alike. But encoded within the words is a small story about the natural systems in which the Yurok lived. By the time the dogwood bloomed each year, Canez said, the great green sturgeon that still inhabit pockets of the Klamath were no longer in the river. That meant it was safe to swim without fear of ripping yourself open on the gigantic creature's ferocious spikes.

This is perhaps the greatest hurdle that young Yurok speakers face in their efforts to reclaim the language—the need to understand not just the words that make up the language, but how to "think Indian" in a way that the language makes sense. ("You say a word, and it doesn't mean what it means in English," someone noted at the strategy session. "It means more.")

There's also the mechanical difficulty common to any attempt to learn a second language: Teaching your mouth to make sounds it is not accustomed to making. For English speakers, this is infinitely harder with Yurok than it is with any other European language. Yurok is filled with noises difficult for an ear used to English to understand. It contains glottal stops—made with the throat rather than the mouth. It contains an unusual vowel, sort of a cross between a short "o" and the consonant "r." One sound, written as "hl," has no close equivalent in English; instructional materials advise a student to place their tongues at the roof of the mouths, then exhale around both sides of the tongue.

But even with these impediments, Yurok isn't as poorly off as many other native Californian languages. First and foremost, students can still draw upon elders who have known the language from birth. The Yurok community can work together with Hoopa and Karuk people, both of whom have active language preservation projects. The UC Berkeley Department of Linguistics has long conducted studies in the language, and is making its material available to students of the language. And the Yurok have a small corps of people—Canez mentioned Carole Lewis and Leroy Halbe of Weitchpec, both in their middle years—who are on the verge of becoming the next generation's master speakers.

In the coming years, the Yurok Elder Wisdom Preservation Project hopes to develop a standard lesson plan for new students in the language, to get more people to attend community classes in the language and to institute an annual summer immersion camp for students, in which only Yurok would be spoken. And the leaders of the project want to continue to record the speech and stories of the elder generation, while they still have time.

Canez takes courage in the way that groups of dedicated individuals devoted to other indigenous tongues, such as Hawaiian, have been able to pull their languages back from the brink. These days, Hawaiian is taught in schools around the state and a growing number of people are speaking it fluently. And even non-indigenous Hawaiians have adopted bits and pieces of the language, giving Hawaiian English a regional flavor that grounds it to the islands. Canez thinks something similar could happen here.

"Everyone knows the Spanish words *uno, dos, tres, hola, adios.* Yuroks know them too," he said. "Why doesn't everyone around here know the Yurok words for those? Where we are now, we can bring that back."

The first word you learn in any language class is "hello." In Yurok, the word is *aiy-yu-kwee´.*

This article originally appeared in The North Coast Journal of Politics, People & Art, *January 12, 2006. Used by permission of the author.*

The Monitor

by Wangari Muta Maathai

By this time, English had become the official language of communication and instruction in Kenyan schools. Those of us who aspired to progress in our studies knew that learning English well was essential. Many schools emphasized that students must speak English at all times, even during holidays.

A common practice to ensure that students kept pressure on one another was to require those students who were found using a language other than English to wear a button known as a 'monitor.' It was sometimes inscribed with phrases in English such as "I am stupid, I was caught speaking my mother tongue." At the end of the day, whoever ended up with the button received a punishment, such as cutting grass, sweeping, or doing work in the garden. But the greater punishment was the embarrassment you felt because you had talked in your mother tongue. In retrospect I can see that this introduced us to the world of undermining our self-confidence.

Not surprisingly, none of us wanted to be caught with the monitor and as a result we spoke English from the time we left church in the morning until we said our final prayers at night. This was remarkable given that everyone in St. Cecilia's had spoken only Kikuyu until then. But the system worked in promoting English: Even when we went home or met children from school in the village, we tended to speak English. The use of the monitor continues even today in Kenyan schools to ensure that students use only English. Now, as then, this contributes to the trivialization of anything African and lays the foundation for a deeper sense of self-doubt and an inferiority complex.

Years later, when we became part of the Kenyan elite, we preferred to speak in English to one another, our children, and those in our social class. While the monitor approach helped us learn English, it also instilled in us a sense that our local languages were inferior and insignificant. The reality is that our mother tongues are extremely important as vehicles of communication and carriers of culture, knowledge, wisdom, and history. When they are maligned, and educated people are encouraged to look down on them, people are robbed of a vital part of their heritage.

Obituary

by Lois-Ann Yamanaka

English class, we got Mr. Harvey. Jerome looks at me and puts his middle finger on the desk to our worst teacher, because Mr. Harvey says for the fiftieth time this year:

"No one will want to give you a job. You sound uneducated. You will be looked down upon. You're speaking a low-class form of good Standard English. Continue, and you'll go nowhere in life. Listen, students, I'm telling you the truth like no one else will. Because they don't know how to say it to you. I do. Speak Standard English. DO NOT speak pidgin. You will only be hurting yourselves."

I tell Jerry, "No make f-you finger to Mr. Harvey. We gotta try talk the way he say. No more dis and dat and wuz and cuz 'cause we only hurting ourselfs."

I don't tell anyone, not even Jerry, how ashamed I am of pidgin English. Ashamed of my mother and father, the food we eat, chicken luau with can spinach and tripe stew. The place we live, down the house lots in the Hicks Homes that all look alike except for the angle of the house from the street. The car we drive, my father's brown Land Rover without the back window. The clothes we wear, sometimes we have to wear the same pants in the same week and the same shoes until it breaks. Don't have no choice.

Ashamed of my aunties and my uncles at baby luaus, yakudoshis, and mochi pounding parties. "Eh, bradda Larry, bring me on nada Primo, brah. One cold one fo' real kine. I rey-day, I rey-day, no woray, brah. Uncap that sucka and come home to Uncle Stevie." I love my Uncle Steven, though, and the Cracker Jacks he brings for me every time he visits my mother. One for me and one for my sister, Calhoon. But I'm so shame.

Ashame too of all my cousins, the way they talk and act dumb, like how they like Kikaida Man and "Ho, brah, you seen Kikaida Man kick Rainbow Man's ass in front Hon Sport at the Hilo Shopping Center? Ho, brah and I betchu Godzilla kick King Kong's ass too. Betchu ten dollas, brah, two fur balls kicking ass in downtown Metropolis, nah, downtown Hilo, brah."

And my grandma. Her whole house smells like mothballs, not just in the closets but in every drawer too. And her pots look a million years old with dents all over. Grandma must know every recipe with mustard cabbage in it. She can quote from the Bible for everything you do in one day. Walks everywhere she goes downtown Kaunakakai, sucks fish eyes and eats the parsley from our plates at Midnight Inn.

And nobody looks or talks like a haole. Or eats like a haole. Nobody says nothing the way Mr. Harvey tells us to practice talking in class.

Sometimes I secretly wish to be a haole. That my name could be Betty Smith or Annie Anderson or Debbie Cole, wife of Dennis Cole who lives at 2222 Maple Street with a white station wagon with wood panel on the side, a dog named Spot, a cat named Kitty, and I wear white gloves. Dennis wears a hat to work. There's a coatrack as soon as you open the front door and we all wear shoes inside the house.

"Now let's all practice our Standard English," Mr. Harvey says. *"You will all stand up and tell me your name, and what you would like to be when you grow up. Please use complete sentences."* Mr. Harvey taps Melvin Spencer on his shoulders. Melvin stands up slowly and pulls a Portagee torture of wedged pants and BVDs out of his ass.

"Ma name is Mal-vin Spenca." Melvin has a very Portagee accent. Before he begins his next sentence, he does nervous things like move his ankles side to side so that his heels slide out of his slippers. He looks at the ceiling and rolls his eyes. "I am, I mean, I wanna. I like. No, try wait. I going be. No, try wait. I will work on my Gramma Spenca's pig farm when I grow up cuz she said I can drive the slop truck. Tank you."

No one laughs at Melvin. Otherwise he'll catch you on the way home from school and shove your head in the slop drum. Melvin sits down. He blinks his eyes hard a couple of times, then rubs his face with two hands.

Jerry stands up very, very slowly and holds on to the edge of his desk. "My name is Jerome." His voice, weak and shivering, his fingers white. "I in. OK, wait. I stay in. No, try wait. OK, try wait. I stay. I stay real nervous." His face changes and he acts as if he has to use the bathroom. He looks out the window to the eucalyptus trees beyond the schoolyard.

Jerry continues, "I am going be one concert piano-ist when I get big. Tank you."

I'm next. Panic hits me like a rock dropped in a hollow oil drum.

Mr. Harvey walks up to my desk, his face red and puffy like a pink marshmallow or a bust-up boxer. He has red hair and always wears white double-knit pants with pastel-colored golf shirts. He walks like Walter Matthau. Mr. Harvey taps my desk with a red pen.

The muscles in my face start twitching and pulling uncontrollably. My eyes begin darting back and forth. And my lips, my lips—

"I'm waiting," Mr. Harvey says.

Jerry looks at me. He smiles weakly, his face twitching and pulling too. He looks at Mr. Harvey, then looks at me as if to say, "Just get it over with."

"Cut the crap," Mr. Harvey spits. *"Stop playing these goddamn plantation games. Now c'mon. We've got our outlines to finish today."* Mr. Harvey's ears get red, his whole face like fire with his red hairs and red face.

"My name Lovey. When I grow up pretty soon, I going be what I like be and nobody better say nothing about it or I kill um."

"OH REALLY," he says. *"Not the way you talk. You see that was terrible. All of you were terrible and we will have to practice and practice our Standard English until we are perfect little Americans. And I'll tell you something, you can all keep your heads on your desks for the rest of the year for all I care. You see, you need me more than I need you. And do you know what the worst part is, class? We're not only going to have to work on your usage, but pronunciations and inflections too. Jee-zus Christ! For the life of me, it'll take us a goddamn lifetime."*

"See," Jerry whispers, "now you the one made Mr. Harvey all mad with us, we all going get it from him, stupid."

I want to tell Jerry about being a concert pianist. Yeah, right. Good luck. How will he ever do it? Might as well drive the slop truck if you cannot talk straight or sound good and all the haoles talk circles around you. Might as well blend in like all the locals do.

Mr. Harvey walks past my desk. *"C'mon, Lovey. Start your outline. You too, Jerome."* Sometimes I think that Mr. Harvey doesn't mean to be mean to us. He really wants us to be Americans, like my kotonk cousins from Santa Ana, he'd probably think they talked real straight.

But I can't talk the way he wants me to. I cannot make it sound his way, unless I'm playing pretend-talk-haole. I can make my words straight, that's pretty easy if I concentrate real hard. But the sound, the sound from my mouth, if I let it rip right out the lips, my words will always come out like home.

Excerpt from "Obituary" from Wild Meat and the Bully Burgers *by Lois-Ann Yamanaka. Copyright © 1996 by Lois-Ann Yamanaka. Reprinted by permission of Farrar, Straus and Giroux, LLC.*

A Piece of My Heart/ Pedacito de mi corazón

by Carmen Lomas Garza

When I was five years old my brother came home crying from the first grade in public school on the third day of classes because the teacher had punished him for speaking Spanish. She had made him hold out his hands, palms down, and then hit him with a ruler across the top of his hands.

This confused us because up to that day my parents had been telling us about how much fun we were going to have in school. So we looked to them for an explanation of this confusing reaction over such a natural act as speaking and why he deserved the unusual punishment. The expression on my parents' faces and their mute silence haunts me to this day. It must have been such a painful moment for them. How could they explain that the punishment was for racial and political reasons and not because he had done something bad?

The incident and the punishment caused much discussion among my parents, their friends and peers whose children were also experiencing the same treatment. Even though it had been seven years since my father and other Mexican Americans had returned from military service during World War II, things had not changed very much in Texas. Now that their children (the baby boom generation) were becoming school age, the discrimination continued. It did not matter that some of our families had been *Tejanos* (Texans) since the days of the Spanish land grants—long before Texas was taken from Mexico. Nor did it matter that almost all of us were *mestizos*, a mixture of Spanish and native Mexican or Native American.

Discrimination against the Mexican American was the main reason my parents became involved with the American GI Forum, a World War II veterans organization of Mexican Americans who fought for civil rights. One of their first activities was to sue a funeral home for refusing to receive the body of a Mexican American hero killed in the Korean War.

My brother's incident still had to be explained. My parents tried to tell us the reasons for the punishment and stressed that from then on at home we would practice speaking only in English and not both languages as we had been doing. I did not make nor understand the distinction between the two languages. And my parents many times spoke in both languages in spite of their decision. All I kept thinking was that I was next in line to go to school the following year.

When I finally did get to school, my first grade teacher was a bit more compassionate and actually took the time to explain the fact that *the* Spanish and *the* English we spoke were not all one language. She demonstrated this by bringing from her bedroom to the classroom a huge fluffy pillow with colorful embroidery and said that the name we knew for it, *almohada*, was Spanish and *pillow* English. I knew and used both words.

The realization that the pillow had a written name and that I knew two languages clicked in my mind just like it had for Helen Keller when she understood the connection between the sign word in her hand for water and the actual water that was falling on her hand. But what had been one world was now two separate entities and it seemed that I had to negate one in order to be accepted and exist in the other.

Knowing the difference between the two languages did not save me from unconsciously using Spanish in the classrooms and on the school grounds so I, too, suffered many physical and emotional punishments. Each time I spoke English I was ridiculed for my accent and made to feel ashamed. At a time when most children start to realize that there is an immense outside world, and communication is an important vehicle toward becoming a part of that world, the educational institution was punishing me for speaking two languages.

When I was in junior high school, I complained to my mother: *"Mami, yo no quiero llevar tacos de tortilla de harina con arroz, frijoles y carne para lonche porque se rien las gringas."* ("Mami, I don't want to take tacos of flour tortillas with rice, beans, and meat for lunch because the white girls make fun of me.") Tacos that were nutritious and made with love, care, and hope had to be replaced with sandwiches of baloney and white bread.

In high school we could take Latin, French, or Spanish classes, but the Mexican American students were still not allowed to speak Spanish in the halls or in other classrooms. It was so ironic to see the white students practicing their new Spanish words and phrases while walking down the halls yet the Mexican American students could expect punishment for doing the same. But the punishment wasn't with a 12-inch ruler across your hands; it was with a 30-inch paddle that had holes drilled into it so that there would be less air resistance as it was slapped across the back of your legs. By the time I graduated from high school I was confused, depressed, introverted, and quite angry.

The Chicano Movement for civil rights of the late sixties and early seventies clarified some of that confusion, started the slow process of self-healing and provided a format to vent some of that anger. I had decided at the age of 13 to become an artist so when I was in college the Chicano Movement nourished that goal and gave me back my voice. But the university art department (which had over 50 percent Chicano students, the highest compared to all other departments) did not offer art history classes about my heritage: neither pre-Columbian, colonial or contemporary Mexican; nor the native American art, even though we were sitting in the middle of South Texas only 120 miles from the Mexican border. Instead we learned about French Rococo and Henry Moore, the English sculptor. I knew more about the Egyptian pyramids than the pyramids in Teotihuacan. I knew more about Greek mythology than Aztec mythology. The only source for formal training about my heritage was in the anthropology department but only after the study of the bones and teeth of Leakey's Lucy.

I was looking for information about the Aztecas, Toltecas, Apaches and Hopi; the Nahuatl language and poetry; the Mayan ceramic sculptures; the gold jewelry and surgical obsidian knives; cultivation of corn, chocolate, cotton, and the vulcanization of rubber. It would have been real cool when I was in high school to have known that way before Columbus invaded this hemisphere the Maya were playing a form of basketball wearing open-toe high top tennis shoes with rubber soles.

Discussions with other Chicano students were the best source of information. It was during one of these discussions, in which I described my revelation about the word pillow, that someone commented that the word *almohada* was of Arab origin as were many other words in the Spanish language.

How does a 6-year-old child in South Texas in 1954 come to use a word from halfway across the world for such a beautiful and intimate object? A word that traveled from a desert across a channel, up and down mountains, across an ocean, over and around islands, through jungles and up to another desert. The history of that word's journey as carried by thousands of people from parent to child, generation after generation had been suppressed or ignored by the two institutions that I had already experienced.

And so the anger, the pride and self-healing had to come out as Chicano art—an art that was criticized by the faculty and white students as being too political, not universal, not hardedge, not pop art, not abstract, not avant-garde, to figurative, too colorful, too folksy, too primitive, blah, blah, blah!

What they failed to see was that the art I was creating functioned in the same way as the *salvila* (aloe vera) plant when its cool liquid is applied to a burn or abrasion. It helped to heal the wounds inflicted by discrimination and racism.

We needed to heal ourselves and each other so we started by choosing a name for ourselves, a name to symbolize our movements for self-determination. The accomplishments of our parents during the 50's civil rights movement were not enough. We started to speak more Spanish in public places; we worked to get better representatives on the school boards and local governments, and we started to explore and emphasize our unique culture in the visual arts, music, literature and theater.

I felt that I had to start with my earliest recollections of my life and validate each event or incident by depicting it in a visual format. I needed to celebrate each special event or reexamine each unusual happening.

We have been doing Chicano art not only for Chicanos, but also for others to see who we are as people. If you see my heart and humanity through my art then hopefully you will not exclude me from rightfully participating in this society.

Aquí les doy un pedacito de mi corazón en mi arte. And now I give you a little piece of my heart in my art.

Putting Black English/Ebonics Into the Curriculum

Early in my teaching career, I initiated the language unit by discussing Ebonics/Black English. I had just returned from a National Council of Teachers of English (NCTE) conference and heard the great and glorious Dr. Geneva Smitherman speak. I read her book *Talkin and Testifyin: The Language of Black America* and returned to Jefferson High School eager to teach about Ebonics. To my surprise, my students, about 80 percent African American, did not see themselves as Ebonics speakers. Clearly, I didn't do Dr. Smitherman's work justice. In fact, my students thought I was insulting them. That experience made me rethink my approach, as a white teacher, to teaching Ebonics in a predominantly black school. As I noted earlier, I worked on and tinkered with this unit for more than 20 years, teaching it to majority black classes, majority white classes, and one class with Native American, black, white, and Latino students. Over the years, I came to

Over the years, I came to realize that I needed to situate Ebonics in a unit about global linguistic domination, rooting it in the context of the broader political and economic domination of languages.

realize that I needed to situate Ebonics in a unit about global linguistic domination, rooting it in the context of the broader political and economic domination of languages.

Prior to discussing Ebonics/Black English—also known as African American Vernacular English (AAVE), I gave students a handout and asked them to fill in a definition of Ebonics, write a few examples, and note where it originated. Out of 31 students, all but one wrote that Ebonics is slang. One student wrote that it was any word ending in "izzle, like shizzle, ma nizzle or drizzle." Another wrote, "Ebonics is the official language of black people. It is the slang that people, many African Americans, use to replace lengthy sentences." Most wrote that Ebonics came out of Oakland or the West Coast or "ghetto." It was clear that their impression was negative.

Even though we had just studied what happened to the Irish, Kenyans, Native Americans, and others, students did not transfer their academic knowledge about the historical oppression of languages into their own contemporary situation because they didn't recognize Ebonics as a language. I wanted students to understand that such an intimate piece of many of their lives, their language, had also been marginalized and ridiculed by powerful others in the same way that Hector Pieterson's and Joseph Suina's had been. What they identified as "ghetto talk" or "slang" carried a piece of their ancestors' languages that had been "stigmatized and marginalized" with the same hammer that bludgeoned Native American, Kenyan, and Irish languages.

None of the black students in my classes use Ebonics exclusively. But many of them use aspects of Ebonics in both their speech and their writing. One of my goals is for students to recognize the difference between slang and Ebonics/Black English when they hear it in their school, churches, and homes—and to be able to distinguish it when they are using it. The term "Ebonics" (from ebony and phonics) was coined by Professor Robert Williams in 1973, during a conference on the language development of black children. In her essay, "Black English/Ebonics: What It Be Like?" Geneva Smitherman writes that Ebonics "is rooted in the Black American Oral Tradition and represents a synthesis of African (primarily West African) and European (primarily English) linguistic-cultural traditions."

During this segment of the language unit, we also discuss code-switching, or moving between home language and the language of power—Standard English—during our readings. As a teacher in a predominantly African American school where the majority of students exhibit some features of African American Vernacular English, I needed to learn the rules and history of the language so I could help students move between the two language systems. In my experience, teaching black students the grammar structure and history of AAVE evokes pride in their language, but also curiosity. All students—not just African Americans—benefit from learning that African American language uses a highly structured grammar system.

Teaching about Ebonics has been a no-go zone for many teachers since the controversy over a 1996 Oakland School District resolution that recognized Black English as a language of instruction. Stanford linguistics professor John Rickford noted in his book *Spoken Soul*:

> Ebonics was vilified as "disgusting black street slang," "incorrect and substandard," "nothing more than ignorance," "lazy English," "bastardized English," "the language of illiteracy," and "this utmost ridiculous made-up language."

As Rickford pointed out, the reactions of linguists were much more positive than those of most of the media and the general public. Although they disagree about its origins, "linguists from virtually all points of view agree on the systematicity of Ebonics, and on the potential value of taking it into account in teaching Ebonics speakers to read and write."

To demonstrate how linguists work, I bring in a small segment of the film *Amistad*. Students watch the scene where Yale linguist Josiah Gibbs discovers that the enslaved Africans speak Mende. After learning to count to ten in this West African language, he walked the wharves in New York repeating: *Ta, fele, sawa, nani, lulu, waeta, waflas, wayaba, talu, pu*—one to ten in Mende—until James Covey, a black sailor who had been born in Africa and sold into slavery as a child, responded. Through this linguistic discovery, the story of how Sengbe Pieh (Cinque) and the 57 other Africans involved in the *Amistad* revolt were kidnapped from Africa unfolds.

We also watch the video *The Language You Cry In* about the linguistic detective work of black linguist Lorenzo Turner, who traces a mourning song from the Gullah Sea Islands off the coast of Georgia to Sierre Leone in the 1930s. The tale continues in the 1990s when two contemporary scholars pick up Turner's trail and discover the village where long-lost kinfolk remember the song and are reunited with their Gullah family.

In the class, we read Rickford's essay "Suite for Ebony and Phonics" aloud together paragraph by paragraph, stopping to discuss each part. Rickford points out that

Ebonics is not just "slang"; it includes "distinctive patterns of pronunciation and grammar, the elements of language on which linguists tend to concentrate because they are more systematic and deep-rooted."

Now is Ebonics just "slang," as so many people have characterized it? Well, no, because slang refers just to the vocabulary of a language or dialect, and even so, just to the small set of new and (usually) short-lived words like chillin ("relaxing") or homey ("close friend") which are used primarily by young people in informal contexts. Ebonics includes non-slang words like ashy (referring to the appearance of dry skin, especially in winter), which have been around for a while, and are used by people of all age groups. Ebonics also includes distinctive patterns of pronunciation and grammar, the elements of language on which linguists tend to concentrate because they are more systematic and deep-rooted.

We also read "From Africa to the New World and into the Space Age: An Introduction and History of Black English Structure," a chapter from Geneva Smitherman's book *Talkin and Testifyin*. Her discussion of the grammar structure of Ebonics leads to a day of conjugating verbs. For example, we discuss the absence of a third person singular present-tense *s* in Ebonics (example: I draw, he draw, they draw, we draw); students then conjugate verbs using this grammar rule. The zero copula rule—the absence of *is* or *are* in a sentence—provides another model for students to practice. Smitherman gives as an example the sentence, "People crazy! People *are* stone crazy!" The emphasis on *are* in the second sentence, she points out, intensifies the feeling. I ask students to write zero copula sentences, and we share them in class.

Ebonics in Literature

In order for students to "hear" Black English in literature, we read pieces that use the language. I want students to understand how sometimes authors write the entire piece in Ebonics and other times only the dialogue is in Ebonics and the narrative is in Standard English—or "Marketplace English," as Rickford calls it. In Alice Walker's *The Color Purple*, Celie uses Ebonics to discuss how her friend Darlene is teaching her how to "talk." During this passage, she also touches on the shame aspect of stigmatized languages and dismisses it:

Plus, Darlene trying to teach me how to talk. She say us not so hot. A dead country give-away. You say US where most people say WE, she say, and peoples think

you dumb.... Every time I say something the way I say it, she correct me until I say it some other way. Pretty soon it feel like I can't think. My mind run up on a thought, git confuse, run back and sort of lay down.... Darlene keep trying. Think how much better Shug feel with you educated, she say. She won't be shame to take you anywhere. But I let Darlene worry on. Sometimes I think bout the apples and the dogs, sometimes I don't. Look like to me only a fool would want you to talk in a way that feels peculiar to your mind.

Alice Walker, reading her poetry.

Bettman Archive/CORBIS

Because I believe it is important for students to understand the conscious decisions writers make when they use language, students read an August Wilson interview from *The Paris Review*. He talked about how his characters came to life once he learned to respect and honor the way black people talk: "When I first started writing plays, I couldn't write good dialogue because I didn't respect how black people talked. I thought that in order to make art out of their dialogue I had to change it, make it into something different. Once I learned to value and respect my characters, I could really hear them. I let them start talking." He went on to describe how he learned to create authentic dialogue by going to a cigar store and listening to people talk:

The language is defined by those who speak it. There's a place in Pittsburgh called Pat's Place, a cigar store, which I read about in Claude McKay's *Home of Harlem*. It was where the railroad porters would congregate and tell stories. I thought, Hey, I know Pat's Place. I literally ran there. I was 21 at the time and had no idea I was going to write about it. I wasn't keeping notes. But I loved listening to them. One of the exchanges I heard made it into *Ma Rainey's Black Bottom*. Someone said, "I came to Pittsburgh in '42 on the B & O," and another guy said, "Oh no, you ain't come to Pittsburgh in '42 … the B & O Railroad didn't stop in Pittsburgh in '42!" And the first guy would say, "You gonna tell *me* what railroad I came in on?" "Hell yeah I'm gonna tell you the truth!" Then someone would walk in and they'd say, "Hey, Philmore! The B & O Railroad stop here in '42?" People would drift in and they'd all have various answers to that. … I used to hang around Pat's Place through my twenties, going there less as time went by. That's where I learned how black people talk.

Rehearsing Ebonics Essays

One day my student Ryan handed me an unexpected gift when he asked if I'd ever heard the rapper Big L's song "Ebonics." I confessed my ignorance, but I looked it up on the web and downloaded the music and lyrics. The song is clever, but because the performer misunderstands Ebonics as slang, he provides a great audience for my students to rehearse their arguments about Ebonics.

After reading linguists Rickford and Smitherman and authors Alice Walker and August Wilson, students have enough evidence to write a response to Big L about Ebonics. "Is this Ebonics?" I ask the class. "Write a letter to Big L. As you write, include evidence from his lyrics and evidence from our study of Ebonics." Harold wrote:

Dear Big L,

Ay, "Ebonics" was fire, but that's not real Ebonics, dude. Your rap was just slang. If you want to know what real Ebonics is, you need to know a few things like Ebonics has five present tenses. Ebonics is Black English and it originally came from Africa.

You were using words like whips, kick, cribs, nose candy, bones, rocks. These words are slang, not Ebonics. This has nothing to do with your roots of West African language.

Ebonics is a ruled-governed language. You said it was some slang shit, but that's not right. There are real Ebonics words that pass down through generations, like kitchen and ashy …

This practice writing, during the unit, helps students collect evidence and embed quotes before they write their final essay.

Jerrell also wove Big L into his essay. Like a number of students who wrote about Ebonics, he worked on embedding quotes into his paper, a skill we practiced during the writing of this essay. What I love about Jerrell's paper is

that he maintained his voice in this academic writing; his essay embodies a love of language in its playful extended list of slang words for money and his tongue-in-cheek incorporation of his classmate's quote:

"Ebonics is slang shit," rapper Big L said in his song titled "Ebonics." In this song he tells a lot about the slang that young African Americans use, but this is the problem. He is talking about slang; there is no Ebonics in his lyrics. The misconception people have is that slang and Ebonics are the same thing. The problem is that slang is just a different way of saying things. For example, in his slang you say money, you can also say bread, cheese, cheddar, cash, dough, green, duckets, Washingtons, chips, guap, and many more. However, when you use Ebonics, there is a sentence structure that you have to use. Don't get me wrong, slang and Ebonics go together like mashed potatoes and gravy, but there is a difference between the two. As my classmate said, "Slang is what I talk; Ebonics is how I speak it."

Students always enjoyed the Ebonics section, but they definitely understood it better when I taught it in the context of the politics of language rather than as an isolated unit. Once they see it in a multicultural setting, they can connect the discrimination against Black English with the suppression of indigenous or colonized languages across the globe.

Code-Switching

I bring the unit back to the lives of many of my students by raising the issue of code-switching, moving between home language and academic or Marketplace English. To put Ebonics in the context of its acceptance in the larger world, I turn to literature again. An excerpt from Bebe Moore Campbell's *Brothers and Sisters* never fails to spark a debate about code-switching and assimilation—and the line between them. In this section of the novel, LaKeesha, a young mother with a desire to get off welfare and become a bank clerk, tries to get a job at a bank. Esther, the African American bank manager, is torn by her desire to give LaKeesha the job even though she speaks "nonstandard English" and her desire to just give the job to a young white man, an "Alex Keaton" who wouldn't raise any eyebrows. "She pictured LaKeesha's face, the yearning in her eyes. No, no, no! She wouldn't sacrifice her career in the name of racial solidarity. Forget it. She was going to pick up the phone and hire an acceptable white boy, with acceptable grammar and short fingernails, because that was the right move to make. The smart move." In the end, she tells LaKeesha what she needs to change in order to be accepted into the bank's world. Students wrestle with the question of how much a person should be willing to change in order to "get ahead." Is speaking Standard English acting white? Does everyone have to code-switch on the job?

Students wrestle with the question of how much a person should be willing to change in order to "get ahead." Is speaking Standard English acting white?

In one class discussion a number of years ago, Brandon, whose father ran a successful nonprofit, argued vehemently that everyone has to change in order to be hired—whites and blacks. According to Brandon, all job seekers have to change their hair, their dress, or their language. These conversations eventually lead to a discussion of code-switching in both our language and our dress—contentious territory, but a real issue for many of my students. Campbell's piece allows them to address a question that will impact their lives, and this unit helps them to see it in the context of a broader awareness of the politics of cultural domination and resistance.

DeShawn started working at a bank when he was in high school. As he demonstrates in the opening to his essay on language, these pieces can reflect the struggles black students deal with daily:

I was born black, raised black, and I live black. But now that I have achieved a job outside the general blackness, some say I'm white because of the language I choose to speak at work. Have I put my culture behind me in order to succeed?

As I wrote earlier, none of my students use Ebonics exclusively. (See "Politics of Correction," p. 264, for how I teach students about their personal grammar and punctuation patterns.) They don't identify their language as Ebonics until after our linguistics and grammar lessons. This unit initially grew out of my desire to help them see that the stigma society puts on their home language is based on ignorance and prejudice, and to help them develop the wisdom to see it as a part of the larger pattern of language discrimination. I want students to have pride in their heritage language, and the tools to switch between languages if they make that choice.

Empowered by Linguistic Knowledge

After I started teaching about Ebonics, many of the students began to understand how assumptions about the supremacy of Standard English had created difficulties in their education. One student, Kaanan, wrote:

When I went to school, teachers didn't really teach me how to spell or put sentences together right. They just said sound it out, so I would spell it the way I heard it at home. Everybody around me at home spoke Ebonics, so when I sounded it out, it sounded like home and it got marked wrong. When I wrote something like, "My brother he got in trouble last night," I was marked wrong. Instead of showing me how speakers of Ebonics sometimes use both a name and a pronoun but in "Standard English" only one is used, I got marked wrong.

Another student, Sherrell, said:

I grew up thinking Ebonics was wrong. My teachers would say, "If you ever want to get anywhere you have to learn how to talk right."…At home, after school, break time, lunch time, we all talked our native language which was Ebonics. Our teachers were wrong for saying our language wasn't right. All I heard was Spanish and Ebonics in my neighborhood. They brainwashed me at school to be ashamed of my language and that almost took away one of the few things that African Americans had of our past life and history.

Throughout the Ebonics unit, I asked students to listen and take notes and see if they could spot the rules of Ebonics at work in the school halls, at home, or at the mall. To celebrate and acknowledge a language that so many of my students spoke without awareness, I pointed out Ebonics in class as students spoke. Often, they didn't hear it or recognize it until we held it up like a diamond for them to examine.

My student Curtina said, "How come I never learned before that I spoke Ebonics? How can people speak a language and not know it?" Hannah and Kahlia walked me to my car one day after class and said, "Why hasn't anyone taught us this before? You can see how excited our class is to learn about Ebonics." In his reflection, Jayme answered the question, "What did you love about this unit?": "The knowledge that was given to us about the language that we speak and how it related to our roots in Africa." Jerrell wrote, "The Ebonics part of the unit was what I loved because that's when I learned the most, and I wrote the best paper I've ever wrote." In her reflection on the unit, Hannah wrote, "This unit is very important. It can give a whole new outlook to students on a language that they didn't know before. Kids who have been taught that the way they speak is wrong their entire lives can now be confident." And I love the sassiness of the final sentences in Ryan's essay, "Ebonics is here to stay and shows no sign of fading away in either the black or white communities. In the words of Ebonics: 'It's BIN here and it's bouts ta stay.'" ■

References

Campbell, Bebe Moore. (1994). *Brothers and sisters.* (pp. 194-199), New York: Putnam.

Delpit, Lisa & Perry, Theresa (Eds.) (1998). *The Real Ebonics Debate: Power, Language, and the Education of African American Children.* Boston: Beacon.

Jordan, June. (August, 1988). Nobody mean more to me than you and the future life of Willie Jordan. *Harvard Educational Review,* 58 (3) pp. 363-374.

LeClair, Thomas. "'The Language Must Not Sweat': A Conversation with Toni Morrison." *New Republic,* 21 Mar. 1981: 25-29.

Rickford, J.R. & Rickford, R.J. (2000). *Spoken Soul: The Story of Black English.* New York: John Wiley & Sons.

Rickford, J.R. (2008). www.stanford.edu/~rickford /papers/ SuiteForEbonyAndPhonics.html

Serrano, Angel & Toepke, Alvaro (Producer and Director). (1998). *The Language You Cry In.* Sierre Leone/Spain: California Newsreel.

Smitherman, G. (1997) *Talkin and testifyin: The language of black America.* Boston: Houghton Mifflin.

Excerpt from Brothers and Sisters

by Bebe Moore Campbell

Esther stared at the scrolling figures on her computer screen. It was hard to comprehend that people could be so careless about their finances that they forgot they had money in the bank, but as she reviewed the dormant accounts, a task she undertook every few months, the evidence was indisputable. In the downtown branch alone, there was nearly three million dollars in accounts that hadn't been active in months, sometimes years. Two million, nine hundred thousand and seventy-eight dollars, to be exact. She logged in the amount. Of course some of the holders of the accounts were deceased, but in those cases, she would have thought that relatives would come and claim the cash. All that money going to waste. She shook her head.

Esther heard a soft knock at the door. She looked at her watch: nine-thirty. She had completely forgotten about her appointment. Well, the interview wouldn't take long. She'd already decided that she was going to hire David Weaver. "Come in," she called.

The door opened slowly, and a young, dark-brown-skinned woman stood in front of Esther's desk. Their eyes met, and Esther could read in them the girl's uncensored surprise. Esther realized immediately the reason for the startled look in the young woman's eyes: she hadn't expected another black person to be interviewing her.

Two months earlier, Angel City had formed a partnership with the city's social service agency. The bank was obligated to interview a certain number of welfare recipients who were involved in a job training program, although they weren't obligated to hire them. Today's interviewee was Esther's first from the program. Office scuttlebutt said the candidates were pretty poorly qualified.

Esther found the girl's astonishment amusing. Why, the child couldn't even speak. "Were you expecting someone else?" Esther said.

"Oh, no. Well, I—" The girl stopped, and they both laughed. "I'm glad it's you," she said, and they chuckled again. "No, I mean, like, it makes me feel good to know that one of us is the boss. You know what I mean?"

"Yes, I know what you mean," Esther said. The girl seemed a little awkward. This was probably her first job interview. Esther felt a twinge of guilt, knowing that her mind was already made up. Thinking, she probably needs a job worse than old Alex Keaton, Esther extended her hand. When the girl shook it, Esther could feel her fingers trembling like a frightened kitten; then she felt something hard and sharp cutting into her palm. She looked down. Good God! Long. Curved. Bright Red with a capital R. And rhinestones were embedded in the pinkie nails. Genuine Hootchy Mama fingernails. "I'm Esther Jackson. Thank you for coming. Sit down, La... La..."

"LaKeesha. LaKeesha Jones." She talks so proper, LaKeesha thought. Just like a white woman.

LaKeesha sat down in the chair near the desk. Esther gave her a quick once-over. The dress was too tight and too short, but not awful. The girl's face was pleasant, even though she wore too much makeup. The braids, well, they weren't the proper hairstyle for a black woman who wanted to get ahead in business. "Tell me a little about yourself, LaKeesha," Esther said. "Have you had any teller experience?"

LaKeesha took a breath, trying not to be nervous in spite of the way Esther was looking at her. Her eyes were like fingers lifting her collar to check for dirt. LaKeesha attempted to concentrate. She'd been through a number of practice interviews. She paused, remembering what Mrs. Clark had told her: Look the person straight in her eyes; smile a lot; speak clearly; sell yourself; don't be nervous. But Esther's language, each word so precisely enunciated, was erecting a brick wall between them. There was nothing to be nervous about, LaKeesha told herself. She smiled at Esther. "I just, like, finished the South-Central Alternative Education Center's bank teller program. I was, like, you know, number one in my class. . . ."

An around-the-way girl if ever I saw one, Esther said to herself as she listened to LaKeesha describe her course work and a month-long internship at one of the city's banks. "The manager wanted to hire me, but they didn't have no openings at the time."

Esther flinched at the double negative. "Well," she said, getting a word in, "it certainly appears that you've been well trained. Tell me about the school you attended."

"See, I dropped out of high school after I had my baby. Then I met this lady named Mrs. Clark; her and her husband run the school, and so she talked me into going there to get my GED. She has a contract with the city to train people, so after I got my GED, I decided that I wanted to take the bank teller course, because, well, I'm on the county and I want to get off." LaKeesha sat back in her chair. She hadn't meant to talk so much, to get so personal. Mrs. Clark told her to be professional. Maybe she shouldn't have mentioned being on the county. She looked at Esther's black suit, the shiny low heels, and all that gold jewelry she wore, not the kind that screamed at you but a nice quiet gold. And words came out her mouth so sharp they could draw blood. She probably thought she was white, sitting up in her own office, being everybody's boss. She shouldn't have said anything about being on the county.

A baby, Esther thought. She could just hear the phone calls, the excuses: the baby is sick; the baby-sitter can't make it. Hiring a single mother with a baby—because of course she wasn't married—was asking for trouble. She looked at LaKeesha, who was staring at her uneasily. "Do you know TIPS?"

LaKeesha grinned. "That's what we was trained in."

Esther scratched the back of her neck. The child wasn't ready for prime time, and the bad thing about it was that she probably had no idea just how deficient she was. Esther thought fleetingly of what that asshole Fred Gaskins would say if he were listening to her conversation with LaKeesha. He'd say that LaKeesha was another product of a substandard high school in South-Central. She could just see the operations manager, his fat little lightbulb head bobbing back and forth, his bantam chest heaving in and out. Fred Gaskins can go to hell, she thought to herself. She glanced at her watch; ten o'clock. "Come with me, LaKeesha. I'd like to see what you can do."

Leading the young woman out the door to the operations area, Esther guided her past the customer reps' desks, around to the back of the tellers' cage. There were five people on duty. Hector Bonilla smiled in his usual polite manner as soon as he saw the two women approaching him. "Hector, I'd like you to meet LaKeesha Jones. Hector, LaKeesha and I have been chatting about the possibility of her becoming a teller here. I'd like for you two to work together for an hour or so, and then I'll come back for you, LaKeesha. Hector, may I see you for a second?"

Esther walked the young man a few feet away from his station. "Listen, I want you to really pay attention to how LaKeesha works. Look at the way she deals with customers, how she handles money, and how well she knows TIPS. I'll talk with you later, all right?"

"Yes, Esther," Hector said, nodding his head so vigorously that his straight black hair rippled over his forehead. In the eighteen months that he had been with the bank, Hector had proved himself to be a good worker, stable and serious. He always came early and stayed late. Esther knew she could depend upon him for a fair assessment. She might not hire LaKeesha this time, but if the girl had decent skills, she might consider her when there was another opening.

One hour later, Esther stepped outside her office, caught Hector's eye, and motioned him over. In a few moments, he appeared at her door, and she ushered him to a seat inside. "How did she do?" Esther asked.

"She is very good worker," Hector said solemnly, his dark, serious eyes looking straight into hers. "She is polite to customers. She is accurate with money. She knows the computer system too. I didn't have to tell her very much at all." His smile was as earnest and diffident as he was.

"Thank you, Hector. Would you tell LaKeesha to come to my office, please."

"Well, Hector told me you did very well," Esther said after LaKeesha settled herself into her chair. The young woman beamed. Esther asked her a few questions about the transactions she'd just made. Finally, she stood up and extended her hand. "I've enjoyed chatting with you, and I'll be in touch."

LaKeesha stood up. "My grandmother, she lives with me and she keeps my baby, even if he's sick, so you don't have to worry about that."

Esther nodded her head. "Well," she said, opening the door just a little wider, "that's just fine."

She felt the girl's eyes on her. "Just fine," Esther repeated, waiting for LaKeesha to leave.

The young woman stepped toward her. "I know I can do a good job for you. I'll come on time. I know how to be a good worker. I can smile at the customers and be polite and hand them their money. I want to work." She knew she was talking too much, that she should just leave, but the words seemed to be bubbling up from some spring. "My whole family's been on the county for as long as I can remember. I didn't tell none of them where I was going, because I didn't want to get their hopes up. I want to be a good example for my younger sisters. They need to see somebody working." She paused and stood up straighter. "If I don't get this job, would you just please call me and, like, tell me what I did wrong, so I won't make the same mistake on the next interview? Because if I don't get this job, I'm gonna get me a job from somebody."

Esther hesitated a moment, then closed the door. "Sit down," she told LaKeesha.

"First of all, get rid of those fingernails. This is a place of business, not a nightclub. Second, your dress is too tight and too short, and your heels are too high. Third, you're wearing too much makeup. Fourth, your grammar is poor. It's 'I didn't tell any of them,' not 'none of them.' And don't say 'like' so much. And another thing: get rid of the braids. I think they're beautiful, but when you're working for white folks you want to fit in, not stand out." Seeing the distraught look on LaKeesha's face, Esther spoke a little more gently. "Now, everything I'm telling you can be corrected. It's up to you."

"If I change all those things, will you give me a job?" LaKeesha's expression was eager, hungry.

"I can't promise you that," Esther said quickly, "but I believe that if you make those adjustments, somebody will hire you. And don't think in terms of a job. You have to think about a career."

LaKeesha's eyes, which seemed to grow larger and more hopeful every minute, didn't leave Esther's face.

"You need to think: I'll start as a teller, then I'll become an operations assistant, then I'll get in the operations training program, and then I'll become an operations manager. That's the kind of mind-set employers want to see in an employee."

LaKeesha's face brightened, and she stood up. Before she realized what she was doing, she was hugging Esther and mumbling in her ear: "Thank you, sister."

Esther felt the word even more than she heard it. There was obligation in that word. And she didn't want any part of that.

She pulled away. "Don't ever call me that here," she said quickly. Esther watched as LaKeesha passed through the bank and out the door. Even after she left, the musky odor of TLC oil sheen spray clung to the air in the room. Esther knew the odor well; it was her scent too.

Esther closed her eyes. She could see herself making those fast deals. Lending millions just on her say-so. If she played her cards right, maybe she could be the one who'd transcend the glass ceiling. Every once in a while, they let somebody black slip through. Why shouldn't she be the one?

Esther walked around her desk with her hands clasped together in front of her and then behind her. She pictured LaKeesha's face, the yearning in her eyes. No, no, no! She wouldn't sacrifice her career in the name of racial solidarity. Forget it. She was going to pick up the phone and hire an acceptable white boy, with acceptable grammar and short fingernails, because that was the right move to make. The smart move.

Sister.

That and a dollar won't even get you a ride on the bus.

Esther picked up the telephone.

From Brothers and Sisters *by Bebe Moore Campbell, copyright © 1994 by Bebe Moore Campbell. Used by permission of G.P. Putnam's Sons, a division of Penguin Group (USA) Inc.*

Hanquan Chen/iSTOCK

Into the World Project

In an effort to make students' learning visible, real, and meaningful, I like to take them beyond the classroom walls to work with diverse audiences, so they can teach others about the politics of language. I attempt to do "into the world" projects two or three times a year. In addition to the essays they write at the end of the unit (described in "Writing Wild Essays from Hard Ground"), students create a project that exhibits their understanding about language. Their task: "Create a project that takes your knowledge about language, naming, assimilation, or Ebonics into the community. Think about an audience for this project. Who needs to know about this? The project must demonstrate knowledge of the topic and include writing and speaking."

The students' task: "Create a project that takes your knowledge about language, naming, assimilation, or Ebonics into the community."

In *Rethinking Our Classrooms*, the editors framed this learning as the "activist" component of a social justice education. Too often, I see this piece misinterpreted as "political brainwashing," taking students to demonstrations that parallel the teacher's politics or enlisting students to write a letter or clean up the streets around their schools. But the intention of this portion of our vision for classrooms was to authentically tie student learning to the world:

> We want students to come to see themselves as truth-tellers and change-makers. If we ask children to critique the world but then fail to encourage them to act, our classrooms can degenerate into factories for cynicism. Part of a teacher's role is to suggest that ideas have real consequences and should be acted upon, and to offer students opportunities to do just that. Children can also draw inspiration from historical and contemporary efforts of people who struggled for justice. A critical curriculum should be a rainbow of resistance, reflecting the diversity of people from

all cultures who acted to make a difference, many of whom did so at great sacrifice. Students should be allowed to learn about, and feel connected to, this legacy of defiance.

To begin the project, I ask students to determine audience, topic, and format for their project. I spend a class period brainstorming audience possibilities with students: elementary schools, other classes at our school, college and university classes, local newspapers. Then I share past projects, so students can think about potential formats for their projects: Children's books my students wrote about Native American issues, including fishing on the Columbia River; books of praise poetry students wrote after studying African American poetry; and the Jefferson Achievement Test, which students created about language and power in the SATs. I have hard copies of previous student work as well as choppy, fading, hand-held video clips of students presenting lessons. Although, obviously, I've saved these over the years, I did not have them initially.

For this project, students may choose to work with a partner. Students developed a wide variety of topics and formats. Michael and Harold created a picture book about Ebonics; Job wrote a children's book about boarding schools for elementary students; Dennise, Jayme, and Ryan created a talk show about Ebonics for college students. Dennise moderated the show, a staged debate between Jayme who played a linguist, fashioned after Smitherman and Rickford, and Ryan, who argued mainstream views about Ebonics. James created a PowerPoint about language assimilation with historical photographs of boarding schools. Jacoa and Alauno worked with the computer teacher to develop their "Ebonics Jeopardy" which included the following categories: Famous quotes, words and phrases, stereotypes, and true/false statements. Students worked on the projects during class for most of a week. Some spent time in the computer lab, some wrote, and some procrastinated.

Once the students completed their projects, I take them through a lesson planning process prior to our engagements. I asked, "What's your hook? What will you say or do when you are in front of the room? Will you ask a question? Tell a story?" Students rarely think of this part. It isn't enough to have the project; they have to write out a plan for how they will introduce their children's book or their talk show to their audience, otherwise they freeze when they get into the room. "Who is in charge of each

Inevitably, the most challenging students in my class are the best teachers in the elementary school. They know how to engage the unengaged.

segment? Who will read the book? What happens after you read the book? Will you get students to write? What are your directions?" We spend a day developing these lessons, but students are rarely prepared. As I recently told my co-teachers at Grant, Russ Peterson and Dylan Leeman, "They aren't ready for prime time, but they will rise to the occasion." And they usually do. After our visit to Faubion Elementary School, one student said, "It's scary when all of those students are looking at you and you're not sure what you're going to do or say." I move from classroom to classroom, giving students hints or reminders, encouraging them to work one-on-one with students. Inevitably, the most challenging students in my class are

The GRANTONIAN

Issue # 11   Volume 123   Portland, Oregon   Grant High School   April 25, 2008

Ebonics and the politics of language: Grant students teach others

Peterson's African American Literature class shares their knowledge about Ebonics. Photo by Sarah Hunter

By Julianne Pike
Grantonian reporter
jpike@grantonian.com

"Language is power, when we get to a point where we see each other as equals, that's when we can overcome and there will be no stereotypes because we'll understand each other."
—Alauno Porter

Continued on page 3

Ryan Halverson discusses AAVE/Ebonics.

the best teachers in the elementary school. They know how to engage the unengaged—and they enjoy it the most.

I try to find supportive places for students to share their projects. Generally, I take them two places: Colleges and elementary/middle schools. We travel after the school day to education classes at our local universities. I take four to eight students at a time, depending on whether or not I can enlist another teacher or administrator to come with me. I take all or almost all of the class to the elementary or middle schools on a field trip during the school day. Sometimes we walk to schools in the neighborhood. Because the school district no longer has money for field trips, I chart out the course on public transportation ahead of time and pray that it doesn't rain on us as we walk to and from the bus stop. And I try to find grant money to buy pizza or snacks after the teaching, so we can celebrate and debrief.

These projects allow students to deepen their knowledge of the language unit by teaching it to others. As Jacoa said after teaching a graduate education class at Portland State University (PSU), "Most of the time, you learn something, then you move on. When we go to teach about language assimilation and Ebonics at colleges, we actually do something with what we learned."

Another positive aspect is that students share their passion about their piece of the topic. After teaching at PSU, Dennise said, "We get to teach people who are going to become teachers about Ebonics and assimilation, so they know and can share this information with their students." Alauno added that he liked teaching adults, to be the one who knows instead of the one always getting taught.

Most of my teaching career I have worked with students who might be the first in their families to graduate high school, and if they attend college, they will be the first in their family as well. So taking students to colleges provides more motivation and promise than a campus tour or a chart about increased income through education. On the way back from Lewis & Clark College, Ryan said, "I am overwhelmed about college. How do I get started?" That conversation led to Ryan going to the college center at Grant to look at colleges. During the same car ride, Jayme asked, "What are the best colleges to become a teacher?" When students not only see themselves on campus, but become bearers of knowledge, they gain confidence in their ability to attend college. As Jacoa noted during our post-PSU dinner, "I feel empowered."

I have taught various forms of this curriculum for over 20 years, and my conviction continues to grow that this unit exemplifies my core beliefs about teaching. The curriculum authentically connects students' lives with an ongoing struggle over a critical issue, language. By examining language policy through the literature and history of those who have fought to keep their language and culture alive, students see how intimately political decisions affect their lives. Students also gain academic skills and knowledge by reading difficult texts and writing poetry, narratives, and essays. And instead of wrapping up the unit with a grade at the end of the quarter, they take their passion about language and power into the world. ■

6: Responding to
Student Work

TEACHING FOR JOY AND JUSTICE

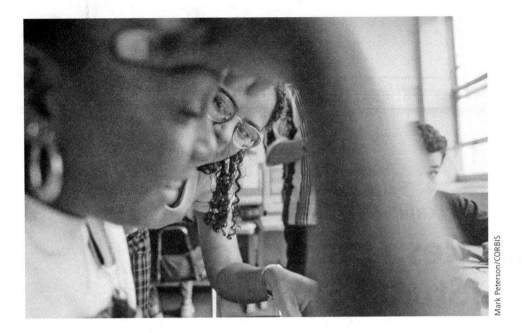

Mark Peterson/CORBIS

The Politics of Correction: Learning from Student Writing

Although I am now the Director of the Oregon Writing Project and should know how to talk right, I still have to watch my words because when I get emotional, home slips out. I say "chimbly" instead of chimney, "warsh" and "crik" when I least expect it. I frequently substitute words because I can't get my tongue around the correct pronunciation. My brother and sisters used to chuckle when our mother talked. Her mouth, grown and raised in Bandon, Ore., had a hard time acquainting itself with foreign words that have become part of our daily language—burrito or futon. As her children, we struggle too, but our language—which has caused us shame in the outside world—bonds us when we're together deliberately mispronouncing words and conjugating verbs the way Mom did.

How do we both nurture students in their writing and help them learn the language of power? We start by telling them what they're doing right.

These days, I'm frequently called into schools to "fix" students' grammar and punctuation errors. I admit to feeling churlish about using conventions—punctuation, grammar, spelling—as the entry point to student writing. I believe writing must begin in students' lives and be generated for real audiences. However, in recent years I've witnessed too many low-income students, students of color, and immigrant students who have not learned how to use Standard/Marketplace English—the language of power. Sure they can write great slam poetry; some can even write killer stories; a few can write essays, but they are often riddled with convention errors. As I discussed in Chapter 5, "Language and Power," failing to learn these skills handcuffs students. Their lack of fluency with the language of power will follow them long after they leave school, silencing them by making them hesitant to speak in public meetings or to write their outrage over public policy because they "talk wrong."

So how do we both nurture students in their writing and help them learn the language of power? We start by telling them what they're doing right. Too many students are scarred by teachers' pens in the margins yelling, "You're wrong. Wrong again. Ten points off for that comma splice. Where is the past tense?" Language Arts teachers become accustomed to looking for errors as if we will be rewarded in some English teacher heaven for finding the most. I know this from experience. I still remember the day when in a frenzy of doing my job right, I corrected every error on Jerald's budding paper and witnessed his transformation from eager to dejected student. I had to turn that practice around and look for what the student does right.

As I've indicated throughout the book, I teach conventions in the context of student writing. While we play with language through poetry and sentence combining, teaching students how to "correct" their writing happens most often within the text of the students' essays and narratives. Yes, there are moments for whole-class lessons on getting rid of passive language, for example, but the real work takes place on the page where students wrestle with their own prose.

Nathan, for example, was a tongue-tied writer when he entered my class in the 9th grade. At the beginning of the year, he gave me very little writing—expecting to be hammered, I suspect. In September, he wrote "My Freshmen Football": "I Realy Injoy the sport. I like Hiting and running. We had a great team and a great year. I would like to encourage all to play the Sporth."

In this writing, it is clear that he's afraid to write. Instead of marking his errors, I asked questions and made comments in the margin of his paper. "*Show* me what you like about football. How do you feel when you're on the field? Tell me about a moment in the game. Make me see the movie." I brought in models written by other writers, especially student writers. In a revision, he wrote:

When the halmut toches my Head my body turns Like doctor Jeckel and Mr. Hide. I become a safage. And there's no one who can stop me when this happens. My blood starts racing my hart pumping. Like a great machine of power. And when that football moves that's the time for me to move and get that quarterback. And anyone who get's in my way is asking for problems.

His paper went on for two error-filled pages. But in this passage he wrote with passion on a topic he cared about. This comes when a student is freed from the teacher as marksman waiting to "correct" every word. In my response to his paper, I pointed out what he was doing right. For example, I love how he uses similes and metaphors throughout the paper. He also uses strong verbs: touches, racing, turns, pumping.

Teacher as Scientist: Looking for Patterns of Errors

Obviously, when a student's paper is filled with errors, giving only positive feedback is a dereliction of duty. Students need to know how to access the "language of power." Clearly, Nathan struggled with conventions. But he had so many errors that as a teacher, I had to choose which ones to first target for change. In her book, *Errors and Expectations*, Mina Shaughnessy wrote, "[T]he teacher must try to decipher the individual student's code, examining samples of his writing as a scientist might, searching for patterns or explanations, listening to what the student says about punctuation, and creating situations in the classroom that encourage all students to talk openly about what they don't understand."

At the beginning of each year I sit with my students' papers and categorize each student's errors, looking for patterns.

Using Shaughnessy's scientist analogy as a model, at the beginning of each year I sit with my students' papers and categorize each student's errors, looking for patterns. I keep this list for myself, so I can work with students to eliminate their errors one at a time. I also create a personalized page for each student on my computer which is ongoing and part of the Patterns of Errors folder I keep for that class. (See "Student Patterns of Errors," pp. 269-270.) When I return students' papers, I attach their "pattern of error" sheet to their drafts and revision, so they can review them to correct their individual "code," as Shaughnessy calls it, before they turn in their next assignment.

As I work with students on their errors, I hold them accountable to self-correct before turning in a final draft. Nathan's paper, for example, demonstrates problems with capitalization, apostrophes, spelling, and basic sentence structure. I tackled capitalization first because it was the easiest problem to solve. Then I made him accountable for checking to make sure that he used capital letters correctly. By correcting just the capitalization problems, Nathan eliminated many errors. Once he mastered that convention, we moved on to another.

When I first explain this process, it sounds so time-consuming that teachers nod and turn away. Believe me, I am not a martyr. At Jefferson, I taught three 90-minute block classes, typically totaling around 90 students, but I would continue to do it even if my student load was 150 or more. Because each student's error chart is on my computer, I can update it regularly and print it out when I hand back papers. It actually takes less time than marking—and remarking—the same errors on paper after paper. It is also more effective. When I mark student errors, instead of making them responsible, I'm doing all of the work. If students read their error sheets and make the changes, they do the work. Also, they have to review their error sheet prior to turning in final drafts, so I see fewer errors as the year moves on.

Like most writers, I have patterns of errors I need to watch out for in my writing. Published writers know their Achilles' heel and return after their draft and revise based on this self-knowledge. For example, I often use passive voice, so after I complete my first draft, I go back, highlight every *is, was, were,* and see if I can rewrite the sentence to make it more active. I also tend to use too many "buts," so I check myself for those as well. This self-knowledge and self-check is a habit I want to instill in student writers.

Teaching Mini-Lessons

Many students in my classes make the same errors—punctuating dialogue, for example—and I can teach mini-lessons on that topic. I find the best way to deal with these problems is to ask students to generate the rules. They remember their rules far longer than when they read the rule and correct the errors in a punctuation exercise.

When I'm teaching students the rules around dialogue, I copy a page from a short story or novel that demonstrates many of the rules—a piece of dialogue interrupted by an attribution, a question, a dialogue where the speakers change but there is no attribution. Then I put the students in small groups and say, "I want you to imagine that you have been consulted by a textbook company to write up the rules for punctuating dialogue. I want your group to examine this passage and figure out the rules. Here are some clues: Look at where the quotation marks are. What do they surround? Look at the punctuation. Highlight it and write up a rule that describes where it is. Look at

where the capital letters are. You need to write the rules so that students across the United States can follow them. Include an example for each rule." Students post their rules on large sheets of paper or the black or white board. After the class checks to see if the rules are correct, we post them on the wall. If I have time, I also type their rules and distribute them, so students can have a reference when they write. At the end of the lesson, I tell students, "If you forget the rules, just pull out a novel that has dialogue and figure them out again." Sometimes I bring in dialogue published in a text from another country so students can see that conventions change from country to country. They are socially constructed, not a part of nature.

Logical Errors from Home Language

Sometimes the "errors" are part of a student's home language. In that case, the "correction" process needs to make it clear that the student isn't "wrong," but that each language has its own way of making plurals or using verb tenses. Students need to learn the differences between their home language and Standard English.

Students need to learn the differences between their home language and Standard English.

In my classes, I attempt to value language variations by studying—and honoring—their use in literature first. After reading authors who use home language and Standard English—for example, Lucille Clifton, Jimmy Santiago Baca, and Lois-Ann Yamanaka—the class discusses which genres and situations call for them to code-switch between their home language and Marketplace English. Students are quick to point out that when writing poetry or dialogue in narratives—genres that call for informal language—they may choose to use their home language. But when they write essays, college or job applications, state writing tests—genres that call for formal language—they may choose Standard English.

As I discussed in the last chapter, as a teacher in a predominantly African American school, where the majority of students exhibited some features of African American Vernacular English (AAVE, also called Ebonics or "Spoken Soul"), I needed to learn the rules and history of the language so I could help students move between the two language systems.

In my student Larry's narrative about shoes, for example, I kept track of his patterns of punctuation errors,

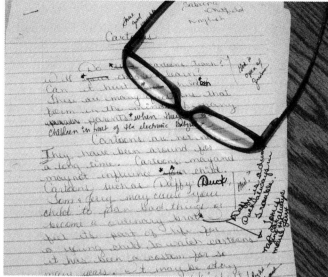

Sabrina Whitfield, a 9th-grade student, revises her own essay.

but I also helped him understand when he used features of AAVE:

> Them old Chuck Taylor high top nasty looking
> Converse these are the ugliest shoes I had ever seen.
> I thought as I put them on.
> "Mom why I have to wear these ugly shoes." My mom say they was in style.
> "Larry be quiet these are in style right now."
> "I don't see how they raggedy."

While Larry made some basic errors in punctuation, many of his "mistakes" correctly use the grammar structure of African American Vernacular English. As I wrote in the last chapter, this can be difficult for a teacher without a linguistic background to understand. Geneva Smitherman noted in *Talkin and Testifyin: The Language of Black America,* "Linguistically speaking, the greatest differences between contemporary Black and White English are on the level of grammatical structure." It *looks* like Larry's errors are simply grammatical, but if a teacher studied the grammar of Ebonics/AAVE, she would recognize that he followed many of the linguistic features of black vernacular.

For Larry, simply correcting these grammar errors without acknowledging their roots in his home language is not only inefficient, it sets Standard English up as the "correct language" and African American Vernacular English as wrong. To walk in the halls of academia or the halls of power, Larry needed to understand how he was transferring the "logic" of his home language into the sentence structure of Standard English, and he needed to know how and when to change that.

For example, in the sentence, "My mom say they was in style," the lack of the third person singular present tense s (*say* instead of *says*) follows the grammar patterns of AAVE. I like the explanation John and Russell Rickford give of this rule in *Spoken Soul: The Story of Black English*: "In getting rid of third-person s, you might think of AAVE as making the rules of English more regular, or as an advocate for equal opportunity: the verb doesn't have special endings with other subjects, so it shouldn't with third-person singular subjects."

The lack of a *be* verb in the run-on sentence, "I don't see how they raggedy" is another example of Larry following the rules of AAVE. In mainstream English, the sentence would read: "I don't see how. They are raggedy." The absence of an *is* or *are* is called "zero copula." Copulas couple, or join, a subject (in this case, "they") and a predicate (what's said *about* the subject—in this case that the shoes are raggedy).

As I mentioned, to code-switch, he must be aware that he used AAVE, which has a complex set of rules and restrictions—especially around the verb *be*. According to the Rickfords, "As with most rules of spoken language, no AAVE speaker has ever been taught these things formally, and few speakers could spell them out for you (unless, perhaps, they had learned them in a linguistics course). But AAVE speakers follow them, almost religiously, in their daily speech." And, I would add, many students incorporate their spoken home language into their writing.

In my experience, teaching African American students the grammar structure and history of Spoken Soul, or AAVE, evoked pride in their language, but also that electric "aha" moment of discovery. All students, not just African Americans, benefited from learning that African American language is a highly structured grammar system.

Teacher Study Groups

In my previous role as a high school language arts specialist, I encouraged teachers to form study groups to analyze the patterns of errors their students bring to class. During one summer, a small group of language arts and ESL teachers looked at the errors their Russian-, Vietnamese-, and Spanish-speaking students made in writing. Once they identified the patterns, they discussed and studied the original languages of their students. In a draft guide for language arts and ESL teachers, they noted the "logical errors" students made. In their introduction, the group reminded teachers that "ELL students: 1) experience linguistic interference from their first language sound system; 2) apply first language rules to Standard English; 3) speak fluently before they learn to write fluently; and 4) over apply newly learned grammatical rules." They also listed common "errors" and related them back to the rules governing the first language. For example, in Vietnamese, the adverb expresses time; the verb remains unchanged; therefore a student whose first language is Vietnamese might write: "Yesterday, I go to the mall."

Teachers at a predominantly African American school formed a study group to analyze their students' errors and study AAVE. The majority of the teachers in the group were African American. During a discussion one morning, a teacher pointed out, "I always told my students what my teachers told me, 'Read your writing out loud and correct those places where it doesn't sound right.' One of my students said, 'But it does sound right.'" The teachers discussed this point for a while. "It sounds right because it sounds like the way we talk at home. It can sound odd when we use Standard English." The study group helped clarify that the old piece of advice might work with Standard English speakers, but not with students whose home language is not the same as school language.

Once students begin—error by error—to understand how to "clean up" their writing, they gain confidence in their ability. They no longer feel like targets in the cross-hairs of the teacher's red pen; they don't need to "wash history from their throats" as poet Patricia Smith so passionately writes in her essay "Talkin' Wrong." Teachers exercise enormous power when we take our pens to student papers. Will we use our power to help students understand that Standard English is one dialect among many or will we use it to whittle away students' voices and home languages one error at a time? ■

References:

Rickford, J. (1997). Retrieved from "Suite for Ebony and Phonics," *Discover Magazine*, December 1997. http://www.stanford.edu/~rickford/papers/ SuiteForEbonyAndPhonics.html

Rickford, J. & Rickford, R. (2000). *Spoken Soul: The Story of Black English*. New York: John Wiley & Sons.

Shaughnessy, M. (1977). *Errors and Expectations: A Guide for the Teacher of Basic Writing*. New York: Oxford University Press.

Smith, P. (2000-2001). "Talking Wrong," *Ms. Magazine*, Dec. 2000-Jan. 2001.

Smitherman, G. (1997). *Talkin and Testifyin: The Language of Black America*. Boston: Houghton Mifflin.

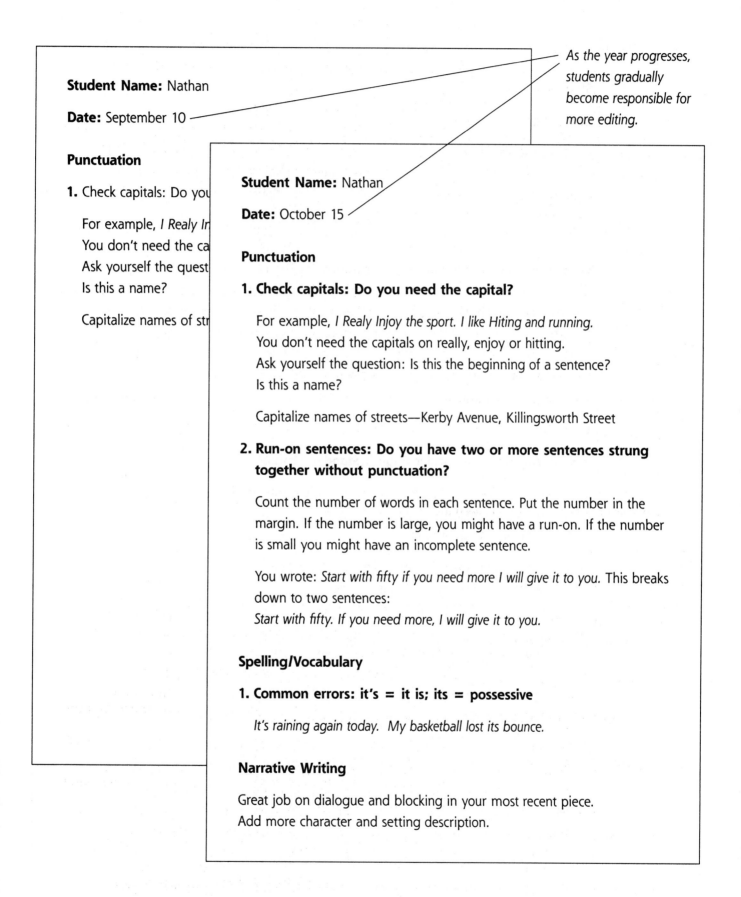

Student Name: Nathan

Date: September 10

Punctuation

1. Check capitals: Do you

For example, *I Realy In*
You don't need the ca
Ask yourself the quest
Is this a name?

Capitalize names of str

As the year progresses, students gradually become responsible for more editing.

Student Name: Nathan

Date: October 15

Punctuation

1. Check capitals: Do you need the capital?

For example, *I Realy Injoy the sport. I like Hiting and running.*
You don't need the capitals on really, enjoy or hitting.
Ask yourself the question: Is this the beginning of a sentence?
Is this a name?

Capitalize names of streets—Kerby Avenue, Killingsworth Street

2. Run-on sentences: Do you have two or more sentences strung together without punctuation?

Count the number of words in each sentence. Put the number in the margin. If the number is large, you might have a run-on. If the number is small you might have an incomplete sentence.

You wrote: *Start with fifty if you need more I will give it to you.* This breaks down to two sentences:
Start with fifty. If you need more, I will give it to you.

Spelling/Vocabulary

1. Common errors: it's = it is; its = possessive

It's raining again today. My basketball lost its bounce.

Narrative Writing

Great job on dialogue and blocking in your most recent piece.
Add more character and setting description.

Student Name: Larry

Date: December 10

What I love about your writing: Your writing is rich in story. It made me laugh out loud when I read your first line: "Them old Chuck Taylor high top red nasty looking Converse shoes." I liked your description of the shoes: "they was way too flexible...I thought they was supposed to support my ankles." You capture the natural sound of dialogue between you and your mother.

What you need to work on for your narrative: This is a delicious first draft. It provides lots of opportunity for you to develop it more. Look back at the narrative criteria sheet and see which elements are missing — add those. Read back over Sarah's "Pro Wings" and notice the way she "blew up" the scene in the store when her mother was buying her shoes. Could you add a scene like that? Could you add a scene where you felt uncomfortable in the shoes as Chetan does in his school scene in "Baby Oil"?

Grammar

African American Vernacular English/Standard English:

- AAVE uses subject and a pronoun, SE uses one or the other.
  You wrote: My *mother she* went to the store.
  In SE: My *mother* went to the store.

- AAVE drops the "s" on the verb when you use he or she:
  You wrote: My *mom say* they was in style.
  In SE: My *mom says* they [are/were] in style.

- AAVE drops *is* or *are* between a subject (in this case, "they") and a predicate (what's said about the subject—in this case that the shoes are raggedy). SE inserts the *is* or *are*.

- You wrote: I don't see how *they raggedy*.
  In SE: I don't see how. They *are raggedy*.

*Note: Due to space limitations, this example does not show: punctuation, spelling, syntax, genre patterns.

7: Letting Go of Grades

TEACHING FOR JOY AND JUSTICE

Jefferson teacher,
Wendy Shelton,
conferences with
students.

Linda Christensen

My Dirty Little Secret:
I Don't Grade Student Papers

I have a secret: I haven't graded a student paper in over three decades. Now, don't get me wrong. That doesn't mean I toss them in the fire, "accidentally" lose them, turn them over to student teachers, stamp them with a six-trait writing analysis and plug in numbers, or push them through some kind of computerized grade machine. I discovered early on that if I wanted to produce writers I needed to let go of grades.

Creating Meaningful Work

Our grading should match our pedagogy. In my classroom I attempt to create aspects of the kind of society I want my students to live in: a society where the work is meaningful and intrinsically rewarding, where people grapple with big ideas they care about, in an environment where they can talk, read, write, and think without worry of failure or ridicule.

Students need to feel that their work is important, relevant, and meaningful. If not, why should they spend time on it?

Students need to feel that their work is important, relevant, and meaningful. If not, why should they spend time on it? I was reminded of this when I demonstrated a narrative lesson in a classroom at Madison High School in Portland. Madison's students come from diverse cultural, racial, linguistic, and economic backgrounds. Students had just read *Breaking Through*, a short memoir by Francisco Jiménez, about growing up in a migrant family and trying to fit in as a teenager. The students and I examined a point in the memoir where Jiménez describes going to graduation wearing a white t-shirt because his family couldn't afford to buy him the required white shirt. We also read Gary Soto's story, "The Jacket," as well as a number of stories written by my former students. (For the complete lesson see "Can't Buy Me Love," p. 70.)

We talked about buying clothes to fit in, desiring clothes we can't afford, receiving clothes that we don't want from people we love. The topic fits my criteria. It's about big ideas—in this case, poverty and acceptance. Students struggle with finding a place to belong, but they also want to avoid being a target for other students' ridicule by wearing the "wrong" clothes or shoes. Many are desperate to fit in—even when "fitting in" means joining a group that rejects the standard teen scene of tight, low-riding jeans and shrink-wrap tops.

As we started writing, I told students, "Find your passion. Write your way into a story that you want to tell."

Daniel didn't write about clothes. He wrote about getting a gift he didn't want from his foster parents:

> "Here you go Daniel," said Matt, my foster dad, while handing me a present. "It's from me and Theresa."
>
> Theresa was my foster mom. Me and her always got along.
>
> "Thank you," I said, trying to put on a big smile, while opening the present at the same time. I was thinking to myself, I wonder what it is. Is it the Golden Sun game I asked for? As I finished tearing off the last piece of paper, taped to the front, I read the name of the present. It was a Tony Hawk's Pro Skater game. Instead of getting me the game I wanted, they got me a different game. I thought to myself, they know that I don't like Tony Hawk. Why would they get me a game that they know I don't like?
>
> The thing is my foster dad was afraid of me. I don't know why, but I know that I didn't like him. Why didn't I like him? Well, that's a good question, huh? I didn't like him because he always hit my foster brothers. For some reason he never hit me. He made me cry once in a while from the verbal abuse, but that was about it.
>
> I had a look of disappointment on my face. Automatically, I put on my biggest smile to the point that the sides of my mouth started to twitch. I hated that smile because I didn't like my mouth to twitch. It got annoying whenever I had to use that smile.

Daniel wrote about living in foster homes, about learning how to lie about gifts he didn't want; he also wrote a list of questions about his next home and his next

school—he was headed into his 12th home the week after I gave the assignment. He wondered if his new "family" would like him. He wondered if he would make friends at his new school. Fitting in meant a lot more to Daniel than wearing the right clothes.

> Ever since I came into foster care four years ago, I have been moving from home to home. I've had to learn skills that even some adults have never had to learn. Right now I am in my eleventh home getting ready to transition into my twelfth home. It has been very hard to move from home to home and from school to school. I hated moving from home to home. Each time before I had to move I have always wondered, what is it going to be like? Is it going to be easy to make friends with them? What's my new school going to be like? Well, each time I have moved, most of the homes were not very good. About three of the homes were good.

The assignment was open enough for Daniel to write about what was important to him, so he did. Because I want Daniel to keep writing, I didn't put a grade on it. Instead we had a conversation at the end of the period where I talked to him about what I loved about the piece, and I told him the truth: Many adults and students needed to read his piece. I gave him a few suggestions for revision.

Instead of rewarding or punishing students with grades, I believe that we need to create situations where students learn to care about the work they produce.

Daniel experimented with taking his story and making it into a narrative essay, tied together with vignettes about the skills he's learned in foster homes. He sent me a draft via email from the library near his new "home." Daniel was not writing for a grade. He didn't even attend Madison anymore. He wrote because this was a topic he cared about. He wrote because someone listened to him, and he hoped that through his writing, more people would understand what it's like to live in a foster home.

Grades as Wages

In too many classrooms, grades are the "wages" students earn for their labor. Teachers assign work, students create products, and grades exchange hands. There are problems with this scenario. Students who enter class with skills—especially reading and writing skills—are rewarded with higher grades. They already know how to write the paper; they just need to figure out what the teacher wants in it. Essentially, they take what the teacher talks about in class and reproduce it in a paper. Students who lack these basic skills are at a disadvantage. Unless there has been an explicit teaching of how to write the papers, they don't know how to produce the products the teacher expects. This doesn't mean they lack intelligence, desire to achieve, or capacity to learn; it means they lack skills. As a result, they receive lower grades.

Instead of rewarding or punishing students with grades, I believe that we need to "live out our ideals" as Myles Horton, cofounder of the Highlander Folk School, exhorts us, by creating situations where students like Daniel learn to care about the work they produce. Of course, this means creating meaningful and important work that students want to do and creating communities where good work can happen. It also means explicitly teaching students how to write essays, articles, stories, poems, and memoirs and finding real audiences to read that work.

I am reminded of Malcolm X's quote, "I have no … compassion in me for a society that will crush people, and then penalize them for not being able to stand up under the weight."

Let me pause to say that sometimes students can't write a better draft. They need more instruction. How fair is it to grade them down on a paper if they don't have the tools to complete the task? Is it their fault that they have made it to my class without academic skills? I don't think so. It's my job to teach them how to write, how to revise. I believe that most students would write a better draft if they could.

For the first years of my career, I lacked the skills to talk with students about what they needed to do to improve their essays or narratives. Once I slowed the writing process down, created ways to teach students the elements of essay and narrative writing, learned to talk with students about revising based on those elements (see "Narrative Criteria Sheet," p. 113, and "Essay Criteria Sheet," p. 145) and developed and saved models, struggling students' writing improved. Their lack of skill was a direct reflection of my ability to teach them.

When I think about grading, I am reminded of Malcolm X's quote, "I have no mercy or compassion in me for a society that will crush people, and then penalize them for not being able to stand up under the weight."

Revision: It's Never "Done"

Numbers on a six-trait analysis or grades for content and mechanics on the top of the papers don't teach students how to write, nor do they push them to their next drafts—even when we promise them an improved grade for a revision. These methods assume that students are "done" or that they will care enough to go back and attempt to fix their drafts in order to raise their grades. Numbers and grades "assess" or judge the paper, rather than provide feedback about how to improve it. Too many of my students learned to negotiate the difficulties of writing by turning in hurried drafts pulled together without much thought. They received their C's or D's, and they were "done" with their writing. The grades let them escape learning how to write.

When Keith Caldwell from the National Writing Project visited the Oregon Writing Project in 1980, he used a great analogy. He compared writing to baking pastries. Grades, according to Caldwell, are the frosting. They signal that the donut or the sugar cookie is heading for the showcase. It's done. He said, "As soon as you put a grade on a piece of writing, it's done. Don't grade it, and you signal that it can still be revised, still worked on."

Because I want my students to view their writing as a process, I refuse to let them be "done." If students turn in drafts that represent their best work at that point in time, they receive full credit for the writing. If students don't have drafts, they receive no credit. If they turn in rushed drafts that clearly aren't their best efforts, I return them and ask them to re-do the papers. Students regularly write and rewrite papers they care about a number of times. I remember Anne Lennon, a senior, lamenting in her end-of-the-quarter portfolio: "Seven drafts on this essay and I'm still not done!"

Too often, writing—and thinking—in school becomes scripted (hence the five-paragraph essay) because scripts are easier to teach and easier to grade. Unfortunately, they fail to teach students how to write. Real writing is messy. And students often don't "get" how to write narratives or essays the first time we teach them. They need lots of practice without judgments; they need to be told what they are doing right, so they can repeat it; they need to examine how to move to the next draft.

But What About Report Cards?

Because I work in public schools that still churn out report cards, I must give students grades at the end of each quarter and semester. And I do—based on the total points earned for each grading period. The difference is that I don't put grades on individual papers. (And I don't give quizzes or tests.) They receive all of the credit possible, or they re-do the papers. For example, a first draft of an essay is typically 150 points; a revision is 300 points. But they only receive the points—all of the points—if they write a paper that meets the criteria. (See "Christensen's Grading Policy," p. 276.)

I'm sure there are folks who will shake their heads at the lack of rigor or standards in my system, but I believe my system is rigorous, and I hold students to meaningful standards. They don't pass my class if they can't write an essay or narrative—even if they complete all of the class work. I will work with them until they can write, but I will not accept work that doesn't meet the exit criteria. And over the years, I ended up working with two or three students over winter and summer vacations.

Student Reaction

Nicole's reaction to my grading philosophy cemented my belief that I was doing the right thing. Nicole enrolled in one of my classes every year, beginning with her sophomore year. The first year, Nicole was frozen by her fear of making a mistake. She attended daily, she responded to other students' papers, but she resisted writing—and this was in Writing for Publication, where writing was essential. In the opening days of her junior year, when a rather smug student made a negative remark about a classmate's paper during a read-around, I didn't have to say a word. Nicole jumped in and talked about the importance of finding what works in a paper. She set the tone for the year—and she finally wrote.

In a mid-year class evaluation of my senior course, Contemporary Literature and Society, Nicole raised her hand. "I like that you don't grade our papers. I went through Sabin Elementary and Beaumont Middle Schools with Mira. Every time the teacher would hand back our papers, Mira's would have an A and mine would have a C. It made me feel like I wasn't as smart as Mira. Now when I look over at Mira's paper, I see that we both have comments from you written all over them. It's a conversation, not a competition."

Mira, the valedictorian, also liked comments instead of grades. "What tells me more about my writing? A grade or the comments and questions you write in the margins?" In fact, Mira looked for colleges where professors wrote narrative evaluations of their students rather than grading them. Now, she teaches writing at the college level and writes magnificent poetry. Nicole writes and performs music.

Peter, a skeptic in the no-grade process, entered my junior class with college-level writing skills. By the end of his second year with me, he wrote in his class evaluation: "The way you have us make comments (What did you like about the piece of writing?) has helped me deal with people. My skin is thick enough to take a lot of abuse just because I've always had a fairly high opinion of some of the things I can do. I didn't realize a lot of other people don't have that advantage. After a while I found out positive criticism helped me more than negative too."

I keep William Stafford's poem "At This Point on the Page" over my desk because it reminds me of the fear I still feel when I turn a piece of writing over to someone to read: Will you like it? Did I do a good job? And what I mean is: Do you like me? Am I OK?

At This Point on the Page*

*Frightened at the slant of the writing, I looked up
at the student who shared it with me—
such pain was in the crossing of each t,
and a heart that skipped—lurched—in the loop of the y.
Sorrowing for the huddled lines my eyes had seen—
The terror of the o's and a's, and those draggled g's,
I looked up at her face,
not wanting to read further, at least by prose:
the hand shook that wrote that far on the page,
and what weight formed each word, God knows.*

When I start a new class with students, I need to remind myself to begin with praise, to find what's working, to find the beauty before I find fault. To remember that when I teach writing, I'm teaching the writer, not the piece. Will my words keep them writing or send them scurrying for cover? ■

"At This Point on the Page" © 1966, 1998 by William Stafford. Reprinted from The Way It Is: New and Selected Poems, *with the permission of Graywolf Press, St. Paul, Minnesota.*

Christensen's Grading Policy

Your grade will be based on several criteria:

- **Basic Concepts of Class:** In order to pass this class, you must demonstrate that you have learned the major concepts of the course. These will change from quarter to quarter, but sample outcomes might include: Writing an essay that demonstrates your understanding of historical or literary material, using historical facts to critique a document.

- **Completion of Daily Work:** Daily work is the place we practice the skills needed for learning long-term skills. On a basketball court, team members might learn passing skills. In here, you will learn to improve your writing by completing shorter writing assignments first, or by completing a reading journal in preparation for class discussions, or by writing an essay about a novel.

- **Class Participation:** This class demands that you participate not only by completing the work, but also by contributing to class discussions. You contribute by listening while others speak, giving positive feedback, speaking on topic, learning how to take turns talking, taking notes during discussion that will help you write later, disagreeing with ideas rather than people. You also contribute by respecting other members of the class. No one should feel vulnerable in this room. We learn best in an atmosphere of respect where people can take risks. So expect positive comments rather than criticism from your classmates and me.

- **Homework:** Homework is an extension of the work in class. Often, it will only be relevant in the context of our class work. For example, if we are studying the Politics of Language and you don't do the reading, you will not be able to participate or understand the class discussion related to the reading. Similarly, we will write essays, narratives, or poetry that parallel our reading assignments. If you do not do your homework, you will miss the connection.

- **Difficulty:** There will be times when emergencies come up or when you do not understand the homework. In the event this happens, call me or email me, and I will either give you more time or explain the work more thoroughly. *You may also set up appointments to work with me after school or during lunch.*

- **Extensions:** Because I expect quality work, from time to time I will return your essays, narratives, and poetry so you can take more time to polish or rework it. I expect that you will take time to learn how to write—which means learning how to rewrite. I will teach you, but in order to learn, you must practice.

About the Author

Linda Christensen is Director of the Oregon Writing Project at Lewis & Clark College in Portland, Oregon. During her thirty year career in Portland Public Schools, she taught language arts at Jefferson and Grant High Schools and worked as Portland's Language Arts Coordinator. She received the National Writing Project's Fred Hechinger Award for use of research in teaching and writing and was named the Western States Teacher of the Year by the U.S. West Foundation. Christensen is the author of *Reading, Writing, and Rising Up: Teaching for Social Justice and the Power of the Written Word*, and co-editor of *Rethinking Our Classrooms: Teaching for Equity and Justice* and *Rethinking School Reform: Views from the Classroom*. She is a member of the *Rethinking Schools* magazine editorial board. Her articles have appeared in *English Journal, Language Arts, Educational Leadership, Democracy and Education*, and other national publications. Christensen has received numerous writing awards from the National Council of Teachers of English and the Oregon Council of Teachers of English. She presents keynotes and workshops nationally and internationally on writing, social justice education, and curriculum development. She is married to Bill Bigelow, and is mother to Anna and Gretchen Hereford. She can be reached at *lchrist@aol.com.*

Index

Note: Page numbers in italics refer to illustrations.

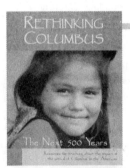

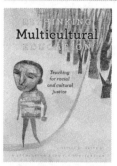
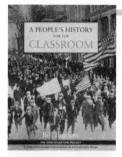
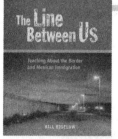

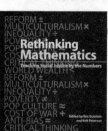

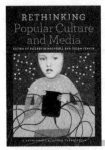

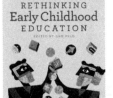

RETHINKING SCHOOLS
F O U R   E A S Y   W A Y S   T O   O R D E R

1. CALL TOLL-FREE: **800-669-4192** 8AM-9PM (ET) M-F
2. SECURE ONLINE ORDERING: **www.rethinkingschools.org**
3. FAX TO: **802-864-7626**
4. MAIL TO: **Rethinking Schools, P.O. Box 2222, Williston, VT 05495**

MASTERCARD, VISA, DISCOVER, AND PURCHASE ORDERS ACCEPTED.

Name

Organization

Address

City/State/ZIP

Phone

Email

METHOD OF PAYMENT

☐ Check or money order made payable to **Rethinking Schools**
☐ Purchase order   ☐ MasterCard   ☐ Visa   ☐ Discover

Credit Card No.

Exp. Date

Authorized Signature

QTY	TITLE/ITEM	UNIT PRICE	TOTAL

MAIL: Rethinking Schools, P.O. Box 2222
      Williston, VT 05495
FAX: **802-864-7626**
CALL: **800-669-4192** FOR A FREE CATALOG
      OF ALL OUR MATERIALS

Subtotal	$
Shipping	$
Donation	$
TOTAL	$

*U.S. shipping and handling costs are 15% of the total (minimum charge of $4.50).
Canadian shipping and handling costs are 25% of the total (minimum charge of $5.50).
Subscriptions already include shipping costs. Payment in U.S. dollars.